Accession no.

D1423229

HERMITS AND RECLUSES IN
ENGLISH SOCIETY, 950–1200

Hermits and Recluses in English Society, 950–1200

TOM LICENCE

LIS LIBRARY

Date	Fund
25/6/12	i-che

Order No

229/654.

University of Chester

OXFORD

UNIVERSITY PRESS

OXFORD
UNIVERSITY PRESS

Great Clarendon Street, Oxford OX2 6DP
Oxford University Press is a department of the University of Oxford.
It furthers the University's objective of excellence in research, scholarship,
and education by publishing worldwide in
Oxford New York
Auckland   Cape Town   Dar es Salaam   Hong Kong   Karachi
Kuala Lumpur   Madrid   Melbourne   Mexico City   Nairobi
New Delhi   Shanghai   Taipei   Toronto
With offices in
Argentina   Austria   Brazil   Chile   Czech Republic   France   Greece
Guatemala   Hungary   Italy   Japan   South Korea   Poland   Portugal
Singapore   Switzerland   Thailand   Turkey   Ukraine   Vietnam

Oxford is a registered trade mark of Oxford University Press
in the UK and in certain other countries

Published in the United States
by Oxford University Press Inc., New York

© Tom Licence 2011

The moral rights of the author have been asserted

Database right Oxford University Press (maker)

Reprinted 2011

All rights reserved. No part of this publication may be reproduced,
stored in a retrieval system, or transmitted, in any form or by any means,
without the prior permission in writing of Oxford University Press,
or as expressly permitted by law, or under terms agreed with the appropriate
reprographics rights organization. Enquiries concerning reproduction
outside the scope of the above should be sent to the Rights Department,
Oxford University Press, at the address above

You must not circulate this book in any other binding or cover
And you must impose this same condition on any acquirer

ISBN 978-0-19-959236-4

Printed in the United Kingdom by
Lightning Source UK Ltd., Milton Keynes

For my students.

Preface

I would not be alone in saying that for most of my life hermits and recluses were half-imagined characters, whose presence in the landscape was sometimes still felt, as an imprint on memory. My grandparents' generation remembered one or two so-called 'hermits' in the Essex marshes. A later prompting urged me to rediscover their appeal.

Carl Watkins, a most inspirational teacher, was responsible for this prompting, which resulted in an undergraduate dissertation on Godric of Finchale. Carl also supervised the thesis, from which this book has grown through various twists and turns. For his many kindnesses, I owe him a mountain of thanks. Second to him, I would thank the AHRC and the Master and Fellows of Magdalene College, Cambridge, who between them funded (and so facilitated) my research for a period of seven years. My book is the fruit of their investment. It is also the fruit of collaborative scholarship, in which the insights of many patient and generous people have quietly interwoven with mine.

Peter Jackson, a friend and mentor, guided my Anglo-Saxon research. His impress is somehow on this book, along with that of Martin Brett and Jonathan Riley-Smith. To them I owe any number of insights. (The errors and oversights, of course, are mine.) Henrietta Leyser, John Blair, Christine Carpenter, and Rosamond McKitterick freely devoted time to reading the manuscript in various recensions and improving my ideas with their advice. Tessa Webber went further than the normal promptings of kindness with her diligent corrections. My thanks go, in addition, to Simon Barrington-Ward, Tom Williamson, Nick Karn, Rebecca Rushforth, Nicholas Vincent, Eamon Duffy, and every other helper. Special thanks go to my family, not least to Ben, who gave me ready encouragement and steadied my footsteps in the course of writing this book.

Tom Licence
Norwich

Contents

List of abbreviations

AB	*Analecta Bollandiana*
Acta SS	*Acta Sanctorum*, ed. J. Bolland et al., 67 vols (Antwerp and Brussels, 1643–)
ANS	*Anglo-Norman Studies* 1- (Ipswich and Woodbridge, 1979–)
ASC	*The Anglo-Saxon Chronicle*, with reference to the collaborative edition, ed. D. Dumville and S. Keynes (general editors), 8 vols (1983–)
ASE	*Anglo-Saxon England*
BAR	British Archaeological Reports
BGAM	Beiträge zur Geschichte des Alten Mönchtums und des Benediktinerordens
BHL	*Bibliotheca Hagiographica Latina*, prepared by the Bollandists, 2 vols (Brussels, 1899–1901, with supplements, 1911, 1986). Cited by item number.
CCCM	*Corpus Christianorum, Continuatio medievalis* (Turnhout, 1966–)
CCM	*Corpus consuetudinum monasticarum*, ed. K. Hallinger (Siegburg, 1963–)
CCSL	*Corpus Christianorum, Series Latina* (Turnhout, 1953–)
CPL	*Clavis Patrum Latinorum*, ed. E. Dekkers and A. Gaar, 3rd edn. (Steenbrugge, 1995). Cited by item number.
CSEL	*Corpus Scriptorum Ecclesiasticorum Latinorum* (Vienna, 1866–)
CSer.	Camden Series
CUL	Cambridge University Library
Eadwold	T. Licence, 'Goscelin of Saint-Bertin and the Hagiography of St Eadwold of Cerne', *Journal of Medieval Latin*, 16 (2007), 182–207
EETS	Early English Text Society
o.s.	original series
s.s.	supplementary series
EHR	*English Historical Review*
EPNS	English Place-Name Society
Gneuss	H. Gneuss, *Handlist of Anglo-Saxon Manuscripts: A List of Manuscripts and Manuscript Fragments Written or Owned in England up to 1100* (Tempe, AZ, 2001). Cited by item number.
GT	'The Life and Miracles of Godric of Throckenholt', ed. T. Licence, *AB*, 124 (2006), 15–43
HBS	Henry Bradshaw Society publications
HRH	*The Heads of Religious Houses, England and Wales, 940–1216*, ed. D. Knowles, C. N. L. Brooke, and V. C. M. London, 2nd edn. (Cambridge, 2001)

JEH	*Journal of Ecclesiastical History*
JMH	*Journal of Medieval History*
L, BL	London, British Library
LC	'The Liber confortatorius of Goscelin of Saint-Bertin', ed. C. H. Talbot, *Analecta monastica, textes et études sur la vie des moines au moyen age, troisième série, Studia Anselmiana*, 37 (Rome, 1955), 1–117
LCM	*The Life of Christina of Markyate: A Twelfth-Century Recluse*, ed. C. H. Talbot (Oxford, 1959)
LG	*Libellus de vita et miraculis s. Godrici, heremitae de Finchale, auctore Reginaldo monacho Dunelmensi*, ed. J. Stevenson, *SS* 20 (London, 1847 for 1845)
MA	W. Dugdale, *Monasticon Anglicanum*, ed. with revisions by J. Caley, H. Ellis, and B. Bandinel, 6 vols in 8 (London, 1817–30, repr. 1846)
MGH	*Monumenta Germaniae Historica*
MGH SRG	*Monumenta Germaniae Historica, Scriptores rerum Germanicarum in usum scholarum separatim editi*
MGH SS	*Monumenta Germaniae Historica, Scriptores*
NL	*Nova legenda Anglie*, ed. C. Horstmann, 2 vols (Oxford, 1901)
ODNB	*Oxford Dictionary of National Biography*, ed. H. C. G. Matthew and B. Harrison, 60 vols (Oxford, 2004)
PL	*Patrologia Latina*, ed. J.-P. Migne, 221 vols (Paris, 1844–64)
PR	Pipe Rolls. Cited by regnal years.
RB	*Revue bénédictine*
RS	Rolls Series (London, 1858–96)
S	P. H. Sawyer, *Anglo-Saxon Charters: An Annotated List and Bibliography* (London, 1968). Cited by item number.
SC	*Sources chrétiennes* (Paris, 1941–)
SCH	*Studies in Church History*
SS	Surtees Society publications
t.r.e.	*Tempore regis Eadwardi* (in reference to entries in *Domesday Book*)
TRHS	*Transactions of the Royal Historical Society*
VB	*Vita Bartholomaei Farnensis* (*BHL* 1015), in *Symeonis monachi opera omnia*, ed. T. Arnold, RS 75, 2 vols (1882–5), I, 295–325
Verba sen.	*Verba seniorum* (BHL 6525, 6527–31)
VRK	'Vitae s. Roberti Knaresburgensis', ed. P. Grosjean, *AB*, 57 (1939), 364–400
WH	*Wulfric of Haselbury by John, Abbot of Ford*, ed. M. Bell, Somerset Record Society, 47 (Frome, 1933)

Note to the reader

After consideration, I decided not to include maps, against my own inclination and the advice of two scholars. Often, maps are invaluable, but a map of hermits and recluses (such as are known) would serve no obvious purpose and could be misleading in that it would display only a fraction of the anchoretic population. I have traced the spread of religious movements and their shifting manifestations at certain locations at various points in the text, but a map of those places would cement them into artificial patterns where the real issue of interest is the free migration of ideas. To reduce footnote baggage, references are usually page numbers rather than full citations of Latin text; with the same aim, only one place of publication is given for books published at more than one location. Part of Chapter 3 is an amplified version of my article 'Evidence of Recluses in Eleventh-Century England', which is listed in the Select Bibliography.

Introduction

THE DEBATE

It is difficult in the twenty-first century to imagine a landscape liberally populated with hermits in their huts or caves, and recluses shut up in cells at countless churches and monasteries. Nine hundred years ago the opposite would have been true: without its anchorites, the land might have seemed like a desert. Even if it had been possible to count them, no one did, so we can only entertain the most impressionistic estimates of their numbers, by collecting assorted evidence from charters, letters, hagiography, chronicles, necrologies, and archaeology. As the evidence comes together, an obscure picture of a landscape peopled by anchorites begins to emerge more clearly, as if an invisible map, gradually appearing, were starting to reveal networks of secret portals by which medieval men and women could access the heavens. The huts and cells of anchorites are the buzzing communication centres, sending and receiving messages via channels linking them to each other and to nearby towns and villages, and also via vertical channels linking them to God above. Far from being eccentric loners cut off from society, medieval anchorites were connected to this living network, using it to escape the suffocating conventions which society imposed and to conduct their lives in accordance with God's will. When a respectable young woman from Huntingdon called Christina sought to escape the marriage her parents had forced on her and vow herself to religion, about the year 1115, this network soon began to buzz with activity.

In one respect, Christina was not unusual, being a young woman betrothed to a man whom her parents wanted as a son-in-law, yet in another respect she broke with convention by resisting their plans and making contrary ones of her own. Her father, fearing the shame it would bring or the lack of a guaranteed income, spurned her plan to renounce the wealth and status she might secure if she married a respectable man and frustrated her attempts to abscond by placing a constant guard on her. Imprisoned in her home, Christina secretly contacted a hermit named Edwin, who came to her by stealth. After learning of her plight, he went to consult his relative, Roger, who was a hermit in the woods off Watling Street, the old Roman road, between St Albans and Dunstable. Roger, however, wanted no part in a plan to dissolve her marriage. Next, Edwin went to see the archbishop of Canterbury, who advised that the marriage was void. On his way back, he spoke to anchorites at various locations before hatching a plan with

Christina. Edwin appears to have used these contacts to identify locations where Christina might hide. She chose to hide with an anchorite named Ælfwen, who lived in the village of Flamstead, two miles from Roger's abode, and who shared the ministrations of his servants. Although her parents opposed Christina's plan to devote her life to God, they were pious enough to make regular trips to a hermitage six miles outside Huntingdon, to consult its occupant. Assisted by a boy in Ælfwen's service, Christina timed her escape to coincide with one of these outings. Later, after hiding for a time with Ælfwen, she prevailed upon Roger, who took her into his hermitage at Markyate and eventually used his influence to secure the annulment of her marriage. At every stage of her adventure, the anchorites involved were informed and guided not only by information brought to them by friends and servants, but also by heavenly messages, visions, and responses to prayer.[1] Such were the channels by which their network proved effective. Mobile hermits such as Edwin, servants moving between different anchorites conveying messages, and the secrecy, influence, and respect these figures enjoyed enabled them to rescue Christina from a marriage bond and the intractable demands of her parents, so that she could fulfil her true spiritual ambition. Dotted across the landscape, aware of what was going on, and visited by members of the local gentry, including Christina's parents, anchorites could open doors which society normally closed, so that God's will might be seen to reach its mysterious ends.

Where did all these anchorites come from? How could they wield such power? What, if anything, was their function? And why did society harbour these people who bypassed its norms and scorned its aspirations? A recluse's cell tucked away in the corner of a churchyard and a hermitage in the woods a little distance from the road could easily be overlooked, but these were nodal points in the landscape at the centre of the parish or near busy routes. By conducting their otherworldly operations where the world went about its business, like an earth-bound community of angels (visible to those who wished to see them), anchorites occupied a paradoxical position. For no other group was more withdrawn from the world and yet so much involved in it. This paradox is the premise of this book: that hermits and recluses, as objects of study, cannot be separated from the societies in which they multiplied but must be viewed within their social, and antisocial, context. The reason they seldom have been is that modern historians, living in a hermitless landscape and a society which views recluses as lonely eccentrics, forget that anchorites might once have performed a valuable role. Our tendency to regard them as eccentrics is a prejudicial tendency, rooted in our literary and historical consciousness by the legacy of Edward Gibbon, who popularized the idea that anchorites were contemptible products of degenerate, irrational fanaticism.[2]

---

[1] *LCM*, 80–92, 98–102, 108.
[2] E. Gibbon, *The History of the Decline and Fall of the Roman Empire*, ed. J. B. Bury, 7 vols (London, 1909), IV, esp. 78–9.

Although Victorian antiquaries tried to repair their reputation, their efforts failed to interest ecclesiastical historians of their era because the latter were concerned with grander subjects such as the papacy, the episcopate, or monastic institutions.[3] Before the mid-twentieth century, moreover, scholars treated hermits and recluses as timeless, universal characters on the medieval stage, whose unchanging appeal derived from eternal spiritual virtues.[4] The idea that their functions altered and their influence waxed and waned in conjunction with the currents of historical change only began to form after historians noticed that hermits were unusually prominent in eleventh-century Italy, Normandy, and France.[5] Other historians had observed that they were also multiplying in Anglo-Norman England. Henrietta Leyser revealed that hermits proliferated in Western Europe across the century *c.*1040–*c.*1140.[6] And it is only in the last few decades that scholars studying recluses (that is, anchorites shut inside cells) have dated the rise of the recluse to between the tenth and the thirteenth centuries in France, Flanders, Lotharingia, Germany, and England.[7] This relatively new interest in anchorites has grown apace with the readiness of social history to search for causes of change beyond the well-trodden territory of elite and institutional activity. As social historians became interested in anchorites, they began to wonder why these people attained greater influence in certain historical contexts – and what their proliferation might reveal about the nature of those societies that nurtured them.

The first and most influential was Peter Brown, who published an article in 1971 titled 'The Rise and Function of the Holy Man in Late Antiquity', dealing mainly with the anchorites of fifth- and sixth-century Syria.[8] It set out to discover

---

[3] E.g. E. L. Cutts, *Scenes and Characters of the Middle Ages* (London, 1872).

[4] E.g. R. M. Clay, *The Hermits and Anchorites of England* (London, 1914); and L. Gougaud, *Ermites et reclus: Études sur d'anciennes formes de vie religieuse*, Moines et monastères, 5 (Vienne, 1928).

[5] See, for example, J. Leclercq, 'La crise du monachisme aux XIe et XIIe siècles', *Bullettino dell'Istituto storico italiano per il medio evo*, 70 (1958), 19–41, translated as 'The Monastic Crisis of the Eleventh and Twelfth Centuries', in *Cluniac Monasticism in the Central Middle Ages*, ed. N. Hunt (London, 1971), 217–37, and G. G. Meersseman, 'Eremitismo e predicazione itinerante dei secoli XI e XII', in *L'eremitismo in Occidente nei secoli XI e XII: Atti della seconda settimana internazionale di studio, Mendola, 30 agosto – 6 settembre 1962*, Pubblicazioni dell'Università cattolica del Sacro Cuore, Contributi Serie 3: Varia 4, Miscellanea del Centro di studi medioevali, 4 (Milan, 1965), 164–79.

[6] H. Leyser, *Hermits and the New Monasticism: A Study of Religious Communities in Western Europe, 1000–1150* (New York, 1984).

[7] E.g. H. Grundmann, 'Deutsche Eremiten, Einsiedler und Klausner im Hochmittelalter (10.–12. Jahrhundert)', *Archiv für Kulturgeschichte*, 45 (1963), 60–90, tr. into Italian as 'Eremiti in Germania dal x au xii secolo: "Einsiedler" e "Klausner"', in *L'eremitismo*, 311–29, at 313; P. L'Hermite-Leclercq, 'La réclusion dans le milieu urbain français au moyen âge', in *Ermites de France et d'Italie (XIe–XVe siècle)*, ed. A. Vauchez (Rome, 2003), 155–73, at 156; A. B. Mulder-Bakker, *Lives of the Anchoresses: The Rise of the Urban Recluse in Medieval Europe*, tr. M. H. Scholz (Philadelphia, 2005).

[8] P. Brown, 'The Rise and Function of the Holy Man in Late Antiquity', *Journal of Roman Studies*, 61 (1971), 80–101.

why they became so important in that predominantly rural setting and what their activities revealed about the society that paid attention to them. Brown called anchorites 'holy men' in respect of his hypothesis that they performed a special function in the East Roman Empire of late antiquity: that their asceticism served as a prolonged, solemn ritual of dissociation by which they severed the normal familial and economic ties which bound society together, intending to stand apart from it. This positioned them to act as mediators and counsellors in an increasingly egalitarian environment, where the dissolution of old hierarchies and great estates was ushering in an aspiring new class of independent, self-respecting farmers. The asceticism of the anchorite impressed such people: '[For it] brought down into the dubious and tension-ridden world beneath the moon a clarity and a stability associated with the unchanging heavens.'[9] Other social historians were quick to embrace Brown's model because it offered a convincing social explanation for a seemingly antisocial phenomenon, while interpreting a religious figure as the product of social forces. Henry Mayr-Harting, in 1975, applied Brown's theory to medieval England by modelling the Somerset recluse Wulfric of Haselbury (d. 1155) in a similar mould. Acknowledging a debt to Brown, his article set Wulfric within a tension-ridden world of economic change, explaining the rise of anchorites like him as the rise of the holy man, modelled by Brown, in the comparable environment of twelfth-century England.[10] Although he was not the first to notice that hermits and recluses were becoming more prominent in that period, he was the first to postulate that the rise of the anchorite in England constituted a 'religious movement'.[11] By this, he did not mean a coordinated, coherent movement, like the Oxford Movement of the nineteenth century, but some favourable shift in society's attitudes towards anchorites.

By spotting this religious movement, Mayr-Harting detected a real phenomenon. Wishing to apply Brown's theory, he needed to explain why twelfth-century England required the sort of counsellor and arbiter that had arisen in late-antique Syria. Brown linked the rise of this figure to the dissolution of established social structures. Mayr-Harting argued that the rise of the anchorite in England was linked to the dissolution of established social structures through the disruptive effects of the Norman Conquest. Some such idea had been forming for more than a generation, for a previous scholar had noticed that hermits and recluses 'were becoming common in England soon after the Conquest', and the impression had hardened and developed in the argument of C. H. Talbot, that, through every account of anchorites in the twelfth century, there was 'an undercurrent of national feeling', alluding to 'differences in tongue and custom' between those who lived as anchorites and the elite of the clerical hierarchy.[12] This seemed to be

---

[9] P. Brown, *The Making of Late Antiquity* (Cambridge, MA, 1978), 17.
[10] H. Mayr-Harting, 'Functions of a Twelfth-Century Recluse', *History*, 60 (1975), 337–52.
[11] *Ibid.*, 338.
[12] *WH*, pp. xlix–l; *LCM*, 12.

evidence for the vocation's special popularity among the English, as did the preponderance of Old English names among known twelfth-century anchorites. Inspired by these findings, Mayr-Harting proposed that the 'great efflorescence of the hermit's way of life in twelfth-century England was not anti-Norman in character, but, as a religious movement, it was a self-consciously English reaction and adaptation to the Norman Conquest'.[13] The idea was that the English desired some arbiter, separate from the Norman elite, who could represent stability in a changing world. Anchorites arose to meet the need for this arbiter in a society where conquest was now blocking the avenues by which the indigenous population had previously advanced its interests.

For a time when little work had been done on anchorites, this was a handy and sensible hypothesis, explaining the most significant observations that had been made by reversion to a plausible theory. It rapidly passed into orthodoxy. Within a few years, it was paraphrased in the statement that twelfth-century anchorites met a need by 'ministering to a people who were not at home with the Anglo-Norman culture'. This statement found its way verbatim into two influential modern studies.[14] A third depicted hermits and recluses 'in their rural ascetic abodes with a clientele of Anglo-Saxon gentry, a post-Conquest conservative response to a changing world'.[15] A fourth claimed that the rise of hermits and recluses 'was partly the result of the fractured lines of authority caused by the Norman Conquest' (sic).[16] These numerous synopses of Mayr-Harting's ideas established the consensus without challenging its premises. Sometimes it was undercut slightly by the intimation that reverence for asceticism was not exclusively English. 'When Englishmen were largely debarred from normal ecclesiastical promotion,' wrote one historian, 'the eremitical life could offer a way to spiritual authority with both the French and the English'.[17] Other scholars maintained that the English were exceptional and that the rise of anchorites after the Conquest seemed to 'reflect a re-appropriation of the Anglo-Saxon and Celtic eremitic heritage in the face of imported Norman ideas of monastic spirituality'.[18] Despite such minor disagreements, the fundamental idea that anchorites functioned principally as arbiters suffered no erosion, but instead crystallized in a metaphor that depicted the anchorite as a bridge. Anchorites

[13] Mayr-Harting, 'Functions', 337–8.

[14] C. J. Holdsworth, 'Christina of Markyate', in *Mediaeval Women: Dedicated and Presented to Rosalind M. T. Hill on the Occasion of Her Seventieth Birthday*, ed. D. Baker, *SCH*, subsidia, 1 (1978), 185–204, at 203; cf. Leyser, *Hermits*, 14, and D. Gray, 'Christina of Markyate: The Literary Background', in *Christina of Markyate: A Twelfth-Century Holy Woman*, ed. S. Fanous and H. Leyser (Abingdon, 2005), 12–24, at 18.

[15] A. K. Warren, *Anchorites and Their Patrons in Medieval England* (Berkeley, CA, 1985), 287.

[16] C. Holdsworth, 'Hermits and the Power of the Frontier', *Reading Medieval Studies*, 16 (1990), 55–76, at 71.

[17] H. E. J. Cowdrey, 'Wulfric of Haselbury [St Wulfric of Haselbury] (*c.*1090–1154/5), Priest and Hermit', in *ODNB*.

[18] S. K. Elkins, *Holy Women of Twelfth-Century England* (Chapel Hill, NC, 1988), 20.

became 'the indispensable bridge between conquered and conquerors'. Their symbolic detachment, or 'liminality' in the idiom of anthropology, turned them into 'a bridge between social groups within Anglo-Norman England'.[19] The metaphor of the bridge harked back to Peter Brown's holy man, whose ritual of separation qualified him to stand across divides that caused conflict in late-antique society. Although the field of anchoretic studies had long seemed barren or, at least, uncultivated, the ideas sown by Brown and Mayr-Harting took root after this fashion, strengthened, and developed, through the cross-fertilization of ideas among historians.

Forty years later, the argument that anchorites arose after the Conquest to heal the wounds and to bridge the gaps created in its aftermath rests on shakier foundations. Since it took shape, many of the developments once associated with the constructed image of 1066 as a cataclysmic event and its romantic concomitant historiography of Anglo-Saxon versus Norman have been reinterpreted in light of the *longue durée*.[20] Mary Clayton, Jane Roberts, Sarah Foot, and John Blair have been studying the place of anchorites or cults of anchorite saints in the Anglo-Saxon era.[21] Their work opens the possibility that hermits and recluses were already influential in England before the Normans arrived. The fact that fewer surface in Anglo-Saxon sources need not reflect the relative scarcity of anchorites in that era so much as the paucity of pre-Conquest sources. In other words, their supposed proliferation could be a trick of the light. The findings of historians working on Continental hermits counter this idea by upholding the hypothesis that hermits were multiplying, but they erode the argument linking that phenomenon to the Conquest. For if anchorites were ascendant in Italy, France, and Normandy before the invaders set sail for England, it is much harder to argue that the phenomenon in England was a distinctively native reaction to a single disruptive event or the peculiar conditions of its aftermath. Whereas the debate on anchorites in England looked to the Conquest as the catalyst or cause of their apparent resurgence, monk-scholars in the Benelux countries, such as Germain Morin and Jean Leclercq, who interested themselves in the history of spirituality (*Geistesgeschichte*), studied it within the context of changing monastic thought. Morin had edited a polemical tract from the 1090s or 1100s in which a hermit named Rainald charged that monasteries were

---

[19] R. I. Moore, 'Ranulf Flambard and Christina of Markyate', in *Christina*, ed. Fanous and Leyser, 138–42, at 141; R. Gilchrist, *Contemplation and Action: The Other Monasticism* (London, 1995), 159.

[20] D. Bates, '1066: Does the Date Still Matter?', *Historical Research*, 78 (2005), 443–64.

[21] M. Clayton, 'Hermits and the Contemplative Life in Anglo-Saxon England', in *Holy Men and Holy Women: Old English Prose Saints' Lives and Their Contexts*, ed. P. E. Szarmach (New York, 1996), 147–75; J. Roberts, 'Hagiography and Literature: The Case of Guthlac of Crowland', in *Mercia: An Anglo-Saxon Kingdom in Europe*, ed. M. P. Brown and C. A. Farr (London, 2001), 69–86; S. Foot, *Veiled Women I: The Disappearance of Nuns from Anglo-Saxon England* (Aldershot, 2000), 179–88; J. Blair, 'A Saint for Every Minster? Local Cults in Anglo-Saxon England', in *Local Saints and Local Churches in the Early Medieval West*, ed. A. T. Thacker and R. Sharpe (Oxford, 2002), 455–94.

far too concerned with easy living, the performance of their offices, and the resolution of lawsuits, to promote the spiritual welfare of their members.[22] To Morin, this was an episode in a wider 'crisis of cenobitism' ('*la crise du céno-bitisme*') in which the monasteries came under attack and alienated their more spiritual inmates because their worldliness or entanglements with society were exposing the brethren to sin and precluding any chance of penance and contemplative prayer. Charles Dereine and Jean Leclercq took up Morin's argument, Leclercq illustrating the novel feeling of frustration by publishing the writings of John of Fécamp (*c.*990–1078), an Italian monk and hermit who became abbot of Fécamp in Normandy in 1028.[23] Vexed by temptations and administrative duties, he wrote of his burning desire to withdraw to a hermitage. 'Free me from these quarrels and controversies', he prayed, 'from the worldly dealings I endure in the monastery ... where every day I multiply my sins'.[24]

Leclercq and others dated the crisis to the century 1050–1150. And although the hypothesis crumbled somewhat when it was subsequently pointed out that recruits to established Benedictine monasteries multiplied over that century, the evidence for a countervailing trend towards the hermitage has not been disputed.[25] Leclercq argued that it grew partly from a concern with the corrupting effects of material wealth, so he allowed the possibility that the apparent shift in spirituality was a reaction to some greater socioeconomic shift. This gave rise to the thesis that a religious movement in favour of poverty and renunciation arose out of the tensions of a transitional economy, neither totally rural nor totally mercantile. In a society confronted with new values, it was argued, the resultant crisis of conscience prompted religious people to reject new ways of thinking and instead seek ways of returning to God.[26] The thesis matured when the appeal of religious renunciation was linked, in particular, to the unforeseen consequences of prosperity. The new argument was that the laity and the clergy alike became increasingly ill at ease with the corrupting influence of money as a means of gaining advantage. By *c.*1040, the perceived sin of simony (the action of buying or selling ecclesiastical office) was rampant in Italy, Germany, and France, and probably in England.[27] Conscientious Christians rejected this creeping evil by

---

[22] G. Morin, 'Rainaud l'ermite et Ives de Chartres: un episode de la crise du cénobitisme au XIe–XIIe siècle', *RB*, 40 (1928), 99–115, at 101–10.

[23] J. Leclercq and J.-P. Bonnes, *Un maître de la vie spirituelle au XIe siècle: Jean de Fécamp* (Paris, 1946); C. Dereine, 'Odon de Tournai et la crise du cénobitisme au XIe siècle', *Revue de moyen âge Latin*, 4 (1948), 137–54.

[24] Leclercq and Bonnes, *Jean de Fécamp*, 194–5, 196, 195.

[25] J. Van Engen, 'The "Crisis of Cenobitism" Reconsidered: Benedictine Monasticism in the Years 1050–1150', *Speculum*, 61 (1986), 269–304, at 284.

[26] L. Genicot, 'L'érémitisme du XIe siècle dans son contexte économique et social', in *L'eremitismo*, 45–69, at 69.

[27] L. K. Little, *Religious Poverty and the Profit Economy in Medieval Europe* (London, 1978), pp. x–xi, 36–40; A. Murray, *Reason and Society in the Middle Ages* (Oxford, 1985), 65–7; F. Barlow, *The English Church 1000–1066*, 2nd edn. (London, 1979), 76, 111–15.

denouncing the greedy world and embracing lives characterized by renunciation, asceticism, and voluntary poverty. Many of them joined monasteries. Others were drawn towards a different form of renunciation and became hermits, often in the numerous loose-knit congregations that multiplied over much of Western Europe during the century 1040–1140. In effect, historians had transformed the crisis of cenobitism into a crisis of conscience by taking a spiritual explanation and setting it within the context of socioeconomic change. More recently the historiography has taken an individualistic turn, interpreting the eleventh century as a period when zealous individuals were breaking free from suffocating institutions to seek God via alternative paths such as pilgrimage, preaching, and the hermitage.[28] The rise of these things has been linked to the growth of individual religious identity and the compulsive new interest in self-exploration in the century after *c.*1050: 'a revolt of individuals against a constricting society'.[29] So strong were the bonds of that society, the theory holds, that empowerment could be gained only by withdrawal. It is perhaps to some extent a reflection of social change over the last few generations, or corresponding changes in historical thought, that the historiography of anchorites has shifted its focus from religion, to society, and, most recently, to the individual. Yet even if each generation of historians has recast these figures in its image, this might enable us to view anchorites as religious individuals in the wider social context – rebellious perhaps, or liberated, or pursuing their own ideal.

The idea that the life of the anchorite was a liberating path to empowerment fits with Christina's experiences – which were recounted earlier – as a woman freed from her unwanted marriage to pursue her true vocation. It could also fit with Brown and Mayr-Harting's model of the anchorite as a figure who achieved unique authority by ritually severing society's normative bonds. Yet it still begs the question whether the social-historical imperative to explain a religious phenomenon in non-religious terms distracts from the fundamental issue. For, although it may be true that hermits and recluses freed themselves from social expectations or acted as authoritative arbiters, these were not their defining characteristics. Perhaps it is time to move, once more, towards a spiritual explanation, now that the historiography is turning full circle, with R. I. Moore, Susan Ridyard, and others reclaiming anchorites as religious figures who performed religious roles.[30] It is a sign of this incipient revolution that historians now are more inclined to link the rise of asceticism in the eleventh

---

[28] P. G. Jestice, *Wayward Monks and the Religious Revolution of the Eleventh Century* (Leiden, 1997), 14.

[29] C. Morris, *The Discovery of the Individual, 1050–1200* (London, 1972), 32.

[30] R. I. Moore, 'Literacy and the Making of Heresy *c.*1000–*c.*1150', in *Heresy and Literacy, 1000–1530*, ed. P. Biller and A. Hudson (Cambridge, 1994), 19–37, at 34; S. J. Ridyard, 'Functions of a Twelfth-Century Recluse Revisited: The Case of Godric of Finchale', in *Belief and Culture in the Middle Ages: Studies Presented to Henry-Mayr Harting*, ed. R. Gameson and H. Leyser (Oxford, 2001), 236–50.

century to the growth of millenarian anxiety than to the sorts of socioeconomic changes previously thought to be its causes.[31] Peter Brown led the way by revising his model of the holy man and reinterpreting his success in light of spiritual concerns. His role, Brown now thinks, was to establish, by his ascetic efforts, an exceptional degree of closeness to God, from which he could intercede on behalf of the ordinary faithful, whose sins cut them off from God, and comfort them, or instil compunction, by wielding holy authority.[32]

By acknowledging spiritual motives of people who became, revered, or visited anchorites, medieval historians have begun to integrate those figures into the broader historiographic tapestry which scholars of piety and religion are increasingly weaving in their many new studies of saints' cults, ritual devotion, pastoral texts, visions, ghost stories, and penitential practices. Carl Watkins, for example, regards the parishes as an interface where the clergy and the laity, responsive to each other, worked out their common faith.[33] But how did anchorites function at this interface? Did they become important during the period 950–1200 because they met spiritual needs, as they did in late antiquity? The shift in the historiography demands answers to these questions; it also exposes how little we really know about anchorites and their distinctive role in English medieval society. First it is necessary to study the route by which anchorites established their reputation, with less attention to the Conquest (although it may have been a factor) and more to the Anglo-Saxon backdrop and their rise through Europe. Next it will be necessary to examine their motives and functions, not to dispel the vision of the arbitrating holy man, or the anchorite set free from society, or the bridge between conquered and conquerors (a figure whom both sets might equally respect), but to understand their rise and role. For until we explain the paradox of the anchorite – why society revered and supported those who bypassed its conventions or renounced its ambitions – a hole will yawn in our understanding of medieval ideals and thought.

The first four chapters of this book aim to discover how and why anchorites made such an impact in the long eleventh century. The last four chapters look more closely at their objectives and functions to *c.*1200. If there is a hinge, the hinge is Chapter 4. Chapter 1 establishes the context by examining the Anglo-Saxon background and the rise of hermits in Continental Europe. Chapter 2 then investigates the influence of hermits in England. The third chapter turns to recluses (anchorites shut inside cells) and the appeal of their distinctive vocation. The fourth chapter moves towards a practical perspective, accounting for the rise of anchorites by reference to the generosity of their sponsors and their

---

[31] E.g. R. Fulton, *From Judgment to Passion: Devotion to Christ and the Virgin Mary, 800–1200* (New York, 2002), 89, 90, 142.

[32] P. Brown, *Authority and the Sacred: Aspects of the Christianisation of the Roman World* (Cambridge, 1995), 57–60, 62, 74–5.

[33] C. S. Watkins, *History and the Supernatural in Medieval England* (Cambridge, 2007).

strenuous efforts as pioneers. Chapter 5 analyses the ways in which anachoresis was presented as a vocation for combating sin, while Chapter 6 illuminates what this meant in practice. Sometimes it entailed hair-raising confrontations with terrifying demons. The seventh chapter seeks to discover what anchorites offered to society that only anchorites could offer (and hence why people turned to them), and Chapter 8 demonstrates the extent of their eventual success, in their recognition as saints both in life and after death. The chronological parameters of the book (950–1200) are notional and flexible: they may represent the period in which anchorites were in the ascendant; alternatively they may serve as markers for demarcating the period normally identified as the central Middle Ages. Practicality too has its parameters. I cannot pretend to have unravelled the numerous traditions pertaining to Wales and Cornwall, or to have conducted much research into Ireland, Scotland, and the Isle of Man. Even my coverage of England was necessarily patchy, while the constraints of constructing an argument left little room for several big topics such as the relationship between eremitism and prophecy, the transformation of hermitages into monasteries, and the anchorite's authority over animal and elemental creation. I can only apologize for passing over the questions arising from these topics and urge other historians to articulate them. I must also apologize to those specialists whose areas of expertise serve as trampling grounds for my historical narratives. It is not my wish to occupy their territory – merely to pass through it. The present book is a study of the development of the anchoretic ideal and how it was perceived and lived in England during the central Middle Ages. The hope is that by seeking to understand a paradox intrinsic to that society, we may come rather closer to seeing how it worked.

DEFINITIONS AND SOURCES

To begin, it would be useful to sketch some outlines of hermits and recluses, to picture each in turn in their typical incarnations. Let us first consider Godric, a forty-year-old fisherman from Wisbech in Cambridgeshire, who abandoned his family and career about the year 1100 and went to live in the woods. When asked his reason, he recounted a vision in which the fisherman saint Andrew had appeared to him and told him to do penance for his sins. His time was spent in prayer, reciting psalms, and in overcoming temptations. Although he had once worn normal clothes, as a hermit he wore coarse garments, selected to chafe against his skin.[34] A girl named Eve, while still in her teens or not much older, left her nunnery at Wilton in Wiltshire, about the year 1080, determined to spend the rest of her life in a cell probably not much bigger than a toilet cubicle.

---

[34] GT, *passim.*

Servants, daily, would have passed her food (pulses, bread, or vegetables) in through a hatch, and others who chose her lifestyle are known to have prayed kneeling in open graves to remind themselves of death.[35] In hard winters, they almost died from numbing cold, but should the summer heat or some accident set fire to the churches which adjoined their cells they would sometimes sooner burn *in situ* than leave their appointed posts.[36] Godric would be called a 'hermit', from the Latin *heremita* or *eremita*. Eve would be called a 'recluse', from the Latin *reclusa*, which was used interchangeably with the noun *inclusa*. (A male recluse would be *reclusus* or *inclusus*.) Throughout the period 950–1200, both categories were usually labelled 'anchorites' from the Latin *anachoreta*, which was an umbrella label for ascetics who embraced withdrawal, either at liberty (hermits) or in the confines of a cell (recluses). The different meanings applied to these words stemmed from their different roots. The noun *anachoreta*, from the Greek equivalent ἀναχωρητής, was the broadest term because it meant 'one who is withdrawn'. The noun for 'hermit' (*eremita*), from the Greek ἐρημίτης, meant 'a person who dwells in the desert', whereas the Latin words for 'recluse' (*inclusus/ inclusa* and *reclusus/ reclusa*) derived from the verb *claudo*, meaning to close, shut off, or enclose.[37] Anchorites could thus be hermits or recluses. To many of their admirers, nonetheless, the distinction between these two divergent lifestyles was less important than their shared vocation for solitary spiritual warfare. Spurning worldly ambition, anchorites were supposed to spend their time on earth preparing their souls for eternity. Heaven was their goal. Their goad was fear of hell. Striving to live in obedience to God, these dedicated ascetics regarded their vocation as a tried and tested route to salvation, trodden over centuries by generations of saints.

How should historians define anchorites? A way to answer this question without engaging in semantics is with reference to prototypes on which anchorites patterned their vocation. Anchorites, in the central Middle Ages, were people who emulated the lifestyle of the earliest ascetics. The eleventh century in particular saw a renewal of interest in the asceticism of the early church.[38] In order to understand anchorites, one must therefore look to their roots. By that date, the solitary life of anchorites, next to the communal life of monks, was viewed as one of two great branches of monasticism that had grown up in Eastern and Western Christendom. Christian monasticism began in the deserts of third-

---

[35] *LC, passim*, and see below, 123–5, 203n. 14.

[36] See below, 70, 77–9.

[37] The key discussion of terminology is still J. Leclercq, '"Eremus" et "eremita": pour l'histoire du vocabulaire de la vie solitaire', *Collectanea Ordinis Cisterciensium Reformatorum*, 25 (1963), 8–30. At 25, Leclercq notes: 'La distinction de deux sortes de solitaires, les *ermites* et les *anachorètes*, est rare et artificielle'. See also C. du Fresne, sieur Du Cange, *Glossarium mediae et infimae latinitatis*, 10 vols (Niort, 1883–7) I, A-BAR, 236. *Anachoreta* corrupted to become *anachorita* in much the same way that *eremita* became *heremita*, in Medieval Latin.

[38] On hermits in this context, see Leclercq, 'The Monastic Crisis'; and Genicot, 'L'érémitisme', 61.

and fourth-century Egypt, where some of its many practitioners lived alone and others in groups, in accordance with the degree of separation which each desired. By the fifth century, a distinction was emerging between the solitary type (anchorites) and the monks that lived together and pooled all their resources (cenobites). In the sixth century, a further distinction was appearing, a subdivision within the first category between the anchorites who moved freely (hermits) and those shut inside cells (recluses). Cenobites, who probably outnumbered anchorites, took the label 'monks', and are the sort of monks to which the label usually applies today. During the Middle Ages, knowledge of famous anchorites and the anchoretic tradition was preserved in the sacred writings of monks and other clerics, although it was also the stuff of legend and oral tradition. Its shape owed much to the scholar, biblical translator, and sometime hermit St Jerome (*c.*341–420). Jerome was one of the first writers to distinguish between the life of monks in communities (cenobitism) and the solitary life of anchorites (anachoresis). He even equipped the latter vocation with a pedigree, identifying its author as the Egyptian hermit St Paul of Thebes (d. *c.*345), whom he called 'the first hermit'. Its exemplar or archetype was St Antony of Egypt (251–356), and St John the Baptist was its 'prince', meaning its forerunner and its most exalted practitioner.[39] Jerome's *Life* of St Paul the Hermit (recounting Paul's achievements) and his *Lives* of the other desert hermits SS. Hilarion and Malchus helped to mould medieval impressions of how virtuous anchorites should behave.[40] Even more influential was the *Life* of St Antony, originally composed in Greek by Athanasios, patriarch of Alexandria, before the fourth-century ascetic writer Evagrius translated it into Latin. St Antony, it claimed, had pursued an exemplary career in the Egyptian desert, first battling demons in the necropolis at Thebes on the west bank of the Nile, before driving Satan's minions from an abandoned fortress and claiming it as a new outpost for Christ.[41] Later he became a role model for monks and hermits alike.

SS. Paul, the first hermit, and Antony were usually numbered among the 'fathers' (though there were similarly some women) who had lived austerely alone or in small groups in the deserts of third- and fourth-century Egypt and the Near East. During the central Middle Ages, accounts of their lives, and collections of their sayings known as 'apothegmata', were staple monastic reading. Collectively these various works were known as the *Vitas patrum* ('*Lives* of the Fathers') and their theme, as the *Vita patrum* ('the *life* of the fathers', singular), which emphasized the unity of their life over any variations

---

[39] Jerome, *Sancti Eusebii Hieronymi epistulae*, ed. I. Hilberg, *CSEL*, 54–6, 3 vols, 2nd edn. (1996), XXII.36.

[40] *Vita s. Pauli Eremitae= BHL*, 6596; *Vitae ss. Hilarionis* and *Malchi= BHL*, 3879, 5190.

[41] The Evagrian *Vita s. Antonii= BHL*, 609. For the saint and his cult, see *Antonius magnus eremita, 356–1956: Studia ad antiquum monachismum spectantia*, ed. B. Steidle, *Analecta monastica, textes et études sur la vie des moines au moyen âge, troisième série, Studia Anselmiana*, 38 (Rome, 1956).

in their individual ascetic practices.[42] The collective labels *Vitas* and *Vita patrum* usually referred to the *Verba seniorum* (the 'sayings of the fathers'), a text so named by its early-modern editor. A collection of aphorisms and anecdotes, it was compiled in Greek in the fourth century, then translated into Latin during the sixth. Typically its sayings dealt with the virtues or temptations of the early hermits. For example: 'The abbot Antony said, "Who sits in solitude and is quiet has escaped from three wars: hearing, speaking, seeing; yet against one thing shall he continually battle: that is, his own heart".'[43] Sometimes the title *Vitas patrum* was also taken to include the *Historia monachorum* (the 'history of the monks'), a slightly later work weaving sayings and stories into an account of a visit by seven Palestinian monks to Egyptian monasteries and hermitages late in the fourth century. Solitary asceticism was no less important a theme in John Cassian's *Conlationes* (Conferences) and in the *Paradisus Heraclides*, or 'Lausiac History', by Palladius of Helenopolis, who was a disciple of Evagrius.[44] Other fathers and mothers of the early Christian period who were widely regarded as hermits during the central Middle Ages included SS. Macarius, Mary Magdalene, and Mary of Egypt, a reformed prostitute who did penance in the desert.[45]

In the early sixth century, the spiritual warfare of the desert fathers and mothers as described in these sacred writings determined how anchorites were depicted in the Rule of St Benedict, a template for life in the cenobium which later spread through Western Europe. There, in his first chapter, St Benedict of Nursia, 'father of monks', defined anchorites as monks who left their monasteries, well trained in asceticism, to perfect their combat with the devil in solitude.[46] In practice, not every anchorite served probation in a monastery, but the author clearly thought it advisable. The patristic encyclopaedist St Isidore of Seville (*c.*560–636) refined St Benedict's definition in his 'Ecclesiastical offices' (*De ecclesiasticis officiis*) by separating his synonymous 'hermits' and 'anchorites' (*heremitae* and *anachoretae*) into two distinct categories. According to Isidore, *heremitae* fled into lonely places far from humanity, whereas *anachoretae*, after attaining perfection in monasteries, enclosed themselves in cells.[47] Although Isidore's work was widely copied, his new distinction did not find its

---

[42] See, further, *Die 'Adhortationes sanctorum patrum' im lateinischen Mittelalter. Überlieferung, Fortleben und Wirkung*, ed. C. M. Batlle, BGAM, 31 (Münster, 1972).

[43] *Verba seniorum* = *BHL*, 6525, 6527–31. I cite *Verba sen.* II.2, tr. H. Waddell, *The Desert Fathers* (London, 1936), 91 (with minor modifications to modernize the prose).

[44] *Historia monachorum* = *BHL*, 6524; *Conlationes* = *CPL*, 512; *Paradisus Heraclides* = *BHL*, 6532.

[45] *Vita eremitica* = *BHL*, 5453–6. *Das altenglische Martyrologium*, ed. G. Kotzor, Abhandlungen (Bayerische Akademie der Wissenschaften. Philosophisch-Historische Klasse). Neue Folge, 88, 2 vols (Munich, 1981), II, no. 133.

[46] *La règle de Saint Benoît*, introd. and tr. A. de Vogüé, ed. J. Neufville, *SC*, 181–6, 7 vols in 6 (1971–2) I, 436–8.

[47] *De ecclesiasticis officiis* = *Clavis*, 1207: *Sancti Isidori episcopi Hispalensis De ecclesiasticis officiis*, ed. C. M. Lawson, *CCSL*, 113 (1989), 75.

way into the influential commentary on the Benedictine Rule penned by the Carolingian abbot Smaragdus of Saint-Mihiel (d. 843); it may not have aroused much interest.[48] The *Vitas patrum* nevertheless, like the Rule itself, became enormously influential in shaping the anchoretic vocation, so that medieval hagiographers and other spiritual writers often supposed that anchorites drew their inspiration from the desert fathers. St Nilus of Rossano (d. 1005), a Greek monk and anchorite from Byzantine Calabria, was thought to have drawn his inspiration from the example of SS. Antony, Saba, and Hilarion.[49] The French hermit Thibaut of Provins (d. 1066) allegedly looked to Elijah, the Baptist, St Paul, the first hermit, and St Antony, the originators of his vocation.[50] At Peterborough abbey in Cambridgeshire, in the early 1080s, the monk Goscelin composed a treatise on anachoresis for the recluse Eve, who inhabited a cell at Saint-Laurent-du-Tertre in Angers, in Anjou. Listing exemplary anchorites, he named the Baptist, Antony, Paul the Hermit, Arsenius, Mary Magdalene, Mary of Egypt, and Jerome. He also complimented Eve by observing that she was coming to be regarded as a solitary worthy of the Baptist's 'family' (*familia*), envisaging, in this comment, an anchoretic cloud of witnesses, which Eve had joined by virtue of her asceticism.[51] In another work, he described how the ninth-century hermit St Eadwold of Cerne Abbas, in Dorset, yearned to follow in the footsteps of Antony, Macarius, and the Baptist, 'prince of hermits' (the epithet appended to the Baptist by Jerome).[52] The idea, in both cases, was that anchorites and their imitators trod a tested road to heaven.

In England, over the period 950–1200, the word *anachoreta*, as previously noted, applied to hermits and recluses alike. At the same time there were still some learned individuals in the monasteries whose awareness of Isidore's differentiation between hermits and anchorites led them to attach the latter term specifically to recluses. One tenth-century copy of the Rule of St Benedict was interpolated to interpose Isidore's distinction as a gloss.[53] This could have been the action of a pedant, but equally the glossator may have thought it desirable to distinguish between solitaries that trained in monasteries and embraced the discipline of a cell and those that did not.[54] At the end of the twelfth century one begins to see more evidence that a special distinction was made. For instance,

---

[48] Compare Isidore with Smaragdus of Saint-Mihiel, *Expositio in regulam s. Benedicti*, ed. A. Spannagel and P. Engelbert, *CCM*, 8 (Siegburg, 1974), 56–7.

[49] C. Lohmer, *Heremi conversatio: Studien zu den monastichen Vorschriften des Petrus Damiani*, BGAM, 39 (Münster, 1991), 11.

[50] 'De sancto Theobaldo, presb. eremita diocesis Vicentinae in Italia', *Acta SS, Jun.* V, 592–5, at 593E.

[51] 'In eius familia tu cepisti censeri anachorita': *LC*, 75.

[52] Eadwold, 200.

[53] R. Jayatilaka, 'The Old English Benedictine Rule: Writing for Women and Men', *ASE*, 32 (2003), 147–87, at 181–2.

[54] Isidore's *De officiis* might have appeared in any well-stocked Anglo-Saxon library: see M. Lapidge, *The Anglo-Saxon Library* (Oxford, 2006), 127, 309–10.

during the reign of Richard I a hermit dwelling in the Forest of Dean could contemplate upgrading to 'the stricter life of an anchorite'; and during the early thirteenth century the prolific ecclesiastic Gerald of Wales (*c.*1146–*c.*1220) defined hermits as those that wandered alone, against anchorites, whom he defined as the strictly enclosed.[55] Even so, by the years around 1200 the distinction had still not caught on. As late as 1170 x 1230, another writer could refer to the hermit Godric of Finchale as *anachorita*. In 1193 x 1213, the Durham monk Geoffrey of Coldingham was applying the same term to the hermit Bartholomew of Farne.[56] How, then, did these terms come to be set apart? The distinction might have begun with Isidore and crystallized after the Conquest in the linguistic process of code-mixing. Old English, unlike Latin, possessed only the one word, *ancer* (anchorite), loaned from the Latin *anachoreta*.[57] This could explain why in pre-twelfth-century Anglo-Latin texts, its Latin equivalent *anachoreta* surfaces far more than *eremita*.[58] Anglo-Norman, on the other hand, used the Old French *hermite* (hermit) as well as *ancre*.[59] If the former term became loaded with a meaning distinct from the latter when it began to circulate in England this could explain their subsequent divergence. At the same time, a growing concern on the part of churchmen to define ecclesiastical institutions was seeking to compartmentalize anachoresis.[60] In eleventh-century England, the term *ancer* covered a spectrum of practices, but the twelfth century's interest in precision began to reduce its elasticity. The publication of the popular manual for recluses, *Ancrene Wisse*, in the early thirteenth century, wedded that term, by association, to the life of enclosure codified in its pages. Thereafter, recluses were more commonly labelled 'anchorites'.

Sometimes hermits and recluses appear in medieval documents without the labels that enable historians to identify them. When those anchorites are well known, this creates few difficulties. When the anchorites are obscure individuals, it matters rather more. Every anchorite who is listed in the anchorites' section of the Durham *Liber vitae* (book of life) is labelled *presbiter* (priest). Only the heading identifies them all as anchorites.[61] Any number of the innumerable

---

[55] Warren, *Anchorites*, 16; E. A. Jones, 'Christina of Markyate and *The Hermits and Anchorites of England*', in *Christina*, ed. Fanous and Leyser, 229–39, at 235.

[56] Blair, 'A Saint for Every Minster?', 489; *VB*, 295, 300, 325.

[57] Ælfric gives *anachoreta* as *ancra* (or *ancer*) in his glossary: J. Bosworth and T. N. Toller, *Anglo-Saxon Dictionary: Based on the Manuscript Collections of the Late Joseph Bosworth, edited and enlarged by T. Northcote Toller* (Oxford, 1972), 38–9.

[58] That is, unless the authors meant to use *anachoreta* in the way that Isidore employed it.

[59] *Anglo-Norman Dictionary*, ed. W. Rothwell, L. W. Stone, T. B. W. Reid, et al. (London, 1992), 354.

[60] *Libellus de diversis ordinibus et professionibus qui sunt in aecclesia*, ed. and tr. G. Constable and B. S. Smith (Oxford, 2003), 15–17, pleads for the recognition of diversity within the eremitical order. See also C. Morris, *The Papal Monarchy: The Western Church from 1050 to 1250* (Oxford, 1989), 250–7.

[61] *Die Gedenküberlieferung der Angelsachsen, mit einem Katalog der libri vitae und Necrologien*, ed. J. Gerchow, Arbeiten zur Frühmittelalterforschung, 20 (Berlin, 1988), 305.

presbiteri who appear in charters, necrologies, and other sources might likewise have been *anachoretae*. The *heremitae* and *solitarii* who appear, on the other hand, might in some instances have been loners who had acquired a nickname. By 1237, one place belonging to Chetwode priory in Buckinghamshire had become known as 'the hermitage', not because any hermit had lived there but because the spot was deserted.[62] Sometimes those living in anchoretic withdrawal were referred to as 'monk' (*monachus*) or 'brother' (*frater*). These labels were even thought appropriate for hermits who had never joined a monastery. Female labels like *inclusa* (an enclosed woman) and *ancilla Dei* (God's handmaiden) could refer to an anchorite, nun, or vowess. Hermitages, in the period covered in this book, evade categorization. Martin Heale's comprehensive study of priories works on the premise that hermitages properly contained only one occupant, but this is a working definition for setting the parameters of his inquiry.[63] Religious houses with several occupants were sometimes called hermitages. One hermitage in Norfolk at Downham Market, mentioned in a charter of 1180 x 1207, supported four brethren.[64] Worcester cathedral priory's dependent monastery at Packington in Warwickshire, by the late twelfth century, had a prior and convent, yet it was still being called a hermitage.[65] Medieval England nurtured all sorts of cells, hermitages, and miniature monasteries. What they were called and how they were perceived depended on how their occupants or patrons viewed them. This illustrates just how much medieval ideas differed from modern perceptions of anachoresis, for although many hermits and recluses lived in solitude, as we picture them in our imaginations, this was not true of all. Some dwelt in communities of sparsely clustered cells, sufficiently far apart to retain some degree of solitude yet close enough to exchange support and consolation. This should be no surprise, given that the terminology – *anachoreta* for 'one who is withdrawn' and *eremita* meaning 'one who dwells in the desert' – did not assume or imply isolation. Of the two words which did carry this meaning, *monachus* (monk), from the Greek μοναχός for 'one who lives alone', came to refer to quite the opposite, whereas the Latin noun *solitarius* ('one who dwells alone') kept its meaning of individual solitude.

No systematic records of hermits and recluses were kept in the Middle Ages, just as no systematic effort was made – beyond the overly zealous efforts of several of the Domesday commissioners – to catalogue every pig, peasant, or parish church. Where they do turn up in the sources they often appear randomly and unexpectedly. Eddie Jones, building on the work of Rotha Clay, is undertaking

---

[62] R. E. Latham, *Dictionary of Medieval Latin from British Sources, Fascicule III D-E* (London, 1986), 792.

[63] M. Heale, *The Dependent Priories of Medieval English Monasteries* (Woodbridge, 2004), 7–8.

[64] *Cartularium monasterii de Rameseia*, ed. W. H. Hart and P. A. Lyons, RS, 79, 3 vols (1884–93), II, 190.

[65] *The Cartulary of Worcester Cathedral Priory, Register I*, ed. R. R. Darlington, Publications of the Pipe Roll Society, 76, n.s., 38 (London, 1968 for 1962/3), no. 313.

the Herculean labour of cataloguing them all.[66] Most anchorites can be found in monastic charter collections (i.e. cartularies). Sometimes they witness charters then vanish from the records, like Walter the hermit of Horwood.[67] In other instances, their hermitages are noticed only to determine the boundaries of estates that happen to have been involved in land transactions. When Roger, son of Payn de Helpston, granted his meadow at Paynesholme to Peterborough abbey in 1233 x 1245, his charter recorded that it lay between the village of Peakirk and the hermitage of St Bartholomew in the marsh.[68] The reference is quite incidental and gives no useful indication of how long the hermitage had been there. Elsewhere anchorites surface erratically. We know about a recluse named Ælfwen only because a contemporary historian retold a couple of her stories.[69] A twelfth-century recluse is known only because the precentor of Salisbury cathedral chose to dedicate a set of meditations to her.[70] Some hermits and recluses are untraceable: inscrutable names in lists of the dead to be comme-morated (necrologies), such as 'John the anchorite' in a necrology from Evesham abbey, and 'Godwine the hermit', in another from Durham cathedral priory.[71] Others have become nameless statistics. The Pipe Roll for 1169 records that Bishop Nigel of Ely supported six recluses from the revenues of his see.[72] Nothing more is known about them. None of these anchorites entered the records by virtue of their vocation, and in this they are representative of the vast majority known. Anchorites whose qualities caught the attention of hagio-graphers were exceptional. As for the rest, with so many glimpses of their hidden networks it is hard to avoid the impression that they were far more numerous than records reveal. To read about the adventures of the runaway bride Christina is to wade into the shallows of an invisible ocean of anchorites. It could be posited that the documentation of these figures was almost mathematically proportional to the volume of documentation that was produced: the more cartularies, necrologies, letters, chronicles, and hagiographies that were written, the greater their chance of being mentioned. Where anchorites left archaeological or onomastic traces, like cells attached to churches or place-names such as *Ancrewic*, the historian can sometimes press these into service. But these are few and far between. Commenting on the situation in Western Europe over the

---

[66] E. Jones, 'Rotha Clay's *Hermits and Anchorites of England*', *Monastic Research Bulletin*, 3 (1997), 46–8; *idem*, 'The Hermits and Anchorites of Oxfordshire', *Oxoniensia*, 63 (1998), 51–77, and 'Christina', in *Christina*, ed. Fanous and Leyser. His final catalogue will greatly benefit research.

[67] *Luffield Priory Charters*, ed. G. R. Elvey, Buckinghamshire Record Society, 15, 18; Northamptonshire Record Society, 22, 26, 2 vols (Welwyn Garden City, 1968–75), II, 89.

[68] CUL, Peterborough Dean and Chapter MS 5, fo. 146r (fo. 150r new foliation).

[69] *Memorials of St. Edmund's Abbey*, ed. T. Arnold, RS, 96, 3 vols (1890–6), I, 38–9.

[70] T. Webber, *Scribes and Scholars at Salisbury Cathedral, c.1075–c.1125* (Oxford, 1992), 124.

[71] L, BL, MS Lansdowne 427, fos. 1–19 (against 3 October); *Liber uitae ecclesiae Dunelmensis: nec non obituaria duo ejusdem ecclesiae*, ed. J. Stevenson, SS, 13 (1841), 146 (against 5 October).

[72] PR, 16 Henry II (1169–70), 96.

period 550–1150, Henrietta Leyser has wisely observed: 'there was . . . no lack of hermits throughout the whole of this period; the evidence for their existence may be varied and scattered but it is also constant'.[73]

It is worth keeping this point in mind, because the frequent opacity, unevenness, and heterogeneity of the sources create false impressions. Sarah Foot's work reveals that in the tenth and eleventh centuries female recluses were seldom clearly labelled.[74] Mary Clayton cautions that a dearth in recorded anchorites in the late ninth and early tenth centuries corresponds all too closely with a dearth in the documentation for that era, generating the illusion of a fluctuating population where the number of anchorites might, in reality, have remained constant.[75] Her caveat applies to the eleventh century too, in relation to the twelfth, and to the twelfth in relation to the thirteenth. For the types of source that were most likely to mention anchorites, namely administrative records such as charters and account rolls, or history and hagiography, proliferated from the twelfth century and were either rarer or absent before that period (and also less likely to survive).[76] If our only way of judging the vitality of anachoresis is to count up the number of anchorites in the sources we are very likely to arrive at a distorted impression, so it is better to assess their impact in other ways. John Blair is sensitive to this problem. His research into patterns of cultic activity through the Anglo-Saxon and Anglo-Norman eras suggests that in the ninth and tenth centuries a number of anchorites were revered as saints, even if the only remaining evidence is from later medieval legends. His provisional list of possible Anglo-Saxon anchorite saints proposes that Hartland in Devon had a hermit saint called Nectan; Somerset, one named Ælfgar, and that Staffordshire and Cheshire had cult centres dedicated to the putative hermit Beorhthelm. Derbyshire might have revered a solitary ascetic called Barloc in certain localities, Sussex, an anchorite named Cuthman, and Warwickshire the female solitary Eadgyth. Stowe in Northamptonshire revered the martyr Ælfnoth, whom the villagers honoured with a feast and who may have been an anchorite, while Oxfordshire had the hermits SS. Freomund and Frithuswith.[77] Blair notes that these putative anchorites represent no more than an accidental scattering of those who attained the status of saints – probably a small minority – and whose legends happen to have survived outside the monasteries, which (because of their interest in written records and the preservation of saints' cults) became the surest vehicles for the transmission of memory.[78] Although the legends of the saints were constantly being

[73] Leyser, *Hermits*, 12.

[74] Foot, *Veiled Women I*, 179–88.

[75] Clayton, 'Hermits', 157.

[76] A. Williams, *The English and the Norman Conquest* (Woodbridge, 1995), 165; M. T. Clanchy, *From Memory to Written Record: England 1066–1307*, 2nd edn. (Oxford, 1993).

[77] J. Blair, 'A Handlist of Anglo-Saxon Saints', in *Local Saints*, ed. Thacker and Sharpe, 495–565, at 546–7, 503, 515–16, 513–14, 523, 527, 505, 535, 536.

[78] John Blair observes that Anglo-Saxon England was 'a world in which a saint's memory could only effectively be promoted in a religious community': Blair, 'A Saint for Every Minster?', 456.

reformulated – and it is hard in any of these cases to know the pedigree of the cult or whether its object really was an anchorite – the relevant point to be drawn from Blair's argument is that we run the risk of overlooking any number of anchorites when we look for them solely in contemporary written sources, where records are so haphazard.

Detailed information about anchorites appears in that genre of historical writing known as hagiography, the objectives of which were to glorify God by recounting the deeds of his saints, to magnify the saints in the process, and to perpetuate patterns of religious conduct, illustrating righteous living. It was a historical genre in as much as its aims accorded with Isidore of Seville's definition of the historian's task, to recount 'whatever is worth recounting'.[79] Yet its concern to perpetuate spiritual truths and depict its subjects as saints took precedence over the classical historical concern to evaluate evidence critically. Hagiography operated by attributing to its subjects the exemplary character traits and feats of established saints. Perceptions of anachoresis were so reliant on these exemplars that to become an anchorite, figuratively speaking, was to be recast in their mould. To appreciate how anachoresis was perceived in the period 950–1200, we must therefore think of it as preconceived, both in the ways the anchorites were depicted and the ways they lived their lives. Preconceptions appear in hagiography as underlying themes, while circumstantial details provide insights into the lives of real, historical anchorites. The saints' *Lives* employed in this book mostly fall into one of two categories: either the sort that was very close to its subject, written when the subject was alive or memories were fresh, or the sort separated from its subject by centuries. The *Life* of the hermit Godric of Finchale (d. 1170) falls into the first category because it was underway before Godric's death. The *Life* of the ninth-century hermit St Eadwold falls into the second because it was written two hundred years after the lifetime of its protagonist.[80] The first sort of *Life* may indicate what anchorites were doing and how they were regarded at the time of writing. The second sort may only reveal what was thought about them at the time of writing (although this in itself is useful for shedding light on attitudes towards them). Earlier chapters in this book rely somewhat less on hagiography than later ones for the reason that less is available from Anglo-Saxon England. Where alternative sources, such as sermons, letters, charters, and wills, touch on anachoresis they are brought into the inquiry. The most prolific late Anglo-Saxon writer was the learned homilist Ælfric (*c*.950–*c*.1010), who trained at Winchester before migrating to Cerne Abbas in Dorset, then from Cerne to Eynsham, in Oxfordshire, where he became abbot in 1005. Ælfric had an ambivalent attitude towards anchorites. His contemporaries

---

[79] Isidore of Seville, *Etymologiarum sive originum libri xx*, ed. W. M. Lindsay, 2 vols (Oxford, 1911) I.44.3. Isidore himself did not identify hagiography as a separate form of historical writing.
[80] *LG*; Eadwold.

too, in their various writings, occasionally offer insights into attitudes towards anchorites during their era.

From the 1060s onwards, more saints' *Lives* survive, although mostly of the sort separated from its subject by centuries. Now and then they reveal what their authors or audiences thought they knew about anchorites. The prolific monk Goscelin is useful in this respect because hermits and recluses often appear in his *Lives* and his treatise on anachoresis, of *c.*1080, written for the nun Eve after she left her monastery and became a recluse in Anjou. This occasionally impassioned work, which conveys Goscelin's sorrow and bitterness at losing an object of his affection, contemplates the anchoretic vocation at length.[81] Like some contemporary works of hagiography, it tells stories about anchorites alive at the time or not long dead. The twelfth century supplies many detailed saints' *Lives* of the sort much closer to its subject. No fewer than ten anchorites alive during the twelfth century became the protagonists of *Lives* before the middle of the thirteenth. Reginald, a monk of Durham, wrote a *Life* of the hermit Godric of Finchale (*c.*1070–1170) in the 1160s and 1170s.[82] The Cistercian John of Ford, *c.*1185, wrote about the recluse Wulfric of Haselbury (*c.*1090–1155).[83] The anchorites Henry of Coquet (d. 1127/8), Caradog (in Wales, d. 1124), and Ælgar (also in Wales, d. *c.*1095) augment the list.[84] The unfinished *Life* of Christina of Markyate (*c.*1096 – after 1155), whose adventures were outlined earlier, was probably composed in the mid- or late twelfth century. *Lives* of the hermits Bartholomew of Farne (d. 1193) and Robert of Knaresborough (d. 1218) were penned before 1213 and *c.*1250, respectively.[85] Less familiar to historians are the anchorites Wulfsige of Evesham (d. *c.*1100), whose miracles – now lost – were collected before 1207, and Godric of Throckenholt (*c.*1060–*c.*1140), whose hagiography is late twelfth century.[86] Their *Lives* supply much of the evidence used in this book. Sources concerning recluses in our period encompass charters, a pontifical enclosure ritual, a handbook of advice put together for recluses in the 1160s by the Cistercian abbot Aelred of Rievaulx, and the famous manual *Ancrene Wisse.*[87] Composed *c.*1215 and reworked *c.*1230 by an anonymous cleric, the revised version notes that by *c.*1230 there were twenty or more anchoresses following its injunctions, in London, Oxford, Shrewsbury, and Chester. They regarded it as a 'rule' (they were 'of anred lif efter a riwle'), but to others it was probably merely a book of advice, hence the designation

---

[81] *LC.*

[82] *LG.*

[83] *WH.*

[84] *NL* II, 22–6; I, 174–6; *The Text of the Book of Llan Dâv: Reproduced from the Gwysaney Manuscript*, ed. J. G. Evans and J. Rhys (Oxford, 1893), 1–5; J. R. Davies, *The Book of Llandaf and the Norman Church in Wales* (Woodbridge, 2003), 96, 124–8.

[85] *VB; VRK.*

[86] For Wulfsige, see below, 175–7; for Godric, GT.

[87] H. A. Wilson, *The Pontifical of Magdalen College*, HBS, 39 (1910), 243–4.

wisse.[88] Where remnants of caves or cells survive, archaeology allows the evidence of written sources to be checked against physical remains. Elsewhere, it is a sobering reminder of how little information is left: for the majority of anchorites mentioned in medieval documents have left no physical trace, and we seldom know who occupied the surviving cells and caves. With so few pieces of the jigsaw, it would be easy to create a false picture, but these, at least, are the sorts of pieces we must try to arrange.

---

[88] *Ancrene Wisse: A Corrected Edition of the Text in Cambridge, Corpus Christi College, MS 402, with variants from other manuscripts*, ed. B. Millett, drawing on the uncompleted edition by E. J. Dobson, with a glossary and additional notes by R. Dance, EETS, 325–6, 2 vols (Oxford, 2005–6), I, 96.

1

The Anglo-Saxon and European background

THE ANGLO-SAXON INHERITANCE, 650–950

The omnipresence of anchorites in England by the early twelfth century bears witness to the appeal of the universal anchorite as a cultural reference point: as a type of imagined persona by which society gave form and substance to notions of virtue, holiness, and renunciation.[1] This reference point, which may have borne little relation to the conduct of real anchorites beyond providing an ideal template of how they should behave, was grounded on certain presuppositions which in turn derived from recurring themes and motifs in the tales that were told, the songs that were sung, and the wisdom that was handed down, from generation to generation, when the subject matter arose. Anchorites, according to Anglo-Saxon tradition, strived to be holy by devoting their attention to God and renouncing the pleasures of this world; they battled vigilantly against the demons which inhabited the untamed wilderness; they restored nature's proper harmony by subordinating their wills to the will of God (although this was a rather sophisticated point). In recognition of this, the wild elements, beasts, and birds of fallen creation submitted to their commands. Anchorites also won fame as seers, prophets, and ascetics, and as the counsellors of nobles and kings. Occasionally a tale described how some anchorite or other fell from grace, but the majority of references to anchorites in surviving Anglo-Saxon sermons, poetry, letters, and hagiography are at least respectful if not openly reverential and full of admiration. It is not within the purview of the present book to ask how solitaries of the seventh and eighth centuries achieved their laudable reputation (we are asking that question of a later period). But to understand why England supported so many anchorites in the period 950–1200 it is essential, nonetheless, to reflect on that legacy of reverence and assess its contribution to the phenomenon in question. Did the inherited attitude of admiration, gathering its own head of

---

[1] The symbolic anthropology of the anchorite is examined in J. Howe, 'The awesome hermit: the symbolic significance of the hermit as a possible research perspective', *Numen* 30, fasc. 1 (1983), 106–119, which interprets the anchorite as a locus of the sacred (i.e. 'that which is specially set apart').

steam, eventually bubble over to flood the realm with anchorites, or was some catalyst required to bring it to the boil? A prevailing tradition of reverence for anchorites in the period 650–950 may not be enough in itself to explain their ubiquity or their benefit to society in the eleventh and twelfth centuries, but it might help to account for both those things if considered in conjunction with other key influences. Accordingly, the first part of this chapter examines the native legacy of reverence for anchorites and the second elucidates the growth of their influence in eleventh-century Europe, which may have been the catalyst that sped their proliferation across England.

England in the age of Bede flourished with prosperity. The period *c.*680–*c.*790 witnessed an increase in long-distance trade and the associated growth of markets and trading centres; an intensification of agricultural production, which advanced apace with population growth; freer circulation of a silver currency than at any subsequent point before the high Middle Ages, and the multiplication of centres of religious life, patronage, and learning.[2] Bede's great monastery at Jarrow sustained its communal spiritual endeavours and intellectual inquiry on the surplus generated by a thriving economy, which also facilitated the commitment to periodic, and in some instances permanent, solitary religious withdrawal, which was an integral part of monasticism wherever Irish or other native British monks moulded monastic spirituality. Many monasteries appear to have been designed to achieve a healthy degree of interaction between the communal life and anchoretic withdrawal, providing hermits' cells within or beyond the precinct so that their members might invigorate their devotions, retreat during Lent for ascetic or penitential purposes, and determine the demands of their vocations by experimenting with different degrees of solitude.[3] In Irish spirituality, voluntary religious exile for the love of God was eulogized as the noblest form of sacrifice. The influence of this ideal in England (as in Ireland) probably had the effect of inspiring a number of the most devoted religious to aspire to anachoresis, which in turn would have perpetuated its reputation for being the pathway trodden by saints. Two who shone forth in Bede's era were St Cuthbert of Farne and Lindisfarne (*c.*637–87) and St Guthlac of Repton and Crowland (*c.*673–715), who, according to their hagiographers, arrived at the vocation by the monastic route set out in the Benedictine Rule, before re-enacting the trials of the desert fathers. The *Life* of St Cuthbert, in its better-known version, is the

---

[2] G. Astill, 'General Survey 600–1300', in *The Cambridge Urban History of Britain, Volume I 600–1540*, ed. D. M. Palliser (Cambridge, 2000), 27–49, at 30–2; M. Blackburn, '"Productive" Sites and the Pattern of Coin Loss in England, 600–1180', in *Markets in Early Medieval Europe: Trading and 'Productive' Sites, 650–850*, ed. T. Pestell and K. Ulmschneider (Macclesfield, 2003), 20–36, at 26–34; and J. Campbell, 'Production and Distribution in Early and Middle Anglo-Saxon England', in *ibid.*, 12–19, at 17–18; D. Hinton, *Gold and Gilt, Pots and Pins: Possessions and People in Medieval Britain* (Oxford, 2005), 84–5.

[3] Clayton, 'Hermits', 153–4; J. Blair, *The Church in Anglo-Saxon Society* (Oxford, 2005), 216–8; A. Macquarrie, 'Early Christian Religious Houses in Scotland: Foundation and Function', in *Pastoral Care before the Parish*, ed. J. Blair and R. Sharpe (Leicester, 1992), 110–33, at 113–14.

work of the Venerable Bede, who closely followed an anonymous *Life* which patterned Cuthbert on St Antony. Initially Cuthbert trained as a monk in the monastery at Lindisfarne before obtaining leave to enter a cell in its outer precincts and embrace the vocation of an anchorite; 'but when he had fought there in solitude for some time with the invisible enemy, by prayer and fasting, he sought a place of combat farther and more remote from mankind, aiming at greater things'. Crossing to the uninhabited island of Inner Farne, he expelled the resident demons.[4] His conflict entailed 'fasting, prayers, and vigils', fixing his gaze on God (that is, by constructing his hermit's cell in such a way that he could see only the heavens), and 'the undisturbed practice of prayers and psalm singing'.[5] Although St Cuthbert was summoned later on to become bishop of the Northumbrian see at Lindisfarne, he remained a hermit at heart. Nearing death, he returned to his hermitage to die as one.

Later, in the eighth century, the monk Felix presented a comparable figure in his *Life* of St Guthlac, whom he patterned on SS. Antony and Cuthbert.[6] After leading an army of freebooters, Guthlac vowed to expunge his sins, so he entered the monastery at Repton in Derbyshire, where he rapidly developed an interest in the desert fathers. Longing to follow in their footsteps, he obtained the permission of his elders to depart in search of a suitable wilderness. 'In the midland district of Britain', Felix observed,

[lies] a dismal fen of immense size, which begins at the banks of the river Granta not far from the camp which is called Cambridge, and stretches from the south as far north as the sea. It is a very long tract, now consisting of marshes, now of bogs, sometimes of black waters overhung by fog, sometimes studded with wooded islands and traversed by the windings of tortuous streams.[7]

Here, on a remote island haunted by demons, after hollowing out his dwelling in a robbed-out tumulus, for the last fifteen years of his life Guthlac lived as an anchorite. During his sojourn at Crowland on the borderlands of the Mercian and East Anglian kingdoms, he earned a reputation as a wise counsellor and a prophet. Notable visitors included Bishop Headda of Lichfield and the future monarch Æthelbald, king of the Mercians (r. 716–57). According to Felix's scheme, Guthlac's achievement lay in successfully recreating, in eighth-century England, the ascetic struggles that Antony had endured four hundred years earlier, in the Egyptian desert. The links which were made with the desert fathers

---

[4] *Anon. Vita Cuthberti* = *BHL*, 2019; *Vita Cuthberti Bedae* = *BHL*, 2021. *Two Lives of Saint Cuthbert: A Life by an Anonymous Monk of Lindisfarne and Bede's Prose Life*, ed. and tr. B. Colgrave (Cambridge, 1940, repr. 1985), 215–17 (Colgrave's translation).

[5] *Ibid.*, 221, 217, 261. On Middle-Saxon Hermitages, see Blair, *The Church*, 216–20.

[6] For the influence of the Evagrian St Antony on Felix, see H. Mayr-Harting, *The Coming of Christianity to Anglo-Saxon England*, 3rd edn. (University Park, PA, 1991), 237–9.

[7] *Vita Guthlaci* = *BHL*, 3723. B. Colgrave, *Felix's Life of Saint Guthlac: Introduction, Text, Translation and Notes* (Cambridge, 1956), 87 (Colgrave's translation). On Guthlac, see H. Mayr-Harting, 'Guthlac [St Guthlac] (674–715)', *ODNB*.

(as much, no doubt, by these hermits themselves, who would have patterned their conduct upon them, as by their monastic hagiographers) hallowed the anchorites' vocation with the authority of antique tradition and justified their claims to possess authority over demonic, animal, and elemental creation, along with prophetic powers and insight into the divine will. Both Cuthbert and Guthlac won admiration at the very highest levels of the social hierarchy, the former being summoned reluctantly from his hermitage when King Ecgfrith (d. 685) wanted a good bishop, the latter attracting the literary attention of the learned scholar Felix, who dedicated his *Life* of Guthlac to Ælfwald, king of the East Angles (r. *c.*713–49). This set a precedent for later kings, nobles, and scholars to admire famous anchorites. After Guthlac's death, in the time of his successor, the hermit Cissa, King Æthelbald enriched his shrine at Crowland. He may have founded the minster dedicated to St Guthlac at Hereford in Mercia, although the dedication is not attested before the late tenth century.[8] Such was the hermit's enduring popularity that Felix's Latin *Life* was translated into English, some time round about Alfred's reign (871–99). Details of his achievements were also included in the *Old English Martyrology* (an eighth- or ninth-century Mercian Who's Who of saints), which celebrated numerous saintly hermits.[9]

Spiritual traditions north of the River Humber rendered that region particularly favourable to anchorite cults. Reverence there for the solitary life was inspired in part by its venerable status in Irish Christianity, the faith that had evangelized the region, and in part by legends of hermits in the golden era of Northumbrian monasticism, the age of Saints Cuthbert and Bede, when saints peopled the north. Even before Guthlac withdrew to his tumulus in the Cambridgeshire fens, northern hermits were perching themselves on fearsome rocky islands battered by the sea. Bede records that St Aidan (d. 651), leader of the Irish mission to Northumbria, retreated periodically to Inner Farne, to be followed in turn on a permanent basis by Cuthbert (d. 687), Oidiluald (d. 699), Felgild, and others.[10] Memory of their sanctity was preserved among successive generations of monks and clerics at Lindisfarne, then a few miles north of Durham at Chester-le-Street, then at Durham itself. This community listed their names among the godly in a ninth-century *Liber vitae* (Book of Life), which is set out hierarchically. The hermits – twenty-eight of them (every one a priest) – outrank even priestly abbots. Oidiluald heads the list; further down are Balthere (d. 756); the hermit goldsmith Billfrith, who, according to the cleric Ealdred, writing at Chester-le-Street in the late tenth century, adorned the Lindisfarne Gospels; and Echha (d. 767), hermit

---

[8] P. Sims-Williams, *Religion and Literature in Western England, 600–800* (Cambridge, 1990), 60, n. 25 and 146, n. 16.

[9] *Martyrologium*, ed. Kotzor, II, no. 63. Clayton, 'Hermits', 154, lists some of the hermits (including late-antique ones) who appear in it.

[10] Clayton, 'Hermits', 153; *Bede's Ecclesiastical History of the English People*, ed. B. Colgrave and R. A. B. Mynors (Oxford, 1969), 263, 455; *Cuthbert*, ed. Colgrave, 100, 154, 349, 359.

of Crayke in the North Riding.[11] Alcuin (*c.*740–804), deacon of the cathedral church at York and scholar in the court of Charlemagne, composed a prayer to Balthere probably in the 780s, praising him as a mighty warrior who had vanquished devils high up on the terrible Bass Rock, encompassed by the sea. He told of the hermit Echha, a prophet, and of Ecgberht, who embraced voluntary exile in search of God (the traditional path of Irish ascetic renunciation). He wrote of Ecgberht's companion Wihtberht, a hermit renowned for godliness who lay enshrined at Ripon minster in North Yorkshire; and of St Wilgisl, whose island hermitage drew visitors from miles around.[12] Away from Mercia and Northumbria, where records are sparser, anchorites are harder to find. Late legends are not to be trusted, for anchoretic credentials easily became attached to saintly careers lost in the mists of time; but a combination of toponymic, topographic, and archaeological evidence suggests that one or two islands in the Somerset Levels, in the vicinity of Glastonbury minster, attracted hermits in the Middle Saxon era.[13] The case of the Irish hermit St Fursa (d. 649), who obtained permission from King Sigeberht of the East Angles to establish a hermitage at a place called *Cnobheresburg*, hints that at least one hermit also found favour with a king of the eastern seaboard.[14]

What, then, can be said about the importance of anchorites in the Middle Saxon kingdoms? Some certainly carried influence at the highest level, but there is no good reason, beyond an acknowledgement of what evidence may now be lost, for thinking that hermits were numerous except perhaps in Northumbria. In the handlist of saints compiled by John Blair, very few plausible examples, noted in contemporary sources, appear, and although there are many more dubious ones even those are outnumbered by the bishops, abbots, monks, abbesses, and nuns who comprise the vast majority.[15] The ninth century ushered in a period of economic stagnation, which was exacerbated by the disruption caused by Scandinavian invasion and settlement. The subsequent atrophy of monasticism robbed anchorites and potential anchorites of institutions that helped promote their vocation and introduce them to the lives of exemplary ascetics. King Alfred's biographer Asser, writing *c.*893, complained that people in England at that time lacked appetite for the monastic life.[16] It may not be surprising, then, that few ninth-century anchorites emerge, and it is telling perhaps that two of the

---

[11] *Katalog*, ed. Gerchow, 305. On the Durham *Liber vitae*, see *The Durham Liber vitae and Its Context*, ed. D. Rollason, A. J. Piper, M. Harvey, and L. Rollason (Woodbridge, 2004).

[12] Alcuin, *The Bishops, Kings and Saints of York*, ed. P. Godman (Oxford, 1982), 83, 105–9; S. Foot, 'Anglo-Saxon Minsters: A Review of Terminology', in *Pastoral Care*, ed. Blair and Sharpe, 212–25, at 217.

[13] Blair, *The Church*, 218, citing the example of Beckery.

[14] *Ecclesiastical History*, ed. Colgrave and Mynors, 269–77.

[15] Blair, 'A Saint for Every Minster?' and 'Handlist'. Blair is the first to accept that the origins of many of these cults, and the identities of the saints they addressed, are now obscure.

[16] Asser, 'De rebus gestis Alfredi', *Life of King Alfred: Together with the Annals of St Neots Erroneously Ascribed to Asser*, ed. W. H. Stevenson and improved by D. Whitelock (Oxford, 1959), ch. 93.

most prominent, Eadwold, who lived near Cerne Abbas in Dorset, and Thancred, who lived on the island of Thorney in the Cambridgeshire fens, were remembered as an exile from and as a martyr to the Vikings respectively. It is doubtful, even in their cases, whether they prove the resilience of anachoresis during this period, because neither is mentioned in any contemporary source: every detail of their legends could be tenth- or eleventh-century fiction.[17] Nevertheless, it would be unwise to ignore them in light of the continuity of oral tradition and the credible topographic elements in each cult: the holy well linked with Eadwold (a feature in many West-Country hermit cults) and the similarity and proximity of Thancred's fen island to the island site chosen by St Guthlac. The comparable site at Plemstall, in Cheshire, where Plegmund, the future archbishop of Canterbury (890–914), supposedly lived as a hermit in the ninth century also has topographic and toponymic elements which favour the legendary tale.[18] These scraps of evidence could support the argument that anchorites continued to thrive in the period 800–950, in Wessex, Mercia, and East Anglia. Even if only a few distinguished themselves, their paucity need not mean that they suffered any loss of reputation. Whoever put together the *Old English Martyrology* admired anchoretic saints. Felix's *Life* of St Guthlac and St Gregory the Great's *Dialogues*, which were translated into English in the era of King Alfred (the latter at the king's command), presented anachoresis as a pathway to sanctity; and an anchorite from Brittany was commended to King Athelstan.[19] Even if the living reality of anachoresis was no longer much in evidence, therefore, the ideal must have retained potency throughout the period, or at the very least lain dormant, ready to awake in more favourable times. Meanwhile, developments in anchoretic life were underway in other parts of Europe.

THE WIDER EUROPEAN CONTEXT, 950–1100

Italy

Like England, the rest of Christianized Europe had already been conditioned to venerate anchorites, for it too had plenty of anchoretic saints. From 950, however, it was brought into closer contact with the vocation as hermits began to make an impact in southern and central Italy. In the past, historians argued that Greek hermits, having inspired emulation among the Latins, initiated an eremitic revival that swept across the West, but their view has since lost

---

[17] Eadwold. For Thorney's saints, see below, 46–7.

[18] J. McN. Dodgson, *The Place-Names of Cheshire*, EPNS, 44–8, 54, 74, 5 vols in 7 (Cambridge, 1970–81), IV (vol. 47), 135–6. I am grateful to John Blair for this suggestion.

[19] C. Brett, 'A Breton Pilgrim in England in the Reign of King Æthelstan', in *France and the British Isles in the Middle Ages and Renaissance: Essays by Members of Girton College, Cambridge, in Memory of Ruth Morgan*, ed. G. Jondorf and D. Dumville (Woodbridge, 1991), 43–70.

ground.[20] It is evident, at least, that from the mid-tenth century the various traditions of Eastern monasticism began to revive and blossom through the Byzantine Empire in a freshly favourable climate of imperial approval and sponsorship.[21] Hermits everywhere were recreating the lifestyle of the desert fathers, prizing asceticism or withdrawal, and reviving the *lavra*: an early type of monastery, associated with St Antony, in which anchorites pursuing contemplative solitude occupied individual cells under the guidance of an abbot. The *lavra* was not so much a community as a recruiting and training ground where enthusiastic but inexperienced ascetics could imitate more seasoned spiritual warriors.[22] Mountainous landscapes with networks of caves most suited its vision of solitude (*eremia*) and individual asceticism (*hesychia*). The movement of recruits between the mountains ebbed and flowed in accordance with the reputations of great ascetics, who attracted numerous imitators and disciples. This form of monasticism won favour in the highest circles; before he became emperor, Nikephoras II Phokas (963–9) planned to occupy the first hermitage in the *lavra* on Mount Athos, although he never took up residence.[23] By the late tenth century, in the westernmost territories of the Empire (the themes of southern Italy), many hermits occupied such settlements. Where saints arose among them, their disciples wrote their *Lives*, recounting the feats of spiritual athletes such as St Elias the Speleote (d. *c*.960) – a cave-dweller – and St Luke of Armento (d. 993).[24] The *Lives* reveal that in Sicily, Calabria, and Basilicata, during the late tenth century, these hermits lived peripatetically among the mountains and forests, founding lavriote monasteries for their followers.[25] They also indicate that many moved away from the predominantly Greek regions of southernmost Italy into Lombard territory, as far north as Campania and Lazio, in some instances to escape Muslim attacks, or in search of lonelier regions.[26] Not long afterwards and not far away, in Abruzzo, Umbria, and Tuscany, a form of eremitic monasticism similar to the lavriote variety took hold among the Latins, chiefly under Romuald of Ravenna (d. 1023 x 1027),

---

[20] See M. Dunn, 'Eastern Influence on Western Monasticism in the Eleventh and Twelfth Centuries', in *Byzantium and the West c.850– c.1250. Proceedings of the XVIII Spring Symposium of Byzantine Studies*, Byzantinische Forschungen. Internationale Zeitschrift für Byzantinistik, 13 (Amsterdam, 1988), 245–59, and S. Hamilton, 'Otto III's Penance: A Case Study of Unity and Diversity in the Eleventh-Century Church', in *Unity and Diversity in the Church*, ed. R. N. Swanson, *SCH*, 32 (1996), 83–94, at 84–5. Leyser, *Hermits*, 25, is similarly sceptical of the Greek connexion.

[21] R. Morris, *Monks and Laymen in Byzantium, 843–1118* (Cambridge, 1995), 19.

[22] On the aspirations and complexities of lavriote monasticism, see *ibid.*, 34.

[23] *Ibid.*, 42, 46.

[24] J.-M. Martin, 'L'érémitisme Grec et Latin en Italie méridionale (X^e–XIIIe siècle)', in *Ermites*, ed. Vauchez, 175–98, at 178; A. Pertusi, 'Aspetti organizzativi e culturali dell'ambiente monacale greco dell'Italia meridionale', in *L'eremitismo*, 382–417, at 394–99.

[25] 'De sancto Elia Spelæote abb. conf. in Calabria', *Acta SS, Sep.* III, 848–888; 'De sancto Luca abb. conf. Armenti in Lucania', *Acta SS, Oct.* VI, 337–42.

[26] Morris, *Monks and Laymen*, 29; Martin, 'L'érémitisme Grec et Latin', 183.

who saw eremitism as the apogee of monasticism. His opinion was at odds with the Western Benedictine tradition, which regarded the cenobium as the optimum environment for spiritual growth, but it did have some basis in the literature of the desert fathers; and the Greek template, of the *lavra*, provided an alternative pre-Benedictine vision by which aspiring ascetics might occupy shared or individual cells.

Romuald of Ravenna and his older contemporary St Nilus of Rossano (d. 1005) were instigators of an eremitic movement in the West, in so far as they brought lavriote monasticism within reach of Rome and the Ottonian court, which was based there.[27] Both hermits impressed the half-Greek emperor Otto III (996–1002), whom Romuald served as a spiritual adviser, and both promoted the virtue of eremitic asceticism by recreating the life of the desert fathers. In doing so, they left a lasting impression, for although the *Vitas patrum* and works with a similar theme were familiar in the West (as they were in the East), no teacher in the West was treating them as a fundamental template for monastic living. This came to the attention of a hermit named John who lived near the monastery of Montecassino at the end of the tenth century. Even during Romuald's lifetime, the imperial chaplain Bruno of Querfurt (d. 1009) quoted John as saying that he 'was the first man of our times' to teach men to live in accordance with the *Conversations* of the desert fathers.[28] This reference to the repository of eremitic wisdom found in Cassian's *Conlationes* implied that Romuald's idea of monasticism was founded on the *lavra*: the backdrop for Cassian's set-piece discussions of ascetic life and practice. Even if John's claim was exaggerated, it reveals how revolutionary Romuald's spirituality must have seemed in the minds of his contemporaries, for up until that point Western monastic reform had largely been concerned with elaborating the liturgy. Asceticism, spiritual warfare, or replicating these primitive visions of the monastic life had been low on its agenda. Romuald's achievement was to capture the imagination of the imperial court by reviving the impressive asceticism of the fathers and playing to the millenarian imaginings of Otto's circle.[29] His reputed influence is evident in Bruno's claim that Otto promised Romuald that he would become a hermit himself, once he had taken care of the realm.[30] Romuald promoted eremitism from its doubtful position in the Benedictine tradition to the summit

---

[27] On the role of St Nilus of Rossano, see E. Sackur, *Die Cluniacenser in ihrer kirchlichen und allgemeingeschichtlichen Wirksamkeit: bis zur Mitte des elften Jahrhunderts*, 2 vols (Halle, 1892–4), I, 329–34; N. Bulst, *Untersuchungen zu den Klosterreformen Wilhelms von Dijon (962–1031)* (Bonn, 1973), 10–11; and S. Parenti, *Il monastero di Grottaferrata nel medioevo (1004–1462): segni e percorsi di una identità*, Orientalia Christiana Analecta, 274 (Rome, 2005), 81–5.

[28] Bruno of Querfurt, *Vita quinque fratrum*, ed. R. Kade, in *MGH SS*, XV, ed. G. Waitz, 2 vols (Hannover, 1887–8), II, 709–38, at 718: Romuald was 'primus nostrorum temporum' to teach men to live 'non propria presumptione' but 'secundum Collationes patrum heremitarum'.

[29] See J. Leclercq, 'Saint Romuald et la monachisme missionaire', *RB*, 77 (1962), 307–22; and Jestice, *Wayward Monks*, 85–6.

[30] Bruno of Querfurt, *Vita quinque fratrum*, ed. Kade, 738.

of monastic endeavour by basing his teaching on a tradition older and fierier than the Benedictine rule. In doing so, he promoted lavriote ideals (which were influential in Byzantium) with his radical belief that monasteries should be ascetic training camps for zealous spiritual athletes. At Camaldoli in the Tuscan hills, in the diocese of Arezzo, his vision took the form of a secluded cenobium built in the foothills to prepare the inmates for hermit cells set higher up in the woody crags. The Camaldolese regime of enforced silence, physical deprivation, and flagellation sought to subordinate the flesh to the will of the spirit.

Romuald's project for reviving the life of the fathers relied to some extent on the ready presence of manpower in the mountains of central Italy, where small, loose-knit networks of hermits were appearing. Some of them were his proselytes, others were like-minded ascetics, and many, such as the hermits at Fonte Avellana in the central Apennines, had come to the vocation as laymen. Romuald met their needs by setting up eremitic monasteries and instructing their inmates with simple precepts based on the wisdom of the fathers.[31] He also preached, thereby setting a pattern for Dominic di Sora (d. 1032), who founded hermitages in the mountains of the Abruzzo region, for the monk-hermit Adalbert di Pacentro (d. *c.*1050), and for many other hermits whose asceticism enhanced their authority as preachers.[32] One of their main concerns apart from a common defence of their lifestyle was that the established Benedictine monasteries were too little interested in asceticism to provide a training ground for spiritual athletes. It is easy to see how such a situation might have arisen, in that the Benedictine expansion of the tenth and eleventh centuries had other objectives in mind, such as accommodating the demands of the nobility and magnifying the liturgy. Another perceived evil denounced by these hermits was the sin of simony, which was usually represented as the sale or purchase of ecclesiastical office. Commitment to their policy of uncompromising renunciation conferred on these hermits a reputation for integrity, which empowered many of them to harness popular resentment against the corruption of the clergy. In Florence, a monk named John Gualberto (*c.*995–1073) left the abbey of San Miniato in protest at the simony of its abbot and went around in the manner of a hermit denouncing him and the archbishop in public and preaching against simony. Another outspoken opponent of simony was the Ravennese hermit Peter Damian (1006/7–72), who wrote a *Life* of Romuald in the early 1040s. In this piece of hagiography, he sought to depict an exemplary hermit who might appeal to a sympathetic audience by voicing Peter's own concerns about the spiritual tepidity of the monks in the monasteries and the corrosive effects of

---

[31] *Ibid.*, 738.

[32] J. Howe, *Church Reform and Social Change in Eleventh-Century Italy: Dominic of Sora and His Patrons* (Philadelphia, 1997), *passim*; J.-M. Sansterre, 'Le monachisme bénédictin d'Italie et les bénédictins Italiens en France face au renouveau de l'érémitisme à la fin du Xe et au XIe siècle', in *Ermites*, ed. Vauchez, 29–46, at 34–5.

simony.[33] Although it is not a reliable treatment of Romuald's aspirations, it affords valuable insights into Peter's.

Peter Damian, over the course of his career, embraced the movement associated with Romuald and made it his own. Joining Fonte Avellana in 1035, he became its superior in 1043 and presided over the foundation of subordinate hermitages, urging on the ascetic efforts of the brethren with tales of how Romuald used to emulate the austerities of the desert fathers.[34] Inspired by Romuald's radical initiative to recreate their asceticism, he poured forth polemic against the sins of the clergy, paying special attention to simony. When, in the 1040s, the German emperor and the papacy at last united to combat the sin, the hermit Peter emerged as a prophet and champion of the anti-simoniacal cause. Soon, his services as a spiritual advisor were being sought in the highest circles. In 1057, the monk-pope Stephen IX appointed him to the post of senior cardinal-bishop, the bishopric of Ostia. From this position of prominence, and later as a legate, he promoted the eremitic life as the pathway to perfection. In his *Life* of St Romuald, Peter had put the argument that salvation was most accessible to holy individuals living in solitude and that life in a religious community threatened to impede the zealous soul.[35] As a papal advisor, he pursued these ideas. For instance, in 1064, in a letter to Pope Alexander II, he praised one of the brethren in his charge, the late hermit Dominic Loricatus (d. 1060), for successfully offloading hundreds of years of penance by interminable self-flagellation and his recitation of the Psalter.[36] Ascetic exercises were only possible when the monk willing to accomplish them had been freed from a monk's normal offices. In Peter's scheme of salvation, obedience to an abbot was essential to success, but any spiritual athlete had to fulfil his vocation outside the cenobium and preferably in the gymnasium of a hermitage. He also saw the hermitage as the perfect environment for undertaking penance and interpreted Romuald's far-famed ascetic exercises in terms of the penances he desired to fulfil.[37]

The legacy of Romuald, his followers, and kindred spirits (not least among them Peter Damian), in Italy by the 1070s, was the successful repositioning of hermits as elite ascetics, spiritual perfectionists, and champions of holiness against the frequent sins of the clergy. Hardly surprisingly their position was not without its challengers. Italian Benedictine hagiographers writing in the

---

[33] Peter Damian, *Vita beati Romualdi*, ed. G. Tabacco, *Fonti per la storia d'Italia*, 94 (Rome, 1957). On the *Life*, see C. Phipps, 'Romuald – Model Hermit: Eremitical Theory in Saint Peter Damian's *Vita beati Romualdi*, chapters 16–27', in *Monks, Hermits and the Ascetic Tradition*, ed. W. J. Sheils, *SCH*, 22 (1985), 65–77. See also Jestice, *Wayward Monks*, 217–24.

[34] *Vita*, ed. Tabacco, 28, 94–5. In arguing that early eleventh-century eremitism drew its inspiration chiefly from the fathers, I contradict a recent claim that it was, at this date, essentially Christomimetic: cf. Fulton, *From Judgment to Passion*, 89, 90.

[35] Phipps, 'Romuald – Model Hermit', 71, 74–5, 77.

[36] *Die Briefe des Petrus Damiani*, ed. K. Reindel, *MGH*, 4 vols (Munich, 1983–93), no. 109.

[37] In his *Life* of Romuald, the reason Romuald enters a monastery in the first place (and similarly his reason for abandoning it) is that he wishes to undertake satisfactory penance.

eleventh century were one obvious set who might have, and often did have, a bone to pick with the idea that the ardent soul could only fulfil its potential in isolation. The tendency in their writings is for saintly hermit protagonists eventually to return to and thereby affirm the cenobium. Whatever their misgivings, nonetheless, they could hardly avoid acknowledging the impressiveness of hermits in accordance with Benedictine tradition but also perhaps in tacit admission that the hermit's vocation had won new approval.[38] Indeed, by the late eleventh century, monastic writers at the great Italian abbey of Montecassino, and also in Norman Apulia, were extolling eremitism as a path to spiritual perfection.[39] This was a paradoxical development, for Romualdian eremitism (whether it was seen as an alternative to Benedictine cenobitism or as a rival to it) was still fundamentally a movement that extolled the hermit's vocation over the monk's. Lay converts to religion, who might previously have opted for a cenobium, would now give serious thought to the possibility of heading for a hermitage instead. Pope Alexander II did nothing to discourage such raw recruits when he canonized the French nobleman Thibaut of Provins (*c.*1030–66) who had left the comital household of Blois-Troyes to live a solitary life without any monastic probation. That the pope did this at the instance of Peter Damian (and the people of Vicenza in Italy, where Thibaut settled and died) indicates that senior ecclesiastics in Catholic Christendom were content to view eremitism as an independent spiritual vocation and not merely as an extension of cenobitism reserved for exceptional monks.[40] Thibaut's canonization was important in this respect because it sanctioned the idea that eremitism was a valid and effective path to salvation, vindicating Peter's teaching on the saving powers of the hermitage.

Normandy

Italian influences played a formative role in the revival and direction of monastic life in the duchy of Normandy, where influential figures nurtured the Romualdian-Italian perception that eremitism could be an independent path to spiritual perfection or, alternatively, an avenue of protest and reform. First steps were taken towards the revival of Norman monasticism when Duke Richard II, in 1001, invited the Italian reformer William of Volpiano (962–1031), who was abbot at the French monastery of Saint-Bénigne in Dijon, to restore monastic observance at Fécamp, a religious house in the diocese of Rouen. William was a

---

[38] Here, I build on Sansterre, 'Le monachisme bénédictin d'Italie', esp. 35.

[39] H. E. J. Cowdrey, *The Age of Abbot Desiderius: Montecassino, the Papacy, and the Normans in the Eleventh and Early Twelfth Centuries* (Oxford, 1983), 89–90; and O. Limone, *Santi monaci e santi eremiti: alla ricerca di un modello di perfezione nella letteratura agiografica dell'Apulia normanna* (Galatina, 1988), 28.

[40] *Alia vita, bullae canonizationis adjuncta*, 'De sancto Theobaldo, etc', *Acta SS, Jun.* V, 596–8, at 596A.

Piedmontese nobleman, a monk and agent of Cluny, though by no means bent merely on replicating Cluny's template in the many monasteries he reformed; rather, he would devise reforms of his own. More than his contemporary, Romuald, he adhered to Benedictine cenobitic ideals, and his efforts to give shape to them in Northern Italy, notably at Fruttuaria in Piedmont, and at the monasteries of Fécamp and Mont Saint-Michel in Normandy, were successful. His Italian recruits included hermits. One of them, John, became abbot of Fruttuaria in 1023.[41] Another was John of Ravenna, who joined his master at Fécamp. John of Ravenna (known as John of Fécamp) had lived as a hermit in his youth; in light of his origins it is likely that he had withdrawn to one of the many eremitic monasteries or hermitages in central Italy. He went on to become one the most profound spiritual authors of the eleventh century, stressing the importance of contrition in the ascetic's struggle against sin. His writings reveal his sorrow that he had abandoned, in his youth, the solitude of his hermitage for the entanglements of monastic administration. They also betray a nagging conviction in common with his contemporary Peter Damian, that the only suitable environment for the spiritual athlete or penitent soul was a hermitage.[42] John became abbot of Fécamp in 1028. His presence there may have contributed to a growth of interest in eremitism among the brethren. A French monk named Maurilius departed to become a hermit in Italy.[43] Later, possibly in the 1050s, Abbot John gave his support to other would-be hermits in his charge, granting the Fécamp monks Peter and Déodat permission to found a hermitage at the ruined chapel of St Martin in the forest of Bonneville-sur-Touques, near Deauville in Lower Normandy.[44] Such was the enthusiasm for eremitism at Fécamp that it even took on a subversive aspect, when monks ran away to live as hermits without John's consent.[45]

John of Fécamp, although less well placed to shape religious thinking than his contemporary Peter Damian in Italy, held influence not only within the duchy but also with successive kings of England. From Cnut, he obtained lands and rents in Sussex. He also harboured the exiled ætheling Edward, who was a rival for Cnut's throne. After Edward became king, he rewarded Fécamp with land in Somerset, and, in 1054, when John crossed the channel to tour his holdings in England, he received him at court with acclaim. Just as Peter, in Italy, held sway with emperors and popes, John was in a strong position to advise dukes and kings on devotional matters. Edward's biographer praised the king for paying attention

[41] Bulst, *Untersuchungen*, 41–2.

[42] Leclercq and Bonnes, *Jean de Fécamp*, 185–7, 189–90, 194–6.

[43] M. de Boüard, 'Notes et hypothèses sur Maurille moine de Fécamp, et son élection au siège métropolitain de Rouen', in *L'abbaye bénédictine de Fécamp: ouvrage scientifique du XIIIe centenaire, 658–1958*, preface by J. Le Povremoyne, 4 vols in 3 (Fécamp, 1959–63), I, 81–92, at 82–3.

[44] M. Arnoux, 'Ermites et ermitages en Normandie (XIe–XIIIe siècles)', in *Ermites*, ed. Vauchez, 115–35, at 119, 124.

[45] This, at least, is the import of John's letter, in Leclercq and Bonnes, *Jean de Fécamp*, 218–20.

to foreign abbots rigorous in their monastic discipline.[46] Duke William may have been equally sympathetic to John's ascetic spirituality, for his biographer noted that the duke promoted anchorites to high offices in the church. The first of them was Maurilius of Fécamp, who returned from his hermitage only to be nominated archbishop of Rouen.[47] Maurilius (*c*.995–1067) was a most unusual choice. Before his nomination the Norman bishoprics had fallen to ducal family members or the relatives of leading nobles. Maurilius, like John, was a scholar and an ascetic; he had trained in the episcopal school at Liège in Lower Lorraine and taught at Halberstadt in Saxony, before taking monastic vows. His appointment was ratified at the provincial council of Lisieux in 1055 under the auspices of the papal legate Ermenfrid of Sion (in modern Switzerland). Ermenfrid, a representative of the reforming pope, may have favoured Maurilius.[48] In England, seven years later, he allegedly expressed a desire that Wulfstan, the ascetic provost of Worcester, should be appointed to the see.[49] Another probable supporter of Maurilius was John himself. It is likely that the duke, amid such admirers of asceticism, was an admirer of Maurilius's eremitic record, for he also promoted a hermit in 1062, when he appointed the hermit Gerbert, as abbot, to reform the abbey of Saint-Wandrille.[50] As churchmen of the highest calibre, John, Gerbert, and Maurilius could in some way have advertised the virtues instilled by eremitism, in their discourse and conduct as pastors. Although Gerbert's background is obscure, John, probably, and Maurilius, certainly, must have learned their eremitism in Italy; and the corollary is that, to some extent, they would have imported characteristics of Italian eremitism into Normandy.

Mont Saint-Michel passed to an Italian disciple of William of Volpiano named Suppo, who was abbot from 1033 until 1048. He too won the favour of the ætheling Edward, albeit probably for political reasons.[51] Problems of leadership spanning the decade after his departure culminated in a disputed election in 1057 or 1058, which brought accusations of simony and opened a rift within the community. Here too the (schismatic) recourse to eremitism was distinctly Italian, in as much as the critics, led by a monk named Robert, seceded from the abbey in protest to live as hermits on the nearby island of Tombelaine. Such action, effective in provoking a scandal, found its nearest precedent in Italy, in the departure of John Gualberto from San Miniato in protest at the simony of its abbot. At any rate, there is no evidence that any monk in Normandy before

---

[46] *Vita Ædwardi Regis: The Life of King Edward*, ed. F. Barlow, 2nd edn. (Oxford, 1992), 62.

[47] *The Gesta Gvillelmi of William of Poitiers*, ed. R. H. C. Davis and M. Chibnall (Oxford, 1998), 90.

[48] See H. E. J. Cowdrey, 'Bishop Ermenfrid of Sion and the Penitential Ordinance following the Battle of Hastings', *JEH*, 20 (1969), 225–42, at 227–9.

[49] John of Worcester, *Chronicon*, edited as *The Chronicle of John of Worcester*, ed. R. R. Darlington and P. McGurk, tr. J. Bray and P. McGurk (Oxford, 1995), II, 591.

[50] *Gesta Gvillelmi*, ed. Davis and Chibnall, 90.

[51] E. van Houts, 'Edward and Normandy', in *Edward the Confessor: The Man and the Legend*, ed. R. Mortimer (Woodbridge, 2009), 63–76.

Robert and his friends became a hermit for this reason. Robert, in his hermitage, began a commentary on the Song of Songs in which he developed a theme beloved of reformers of his generation: a hidden church of the pure – another Italian preoccupation.[52] His companions in exile included a second spiritual author, Anastasius the Venetian, who had been educated both in Latin and in Greek.[53] Like many hermits of this period, they went on to distinguished careers. The former was summoned from his hermitage in 1066 by Duke William's half-brother Bishop Odo of Bayeux (bishop 1049/50–97) to restore and head the abbey of Saint-Vigor in the suburbs of Odo's episcopal city. The latter became a monk at Cluny and, later, a papal missionary in Spain. Far from landing these men in obscurity, their withdrawal to hermitages had enlarged their reputations and caught the eye of talent scouts. In Normandy as in Italy, hermits were positioning themselves as opponents of simony and as the guardians of a purer spiritual vocation. They were also winning promotion.

The careers of two other prominent churchmen of that era show how new ideas about eremitism could have travelled between Italy and Normandy, ultimately, into England.[54] One was Italian, the other from southernmost Burgundy; both became monks at the same abbey in Normandy and both ended their careers as archbishops of Canterbury: Lanfranc of Pavia (*c.*1010–89) and Anselm of Aosta (*c.*1033–1109). After a decade as a wandering scholar and teacher, Lanfranc became a monk at the abbey of Bec in Normandy, which was a recent foundation still simple and austere in its outlook. Even so, Lanfranc worried that the monks were insufficiently zealous, so he devised a plan, in the early 1040s, to leave and to live as a hermit. (It is a question of little consequence whether this tale was invented to add drama to his posthumous dossier, for the scenario is plausible, in that monks at that date were indeed leaving monasteries to become hermits, especially in the region where Lanfranc grew up.)[55] Lanfranc's dilemma mirrored Peter Damian's concern that a cenobium could impede the soul's progress. Like Robert's secession from Mont Saint-Michel, it presents an instance of how an uncompromising Italian conviction could have sown its seeds in Normandy. Anselm, after studying under Lanfranc and considering the paths open to him, could not decide whether to become a monk or a hermit.[56] This

---

[52] E. A. Mather, *The Voice of My Beloved: The Song of Songs in Western Medieval Christianity* (Philadelphia, 1990), 106. On Robert, see P. Quivy and J. Thiron, 'Robert de Tombelaine et son commentaire sur le Cantique des cantiques', in *Millénaire monastique de Mont Saint-Michel*, ed. J. Laporte, R. Foreville, et al., 4 vols (Paris, 1966–71), II, 347–56.

[53] M. Arnoux, 'Un Vénitien au Mont Saint-Michel: Anastase, moine, ermite et confesseur († vers 1085)', *Médiévales*, 28 (1995), 55–78.

[54] One might also add 'into Norman Apulia'. See Limone, *Santi monaci, passim.*

[55] Lanfranc's modern biographers have accepted the story, most recently H. E. J. Cowdrey, *Lanfranc: Scholar, Monk, and Archbishop* (Oxford, 2003), 11 (where the relevant sources are cited in n. 1), 14.

[56] Eadmer, *The Life of St Anselm, Archbishop of Canterbury*, ed. and tr. R. W. Southern (Oxford, 1972), 10–11.

was about the year 1060, and it shows what in-roads Romuald and others had made, that a learned man like Anselm, after studying in a Benedictine monastery, looked to eremitism as an independent vocation, despite Benedictine tradition. His English biographer, the monk Eadmer of Canterbury, also saw nothing strange in this. Lanfranc took Anselm to Maurilius, who advised him to enter a cenobium. The archbishop's advice should not be taken as an indication that he had turned his back on eremitism, for it was in line with the Benedictine tradition in which he had been trained. Still, there may have been a generational and cultural gap between the ageing Frenchman and the young Italian making it harder for the former and easier for the latter to discern virtue in the uncompromising renunciation which conversion directly to eremitism entailed. At Bec, Anselm wrote affectionately to Robert of Tombelaine, expressing a great desire to meet Anastasius, whose work he knew.[57] Yet the path he eventually chose reveals that the Norman commitment to a Benedictine template did curb some of the wilder impulses to bypass a cenobitic probation and convert to eremitism directly that had found an outlet in Italy. It also shows (like the canonization of Thibaut of Provins) that eremitism, by the 1060s, was coming to be viewed as a vocation in its own right.

The influences and possible influences of Italian eremitism in Normandy serve to illustrate processes whereby new spiritual ideas could be transmitted from one realm to another. They also account for the alterations that occurred in their transmission. Seldom are the links straightforward, but if we wish to explain why John of Fécamp saw eremitism as the proper calling of the penitent, or why Robert of Mont Saint-Michel treated it as an avenue of protest, or why Lanfranc felt that even an austere religious community might impede his progress, or why Anselm saw eremitism as an independent vocation, we need only look to their Italian roots and connexions, seeing that all these ideas had apparently developed in Italy. If, on the other hand, we are perplexed that Lanfranc chose to remain at Bec, or that Maurilius advised Anselm to enter a monastery, an explanation could lie in the comparative strength of the Norman Benedictine tradition. For in Normandy there was no separate movement of hermits, as there had been in Italy, perhaps because William of Volpiano and his disciples had noted the concerns of that movement and resolved to cater for its needs within their own normative Benedictine environment. Already two themes were emerging which would influence subsequent permutations of eremitism. The first was an incremental realization of the threat which money posed to the practice of good religion. Simony brought home the impact of the corrupting power of wealth, and in preaching against it Peter Damian in particular excoriated avarice as the new worst clerical sin. Pride, according to Lester K. Little's analysis, was knocked into second place.[58] The second theme was the burgeoning apprehension that the

---

[57] *S. Anselmi Cantuariensis archiepiscopi opera omnia*, ed. F. S. Schmitt, 6 vols (Edinburgh, 1946–61), III, no. 3, at 1023; Arnoux, 'Un Vénitien', 58.

[58] Little, *Religious Poverty*, 36.

communal life might offer little to nurture spiritual growth. So various were the associated criticisms that the underlying refutation became like a hydra, difficult for Benedictine communities to slay. Either observances were thought too lax, or too much time was given over to the liturgy; lukewarm brethren might be a malign influence, or an over-involved patron threaten to entangle monks in worldly affairs; there was too little space for contemplation, or else no freedom to practise penance. In these and like complaints, the hydra reared its many heads, and communal religion, although it continued to gain in popularity, lost many potential recruits, to a movement obsessed with the perfection of the individual.

The new hermits

Despite their different visions of the ideal religious life, monks and hermits of the eleventh century were united in at least one respect: that they called the laity to repent, convert to a life of religion, and thus increase their hope of salvation. The summons did not go unheeded. More than any century before, the eleventh became the century of adult conversion, swelling the ranks of the religious with innumerable recruits who were often bent on determining their own paths to salvation and persuading others to do the same. Soldiers became penitents to make amends for past careers embroiled in bloodshed; scholars disillusioned with the vacuous pursuit of knowledge gave thought to the needs of their souls; even the poor aspired to salvation. Some of these various converts chose to enter monasteries; others embraced lives of poverty, simplicity, and seclusion. Historians refer to the latter as the 'new hermits'. They were 'new' in that they multiplied as never before. They were 'hermits' in as much as they achieved a degree of ascetic austerity and solitude comparable to that of the desert fathers.[59] The category 'new hermits' is a handy scholarly invention. We owe it to Henrietta Leyser, and it captures something of the inspiration and the spirit that communities of this sort possessed. These hermits were wandering, preaching, monastery-founding hermits, different from the old sort, which tended neither to wander nor preach nor found monasteries. Every congregation of new hermits possessed no fewer than three of the following characteristics: namely charismatic leadership capable of attracting a good number of adult converts; interest in pursuing a better expression of monasticism than any sort that was available; a life of austerity, asceticism, and separation realized in an unconventional setting (i.e. not within a cenobium or a subordinate hermitage); and blending of or alternation between the solitary life and the communal life. Romuald's followers were new hermits, yet they differed from their contemporaries in Germany, Normandy, and France in two respects: Romualdian hermits were interested in severe asceticism and in opposing simony, whereas their

---

[59] Leyser, *Hermits*, 18–28.

counterparts in other countries were often more interested in simplicity and poverty. And whereas the former sort desired freedom from Benedictine cenobitism, the latter sort usually ended up embracing it.

The congregation of new hermits at Rinchnach in Bavaria, under the leadership of the famous hermit Gunther (d. 1045), stood somewhere between these two models.[60] Gunther, like Peter Damian and John of Fécamp, was a vocational penitent, whose sermons on John the Baptist, according to an eyewitness who knew him, moved his audiences to tears.[61] Like other hermits, he adopted the Baptist as his patron probably because the saint was regarded as an archetypal hermit or because he was a preacher of penitence. If so, Gunther, like his Italian contemporaries, might have believed that penance was most effectively performed in a hermitage. Even so, his community was apparently content to embrace a Benedictine template. In the case of another new hermit, Herluin of Bec (d. 1078), simplicity, poverty, and the Benedictine template were the defining features of a new eremitic community. Herluin, a soldier, converted to religion then sought to discover what life was like in a monastery. Whichever he visited fell short of his expectations, so he opted instead for an austere life of poverty, manual labour, and seclusion on his estates.[62] A comparable case is that of Herluin's contemporary Robert de Turlande (*c*.1001–67), who is better known as Robert of Chaise-Dieu. He was a canon of the church of St Julien at Brioude, in the Auvergne region of France, who left his position, initially, to enter the abbey of Cluny, before settling, at last, in the year 1043, at a ruined chapel in a remote part of the forest at Brioude. With the help of his uncle, the bishop of Clermont, he founded an abbey there along with a number of dependant priories. Recruits were abundant and by the time of Robert's death are said to have numbered three hundred.[63] The success of Gunther, Herluin, and Robert in founding these communities proceeded partly from their leadership and vision (which were characteristic qualities of the new hermits); yet they would hardly have been so successful had the eremitic vocation not acquired the degree of prestige which Romuald, his

---

[60] Grundmann, 'Eremiti in Germania', 320–1; G. Lang, 'Gunther, der Eremit, in Geschichte, Sage und Kult', *Studien und Mitteilungen zur Geschichte des Benediktinerordens und seiner Zweige*, 59 (1941), 3–83.

[61] Wolfhere, *Vita Godehardi episcopi Hildensheimensis*, in *MGH SS*, XI, ed. G. H. Pertz (Hannover, 1854), 162–219, at 201–2.

[62] Gilbert Crispin, *Vita Herluini*, in *The Works of Gilbert Crispin*, ed. A. S. Abulafia and G. R. Evans, Auctores Britannici medii aevi 8 (Oxford, 1986), 183–212. Although Gilbert's account was written perhaps eighty years after these events, its portrait of Herluin, not as a would-be hermit sighing after solitude but as a convert interested in monasticism who received the habit from his bishop in a church on his own estate, resembles other cases from the 1030s and 1040s. There are also signs that Gilbert stuck to what he knew: his account of the monastery's growth is decidedly vague (at 192, for example).

[63] *Marbodo di Rennes, Vita beati Roberti*, ed. A. Degl'Innocenti (Florence, 1995), 34. Following an earlier work by one of Robert's disciples, Marbod of Rennes composed his *Life* at some point between 1067 and 1096. Marbod was rather sceptical of hermits by the 1090s (as we shall see), so, although he employs some eremitic rhetoric to decorate his prose, it is doubtful that he would have endeavoured to exaggerate Robert's eremitic credentials *per se*.

admirers, and like-minded ascetics brought to it, or without their lucid, attractive idea of portraying it as a revival of the purity and austerity associated with the fathers. The cases of Gunther, Herluin, and Robert date the irruption of the eremitic movement in Germany, Normandy, and France to the 1040s or thereabouts – when Peter Damian began championing eremitism in Italy.

The rise of eremitic communities in places where Benedictine cenobitism was traditionally the most prominent incarnation of monasticism had the effect not only of challenging the assumption that religious endeavour should be communal (as opposed to individualistic); it also forced monks and hermits to compete with each other in the activity of persuading would-be converts of the benefits of their respective vocations. The great Burgundian abbey of Cluny, which together with its satellites and affiliated monasteries had built its reputation on the intercessory power of its cycle of perpetual liturgy, claimed, on the strength of that attribute, to be a haven for penitent souls.[64] New hermits conversely implied and preached that penitents should embrace lives of austerity and solitary ascetic endeavour. Inevitably, with two paths being advocated, the question soon arose, which was preferable? By the middle of the eleventh century, Cluny could hardly have failed to notice that eremitism was competing with it as an independent monastic vocation, offering its own unique spiritual benefits and exerting its own individual pull on recruits. Consciously or not, those drawn by the current of eremitism were rejecting the Cluniac vision. Cluny's response may be apparent in a clever piece of propaganda, which makes a hermit a spokesman for its cause. The tale first appears in the chronicle of Rodulf Glaber (d. *c.*1046), sometime monk of Cluny, who described a traveller's encounter with a hermit in Africa. This hermit had seen nobody for twenty years, yet he knew of Cluny and that its continuous celebration of masses was more effective than the offices of any other monastery in freeing souls from the clutches of evil angels. After Glaber, in the 1050s, a monk of Cluny named Jotsald reworked the story in his hagiography of its saintly abbot Odilo (*c.*962–1049). This time a pilgrim, shipwrecked en route from Sicily to Thessalonike, meets a hermit and hears him recount a vision in which the prayers of the monks of Cluny and their abbot free souls from otherworldly torments. The pilgrim was to make this known to the brethren and get them to redouble their efforts. When he returned and told them, the monks rejoiced and redoubled their prayers, fired with determination. Moreover, Odilo decreed that in every Cluniac monastery a special day should be reserved for prayers for the dead, thereby instituting the feast of All Souls (2 November).[65] This legend was a clever piece of propaganda because it employed the hermit in his conventional role

---

[64] H. E. J. Cowdrey, *The Cluniacs and the Gregorian Reform* (Oxford, 1970), 128.

[65] Rodulfus Glaber, *Historiarum libri quinque*, in *idem, Opera*, ed. and tr. J. France, N. Bulst, and P. Reynolds (Oxford, 1989), 3–253, at 234–7; Jotsald of Cluny, 'De uita et uirtutibus sancti Odilonis abbatis', PL, 142: 897–940, cols 926–7. On the significance of this story, see M. McLaughlin, *Consorting with Saints: Prayer for the Dead in Early Medieval France* (Ithaca, 1994), 231–4.

as a visionary seer to acknowledge the efficacy of Cluny's liturgical intercession. For all its austerity, eremitism was no match for Cluny when it came to freeing souls.

Cluny's power and empire continued to expand, but communities of new hermits multiplied apace, as eremitic nurseries similar to those that had appeared earlier in the mountains of central Italy, then at Rinchnach, Bec, and in the forest of Brioude, began to appear in the forests of Colan and Molesme in Burgundy, at Muret near Limoges, and in the forest of Gironde near Bordeaux in the last quarter of the century. Some of these locations became known as the haunts of great ascetics or as the nearest modern equivalents to that region of Upper Egypt called the Thebaid, where the desert fathers had lived. The most famed and notorious by the end of the century was a vast swathe of heath and woodland on the marches of Maine and Brittany where converts from all sorts of backgrounds were settling individually or in small congregations to pursue an eremitic vocation. In the 1090s, this modern Thebaid became a recruiting ground for charismatic leaders who sought to establish new religious communities. One was the Breton Robert of Arbrissel (*c.*1055–1117) who had taught philosophy at Angers then resigned his post as archpriest of Rennes to live among the hermits in Craon. Another was a monk named Bernard (*c.*1046–1117) from Abbéville in the County of Ponthieu. A lover of solitude yet dutiful to the interests of his abbey, he had been deposed from the abbacy of Saint-Cyprian near Poitiers in the wake of a Cluniac takeover.[66] A third was the Norman cleric Vitalis of Mortain (*c.*1060–1122), who had exchanged his chaplaincy in the service of Count Robert of Mortain (the brother of Bishop Odo of Bayeux) for a canonry at the count's collegiate church. That church, as it happened, was dedicated to the seventh-century monk St Evroul (d. 706), who had retired to live in solitude, attracted followers, and founded monasteries to accommodate them. This sort of career path, of course, was enjoying a renaissance. Before the century was through, Robert of Arbrissel, Bernard, Vitalis, and many others (such as Ralph de la Futaye, founder of the abbey of Saint-Sulpice-la-Forêt, *c.*1096), would make it their own profession by establishing eremitic monasteries given to rigour and asceticism.[67]

The hermits of Maine and Brittany, unlike some of their predecessors at Bec or Brioude, nurtured the sorts of traits that had characterized Romuald's followers, such as denunciatory ardour, ostentatious asceticism, and readiness to experiment with new forms of monasticism. Like the Italian hermits fifty years earlier who had embraced renunciation in order to achieve the spiritual authority to denounce simony, these new hermits lived austerely in order to underline

[66] Potted biographies can be found in Little, *Religious Poverty*, 78–9 and 76–7. For a fuller account of the movement, see J. von Walter, *Die ersten Wanderprediger Frankreichs. Studien zur Geschichte des Mönchtums*, 2 vols (Leipzig, 1903–6).

[67] For a brief synopsis, D. Knowles, *The Monastic Order in England: A History of Its Development from the Times of St Dunstan to the Fourth Lateran Council, 940–1216*, 2nd edn. (Cambridge, 1963), 200–2.

their opposition to the luxury and laxity they discerned in the lives of Benedictine monks. In his assaults on cenobitism, in the 1090s or 1100s, the hermit Rainald charged that the monasteries were too reliant on comfortable living, the performance of their offices, and the resolution of lawsuits, to promote the spiritual welfare of their members.[68] Against the perceived torpor of Cluniac monasticism, these new hermits of Maine and Brittany advocated voluntary poverty, allying to this their vocational preaching and mendicancy, these preachers symbolizing visually in their rag-clad appearance their path to spiritual purity. Robert of Arbrissel, Bernard, and Vitalis set out on preaching missions through France and Normandy, criticizing the sins of the clergy and laity and summoning them to repent. Courting controversy, the preachers opened themselves to criticism. One delegation of hermits annoyed Bishop Ivo of Chartres (1090–1115) by arriving at an abbey in his diocese and urging the brethren to leave.[69] In Ivo's opinion, they were too assured of their own salvation. His colleague, Bishop Marbod of Rennes (1096–1123), thought that the influential preaching hermit Robert of Arbrissel trusted too much to his own holiness. With uncovered legs, bare feet, full beard, and scruffy haircut, he 'lacked only a stick to look like a lunatic'.[70] The accounts of the desert fathers abounded with cautionary stories of hermits developing inflated opinions of their own achievements. Ivo and Marbod may have been thinking along similar lines. As bishops, they would have known that wandering hermits were not easily disciplined and were a threat not only to themselves but also to the gullible. Voices, by now, were calling for tolerance with respect to the different religious vocations, while some of the new hermits were getting a bad name for demanding intractable standards which only a few could attain.

The firebrand hermits of the 1090s, like other new hermits before them, were all searching for the same thing: the optimal religious life. A hundred years beforehand Romuald had equated it with the life of the desert fathers, which subsequent hermits endeavoured to emulate. Now, however, these radical preachers were looking for an earlier, purer template, less concerned with competitive asceticism and better suited to conveying their message of salvation to the world beyond the hermitage. Monks had traditionally depicted cenobitism as the continuation of the communal life lived by Christ's apostles, but two elements of the apostolic life had long since fallen out of it. These were evangelism and poverty, the latter bearing the implication of reliance on God's provision. Seeing their chance, the preaching hermits sought to restore these elements to the monastic life and, in the process, claimed to be reviving the apostolic life itself. Their bare feet, clothing, and donkey for a mount were carefully chosen symbols signifying their restoration of the lifestyle and mission of Christ's

---

[68] Morin, 'Rainaud', 101–10.
[69] Ivo of Chartres, *Epistolae*, PL, 162: 11–290, no. 192 (cols 198–202), at 201–2.
[70] G. Constable, *The Reformation of the Twelfth Century* (Cambridge, 1996), 26, with references.

apostles.[71] Dissatisfaction with contemporary monasticism had became so en-
trenched within the movement that its leaders had no wish to found more
monasteries on existing models. For this reason, the new hermits of the 1090s
and 1100s followed their own instincts by creating new monastic regimes that
were sensitive to the apostolic ideal, stricter in their adherence to neglected
Benedictine precepts, such as the obligation to perform manual labour, and
committed to eremitic principles, such as seclusion and austerity. Robert of
Arbrissel, on the pattern of the apostolic church, founded a community of priests,
lay workers, and women, which eventually mothered the order of Fontevrault.
Bernard and Vitalis founded the orders of Tiron and Savigny respectively, looking
to St Benedict's precepts of solitude and manual labour. Robert of Molesme, in
1098, founded the monastery of Citeaux in Burgundy. And from these humble
beginnings arose the most influential order of all, the Cistercian order, which,
within the space of half a century, overtook Cluny in prestige and power as the
self-styled reformed order of St Benedict. It also overtook eremitism, by yoking
eremitic ideals of simplicity, austerity, and solitude to the cenobitic safeguards of
collective scrutiny, a regulated regime, and a hierarchical system of discipline. The
Cistercian order, in this respect, was the happiest synthesis to emerge from the
eleventh-century dialectic between the eremitic and cenobitic vocations, for it
combined the best qualities of both, while eliminating the negative attributes
which had caused so much controversy: luxury and worldliness on the part of the
established Benedictine monasteries; proud wilfulness and unruliness where
vagabond hermits were concerned. In the twelfth century, most of the converts
who might previously have joined communities of hermits joined new orders of
monks or communities of canons, which provided for their ascetic needs in
regulated spiritual environments.[72] Consequently, fewer eremitic communities
arose.

---

[71] M. Lambert, *Medieval Heresy: Popular Movements from the Gregorian Reform to the Reformation*,
3rd edn. (Oxford, 2002), 49.

[72] On the transformation of eremitic congregations into communities of regular canons, see
L. Milis, 'Ermites et chanoines réguliers au xii⁵ siècle', *Cahiers de civilisation médiévale*, 22 (1979),
39–80 (which has been translated into English as Milis, 'Hermits and Regular Canons in the
Twelfth Century', in *idem, Religion, Culture and Mentalities in the Medieval Low Countries: Selected
Essays*, ed. and tr. J. Deploige, M. De Reu, et al. (Turnhout, 2005), 181–246); and Milis,
'L'evolution de l'érémitisme au canonicat régulier dans la première moitié du douzième siècle:
transition ou trahison?', in *Istituzioni monastiche et istituzioni canonicali in occidente (1123–1215),
Miscellanea del centro di studi medioevali*, IX (Milan, 1980), 223–38.

2

The rise of the hermit in England

THE EREMITIC IDEAL, *C*.950–*C*.1050

Chapter 1 has now sketched the background, noting that Anglo-Saxon England nurtured a tradition of admiration for anchorites and that in parts of Western Europe, from *c*.950 to *c*.1100, hermits earned a reputation for their opposition to sin. The aim of the present chapter is to discover whether hermits or their distinctive form of asceticism were also flourishing, gaining influence, and winning support in England in the period between 950 and the early twelfth century. Historians have argued that they were, but they linked this development to the effects of the Norman Conquest, and the strength of that link must now be tested against the case for continuity (with regard to the Anglo-Saxon tradition) and the impact of the European movement that was extolling anchoresis at that time. To weigh these different factors, it is necessary to determine when, whether, and why hermits were building a reputation in England. Recluses are left to the next chapter. More specifically, the questions to be resolved are whether the behaviour of hermits or people's attitudes towards them changed over the duration of the period 950–1100; when such changes occurred, and whether they bore any resemblance to those changes noted in the previous chapter, which occurred elsewhere in Europe, or were uniquely linked to circumstances in England. The best way of solving these conundrums is to focus on monasticism, for although this may have the drawback of narrowing our historical perspective, it also has the advantage of providing unbroken commentary, in the form of religious writing, from the people most interested in asceticism and withdrawal. Monks indeed (and less often nuns) were usually the only people to leave such records – so we have little choice but to go down this avenue. Yet what they say or indicate about hermits was not thought up in a vacuum. Sometimes it sheds light, if inadvertently, on people's attitudes generally.

While hermits multiplied in Italy during the late tenth century, England, which had learned to admire asceticism, witnessed a minor revolution in organized religion. Historically, the clergy could be divided into two camps: those committed to chastity, common ownership of property, and a monastic horarium and liturgy (the monks and nuns); and those following secular forms of liturgy, who possessed their own estates and were content to marry (secular clerics). In England, during the third quarter of the tenth century, a reformed variety of monasticism was imposed on both categories of clergy at a few important religious houses and promulgated through the foundation of new monasteries and the resurrection of defunct ones. Its features were assembled after influential English monks examined prominent monasteries abroad, such as the French abbey of Fleury-sur-Loire, with an eye to recasting native monasticism in a Continental mould while retaining its better customs.[1] Liturgies already in use were replaced with the *cursus* of psalms prescribed by St Benedict and amplified by his namesake, the Carolingian reformer St Benedict of Aniane (750–821). By the 970s, the leading advocates of reform, namely Æthelwold (d. 984), Oswald (d. 992), and Dunstan (d. 988), who were reformers to different degrees but united in their vision, held several of the most powerful abbeys and bishoprics in the realm. The king liked their plans, and, seeing that the apparatus of ecclesiastical and royal power had come into friendly hands, Æthelwold masterminded a template for reformed monasticism – a customary called the *Regularis concordia* ('The monastic agreement'), which King Edgar duly enjoined on his monks and nuns. The farthest-reaching result of all this, from the historian's viewpoint, is that a small coterie of monastic writers, interested principally in the values associated with their own liturgical and cenobitic variety of monasticism, weigh in disproportionately among sources surviving from that period. These reformers were the least likely to admire a vocation which preferred individual exertion, solitude, and the unadorned wisdom of the desert fathers to the most up-to-date fashions in cenobitism. Everyone else, on the other hand, had no such obvious ideological conflict with anachoresis. They were more likely to admire anchorites, in acknowledging the legacy of respect for them, which their ancestors had passed down.

Reformers like Æthelwold wanted to free religious houses from lay overlordship, break vested interests where opposition threatened, and build their own ecclesiastical patrimonies. Sometimes they positioned their revolution at nodal points in the sacred landscape, setting up reformed monasteries at sites associated with the cults of saints, to draw on their power and prestige.[2] Wherever they did so it was a testimony to the authority and enduring potential of the cults they sought to harness, for, in the tenth century, the laity and religious alike looked to the saints for assistance in exceptional circumstances and everyday enterprises.[3] If

---

[1] See P. Wormald, 'Æthelwold and His Continental Counterparts: Contact, Comparison, Contrast', in *Bishop Æthelwold: His Career and Influence*, ed. B. Yorke (Woodbridge, 1988), 13–42; and J. Nightingale, 'Oswald, Fleury and Continental Reform', in *St Oswald of Worcester: Life and Influence*, ed. N. Brooks and C. Cubitt (London, 1996), 23–45. Cultural connexions with the Continent are examined in V. Ortenberg, *The English Church and the Continent in the Tenth and Eleventh Centuries: Cultural, Spiritual, and Artistic Exchanges* (Oxford, 1992).

[2] A. Thacker, 'Saint-Making and Relic Collecting by Oswald and His Communities', in *St Oswald*, ed. Brooks and Cubitt, 244–68.

[3] Blair, 'A Saint for Every Minster?' and 'Handlist'; D. W. Rollason, *Saints and Relics in Anglo-Saxon England* (Oxford, 1989), 186–8; and A. Thacker, 'The Making of a Local Saint', in *Local Saints*, ed. Thacker and Sharpe, 45–73, at 70–1. C. Cubitt argues for the lay origins of certain cults in 'Sites and Sanctity: Revisiting the Cult of Murdered and Martyred Anglo-Saxon Royal Saints', *Early Medieval Europe*, 9 (2000), 53–83.

anchorites were popular in this period it would stand to reason that their cults should have attracted promoters who wished to exploit their potential. This, apparently, is what happened at Crowland, when a cleric named Thurketel acquired the site. Thurketel was a relative of the diocesan bishop, Osketel of Dorchester and, later, of York (d. 971). Osketel was a pluralist, interested in expanding his patrimony and probably instrumental in securing Crowland for his kinsman; indeed it may have been the dynasty's proprietary monastery. Much later, the historian Orderic Vitalis, who stayed at Crowland in 1109 x 1124, claimed that Thurketel was a reformer, but he also let slip that after his death the abbey passed to his nephew Æthelric, who in turn left it to his kinsman Æthelric II.[4] There is a clue that the fourth abbot may have been yet another kinsman, for he shared the name of Thurketel's uncle Osketel. Orderic may be a late source, but abbeys seldom erred in keeping lists and basic details of their abbots. The two reformist principles at stake here, that abbots should be elected and secular overlordship opposed, exercised the reformers sufficiently to find mention in the prologue of the *Regularis concordia*. Crowland, it would seem, neglected both. In view of this, Thurketel's acquisition of the shrine may be seen as the takeover of a promising hermitage by a clerical dynasty headed by the pluralist (maybe the proprietor) Osketel. Orderic dates this takeover to Eadred's reign (946–55).[5] If he is right, Guthlac's was one of the first hermit shrines to attract investors in our period. The fact that it was thought to be a suitable site for establishing a clerical, or possibly a monastic, dynasty implies that the cult of the archetypal hermit St Guthlac retained a promising measure of popularity or potential.

In Guthlac's case, there is considerable evidence that the saint was well regarded through much of the realm, at least within a generation of Thurketel's acquisition and endowment of his shrine. By the eleventh century, most major monasteries were commemorating his feast. A tenth- or eleventh-century calendar from St Augustine's abbey in Canterbury suggests that the monks there venerated Guthlac on 11 April in a major solemnity, ranking his feast as an unusually important occasion.[6] Many such calendars identify him specifically as an anchorite, leaving no doubt about the role in which he was remembered. His anchoretic identity was also proclaimed in litanies and the Proper of the

---

[4] Orderic Vitalis, *The Ecclesiastical History of Orderic Vitalis*, ed. and tr. M. Chibnall, 6 vols (Oxford, 1969–80), II, 343; cf. London, College of Arms, MS Arundel 10, fo. 62r (on which, see R. Kay, 'Walter of Coventry and the Barnwell Chronicle', *Traditio*, 54 (1999), 141–67).

[5] *Ecclesiastical History*, ed. Chibnall, II, 341. D. Whitelock rejected this date because a man named Thurketel was abbot of Bedford until 971. However, if this was the same man, he might have held the abbeys in plurality: 'The Conversion of the Eastern Danelaw', *Saga Book of the Viking Society for Northern Research*, 12 (1941), 159–76, at 174–5. For the reference to Thurketel of Bedford, see *Liber Eliensis*, ed. E. O. Blake, CSer. 3rd ser. 92 (1962), 96n, 105n.

[6] Guthlac is entered in majuscules: *English Kalendars before A.D. 1100*, ed. F. Wormald, HBS, 72 (1934), 61; on the origins of the calendar, see *The Leofric Missal*, ed. N. Orchard, HBS, 113–14, 2 vols (2002), I, 173–4.

Mass.[7] Two extant copies of Felix's *Life* of St Guthlac, which date from the early and the mid-tenth century respectively, may have been made at Worcester cathedral priory; another two, from the late tenth or early eleventh century, may have emanated from Canterbury.[8] Their preservation suggests that the hermit's career was known, re-read, and studied in different locations. A book probably made at St Augustine's abbey, Canterbury, in the late tenth century, contains Jerome's *Life* of St Paul the hermit and Felix's *Life* of St Guthlac together and alone in the hand of a single scribe.[9] Whoever brought the careers of these two archetypal hermits together in one volume apparently intended to assemble a little book for someone interested in anachoresis, both in its desert origins and its achievements in England. Perhaps it was intended to function as an anchorite's handbook. Vernacular literature, including a translation of his *Life* and poems eulogizing the saint, may attest Guthlac's popularity among the laity. Jane Roberts comments, 'there is a surprising amount written about Guthlac in Old English'.[10] There may be more about him than about any other saint. One effect of his popularity was the appearance of what one might call satellite cults in the vicinity of his shrine at Crowland, where characters that appeared in his legend, or hermits with similar credentials, eventually came to be venerated in their own right.

Among the shrines and holy places dotted throughout the fenland region were a number of holy sites mentioned by Bede, including Ely and Peterborough, the sites of early monasteries, which by the late tenth century had devolved to the royal fisc. Æthelwold now came hunting through the region, looking for places where he could fit his new form of monasticism into the existing sacred landscape. He purchased Ely and Peterborough about the year 970 and peopled them with his monks.[11] Crowland might have tempted him if Thurketel had not already acquired it, but instead he went for the next best thing: another fen island nearby, where there was a credible satellite cult. This lush fen island of Thorney, five miles to the south-east of Crowland, was known as 'Anchorite Island' after the semi-legendary brothers Thancred and Torhtred and their sister Tova, who were thought to have lived on the island as anchorites.[12] Æthelwold presumably

---

[7] See *Anglo-Saxon Litanies of the Saints*, ed. M. Lapidge, HBS, 106 (1991), and the *Propria* in *The Missal of Robert of Jumièges*, ed. H. A. Wilson, HBS (1896), 3, 153; and also in *The Leofric Missal*, ed. Orchard, II, 306, 380.

[8] Gneuss, nos. 88, 484, 781, 804. For the argument that Arras, Bibliothèque municipale MS 1029, was produced at Canterbury (or in Flanders), as opposed to Bath, see H. A. McKee, 'St Augustine's Abbey, Canterbury: Book Production in the Tenth and Eleventh Centuries', PhD thesis, University of Cambridge, 1997, 161–8. Similar arguments may apply to Gneuss, no. 804.

[9] Corpus Christi College, Cambridge, MS 389; Gneuss, no. 103: M. Budny, *Insular, Anglo-Saxon, and Early Anglo-Norman Manuscript Art at Corpus Christi College, Cambridge: An Illustrated Catalogue*, 2 vols (Kalamazoo, 1997), no. 23.

[10] Roberts, 'Hagiography and Literature', 69–86, 82 (referring to Gneuss, nos. 657, 941).

[11] *Liber Eliensis*, ed. Blake, 74. On this, the *Libellus Æthelwoldi* agrees with the saint's biography.

[12] C. R. Hart, *The Early Charters of Eastern England* (Leicester, 1966), 166.

knew of them, for an account of them appears in what is probably a late tenth-century charter, describing how he founded the monastery, and the other sites which he acquired in the region at that time were chosen for their religious associations.[13] Early in the eleventh century these three hermits were listed in the 'List of saints' resting places in England' (the *Secgan*) among the saints then resting at Thorney.[14] The others included Guthlac's successor Cissa, whom Felix depicts as a hermit.[15] An early twelfth-century relic list from Thorney, which lists relics of *S. Cissi anach'* (St Cissa the anchorite), suggests that his identity had not changed in the interim.[16] His appeal probably derived from his proximity to Guthlac in the Guthlac legend, just as the two hermits who succeeded St Cuthbert on Inner Farne, SS. Oidiluald (d. 699) and Felgild (d. *c.*725), attained their sanctity largely by following in Cuthbert's footsteps. Whether or not he followed Thurketel's example, Æthelwold, by establishing a base on Thorney and embracing hermit saints, provided further evidence that hermits were potent symbols in the locality. Another cult still thrived five miles to the south-west of Crowland, at Peakirk, long associated with Guthlac's sister Pega.[17] Early in the eleventh century a minster stood there, on the lands of a man named Sigefyrth, who may or may not have built it.[18] Sigefyrth was probably the leading thegn of the East Midlands murdered at the Council of Oxford in 1015. The presence of a new minster on his estates, associated with the cult of the anchorite Pega, could indicate that the lay nobility were as interested in hermits as the clerics Thurketel and Æthelwold were.

Was such interest confined to the locality of Crowland? Certainly, the popularity of Guthlac and the presence of anchoretic satellite cults are enough to explain it. And these things may also explain why Æthelwold chose an eremitic site for his monastery there; for, with the exception of Thorney, no monastery founded by him or through the influence of his fellow reformers, Oswald and Dunstan, set out to exploit a hermit cult. Æthelwold's decision to do so appears to reflect the spirituality of the locality rather than any interest of his own. Moreover, the saints' *Lives* written in reforming circles in the late tenth and early eleventh centuries, notably those by the homilist and hagiographer Ælfric (d. *c.*1010), Abbo of Fleury's *Life* of St Edmund, Wulfstan of Winchester's *Life* of St Æthelwold, Byrhtferth of Ramsey's *Life* of St Oswald, and the anonymous

---

[13] S 792. See Hart, *Early Charters*, 165–86; and *Wulfstan of Winchester: The Life of St Æthelwold*, ed. M. Lapidge and M. Winterbottom (Oxford, 1991), p. xlix.

[14] F. Liebermann, *Die Heiligen Englands, angelsächsisch und lateinisch* (Hannover, 1889), 16; D. W. Rollason, 'Lists of Saints' Resting-Places in Anglo-Saxon England', *ASE*, 7 (1978), 61–93, at 91.

[15] *Guthlac*, ed. Colgrave, 175–6; Blair, 'Handlist', 521.

[16] L, BL, MS Add. 40,000, fos. 11v–12r, and *ibid.*, fo. 11v; printed in *Kalendars*, ed. Wormald, 129–30.

[17] For evidence of her cult, see Blair, 'Handlist', 552.

[18] S 947; *Charters of the New Minster, Winchester*, ed. S. Miller (Oxford, 2001), p. xxxvii, n. 72; Blair, *The Church*, 356.

Life of St Dunstan, reveal not the faintest inclination to represent their subjects as anchorites or praise anachoresis. If ever they speak of desert solitude they speak of it as an ornament to the cenobium. Ramsey abbey, which Oswald founded in the 970s, lay on an isolated fen island roughly sixteen miles south of Crowland. Abbo of Fleury, a French scholar from Fleury-sur-Loire who taught there in the 980s, described it rhetorically as a paradisiacal haven in the desert.[19] He also described The Fens as a bosom of the solitary life, embracing flocks of monks who attained a degree of solitude there equal to that of the desert.[20] The latter reflection employed an idea from the *Life* of St Martin of Tours (*c.*316–97), a saint of enormous influence in the Frankish domains: that the ideal site for a monastery should possess desert solitude.[21] Abbo's pupil at Ramsey, the monk Byrhtferth, went even further with his eremitical rhetoric, reporting that Oswald 'appropriately enough' visited that 'desert' – while preparing to establish his monastery – on the feast of St John the Baptist, who had 'always aspired to the desert'.[22] He linked Oswald to the Baptist in order to associate him metaphorically with the origins of his cenobitic monastery and edify the monks by recalling their eremitical origins. The reformers might also have appropriated St Guthlac, for it has been proposed on thematic, stylistic, and linguistic grounds that the Old English poem on the saint, *Guthlac A*, represents an attempt by some monk writing in the third quarter of the tenth century to reinvent the hermit for a cenobitic audience.[23] All in all, then, it would seem that the reformers' vision of the desert was communal, not solitary, and that where they appropriated hermits and eremitical rhetoric they did so to recall their dedication to austerity and solitude. Nevertheless, the fact that they presented themselves rhetorically in eremitical terms conveys the same impression, but on a wider scale, as their interest in hermit cults on Thorney: that they could not help participating in a culture of admiration for solitary asceticism.

---

[19] On the depiction of monasteries as oases in the desert, see Constable, *The Reformation*, 136–7, 138–9.

[20] 'Ut noua sint heremi claustra reperta tibi' (a variant gives 'heremita' for 'heremi claustra'): Byrhtferth of Ramsey, *The Lives of St Oswald and St Egwine*, ed. and tr. M. Lapidge (Oxford, 2009), 92–3; *The Historians of the Church of York and Its Archbishops*, ed. J. Raine, RS, 71, 3 vols (1879–94), I, 431. 'Quae paludes prebent pluribus monachorum gregibus optatos solitariae conuersationis sinus, quibus inclusi non indigeant solitudine heremi': Abbo, 'Life of St. Edmund', in *Three Lives of English Saints*, ed. M. Winterbottom (Toronto, 1972), 67–87, at 70.

[21] Sulpicius Severus, *Vie de saint Martin*, ed. J. Fontaine, *SC*, 133–5 (Paris, 1967–9), I, 272–4; A.-M. Helvétius, 'Ermites ou moines: solitude et cénobitisme du Ve au Xe siècle (principalement en Gaule du Nord)', in *Ermites*, ed. Vauchez, 1–27, at 5–7.

[22] 'Satis apte euenit ut in illius die ad heremum uenirent, qui semper dilexisse heremum nouit, sicut canit sancta ecclesia': Byrhtferth, *The Lives*, ed. Lapidge, 90. He referred here to a hymn, sung on the Baptist's feast day, which described how the saint from his 'tender years' had 'sought the desert caves': I. B. Milfull, *The Hymns of the Anglo-Saxon Church: A Study and Edition of the 'Durham Hymnal'* (Cambridge, 1996), no. 86.

[23] P. W. Conner, 'Source Studies, the Old English Guthlac A and the English Benedictine Reformation', *RB*, 103 (1993), 380–413. See also C. A. Jones, 'Envisioning the *Cenobium* in the Old English *Guthlac A*', *Mediaeval Studies*, 57 (1995), 259–91.

Ælfric the homilist, who trained under Æthelwold at Winchester and embraced his commitment to liturgical cenobitism, was a product of the reform movement. For this reason, he may not have been altogether comfortable with anchorites. Mary Clayton has suggested that in his collection of English saints' *Lives* 'there is a clear avoidance of eremitic saints' and that Ælfric 'seems to have deliberately refrained from presenting the life of the contemplative hermit as an ideal'.[24] The avoidance of St Guthlac is comprehensible. Ælfric's aim in translating Latin saints' *Lives* into the vernacular was to make them accessible to a wider audience, but a vernacular *Life* of Guthlac and poems about his deeds were already circulating.[25] Yet Clayton's point remains valid, for whereas Ælfric approved of apostles, martyrs, and confessors he nowhere attends to saintly hermits. Even when he extracted sermon material from the *Vitas patrum*, he avoided the central theme of anachoresis.[26] At the same time, his sermons anticipate that the laity who comprised his intended audience would regard anchorites as saints. In one sermon, a story from the *Verba seniorum* warns of the fate of an evil soul. Another, on the devilish snares of auguries, borrows a tale from the *Historia monachorum* about the hermit Macarius and some wicked magicians, to warn against devilish illusions.[27] The first tale dupes the audience into thinking that a hermit will go to heaven because of his reputed holiness; instead he is dragged off to hell. The second casts Macarius as an expert in discerning devilry. In each sermon, Ælfric plays to the expected assumptions of his audience. The assumption anticipated in the first is that hermits are exceedingly holy; the assumption in the second is that they are qualified to outwit the devil. It is telling that in the first tale Ælfric aimed to demolish the myth that hermits were invulnerable to sin. In the world's eyes, the hermit in the tale is a holy man. In God's eyes, he is a sinner. This tale was meant for an audience that was rather too inclined to put anchorites on pedestals. Ælfric's assumption about his audience suggests that the laity then held hermits in high regard.

Near the end of his life, when he was abbot of Eynsham in Oxfordshire, Ælfric wrote a letter to a nobleman named Sigefyrth who retained an anchorite on his estate. Ælfric described the anchorite as 'your anchorite at home with you', as though this arrangement was nothing unusual.[28] If Sigefyrth kept an anchorite, other rich thegns might have kept them. This anchorite was teaching that mass-priests were permitted to marry. Referring to him in respectful terms as 'God's

[24] See Clayton, 'Hermits', 162–4.

[25] On Ælfric's intention in translating Latin saints' *Lives*, see H. Magennis, 'Warrior Saints, Warfare and the Hagiography of Ælfric of Eynsham', *Traditio*, 56 (2001), 27–51, at 50.

[26] P. Jackson, 'Ælfric and the "Uita patrum" in Catholic Homily I.36', in *Essays on Anglo-Saxon and Related Themes in Memory of Lynne Grundy*, ed. J. Roberts and J. Nelson (London, 2000), 259–72, at 270–1.

[27] *Homilies of Ælfric: A Supplementary Collection*, ed. J. C. Pope, EETS, o.s. 259–60, 2 vols (1967–8), nos. xxvii, xxix. Pope thought that only part of no. xxvii (the relevant part) was Ælfric's.

[28] 'Eower ancor æt ham mid eow': *Angelsächsische Homilien und Heiligenleben*, ed. B. Assmann, Bibliothek der angelsächsischen Prosa, 3 (Kassel, 1889), 13.

friend', Ælfric wrote to rebut his argument by proceeding to list various anchorites who had vowed themselves to chastity, namely the desert fathers Antony, Paul, Hilarion, Macarius, John, Arsenius, and Paphnutius, reeling off their names as though Sigefyrth or his anchorite ought to have been familiar with them.[29] This brief glimpse of a nobleman not only retaining an anchorite but also listening to his advice and probably possessing knowledge of saintly anchoretic role models lends weight to the argument that the laity admired them. Sigefyrth, whose name was uncommon, may have been the owner or founder of the monastery at Peakirk.[30] In that locality, it would not be surprising if modern-day Guthlacs were able to set themselves up as oracles and win the patronage of the local nobility. The anchorite's teaching contradicted one of Ælfric's most cherished precepts: that the clergy should try to be chaste. It may have galled him all the more that someone as holy as an anchorite held such little regard for chastity. This case reveals that, although a reformer like Ælfric could generate innumerable sermons and letters offering pastoral guidance on various matters, anchorites were able to find an attentive audience – and contradict the reformers, in the most influential social circles.

Further evidence of their influence in the early eleventh century surfaces in the cases of Mantat, an anchorite somehow connected to Thorney, and Withman, an abbot of Ramsey who became a hermit in the 1020s. Mantat is known because he identifies himself in his will, which survives in the archive of Thorney abbey, as 'Mantat *ancer*' (Mantat the anchorite). Datable to 1017 x 1035, it bequeathes land at Twywell in Northamptonshire and Conington in Huntingdonshire to Thorney abbey in return for the annual recitation of 200 masses, 200 psalters, and numerous holy prayers for the testator's soul.[31] A cryptic comment in his will hints that Mantat performed some important spiritual service on behalf of the king and queen. Addressing Cnut and Emma he wrote: 'God knows that no tonsured man has been more useful to you both than I, and that shall be known to you in the future life.' Perhaps he had served as their confessor, counsellor, or intercessor – the matter is obscure. Given that Cnut and a number of his entourage entered into confraternity with the monks of Thorney, Mantat's connexion with that abbey could derive from his association with the royal circle.[32] Alternatively, Thorney might have attracted him (or inspired him to become an anchorite, if he was already a monk there) because it venerated anchoretic saints. The fact that Mantat addressed his will to Cnut seems to indicate that he saw the king as his temporal lord, a scenario which raises the

---

[29] *Homilien*, ed. Assmann, 13, 23.

[30] I am grateful to John Blair for this suggestion (personal communication).

[31] S 1523. See Hart, *Charters*, 204–5, and *Anglo-Saxon Wills*, ed. and tr. D. Whitelock (Cambridge, 1930), no. 23 (though in regard to her argument against the name, note the presence of a certain Mantat in S 1497). The antiquary Robert Cotton transcribed a variant, from a lost cartulary of Thorney Abbey, in Cambridgeshire County Record Office, MS 588DR/Z3 (unfoliated).

[32] C. Clark, 'British Library Additional MS. 40,000, ff. 1v–12r', in *Words, Names and History: Selected Writings of Cecily Clark*, ed. P. Jackson (Cambridge, 1995), 301–19, at 308.

possibility that Cnut was his patron and sponsor, as Sigefyrth had been patron to the anonymous anchorite on his estate. There is, nevertheless, an alternative scenario, in that Mantat may have addressed the king and queen as a cleric or as a foreigner whose property the king was legally bound to protect.[33] The estates he possessed would have been more than enough to sustain him. Whatever his connexion to the monarch, his spiritual claim on Cnut is striking.

Withman, a German, may also have been a monk in the service of King Cnut. After the conquest of 1016, when Abbot Wulfsige of Ramsey was killed in battle, he was put in charge of the abbey; but being a strict disciplinarian he soon fell out with the monks and, in the fourth year of his abbacy, escaped on pilgrimage to Jerusalem. In his absence, the monks made their own man abbot, and when Withman returned in 1020 or 1021 he accepted the change. According to Ramsey's twelfth-century 'Book of Benefactors' (*Liber benefactorum*), the usurper offered to resign, but Withman declined the restoration of his old office and elected instead to live as a hermit on a nearby island surrounded by muddy fens, barely a stone's throw from the abbey. It is a plausible story, in that there was little that an unpopular abbot, who had already once absconded, could have achieved by returning to his post. Moreover, the pay-off that he would have received in the form of a pension, coupled with the prospect of peace and quiet, could have made for an attractive retirement. During his twenty-six or more years there (he died *c*.1047), a monk of Ramsey named Oswald joined him on the island. Ramsey's twelfth-century chronicler claimed that King Edward would visit these hermits whenever he came to Ramsey, presumably for spiritual counsel, and that they persuaded him to give alms to their abbey. The gifts, he claims, included an estate at Ringstead (near Hunstanton) with appertaining liberties and rights of wreck; the hundred and a half of Wimbotsham (i.e. Clackclose); Downham Market, also in north-west Norfolk, and sixty-four soke-men. Whereas Withman supposedly secured Ringstead for the abbey, Oswald supposedly used his influence with King Edward to obtain its interests in Clackclose and Downham Market. Although the chronicler probably based these claims partly on one or more forged charters, which seem to exaggerate the extent of the royal gift, the story still suggests that the hermits held influence with the king.[34] This fits with the statement of a cleric connected with Edward's court, that the king looked on ascetic monks with favour.[35]

---

[33] Cnut's laws obliged the king to defend the property of a man in holy orders or a foreigner: *English Historical Documents, c.500–1042*, ed. D. Whitelock, 2nd edn. (London, 1979), 461. The Mantat named in S 1497 was a slave in Bedfordshire who was freed by the lady Æthelgifu in the 990s or thereabouts. Might this have been the same man?

[34] *Chronicon abbatiae Rameseiensis*, ed. W. D. Macray, RS, 83 (1886), 120–5, 159–60, cf. S 1030 and S 1109; *Cartularium monasterii de Rameseia*, ed. W. H. Hart and P. A. Lyons, RS, 79, 3 vols (1884–93), II, 73; and C. P. Lewis, 'Withman [Leucander; name in religion Andrew] (d. *c*.1047), abbot of Ramsey', in *ODNB*.

[35] *Vita Ædwardi*, ed. Barlow, 62. Foreign clergy were Edward's favourites. Withman was German.

It is possible to account for this influence in light of the Anglo-Saxon inheritance, because tales like the story of Æthelbald's visit to Guthlac had established the idea that rulers should befriend anchorites. Yet it can also be explained with reference to patterns of kingly piety across Europe; for neither Cnut nor Edward had grown up in England. Parallel examples can be found in the German Empire, where rulers at that date sought out hermits for counsel or made gifts at their request. The emperor Henry II (1002–24) and his nobles consulted and sponsored the hermit Wanlef (d. 1013), who dwelt near Islenburg at the foot of the Harz Mountains in Saxony, in the imperial domain.[36] While Henry was at Ravenna in December 1021, the hermit Romuald persuaded the emperor to make a gift to one of his monasteries.[37] Romuald, indeed, had been getting his way with the imperial court since the reign of Otto III (996–1002). In the early 1040s, Peter Damian applauded his ability to intimidate an Italian nobleman, who had remarked: 'Not the emperor, not any other man, is able to strike great fear into me in the way that the appearance of Romuald terrifies me – before his face I do not know what to say, nor can I find any excuses by which I could defend myself.' Peter himself then commented: 'whatever sinners, especially powerful men of the world, would come into Romuald's presence would soon be struck with inner trembling, as if in the presence of the very majesty of God'.[38] Conrad II (1024–39) made gifts to the hermits at Rinchnach in Bavaria, probably in recognition of his admiration for their leader Gunther, a converted Thuringian nobleman, who later forged a friendship with the emperor Henry III (1039–56).[39] The French chronicler Rodulf Glaber (d. *c*.1046) certainly thought it plausible that a hermit might prevail upon an emperor, for he recounts the story of how a hermit in southern Italy persuaded Henry II, in 1022, to have mercy on the people of Troja in Apulia.[40] Whether there is any truth in these stories is less interesting than the fact that writers in the second quarter of the eleventh century imagined that hermits possessed the authority to influence monarchs and nobles. In view of this, it appears plausible that King Cnut would have sought the services of the anchorite Mantat and that King Edward visited Ramsey's anchorites and granted gifts to the abbey at their instigation.

---

[36] Grundmann, '"Einsiedler" e "Klausner"', 314–15.

[37] G. Tabacco, 'Romualdo di Ravenna e gli inizi dell'eremitismo camaldolese', in *L'eremitismo*, 73–119, at 99.

[38] Adapted from the translation in Howe, 'The Awesome Hermit', 106; see *Vita beati Romualdi*, ed. Tabacco, 83.

[39] Grundmann, '"Einsiedler" e "Klausner"', 320–1.

[40] *Opera*, ed. France, 102–3. There is a touch of humour in this story, in that the people of Troja grabbed hold of a hermit (one of the many then available, Glaber notes) and sent him out reciting the standard eremitic mantra (*Kyrieleison*) like some automaton, leading all the children in his wake, in a ploy to move the emperor to pity.

ASCETICS AND HERMITS, C.1050–C.1080

While anchorites were apparently finding favour with King Edward, one or two ascetics were being promoted to high clerical office, just as others were in Normandy. These included Bishop Wulfstan of Worcester (1062–95), whose election in 1062, on the advice of a papal legate, marked an abrupt change of direction from the reign of his worldlier predecessor. Wulfstan's asceticism is an important theme in William of Malmesbury's Latin revision of a lost Old English *Life* of Wulfstan composed by his chaplain Coleman (d. 1113).[41] Twice removed from its subject and written with the intention of presenting Wulfstan as a credible saint, its claims are open to suspicion. Nevertheless, they are consistent with the spirituality of some of Wulfstan's European contemporaries who promoted solitude, such as Jean of Fécamp and Peter Damian. According to William of Malmesbury, when Wulfstan was provost of Worcester during the 1050s he was noted for his austerity. Two of his customs were to lock himself in a chamber for the purpose of solitary prayer and to undertake solitary vigils at churches; he also maintained a penitential diet, fasting three days a week. During Lent, he withdrew into solitude.[42] In 1062, after attempts to persuade Wulfstan to accept the bishopric had failed, a respected recluse named Wulfsige, who lived at the monastery of Evesham, allegedly managed to persuade him. Factual or symbolic, the story about Wulfsige suggests that Wulfstan's personal asceticism and penitential regimen may have gone together with reverence for living anchorites.[43] William of Malmesbury relates that every one of his episcopal estates had an isolated chamber or oratory, 'where he enjoyed solitude as profound as any he could have found in the desert'. The number of these cells is perhaps an exaggeration, but the belief that a bishop might possess such retreats was well founded. Similar retreats are mentioned in the early eleventh-century *Life* of the saintly German bishop Burchard of Worms (d. 1025).[44] Seventh- and eighth-century Anglo-Saxon bishops had also used them for Lenten withdrawal. Eadberht, bishop of Lindisfarne (d. 698), withdrew to a hermitage during Lent, while St John of Beverley (d. 721) would retire to an oratory he had built near Hexham in Northumbria.[45] Wulfstan may have been reviving an old practice. His retreats reflected both his native tradition and Continental ascetic trends.

---

[41] William of Malmesbury, *Saints' Lives: Lives of SS. Wulfstan, Dunstan, Patrick, Benignus and Indract*, ed. and tr. M. Winterbottom and R. M. Thomson (Oxford, 2002), pp. xv–xvi. See also A. Orchard, 'Parallel Lives: Wulfstan, William, Coleman and Christ', in *St Wulfstan and His World*, ed. J. S. Barrow and N. P. Brooks (Aldershot, 2005), 39–57.

[42] *Saints' Lives*, ed. Winterbottom and Thomson, 25–7, 45, 119.

[43] *Chronicle*, ed. Darlington and McGurk, II, 591.

[44] *Vita Burchardi episcopi Wormatiensis*, ed. D. G. Waitz, in *MGH, SS* IV, ed. G. H. Pertz (Hannover, 1841), 829–46, at 837.

[45] *Cuthbert*, ed. Colgrave, 293, 358; *Ecclesiastical History*, ed. Colgrave and Mynors, 457.

During Wulfstan's time at Worcester, and perhaps through his influence, interest in the desert fathers blossomed there.[46] Among the manuscripts probably copied at Worcester about mid-century, one contains 171 selections (out of some 700 sayings) from the *Verba seniorum*, with many eleventh-century interlineations, the proofs of careful study.[47] Through the second half of the century, and into the twelfth, the monks there copied Jerome's *Lives* of SS. Paul, Hilarion, and Malchus, the *Life* of St Antony, and the *Historia monachorum*.[48] Felix's *Life* of St Guthlac was the only hagiography that they chose to add to the large collection of saints' *Lives* known as the 'Cotton-Corpus Legendary', which arrived in England in the eleventh century.[49] They also acquired a translation of Jerome's *Life* of Malchus and may themselves have translated extracts from the *Verba seniorum*.[50] Scholarly activity such as this went beyond commemorative duties and could only have stemmed from an interest in the lives of desert saints. It upholds William of Malmesbury's portrait of a prelate who was interested in solitary asceticism. Although the paucity of surviving books and book-lists, and difficulty of attributing them to known libraries, leaves it unclear whether other English monasteries were developing similar interests at that date, interest in the desert fathers at Worcester, coupled with Wulfstan's enthusiasm for emulating their austerity, suggests that the spirituality of Romuald, Peter Damian, and John of Fécamp had found a foothold in England. It may have touched Wulfstan's episcopal neighbour and colleague, Bishop Ælfwold of Sherborne (*c*.1046–*c*.1065). In the 1120s, William of Malmesbury reported what he had heard from old men, that Ælfwold had lived frugally in devotion to St Cuthbert, who appealed to him over and above other saints because he had lived like a monk in the surrounding turmoil.[51] If Wulfstan was patterning his own conduct on the desert fathers, Ælfwold might have patterned his on the vocational anchorite Cuthbert, who had taken up the crozier with reluctance. Although the alleged rigours of Wulfstan and Ælfwold are not otherwise in evidence among their episcopal colleagues, they may signal the beginnings of a shift. Fifty years before Ælfwold's era the most prominent monks in the realm – the reformers – had stressed the liturgy and communal life. Now there was a revival of interest in solitary

---

[46] P. Jackson, 'The *Vitas patrum* in Eleventh-Century Worcester', in *England in the Eleventh Century: Proceedings of the 1990 Harlaxton Symposium*, ed. C. Hicks (Stamford, 1992), 119–34.

[47] Gneuss, no. 761; and see R. M. Thomson, *A Descriptive Catalogue of the Medieval Manuscripts in Worcester Cathedral Library* (Woodbridge, 2001), 29–30.

[48] Gneuss, nos. 359, 761. Dates attributed to these range from *s*. xi*med* to *s*. xii*in*.

[49] *Three Eleventh-Century Anglo-Latin Saints' Lives: Vita s. Birini, Vita et miracula s. Kenelmi and Vita s. Rumwoldi*, ed. and tr. R. C. Love (Oxford 1996), p. xxi.

[50] Jackson, 'The *Vitas patrum*', 127; and K. S. Beckett, 'Worcester Sauce: Malchus in Anglo-Saxon England', in *Latin Learning and English Lore: Studies in Anglo-Saxon Literature for Michael Lapidge*, ed. K. O'B. O'Keeffe and A. Orchard, 2 vols (Toronto, 2005), II, 212–31, at 218–23.

[51] William of Malmesbury, *Gesta pontificum anglorum: The History of the English Bishops*, ed. M. Winterbottom, with the assistance of R. M. Thomson, 2 vols (Oxford, 2007), I, 282–4. D. P. Kirby, 'Notes on the Saxon Bishops of Sherborne', *Proceedings of the Dorset Natural History and Archaeological Society*, 87 (1965), 213–22, at 219.

asceticism and austerity. Such a shift is hard to explain without reference to the Continental developments examined in the first chapter, which seem to have led increasingly to the ecclesiastical promotion of ascetics. Wulfstan and Ælfwold were probably buoyed on the tide of reverence for asceticism, solitude, and renunciation, which was rising, at that time, over a large part of Western Christendom.

About that time, during the third quarter of the century, new hermits began to appear in the woods of Great Malvern in Worcestershire and at various sites north of the River Humber. Their arrival on the scene is also best explained in view of the eremitic movement then thriving in Western Europe, but the nature of their impact owed a lot to conditions in England after the Conquest. Before their arrival, about the 1070s, the phenomenon of master hermits who attracted disciples was not commonly seen in England, although some examples could be given.[52] Then within the space of a decade there were several. The account of Great Malvern provided by William of Malmesbury reports that a hermit named Ealdwine gained recruits one by one and eventually assembled thirty followers in the woods.[53] In the 1080s, they began to build a church and adopt Benedictine observances under the patronage of the sheriff Urse d'Abetot (sheriff *c.*1069–1108).[54] Thirty was a lot of converts, but the number is not implausible in light of the expansion of eremitic communities in France and Normandy and the size of other convents in the diocese at that time.[55] It is possible that in England the Norman Conquest of 1066 acted as a catalyst in the expansion of these communities because its aftermath was a time of soul-searching and upheaval. Early in 1070, during the winter, the armies of King William I (or perhaps rebel or Danish soldiers) wreaked enough havoc in the north to generate a number of refugees. According to the Evesham chronicler Thomas of Marlborough (d. 1236), who was using a lost account written by the monk Dominic of Evesham in the first decade of the twelfth century, one outcome of this devastation was that a large number of those displaced by famine and war fled to Evesham.[56] Abbot Æthelwig (1058–77) did all he could to feed them and entrusted many to the officials, servants, and capable brethren of the monastery, but many died throughout the vill. Nothing more is said about the dispersal of these refugees, probably

---

[52] E.g. St Fursa (d. 649) at *Cnobheresburg* (*Ecclesiastical History*, ed. Colgrave and Mynors, 269–77) or Wulfric at St Benet's at Holme, if we believe a later account: see T. Licence, 'Suneman and Wulfric: Two Forgotten Saints of St Benedict's Abbey at Holme in Norfolk', *AB*, 122 (2004), 361–72.

[53] *Gesta pontificum*, ed. Winterbottom and Thomson, I, 434–5. Our earliest accounts of Ealdwine are from William of Malmesbury's writings, the first from his *Deeds* of the bishops (*Gesta pontificum*), the second from his *Life* of St Wulfstan. In the earlier work, William portrays Ealdwine as a monk, ordained by Wulfstan, 'living as a hermit' in the Malvern Hills. In the later work, he introduces him not as a hermit but as an uneducated monk – a lay convert, presumably – endeavouring to establish a religious community (in the manner of a new hermit).

[54] *Annales monastici*, ed. H. R. Luard, RS, 36, 5 vols (1864–9), IV, 373.

[55] Worcester, *c.*1080, had about thirty monks. Evesham in 1077 or 1078 had thirty-two. *English Episcopal Acta 33: Worcester, 1062–1185*, ed. M. Cheney, D. Smith, C. N. L. Brooke, and P. M. Hoskin (Oxford, 2007), nos. 8 and 7.

[56] Thomas of Marlborough, *History of the Abbey of Evesham*, ed. and tr. J. Sayers and L. Watkiss (Oxford, 2003), p. xxxii, 167. Historians still dispute the impact of the harrying of the north.

because the chronicler's interests were directed elsewhere. Still, it is unlikely that every refugee headed straight towards Evesham. Sixteen miles to the west lay the hermitage at Great Malvern. Some of the refugees could have ended up there. This may explain how Ealdwine managed to acquire so many recruits, for many of the displaced probably had nowhere else to go. More than one of those taken on board at Evesham remained at that location, as others may have done at Malvern. It is reasonable to suppose, moreover, that the hermits at Malvern sympathized with the plight of their native people and that the woods there could be cleared and farmed by any that were willing to join them and embrace a religious life.

In 1070, when it was still a war-torn region, there were no monasteries north of the River Trent. Yet this need not imply that its inhabitants lacked interest in their ascetic heritage. In the second quarter of the century or thereabouts, the Durham cleric Ælfred, who held Hexham church in Northumbria, had visited ruined minsters in the region and 'raised from the earth the bones of those saints whom he knew to be buried in these places, enshrining them above ground, that they might be better known to the people and venerated by them'.[57] It was said that these relics included bones of the anchorites Balthere and Billfrith and of other saints such as Oswine, the martyred king of Deira (d. 651). Ælfred's hope, apparently, was to stimulate devotion. He may have been successful, for in the days of Earl Tostig (1055–65), at St Mary's church in Tynemouth, a God-fearing man kept vigil before Oswine's shrine. He was probably its sacristan, Edmund. According to a twelfth-century writer – whose meaning may be figurative – he resembled a monk or anchorite, although he had taken no vow.[58] So little is known of religious life in the north at this time that many similar figures have probably been forgotten, even if a few can still be identified. Among the latter was a monk named Benedict from the Burgundian abbey of St Germanus at Auxerre, who settled in the year 1069 at Selby on the River Ouse. The narrative of his adventures, written in 1174, is somewhat tongue-in-cheek. At the saint's recommendation, its protagonist escapes from Auxerre with a finger of St Germanus sewn inside his arm. The saint sends him on to *Selby*, he interprets this as *Salisbury*, and more silliness follows.[59] Even so, the core biographical details may be reliable. These maintain that Benedict first served

---

[57] Symeon of Durham, *Libellus de exordio atque procursu istius, hoc est Dunhelmensis, ecclesie = Tract on the Origins and Progress of This the Church of Durham*, ed. and tr. D. Rollason (Oxford, 2000), 163–5 (adapted from Rollason's translation). I. G. Thomas, 'The Cult of Saints' Relics in Medieval England', PhD thesis, University of London, 1975, 76–8, locates the translations within the context of the consolidation of Durham's patrimony.

[58] *Miscellanea biographica*, ed. J. Raine, the Elder, SS, 2 (London, 1838), 12, 20; P. A. Hayward, 'Saint Albans, Durham and the Cult of Saint Oswine, King and Martyr', *Viator*, 30 (1999), 105–44, at 130.

[59] The relevant section appears in *The Coucher Book of Selby*, ed. J. T. Fowler and C. C. Hodges, The Yorkshire Archaeological and Topographical Association, Record Series 10, 13, 2 vols (1891–3), I, 6–16. J. Burton, 'Selby Abbey and Its Twelfth-Century Historian', in *Learning and Literacy in Medieval England and Abroad*, ed. S. Rees-Jones (Turnhout, 2003), 49–68, does not report the humour.

in Auxerre as a layman, became a monk and priest, and later fled without permission. Like other new hermits he may have desired greater solitude. When he got to Selby, he built a crude hovel under an enormous oak and erected a large cross on the bank of the Ouse. This came to the attention of the sheriff of York, Hugh fitzBaldric (sheriff 1069–*c.*1087), who took him into his protection. When the sheriff introduced him to King William I at York, the king granted him one plough-land – a substantial unit of potential or real arable, which commonly approximated to 120 acres – for the foundation of a monastery. Benedict, or the enormous gift of land, attracted brethren to the settlement, its holdings increased, and a monastery appeared.

The hermitage at Selby had not been established long when three monks from the diocese of Worcester decided to journey north, with aims not dissimilar to Benedict's. One came from Winchcombe abbey, which lay nineteen miles south-east of Malvern and eleven south of Evesham; the others came from Evesham itself. To summarize events: some time in the early 1070s, Prior Ealdwine of Winchcombe (who is not to be confused with Ealdwine the hermit of Malvern) and the Evesham brethren Ælfwi and Reinfrid journeyed north, where over the next twenty years they played leading roles in fostering the establishment of several monastic communities. They settled first at Monkchester (now Newcastle), before relocating to the ruins of Bede's old monastery at Jarrow, at the invitation of the Lotharingian bishop Walcher of Durham (1071–80). There they set up crude dwellings, and a community grew, comprising northerners and southerners. After some space of time, Ealdwine departed with one of the recruits, a Lincolnshire cleric named Turgot (Thorgod). He had recently returned to England from Norway after fleeing there as a fugitive from Norman captors.[60] Ealdwine and Turgot settled at a site associated with St Cuthbert: the deserted monastery of Melrose in the Scottish Borders. Reinfrid also relocated, to the ruined abbey of Streoneshalh (Whitby), which was originally founded by St Hilda (614–80), a saint lauded by Bede. Others joined him, but a group broke away under a convert named Stephen. In the meantime, Durham's new bishop, William of St Calais (1080–96), wished to reform his cathedral community, so he summoned Ealdwine to lead the monks who were to replace the cathedral clerics. William, a monk himself, had been educated under Odo of Bayeux and may have followed his lead in choosing a hermit to head his new monastery. (Bishop Odo had summoned Robert of Tombelaine to restore Saint-Vigor.) A more obvious possible reason for choosing Ealdwine was the pastoral experience that he had gained since coming to the north. Ealdwine became Durham's first prior (1083–7) and Turgot its second (1087–1109). Stephen and his followers, after various travails, ended up at York, where an abbey was founded in honour of St Mary. Stephen became its abbot (*c.*1088–1112). His followers made up the convent.

---

[60] On Turgot, see Simeon of Durham, *Historia regum*, in *Symeonis monachi opera omnia*, ed. T. Arnold, RS, 75, 2 vols (1882–5), II, 3–286, at 202–5.

By 1115, and probably rather earlier, historians of the convents at York and Durham had produced *narrationes fundationis*: accounts of their respective origins. York's is presented and generally accepted as a first-hand narrative penned by Abbot Stephen himself, perhaps *c*.1094.[61] Durham's is the work of the French or Norman monk Simeon, who composed it some time between 1104 and 1115 under Turgot's auspices.[62] A third *narratio fundationis* was produced at Whitby and augmented with records of benefactions to the monastery up to *c*.1176.[63] Scholars who have studied these sources have been content to interpret Ealdwine, Reinfrid, and Ælfwi as seekers after a simple life of solitude, much in the mould of new hermits.[64] Above all, Janet Burton has laboured to venture a critical reconstruction of the various stages of events outlined by the *narrationes*.[65] She attributed the northern revival to the combination of three powerful influences: the desire to recover an Anglo-Saxon northern monastic heritage; the inspiration of the eremitic tradition, 'that is, the notion of withdrawal, as hermits, from the secular world, and a stress on simplicity and poverty'; and lordly interest in founding and regulating new monasteries.[66] Far from setting out to inculcate a cenobitic revival, Ealdwine, Ælfwi, and Reinfrid, at least in Burton's thinking, journeyed north to pursue a life of poverty and prayer as anchorites. The revival came as the result of a consequent dialectic. In Burton's words: 'The first generation of monastic growth in Yorkshire was characterized by the twin impulses of the eremitical aspirations of monks and the desire of lay patrons for full, corporate monastic communities.'[67] Where hermits encountered patrons, monasteries appeared.

In addition to the dialectic observed by Burton, another dialectic is evident in these accounts: for the Durham and York *narrationes* betray a conflict of interests in which at least two seekers after solitude were forced to confront their duty to provide for recruits by establishing them in regulated communities. Ealdwine and Reinfrid, if not Ælfwi too, journeyed north in search of solitude. Simeon's assertion that when they arrived they strove to teach anyone they could to enter with them on their path to salvation need not militate against this supposition, for its author casts doubt (as does Stephen) on Ealdwine and Reinfrid's initial

---

[61] A new edition by N. Karn is forthcoming. I am grateful to Dr Karn for granting me prior viewing.

[62] *Libellus*, ed. Rollason, p. xlii. J. E. Burton, 'The Monastic Revival in Yorkshire: Whitby and St Mary's, York', in *Anglo-Norman Durham, 1093–1193*, ed. D. W. Rollason, M. M. Harvey, and M. Prestwich (Woodbridge, 1994), 41–51, at 43.

[63] *Cartularium abbathiæ de Whiteby, ordinis s. Benedicti fundatae anno MLXXVIII*, ed. J. C. Atkinson, SS, 69, 72, 2 vols (1879–81, for 1878–79).

[64] Knowles, *Monastic Order*, 166; Leyser, *Hermits*, 36.

[65] J. E. Burton, 'The Eremitical Tradition and the Development of Post-Conquest Religious Life in Northern England', in *Eternal Values in Medieval Life*, ed. N. Crossley-Holland, Trivium, 26 (1991), 18–39. See also J. E. Burton, 'The Monastic Revival', and *The Monastic Order in Yorkshire, 1069–1215* (Cambridge, 1999), 23–44.

[66] Burton, 'Monastic Revival', 41.

[67] Burton, *Monastic Order*, 23.

willingness to care for their recruits.[68] Stephen does so by differentiating between eremitically inspired withdrawal, which could be communal, and solitary isolation. Reinfrid, he states, lived at Jarrow as a solitary (*solitarius*) and later left 'to pursue the solitary life' (*solitaria uita*) once again at Whitby. Afterwards a change occurred, for when Stephen arrived at Whitby in 1078 the brethren then multiplying there were living 'the eremitic life' (*heremitica uita*).[69] Stephen's distinction between *heremitica uita* and *solitaria uita* is significant in this context. As Colin Morris has noted of new hermits on the Continent, those involved in the eremitic movement 'remembered that the word "hermit" properly means a wilderness-dweller' and sought 'an alternative way of life, which was severe but not necessarily solitary'.[70] Typically, they alternated between solitude and communal eremitism, as Ealdwine and Reinfrid did. They also typically shared these hermits' inclination to run from the pastoral responsibility that beckoned, while feeling duty-bound to yield to its embrace. Having yielded in the end, Ealdwine and Reinfrid emerge as dutiful individuals who sacrifice their desire for solitude to provide for the souls of their followers. Ælfwi, who remained at Jarrow, may have done so sooner. Not only did all three possess the attributes of new hermits; Stephen's reference to the 'eremitic life' as lived at Whitby when he arrived there suggests that they and their recruits thought of themselves as an eremitic community. Burton concluded that the northern revival 'was characterized by the twin impulses of the eremitical aspirations of monks and the desire of lay patrons for full, corporate monastic communities'.[71] However, it is clear now that there were two dialectics in operation. The first forced monks who went to find solitude to confront their duty towards their disciples. The informal communities thereby created had then to reach an arrangement with patrons who wished to sponsor conventional establishments. Fashion favoured Benedictine monasteries. The new communities of new hermits at Bec, La Chaise-Dieu, Malvern, Whitby, York, and Jarrow were duly transformed into Benedictine monasteries.

Taken altogether, the evidence of Ælfred's elevation of the saints early in the century; of the God-fearing man who kept watch at St Oswine's shrine in the 1060s; of Benedict's recruitment at Selby, and of the communities formed by Ealdwine, Ælfwi, and Reinfrid, contends that what was lacking at that time in the north was neither the will to revive the ascetic tradition nor potential recruits, but rather the leadership and expertise necessary to galvanize the indigenous population. The arrival of outsiders with monastic training was a godsend, for it meant that anyone seeking or living some form of religious life could join one of their monasteries. The hermit who kept watch at St Oswine's shrine, for example, became a monk of

---

[68] *Libellus*, ed. Rollason, 209.

[69] *Cartularium*, ed. Atkinson, I, p. xxxv.

[70] Morris, *Papal Monarchy*, 69. Cf. Adam of Eynsham (who uses *solitarii* to mean *inclusi*): 'set nec heremite tantummodo atque solitarii': *Magna vita sancti Hugonis = The Life of St Hugh of Lincoln*, ed. and tr. D. L. Douie and D. H. Farmer, 2 vols (Oxford, 1985), II, 43.

[71] Burton, *Monastic Order*, 23.

Durham.[72] Had the region not been ready for religious revival, and had barons and bishops not been anxious to extend their influence, build relations with the indigenous population, and express their religious allegiances by sponsoring eremitism, monks who fled there to live in solitude, such as the trio from Worcester diocese, should have attained the solitude they sought. Instead they were obliged to found monasteries. The land that became available when patrons endowed their communities provided a further incentive for their recruits. In the aftermath of the Conquest, people were driven from their lands or lost the capital to farm them, or – like Turgot – were forced into hiding or exile. By joining a new eremitic monastery, as brethren or lay servants, such refugees could hope to make a new start. From a Europe-wide perspective, this development may be interpreted as the middling stage of the eremitic movement waxing strong in England. From an English perspective, it may have exerted a particularly powerful influence in the locations where it is visible (principally Great Malvern and the north) because of the presence of refugees in the wake of recent upheavals, the readiness of Norman barons and would-be monastic converts to unite in their promotion of eremitism, and the potent northern inheritance of reverence for anchorites and the eremitic vocation. Finally, there may be something in the fact that most of the leading new hermits in this period, namely the two Ealdwines, Reinfred, and Ælfwi, ventured forth from the diocese of Worcester, where there was an unusually strong interest in the life of the desert fathers from about the middle of the eleventh century. This could account for their fashion of asceticism and fit them into the broader European eremitic movement.

HERMITS AND THEIR ADMIRERS, C.1080–C.1120

As the new hermits multiplied in the last third of the eleventh century, something else was happening too, in the realm of hagiography, in response to the prestige which eremitism was coming to enjoy. The change is clearest in the work of the prolific hagiographer Goscelin, who journeyed to England as a young man from the abbey of Saint-Bertin at Saint-Omer in Flanders. He was plunged soon or immediately into a land in the birth pains of conquest, albeit sheltered from its vicissitudes by Herman, bishop of Ramsbury-Sherborne (d. 1078), a survivor from the old regime. Sherborne cathedral priory became his home, but after Herman died he was forced to wander, stopping at monasteries in Wessex, the East Midlands, Essex, and Kent, and writing liturgical materials and *Lives* of native saints for mostly English audiences.[73] What is striking about his work

---

[72] *Miscellanea biographica*, ed. Raine, 20.
[73] Goscelin wrote for the convents of Sherborne, Wilton, Peterborough, Barking, St Augustine's, and Ely, among others. For the composition of convents in this period, see Williams, *The English*, 131–5.

from our perspective is that nearly every saint he wrote about is invested with eremitic credentials. The overall impression is that experience as a hermit was prerequisite to sainthood. There are anchorite-virgins who hanker after solitude, a saintly bishop who periodically retreats like a hermit, hermit penitents in flight from life's false pleasures, solitaries who attain fame through their martyrdom, and recluses blessed with miracles. Of the works attributable to Goscelin, the *Life* of St Eadwold of Cerne is possibly one of the earliest. It is a paean to the solitary life, praising its protagonist for casting aside the world's false riches and living virtuously in secret. Eadwold becomes a prince in wilful exile.[74] In defiance of the Benedictine Rule, it is nowhere said that he trained in a monastery. Another early work, written soon after the death of Goscelin's patron Bishop Herman, is the *Life* of St Wulfsige, Sherborne's saintly reformer.[75] The saint here is a bishop, but – as if this were not enough – Goscelin stresses the anchoretic element in his spirituality, claiming that he habitually withdrew during Lent, 'more like a hermit than a church dignitary'.[76] Seemingly, it was not enough, that St Wulfsige had been a devoted and dutiful bishop.

Goscelin also wrote for the nuns of Wilton, penning a *Life* of their saintly sister Edith (d. 984). Edith was a royal nun, but here too Goscelin thought fit to weave an anchoretic thread into his subject's spirituality. In her contemplative moments, he ventured, she would switch into anchorite mode (*mente ... anachoritica*), embracing solitude 'like Antony and Macarius', or like Martha's sister Mary, the exemplary contemplative. Preferring animal company, she withdrew among birds and beasts, fleeing the whirlwind of the world.[77] At Ely in the 1080s he undertook a *Life* of St Wihtburh, an obscure saint once venerated in Norfolk at East Dereham before the monks of Ely acquired her remains.[78] Legends first recorded by Ælfric identified her simply as the sister of Ely's patron St Æthelthryth. Goscelin recast her as a hermit, patterning her on Eadwold, as a soul grown sick of the world's false riches, desirous of solitude in Christ. Longing to be freed 'from the whirlwind of the world as a solitary', she 'desired fervently to escape from the predatory charms of wealth which entrap the souls of mortals'. Of Eadwold, he wrote, similarly: 'isolation he preferred to royalty, to worldly wealth Christ's poverty'.[79] Such images reappear throughout Goscelin's oeuvre, and anchorites

---

[74] Eadwold, 201.

[75] C. H. Talbot, 'The Life of Saint Wulsin of Sherborne by Goscelin', *RB*, 69 (1959), 68–85; R. Love, 'The Life of St Wulfsige of Sherborne by Goscelin of Saint-Bertin', in *St Wulfsige and Sherborne: Essays to Celebrate the Millennium of the Benedictine Abbey 998–1998*, ed. K. Barker, D. A. Hinton, and A. Hunt (Oxford, 2005), 98–123.

[76] 'Magis anachorita uidebatur quam [ierarcha]': Talbot, 'Saint Wulsin', 76.

[77] Iwi's *Life* is printed in *NL*, II, 91–2; for Edith the hermit, see A. Wilmart, 'La légende de ste Édith en prose et vers par le moine Goscelin', *AB*, 56 (1938), 5–101, 265–307, at 66.

[78] Goscelin of Saint-Bertin, *The Hagiography of the Female Saints of Ely*, ed. and tr. R. C. Love (Oxford, 2004), 56; Blair, 'Handlist', 559; *Liber Eliensis*, ed. Blake, 13, 120–3.

[79] C. E. Fell, 'Saint Æðelþryð: A Historical-Hagiographical Dichotomy Revisited', *Nottingham Medieval Studies*, 38, ed. M. Jones (1994), 18–34, at 32; *Saints of Ely*, ed. Love, 57; Eadwold, 195, 204.

are found in ten of his known works: his treatise on anachoresis (the *Liber confortatorius*); his *Lives* of SS. Eadwold, Mildburg, Wulfsige, Edith, Ivo, Wihtburh, Wærburh, and Augustine, and in the *Miracles* of St Mildthryth. The intended audiences were the recluse Eve, enclosed at Saint-Laurent du Tertre in Angers, the monks of Cerne Abbas, the nuns of Much Wenlock in Shropshire (who were the custodians of St Mildburg), Goscelin's brethren at Sherborne cathedral priory, the nuns of Wilton, the monks of Ramsey (who by that date were venerating the hermit St Ive), the monks at Ely abbey and those of St Augustine's at Canterbury, as well as the prelates addressed in his prologues. Six works give the male or female protagonist anchoretic credentials of the sorts already described; a seventh (the *Liber confortatorius*) addresses the recluse Eve on the austere spirituality of anachoresis.[80]

Goscelin's interest in anchorites may have stemmed from his own experiences. It could be, for example, that St Eadwold proved an early, formative influence on his perception of how sanctity was best attained, or that the flight of his beloved Eve into solitude at barely twenty years of age, or some other event or influence now forgotten, moulded his spirituality. Herman's death, Goscelin's expulsion from Sherborne by the bishop's unsympathetic successor, and Eve's flight abroad within the space of a few years rendered Goscelin not unlike the loners, exiles, and wanderers he eulogized. Occasionally he hankered after a solitary life himself, he claimed.[81] Yet when placed alongside his contemporaries, Goscelin is relatively normal. Take his fellow Fleming Folcard, for example, who probably also reached England during the 1060s. Folcard attached anchoretic credentials to five of the seven saints he wrote about, namely SS. Thancred, Torhtred, Tova, John of Beverley, and Æthelwold, though not to Botulf or Athulf. He wrote for a monastic audience at Thorney, regular canons at York, and at least two bishops, to whom he dedicated his works. These audiences were similar to Goscelin's, and the references to anachoresis in the writings of both monks suggest that their audiences would have approved of hermits. Had hermits not been popular it would have been easy enough (except in the cases of Thancred, Torhtred, and Tova) to suppress stories of a saint's anchoretic inclinations. Yet the stories appear again and again, as though these writers found many different audiences to appreciate them.

Folcard, who was acting abbot of Thorney *c.*1068–85/6, wrote a joint *Life* of Thancred, Torhtred, and Tova, following a source attributed to Bishop Æthelwold.[82] This may have been the abbey's charter or an unidentified narrative it

---

[80] For the two anchorites in the *Vita Augustini*, see Goscelin, *Historia, miracula et translatio s. Augustini* (*BHL*, 777, 779, 781), *Acta SS, Maii* VI, 375–443, at 429F. I am grateful to Rosalind Love for allowing me to consult her forthcoming edition of Goscelin's *Life* of Mildburg.

[81] *LC*, 34.

[82] W. de G. Birch, *Liber vitae: Register and Martyrology of New Minster and Hyde Abbey, Winchester*, Hampshire Record Society (London, 1892), 284–6; C. Clark, 'Notes on a Life of Three Thorney Saints, Thancred, Torhtred and Tova', *Proceedings of the Cambridge Antiquarian Society*, 69 (1979 for 1980), 45–52.

drew upon.[83] He also offered a novel depiction of the bishop's activities at Thorney:

Not far from the same abbey, in the very place where Christ's blessed virgin Tova had had her anchorhold [Æthelwold] had built a tiny stone chapel in the shape of a pyramid, encompassed by the slenderest railings, where three miniature altars were dedicated within a double court. Trees of many kinds sheltered it up to its very walls and it was intended as a personal retreat . . . whenever he was able to visit the island of Thorney he withdrew to this place. Here he performed his prayers and holy vigils; [to this place], after addressing the brethren and organizing whatever was needed for the house, God's friend at once retired.[84]

Æthelwold, of course, was not remembered as a hermit. He was known as a reformer, bishop of Winchester, and a monastic legislator. Folcard's portrait is remarkable for depicting a prelate who venerated an anchorite and periodically lived as one. The fact that neither of Æthelwold's contemporary hagiographers paints such a picture leaves us wondering whether Folcard reinvented the saint to suit more ascetic tastes. During the 1060s, Folcard had written a *Life* of the celebrated bishop of York, St John of Beverley (d. 721), which he had dedicated to the saint's statesman-like successor, Archbishop Ealdred (1061–9). According to Folcard, the saint would periodically retire to his oratory near Hexham to engage in fasting, prayer, and almsgiving. His eremitic credentials were not Folcard's invention, for Folcard was closely following Bede's account of the saint.[85] Yet the parallel between Folcard's account of St John of Beverley and his account of St Æthelwold suggests that he patterned his portrait of the latter on the former, inspired, perhaps, by the remains of some overgrown chapel on Thorney. His anchoretic vignette has the sole purpose of augmenting Æthelwold's sanctity by revealing his hermit-like behaviour. It indicates, therefore, that Folcard, as much as Goscelin, believed that anchoretic credentials enhanced a saintly reputation.

Goscelin and Folcard were not the only monks of their generation who were keen to represent their saints as anchorites. The monk, hagiographer, and musician Osbern (d. *c.*1094), who was probably somewhat younger than the two Flemings, was also interested in solitude as an attribute of sanctity. Osbern grew up in the years before the Conquest among the monks of Christ Church, Canterbury, though he later spent a period studying at the monastery of Bec in Normandy.[86] Writing primarily for the members of his own monastery,

---

[83] 'Sicut . . . Aetheluuoldus in suis testatur scriptis'; 'ut predictus Dei pontifex Atheluuoldus eadem scriptis suis edocet' (referring to details about Tova and Torhtred, respectively): Birch, *Liber vitae*, 285. Clark, 'Notes', 45, argues that Folcard used the foundation charter, S 792.

[84] The translation is adapted from Clark, 'Notes', 51n.

[85] *Ecclesiastical History*, ed. Colgrave and Mynors, 457.

[86] For Osbern's career, see J. Rubenstein, 'The Life and Writings of Osbern of Canterbury', in *Canterbury and the Norman Conquest: Churches, Saints and Scholars 1066–1199*, ed. R. Eales and R. Sharpe (London, 1995), 27–40.

he enriched the careers of its saintly archbishops Dunstan and Ælfheah with anchoretic credentials. He turned his pen first to a *Life* of St Ælfheah (d. 1012), the martyred archbishop of Canterbury, casting him as a one-time recluse who had founded the monastery at Bath. 'Arriving there he built a hut and, with this built, enclosed himself and, thus enclosed, confined himself with startling severity.'[87] We have no way of checking this story, and neither did Osbern (as far as we know), so there is no reason to think that it went back any further than the late eleventh century. Later, Osbern wrote a new *Life* of St Dunstan (d. 988), the reforming abbot of Glastonbury who died as archbishop of Canterbury. Two other clerics had already written hagiographical accounts of his activities, but by the time Osbern picked up his pen their accounts were decades old. Neither of them depicted Dunstan as a recluse, but Osbern gave much attention to the matter. First he reveals that among the showpieces at Glastonbury in the late eleventh century was a tiny rock-hewn cell, formerly occupied by Dunstan. Osbern, a visitor to the abbey, wrote that he marvelled tearfully at its nearly uninhabitable dimensions.[88] Such strictures, he implies, set a high standard of religion and were proof of Dunstan's great sanctity.

Though varying in their representations of it there can be little doubt that these three hagiographers saw solitary withdrawal as an ideal to which saints should aspire. Writing to please target audiences, they must also have anticipated that a range of monks, nuns, and regular clergy, English and Norman alike, would agree with their sentiment. Had this not been so, the sentiment should hardly have found currency. Yet it is found in many other works, such as the *Passio* (a martyrdom narrative) of St Æthelberht, king of East Anglia (779/80–94). Preserved in a manuscript of *c.*1100, the *Passio* is written in the ornate though not impenetrable Latin style cultivated in the late eleventh century. The hermit in this tale is Ælfthryth, daughter of King Offa of Mercia (d. 796), who vows to live a solitary life at Crowland to make atonement for her parents' sin in having arranged King Æthelberht's murder.[89] She departs with a pious speech. If the fourteenth-century abridgement of the *Life* of the Peterborough saints Kyneburga, Kyneswitha, and Tibba derives from a late eleventh-century source, it would provide another example from that era, of special attention paid to a saint's anchoretic credentials (Tibba).[90] The *Life* of the Cornish monk and hermit St Neot (d. *c.*877) is a stronger case in point. According to his first hagiographer, the saint had settled in a spot of extreme solitude: 'a well-wooded place completely

---

[87] Osbern of Canterbury, *Vita s. Elphegi*, in *Anglia sacra sive collectio historiarum antiquitus scriptarum de archiepiscopis et episcopis Angliae, a prima fidei Christianae susceptione ad annum MDXL*, ed. H. Wharton, 2 vols (London, 1691), II, 122–42, at 124.

[88] *Memorials of St Dunstan, Archbishop of Canterbury*, ed. W. Stubbs, RS, 63 (1874), at 83–4.

[89] M. R. James, 'Two Lives of St. Ethelbert, King and Martyr', *EHR*, 32 (1917), 214–44, at 240. The *Passio* is *BHL*, 2628; see also Blair, 'Handlist', 505.

[90] *NL*, II, 130–2. Many of the saints' *Lives* abridged by John of Tynemouth in the fourteenth century dated from the late eleventh century or the first part of the twelfth.

surrounded by trees', where for seven years he had weakened his body with fasting, vigils, prayers, and mortifications.[91] His *Life* (*Vita prima*) and the accompanying *Translatio* – an account of the removal of his relics from St Neots (called *Neotestoc*) in Cornwall to St Neots (called Eynesbury) in Cambridgeshire – date from the tenth or eleventh century.[92] Its editors favour a date in the middle or late eleventh century because an anachronistic claim, that the reformer St Æthelwold was St Neot's tutor, militates against a tenth- or early eleventh-century provenance. If the editors are right – and their case is plausible – Neot's *Life* might provide another example of a saintly career enriched with anchoretic credentials in an age when hagiographers were touting them.

During the early twelfth century, the practice of reinventing saints as anchorites continued and spread. Between 1109 and 1131, two Ely hagiographers recast the great St Æthelthryth in this mould by revealing in her new hagiography her previously undocumented desire to live as an anchorite.[93] The Welsh hagiographer Caradog, not long after 1120, represented St Gildas as a hermit in the tradition of St Antony.[94] And Peterborough abbey, by the 1120s, was bolstering its credentials by claiming that it had colonized 'Anchorite Island' (i.e. Thorney) before Æthelwold had ever got there. Writing in the 1120s, the Peterborough chronicler claimed that as far back as 656 their abbot Seaxwulf had begged King Wulfhere of Mercia (d. 675) to let him found a retreat on the island. Wulfhere assented, and a monastery was founded, in which the monks were supposed to live communally but in separate, isolated cells.[95] The whole tale may be fiction, for the charters that Peterborough ascribed to King Wulfhere are late eleventh- or early twelfth-century forgeries, and the story concerning Seaxwulf's monastery, which could have been patterned on the type of monastery in the *Vitas patrum*, is uncorroborated. The incentive for inventing such fiction was not only to link Peterborough to long-dead saintly anchorites, it also would have allowed Peterborough's abbot to claim precedence over the abbot of Thorney, thereby resolving the vexed question of seniority. (Both abbeys were founded at much the same time.) The significance of this new legend, of course, lies in the ostentatious integration of anchoretic tales into the traditions of a Benedictine abbey. New interest in hermits, visible from the late eleventh century, had burgeoned into a commonplace.

[91] D. Dumville and S. Keynes (general editors), *The Anglo-Saxon Chronicle: A Collaborative Edition, Vol. 17: The Annals of St Neots, with Vita prima sancti Neoti*, ed. D. Dumville and M. Lapidge (Cambridge, 1985), 118–20. On Cornish saints, see N. Orme, *The Saints of Cornwall* (Oxford, 2000); and G. H. Doble's Cornish Saints Series, 46 vols (pub. various, 1924–41).

[92] *Annals*, ed. Dumville and Lapidge, pp. xcvi–vii. On Eynesbury's origins, see *ibid.*, pp. lxxxvii, xcv; Hart, *Charters*, 28–9; M. Chibnall, 'History of the Priory of St Neots', in C. F. Tebbutt, 'St Neots Priory', *Proceedings of the Cambridge Antiquarian Society*, 59 (1966), 33–74, at 67–74.

[93] She 'appetit desiderantissime uiuere solitarie': *Saints of Ely*, ed. Love, 194.

[94] Davies, *Book of Llandaf*, 199.

[95] CUL, Peterborough Dean and Chapter MS 5, fo. 23v; *The Chronicle of Hugh Candidus, a Monk of Peterborough*, ed. W. T. Mellows (London, 1949), 12.

It is difficult not to conclude that monks of Goscelin's era, more than Ælfric's, thought of solitary withdrawal as a laudable vocation. This at least is the impression created by self-selecting commentators. Whereas the reformers had appropriated the imagery of anachoresis, later hagiographers contrived to enhance the reputations of saints by depicting them as hermits. Whereas Ælfric's contemporaries were content to liken themselves to the desert fathers without leaving their monasteries, for Goscelin's generation the old distinction between communal solitude and individual solitude demanded a differentiation of rhetoric. By the late eleventh century, it was no longer enough for a saint under literary construction to have spent time in a secluded monastery: the saint in question had to have yearned for solitude or spent time alone. The shift that occurred between the 1000s and the 1080s, in the minds of monastic hagiographers, was the transference of eremitic imagery from the monastery to the hermitage, along with the recognition of eremitism as a mainstay of sanctity. In its timing and essence, this shift mirrored the shift on the Continent, where the life of the desert fathers became associated with anachoresis, after Romuald and other hermits made it their own, won admiration, and gained recognition for their vocation as a path to sanctity. It also mirrored a shift in the qualities expected of the higher clergy, for asceticism had also become a desirable credential in the competition for ecclesiastical promotion. In England, the native legacy of reverence for hermits had combined with the European ascetic movement to promote their reputation in the monasteries and probably – although the laity may always have admired them – beyond. It is possible to find this combination at work in late eleventh-century hagiography, which seized upon old images that had long been associated with England's hermits, such as their asceticism, fasting, skill in outwitting the devil, and authority over elemental creation, while tying them to the concerns of contemporary reformers, such as the desire to escape false riches and worldly entanglements. One offshoot of the movement that was not evident in England was the ragged hermit preacher. By the 1090s, when this figure appeared in Maine and Brittany, English monasticism may have obviated the need for any such radical reformers by providing outlets for aspiring ascetics in its hermitages and in the many monasteries that had recently grown out of hermitages, which presumably still cultivated something of their prior austerity. This could also explain why only one new order was founded in England (the Gilbertines). Here too, a blend of native and Continental influences determined the tone of English eremitism.

3

The rise of the recluse

RECLUSES IN THE GERMAN EMPIRE

Unlike hermits, recluses were shut inside cells, although they drew inspiration from the same anchoretic tradition, prizing solitude, renunciation, and asceticism as devices for purifying the soul. Their ideal attributes were depicted in familiar cameos such as the portrait of Patroclus the recluse in the History of the Franks by the sixth-century bishop St Gregory of Tours.[1] By the ninth and tenth centuries, through the Frankish territories, recluses were attracting attention. Phyllis Jestice has reinforced Herbert Grundmann's argument that in eastern Francia, Lotharingia, and Germany, across the period 800–1050, reclusion overtook eremitism as the preferred form of asceticism.[2] In other words, the strictures of withdrawal into a cell were regarded with greater admiration than the uncontained rigours of eremitism. In these territories, reclusion was on the rise in the tenth and eleventh centuries, usually as an extension of asceticism for monks and nuns. Afterwards it spread more widely among the laity. Anneke Mulder-Bakker observed that a new figure began to emerge in the eleventh and twelfth centuries through France, Normandy, Flanders, and Lotharingia. This was the urban recluse that inhabited a cell at a church in a town or city. More often than not she was a lay, female convert.[3] Paulette L'Hermite-Leclercq's research on reclusion in France concluded similarly, that towards the end of the eleventh century the reclusive vocation became more prominent and increasingly dominated by laywomen and the laity generally.[4] In light of these findings, it would appear that a new sort of recluse that neither trained in nor lived in a monastery was emerging at roughly the same time as the new hermits. Perhaps this vocation became popular in the eleventh century for the same sorts of reasons that eremitism gained new approval.

From the pastoral perspective of bishops and monastic communities, reclusion may have been the preferred form of anachoresis from an early date on account of its disciplinary advantage, in that an anchorite who was committed to a cell was

---

[1] Gregory of Tours, *Historia Francorum*, in *S. Georgii Florentini Gregorii Turonensis episcopi opera omnia*, PL, 71: 161–604, at col. 325.
[2] Grundmann, 'Deutsche Eremiten', or 'Eremiti in Germania', where the case is made at 313. Jestice develops the argument in *Wayward Monks*, 94–5.
[3] Mulder-Bakker, *Lives of the Anchoresses*, 14.
[4] L'Hermite-Leclercq, 'La réclusion', at 156.

less able to stray and had to fulfil her vow. The canonical rulings, established at ecclesiastical councils between the fifth and eighth centuries to regulate reclusion, ordained that no recluse should build or enter a cell without the permission of the bishop or abbot; that anyone wishing to become a recluse should first spend a probationary period inside a monastery, getting a feel for the solitary life (to determine whether the candidate had a genuine vocation and in preparation for entering a cell), and that no recluse should ever rescind his or her vow.[5] These precepts and others were set down in a rule for monks and recluses written by a priest named Grimlaïc, who was probably a recluse himself. The first extant of its sort, it was composed probably in Lotharingia, either at the turn of the tenth century or *c.*950.[6] Grimlaïc required that any postulant recluse should spend at least a year's probation in a monastery, obtain the permission of his bishop, abbot, and brethren before entering his cell, and remain in it thereafter. He also recommended, as a matter of course, that the bishop should put his episcopal seal on the door with his signet ring. In Grimlaïc's scheme, these conventions were to be waived only in exceptional cases: for instance, if a postulant wished to follow in the tradition of the desert fathers by fleeing into solitude with no monastic probation.[7] Even so, it was up to individual bishops to decide whether, and to what extent, they wished to regulate reclusion, if indeed they cared enough or had the power to do so. Archbishop Bruno of Cologne (953–65), who was duke of Lotharingia and brother to the emperor Otto I, was conscientious and powerful enough to attempt reform in his diocese. He gave out the order that all recluses should occupy cells at monasteries or churches, with no more than one or two in each cell.[8] This may indicate that cells were multiplying on private estates, or that recruits to the vocation outnumbered the cells that could realistically be sustained and supervised by the bishop and his clergy.

From the late ninth century, recluses began to multiply across various parts of the Empire, including Lotharingia. Their activities are unusually well documented at the monastery of Saint Gall – now in Switzerland – in the diocese of Constance, where a steady stream of votary recluses entered cells attached to churches in the precincts of the monastery or nearby. One of the first was Wiborada, a nun at the abbey, who had sought permission to become a recluse. Her abbot, Bishop Solomon III of Constance (890–919), responded by installing her initially in a cell attached to the abbey church of St George, before moving her to a cell attached to his newly built church of St Magnus. In 926,

---

[5] Warren, *Anchorites,* 53–5 and references.

[6] *Grimlaici presbyteri, regula solitariorum,* PL, 103: 574–663; on the date, see Jestice, *Wayward Monks,* 92n; and K. S. Frank, 'Grimlaïcus, "Regula solitariorum"', in *Vita religiosa im Mittelalter: Festschrift für Kaspar Elm,* ed. F. J. Felten and N. Jaspert, with S. Haarländer, Berliner historische Studien, 31; Ordensstudien, 13 (Berlin, 1999), 21–35.

[7] *Grimlaici . . . regula,* 593–4, 593A.

[8] Ruotger, *Vita Brunonis archiepiscopi Coloniensis,* in *MGH SRG,* n.s. 10, ed. I. Ott (Weimar, 1951), 1–50, at 34.

she was killed in a Magyar raid. Her fellow recluse Rachild (d. 947) survived. As the years went by, their cells were almost continuously occupied, their popularity no doubt fuelled by Wiborada's burgeoning martyr-cult. Another female recluse, Kerhild, held the cell at St Magnus's between 952 and 1008. The cell at St George's went to the widow Bertrada, enclosed there in 959. When she died, in 980, it passed to Hartker (d. 1011 or 1017), a priestly monk of Saint Gall.[9] Brethren of the monastery commemorated these recluses and apparently held reclusion in esteem as a form of 'white martyrdom': that is, severance from the world's pleasures for the love of God. Wiborada's epitaph contemplates this vision of martyrdom by treating her entry into her cell as a metaphorical death, chosen by the recluse (who eventually suffered 'red martyrdom' at the hands of the Hungarian raiders) as a way of devoting herself to her heavenly bridegroom.[10] A metrical epitaph composed to commemorate Hartker described him as a martyr and living sacrifice, imprisoned for thirty years (the noun used is *carcer*), who used to lie cruciform on the floor in a customary gesture of penance. Similar imagery was used of the nun Kotelinde (d. 1015), another recluse linked to Saint Gall, and likewise immured out of love for Christ, her bridegroom.[11]

The imagery that was applied to these recluses could equally apply to the abbey's saintly patron, St Gall, who was remembered as an Irish *peregrinus* and anchorite.[12] In Irish tradition, the *peregrini* (pilgrims) were the most exalted ascetics because their intense love of God urged them to depart from their native land for the wilderness of exile, to search for God through their wanderings by forcing themselves to depend on his provision.[13] The fact that a number of *peregrini* who came to the Empire chose to become recluses may reflect the parallel between their own form of white martyrdom and reclusion, or the parallel esteem in which these paths were held in Ireland and in the Empire respectively. For although the *peregrini* were, by definition, wanderers, whereas recluses were anchored to one spot, the two had much in common, in so far as both undertook ritualized acceptance of social death in pursuit of spiritual rebirth. An early example was St Findan (d. 878?), who entered a cell at his monastery on an island near Rheinau in Swabia.[14] Another Irishman, Abbot Columbanus, withdrew to Flanders, to the city of Ghent, where for the last two years of his life (957–9) he

---

[9] Sources relating to these recluses are gathered in E. Schlumpf, *Quellen zur Geschichte der Inklusen in der Stadt St. Gallen,* Mitteilungen zur vaterländischen Geschichte. Herausgegeben vom historischen Verein des Kantons St Gallen, 41 (St Gallen, 1953), 1–4.

[10] *Vita s. Wiboradae,* in *MGH SS* IV, ed. Pertz, 452–7, at 457.

[11] Schlumpf, *Quellen,* 4 and 6 (of Kotelinde): 'Sponsi celsa subit, cui se uiuam sepeliuit'.

[12] See further, W. Berschin, *Eremus und Insula: St. Gallen und die Reichenau im Mittelalter – Modell ein lateinischen Literaturlandschaft,* 2nd edn. (Wiesbaden, 2005).

[13] For an introduction to *peregrini,* see T. M. Charles-Edwards, 'The Social Background to Irish *peregrinatio*', *Celtica,* 11 (1976), 43–59.

[14] *Vita Findani,* ed. O. Holder-Egger, in *MGH SS* XV.i, ed. Societas Aperiendis Fontibus (Hannover, 1887), 502–6, at 504.

lived in a cell within the cemetery attached to St Bavo's monastery.[15] The Irish chronicler Marianus Scotus (1028–82?) identifies three more Irish recluses. Anmchad (d. 1043) inhabited a cell at the royal monastery of Fulda in Hesse. Another Irish recluse, the monk Paternus, spent many years in a cell attached to a monastery at Paderborn in Saxony. According to Marianus, when the city was destroyed in 1058, Paternus was so keen to become a martyr that he refused to leave his cell and was burned to death (appropriately enough on Good Friday). His resolve was evidently inspirational, for only a couple of weeks later Marianus went to pray on the dead recluse's mat. The next year, he sought enclosure at Fulda, spending a decade (1059–69) in Anmchad's old cell, where heavenly lights were seen over the dead recluse's tomb and psalmody was heard.[16] Marianus then spent the remainder of his life in a cell at Mainz cathedral in Rhenish Franconia. The kings, bishops, and religious communities who sponsored these recluses in the imperial heartlands may have prized the *peregrini* on account of their reputation for uncompromising renunciation, and seized on them for this reason.

Apart from the Irish and native recluses there was also the occasional Greek who found his way into the Empire's cosmopolitan community of ascetics: indeed, one of the first recluses to inspire a canonization campaign and win the posthumous prize of a papally approved cult was Simeon of Trier (d. 1035), who was born in Syracuse, to a Greek father and a Calabrian mother, and educated in Constantinople. Dropping out of school, he spent several years as a pilgrim-guide before deciding to become an anchorite, and, after tracking down a recluse who occupied a tower on the bank of the Jordan, he entered his service, inhabiting the lower room, in order to learn from his example. Forced to depart, he became a monk in Bethlehem then at the foot of Mount Sinai, before retiring to live as a hermit on the shore of the Red Sea. Later, his abbot sent him to collect alms in the lands of Duke Richard II of Normandy (996–1026), but after many adventures he arrived to find that the duke was dead. It was at roughly this juncture that archbishop Poppo of Trier (1016–47) learned about Simeon and recruited him to guide his pilgrimage to Jerusalem. Simeon was not only an experienced guide; he could communicate in Coptic, Syriac, Arabic, Greek, and Latin. Returning to Trier about the year 1030, he sought Poppo's permission to live as a recluse inside the great Roman gate known as the *Porta Nigra*. Poppo consented and enclosed him with great ceremony before all the clergy and the people in a cell high up in the tower. Not long after he had been enclosed, Trier suffered a great flood, which the people attributed to his sorcery, so they threw stones up at his cell and smashed the window. Despite this unfortunate episode, after his death in June 1035 miracles began to be reported within only a few months; a ladder was erected so that suppliants could climb up to his tomb, and within a year or two a companion from one of his pilgrimages, Abbot Eberwin of

[15] *Annales s. Bavonis Gandensis*, in *MGH SS* II, ed. G. H. Pertz (Hannover, 1829), 188.
[16] *Chronicle*, ed. Darlington and McGurk, II, 536, 584, 586.

St Martin's in Trier, had written his *Life* and *Miracles*, and Poppo had managed to secure Simeon's official canonization by procuring a bull consenting to his cult from Pope Benedict IX (1032–44, 45, 47–8). The speed of this process was extraordinary, and, although the tale suggests that in the thinking of the inhabitants there was a rather fine line between a recluse and a sorcerer, it does indicate that there was considerable enthusiasm for recluses in Lotharingia in the 1030s (unless Simeon's other credentials or the designs of his supporters somehow account for his posthumous popularity).[17]

Sources from the early decades of the eleventh century support the argument for enthusiasm, by revealing that other recluses were greatly admired in other parts of the Empire. Their prestige is clearly apparent in a story told by a cleric of the cathedral at Worms, in Rhenish Franconia, who wrote the *Life* of Bishop Burchard (*c*.950–1025) soon after the latter's death. According to the cleric, Burchard of Worms preached at a ceremony to enclose a nun and postulant recluse named Caritas at a local monastery. In doing so, he reproached both young and old in his congregation, which was mainly made up of vowed religious, for lacking her zeal.[18] At Drübeck in Saxony the recluse Sisu (d. 1018) impressed the chronicler Bishop Thietmar of Merseburg (1009–18) to the extent that he likened her to one of the desert fathers. When she died, he reported that she had lived in her prison for sixty-four years, allowing her body to be eaten up by maggots, like the fifth-century Syrian hermit St Simeon Stylites, who dwelt on top of a pillar.[19] The canonization of Simeon of Trier, *c*.1036, was eventually followed by the official canonization of St Wiborada in 1047 – the second recluse and the first woman to be canonized by a pope – after an account of her life and miracles was read out loud in the presence of Pope Clement II. Recently created pontiff by the emperor Henry III (1039–56), Clement was a German ecclesiastic who took a keen interest in restoring the purity of the early church. Wiborada's suffering, re-enacted differently but recalled in the career of Paternus, who burnt to death eleven years later in 1058, united the white martyrdom of a recluse's metaphorical death with the martyrdom of her real death in a doubly impressive feat of renunciation and self-sacrifice. Recluses like Caritas and Sisu, Simeon, Wiborada, and Paternus may have inspired any number of recruits to the reclusive vocation, Marianus Scotus among them. During the next few decades and through the twelfth century, recluses proliferated in the Empire and also in northern France, and through the territories now known as the Low Countries, as scholars have shown.[20] Most of them were

---

[17] Eberwin, 'De sancto Symeone, recluso in porta Trevirensi', *Acta SS, Jun.* I, 89–101; M. Coens, 'Un document inédit sur le culte de s. Syméon, moine d'orient et reclus a Trèves', *AB*, 68 (1950), 181–96.

[18] *Vita Burchardi*, ed. Waitz, 838.

[19] Jestice, *Wayward Monks*, 99–100, 108. *Die Chronik des Bischofs Thietmar von Merseburg, und ihre korveier Überarbeitung*, ed. R. Holtzmann, *MGH SRG*, n.s. 9 (Berlin, 1935), 502–4.

[20] L'Hermite-Leclercq, 'La réclusion'; Mulder-Bakker, *Lives of the Anchoresses*.

women; few had undertaken any form of monastic probation. Their multiplication shows that, by the late eleventh century, reclusion, just like eremitism, had come to be regarded as a vocation in its own right.

THE RISE OF THE RECLUSE IN ENGLAND

Identifying the recluses

In the late eleventh century, through the German Empire, Flanders, France, and along the North Sea littoral, at focal locations in the devotional landscape, recluses occupied cells typically situated at monastic churches or at parish churches in cities, towns, and villages, or in the adjoining cemeteries – with one or two inhabiting ruins, after the example of St Antony, such as the saintly recluse Simeon at the *Porta Nigra* in Trier. For all the recluses mentioned in the sources, the occasional discovery of the remnants of unknown cells indicates that very many more have been forgotten. What references chance to survive, nevertheless, are sufficiently numerous to demonstrate that recruits and sponsors were abundant through our period. The questions for this section are whether this was also the case in England and whether reclusion became more popular in the period 950–1100. Little attention has been paid to recluses in these centuries.[21] Ann Warren's book on recluses and their patrons in England starts in 1100 and infers that recluses multiplied in the twelfth century and even more so in the thirteenth from the numbers which appear on record. Specifically Warren counted about a hundred individuals alive in the twelfth century and roughly two hundred on record for each century from the thirteenth to the fifteenth inclusive.[22] Quantitative analysis of this sort can be misleading because it is more likely to reflect the survival rate of information than any fluctuation in the number of recluses. Statistics aside, for all we know the reclusive population might have declined over that period. A better method for examining the population is to adopt a qualitative approach by basing our assessment of its vitality on the evidence of its sites and sponsors. Warren found, by employing such methodology, that the vocation was popular with assorted patrons up and down the social hierarchy. But was this also true in the period 950–1100? Was its success in England linked to its popularity on the other side of the North Sea, and did the growth of the vocation result from an orchestrated initiative of the bishops or spontaneous initiatives in monasteries and parishes? Answering these questions will enable us to see whether, and – if so – why, the reclusive vocation was flourishing. Earlier, we encountered the Lotharingian cleric Grimlaïc who advised that a postulant recluse should spend at least a year in a monastery,

---

[21] T. Licence, 'Evidence of Recluses in Eleventh-Century England', *ASE*, 36 (2007), 221–34.
[22] Warren, *Anchorites*, 18–21.

obtain permission from his bishop, abbot, and brethren before entering his cell, and spend the rest of his life inside it. Yet there is no evidence that his manual was known in England, where procedures appear to have deviated from the protocol and injunctions which Grimlaïc carefully set out. In the past, there was a tendency to treat Grimlaïc's regulations as though they were relevant to England.[23] For the period up to *c.*1150 (at least), this cannot be sustained.

In Germany, France, and Flanders, reclusion was already being seen as a vocation with distinctive terminology and imagery.[24] Gregory of Tours, for example, used the noun *reclusus* (or *reclausus*) and the verb *includo* when he referred to this category of anchorites.[25] In Anglo-Saxon England, where recluses are less visible, these terms may not have been familiar. Prior to the twelfth century the label most commonly appended to solitary religious in England was the all-encompassing noun *anachoreta* (OE *ancer*), which could refer to any type of anchorite, from a recluse enclosed in a cell to the freer occupant of a hermitage. As far as I can discern, the participle and noun inclusus (f. *inclusa*, or *reclusus* / *reclusa*), used to refer to a recluse, found no currency in Anglo-Saxon England. Its earliest appearance in a work written in the country is in Goscelin's treatise on the solitary life, composed at Peterborough in the early 1080s, in which it interchanges with and qualifies the flexible *anachoreta*. The verb *includo* and its participle surface in Osbern's *Life* of St Ælfheah, which claims – as we have already seen – that the saint shut himself in a cell.[26] It would be useful to know the circumstances in which Osbern had learned this term. Unlike Goscelin, he may have grown up in England, but he also studied at Bec in Normandy, in the late 1070s, where *inclusus* was probably already in use. A letter Anselm wrote in 1078 x 1093 when he was still abbot of Bec addresses Hugh 'the recluse' ('ad Hugonem inclusum').[27] The monk Herman of Bury St Edmunds, who wrote in the 1090s, employed the noun *reclusa* ('religiosa reclusa') to describe a woman 'living alone' ('solitarie uiuens') at the abbey of St Benedict at Holme in Norfolk.[28] These writers show that by the 1080s and 1090s terminology already current across the Channel and over the North Sea had entered the Latin vocabulary of monks in The Fens, Kent, and East Anglia. For comparison, a lead funerary plaque found at the abbey church of Saint-Amand in Flanders (now situated at Nord in northern France) commemorates a recluse (*reclusa*) named Olardis, who died in 1078.[29] This plaque was deposited in her grave. To

---

[23] E.g. Clay, *Hermits*, 79, 128, 141, 167.

[24] Du Cange, *Glossarium*, IV, G-K, 328–9; O. Doerr, *Das Institut der Inclusen in Süddeutschland*, BGAM 18 (Munster, 1934), 1–4; and J. Heuclin, *Aux origines monastiques de la Gaule du Nord: ermites et reclus du Ve au XIe siècle* (Lille, 1988), 243–51.

[25] E.g. Gregory of Tours, *Historia Francorum*, cols. 325, 473, 519, and 396.

[26] *LC*, 26 and *passim*; Osbern of Canterbury, *Vita s. Elphegi*, 124.

[27] 'To Hugh the Recluse': *Opera*, ed. Schmitt, III, no. 112 (244–6), cf. no. 45 (158–9).

[28] *Memorials*, ed. Arnold, 38.

[29] L. Serbat, 'Inscriptions funéraires de recluses a l'abbaye de Saint-Amand (Nord)', *Mémoires de la sociéte nationale des antiquaires de France*, 71, 8th ser. 1 (1912), 193–224, at 196.

my knowledge, no native Englishman employed the participle or noun *inclusus /
reclusus* (except for Osbern, who could have learned it at Bec) before Prior Turgot
of Durham, who mentions recluses in his *Life* of Queen Margaret of Scotland,
written in 1100 x 1107.[30] And, although it is worth noting that few Englishmen
are known to have composed within the Latin historical-hagiographical genre –
the source of most of the early references to recluses – during the post-Conquest
generation, the absence of these terms from the not insubstantial pre-1066
corpus of Anglo-Latin hagiography fortifies the hypothesis that their application
to enclosed solitaries was a Continental usage only newly taking hold in England
in the last quarter of the century.

Before that date, and perhaps partly for that reason, few recluses are discernible
in England, although some of English origin are discernible overseas.[31] In
England, it is hard enough to distinguish between hermits and recluses, and
doubtful that the distinction carried much meaning. Ælfric's letter to the
nobleman Sigefyrth provides a case in point, for it could refer either to a recluse
inhabiting a cell or to a hermit in a hermitage.[32] Mantat (at Thorney?), similarly,
may have been either. There is better evidence for the argument that Dunstan
lived as a recluse at Glastonbury in the mid-tenth century. Early in the eleventh,
the monk Adelard of Ghent wrote a series of lessons for St Dunstan's feast at the
request of Archbishop Ælfheah of Canterbury (1006–12), in which he referred to
St Dunstan 'in his cell' (*in cella sua*). In the absence of an alternative explanation
for this reference, the cell could be that which Osbern inspected there some
eighty years later.[33] Were we to set this case alongside Osbern's account of
Ælfheah's own reclusive past we might mount an argument that two archbishops
of Canterbury experimented with solitary confinement in the early stages of their
careers. In light of religious trends then emerging in Flanders and the eastern
Frankish realm, the possibility does not seem strange; Dunstan certainly had
links to Ghent, where there were recluses at that date. Nevertheless, the evidence
is late and the incentives for myth making were too strong for it to count for very
much. All that Adelard shows is this: that in the early eleventh century Adelard
imagined Dunstan in a cell. From the early part of the eleventh century, the only
male recluses that are clearly labelled, albeit in later records, are Basing, Ælfwine,
and Wulfsige, of the abbey of Evesham in Worcestershire. They are noticed in an
early twelfth-century account of the abbey's greatest members, which was written
by the monk Dominic of Evesham. Dominic mentions 'three anchorites [*anachor-
itae*], Basing, Ælfwine, and Wulfsige who dwelt in different places as a recluse
[*reclusus*] for seventy-five years, although Basing served seventy-two.' He utilizes
reclusus to sharpen the meaning of *anachorita*, just as Herman employs *reclusa* in

---

[30] J. H. Hinde, *Symeonis Dunelmensis opera et collectanea*, SS, 51 (1868), 247.
[31] Heuclin, *Aux origines*, 243, 246.
[32] 'Eower ancor æt ham mid eow': *Homilien*, ed. Assmann, 13.
[33] *Memorials*, ed. Stubbs, 56.

his description of the woman 'living alone'.[34] Of these three recluses only Wulfsige is independently attested. According to the chronicler John of Worcester, this recluse [*inclusus*] Wulfsige, as noted earlier, persuaded Wulfstan to accept the bishopric of Worcester in 1062.[35] John reports that he had then lived in solitude for over forty years. If Dominic's claim that he was enclosed for seventy-five years (*c.*1020–*c.*1095) is correct, he must have adopted that lifestyle in his youth or in childhood. Goscelin's protégé Eve provides a point of comparison. When she entered her cell, *c.*1080, she was barely twenty, and Goscelin gloomily pictured her sitting within its confines until her fiftieth or hundredth year.[36]

Basing and Wulfsige, unless blessed with exceptional longevity, must have entered their cells as oblates. Evidence for such a practice is found in a historical tract composed in the late twelfth or early thirteenth century at Bury St Edmunds. This tract, which describes some of the abbey's major building works, notes that among the churches, towers, and porticoes that had been demolished over the years a large tower once stood in the place of the infirmary. The builder was the powerful thegn Ælfric, son of Wihtgar, who had put into the tower, with the permission of Abbot Ufi (d. 1044) and his successor Abbot Leofstan (1044–65), a son who was invalided or disabled (*infirmus*). He had attached to this gift the rent from his manor of Long Melford, not far from Bury, which was worth £20, *t.r.e.* The tract's author may have obtained these details from memorial inscriptions or lists of the abbey's benefactors, several of which survive. One of these lists notes that the son in the tower was called Wihtgar.[37] Where they can be checked against extant charters, the details in these lists are frequently shown to be reliable. In Wihtgar's case, the arrangement is best explained as the endowment of a recluse's cell. Other cells of that date are probably now forgotten. We only know about Wihtgar because the terms of his father's gift required that his existence be recorded. Basing and Wulfsige, no less arbitrarily, entered the historical record because their exceptional longevity attracted comment. These accidents of documentation virtually require the corollary that other recluses failed to leave any trace. Those that have left traces raise additional questions. Why a relatively minor abbey such as Evesham should have acquired three, for example, remains a mystery. If the men were contemporaries, one of them might have won converts to the vocation, thereby generating a brief, localized outburst of reclusion. The alternative scenario, that one recluse succeeded another as at Saint Gall, would have required a steady supply of

---

[34] *Chronicon abbatiae de Evesham, ad annum 1418*, ed. W. D. Macray, RS, 29 (London, 1863), 322.

[35] *Chronicle*, ed. Darlington and McGurk, II, 591.

[36] *LC*, 70.

[37] L, BL, MS Harley 1005, fo. 218v, edited as Appendix ix in *The Customary of the Benedictine Abbey of Bury St. Edmunds in Suffolk*, ed. A. Gransden, HBS, 99 (1973), 114–22; Hart, *Charters*, 71; *Anglo-Saxon Charters*, ed. A. J. Robertson, 2nd edn. (Cambridge, 1956), 425.

volunteers or oblates; but Dominic's claim that all three flourished in the days of Abbot Mannig (abbot 1044–58, d. 1066) undermines it.

Female recluses, who account for the bulk of those recorded in later centuries, are scarcely more recognizable than their elusive male counterparts. An entry in an Ely necrology in commemoration of an *anachorita* named Herewen may date to the tenth or eleventh century, but even this degree of terminological precision is exceptional.[38] In most cases, female recluses were probably described in imprecise terms with the sort of terminology that Sarah Foot associates, in her typology of women religious, with the 'single vowess'. Foot uses the term 'single vowess' for any woman who had taken a religious vow and who lived alone or independently, not within a cenobium, although monasteries often supported these vowesses by granting them corrodies or making provisions for their spiritual requirements. Charters refer to them as [*sancti-*] *moniales* or *nunnan* (nuns), *religiosae feminae* (religious women), and *ancillae Dei* (God's handmaidens).[39] Before Foot brought any number of single vowesses to our attention, historians of Anglo-Saxon England seldom searched for female religious outside monasteries for nuns. This would help to explain why recluses have been so neglected, because they fall within a category which is not rigidly defined and which has only recently been identified in the sources. These vowesses were dotted around, living in their own homes or cells in the precincts of monasteries for monks. In many cases, their individual spiritual aspirations (if not the guidance of some priest or monk) would have determined the nature of their particular religious regimes; and there can be little doubt that at least some of them would have adhered to the reclusive tradition by choosing lives of solitude, asceticism, and enclosure within cells of the typical sort.

Two likely cases turn up in the tenth century, although more may come to light. Abbo of Fleury, writing in the 980s, stated that for many years 'a venerable woman' named Oswen dwelt at the tomb of St Edmund, praying and fasting, and tending the martyr's incorrupt body. According to Abbo's reckoning, she had dwelt there 'about a generation ago'.[40] The only literal sense in which this holy woman could have dwelt 'at the tomb' was in a cell that communicated with the chancel of the minster. This sort of arrangement would have matched the living arrangements of eleventh- and twelfth-century recluses at other important churches. In another case, in 948, King Eadred granted land to an unnamed *religiosa femina* at the village of Wickhambreux near Canterbury. About a century later a female recluse occupied a dwelling (*mansio*) there, which another recluse hoped to inhabit after her death. A church not far away in a suburb of Canterbury witnessed reclusive occupation over a two-hundred-year period, first in the late eleventh century, then again during the thirteenth, though it is not

---

[38] *Katalog*, ed. Gerchow, 344.
[39] Foot, *Veiled Women I*, 179–88.
[40] *Three Lives*, ed. Winterbottom, 82–3: 'paulo ante haec nostra moderna tempora'.

known whether it did in-between. Perhaps the same was true of Wickhambreux across the tenth and eleventh centuries.[41] If the *religiosa femina* there was a recluse, King Eadred's benefaction could possibly represent the endowment of a long-lasting anchorhold. Other clues also suggest that there were more female recluses than the records reveal. Domesday Book names ten single religious women as holders of land without once using the terms *reclusa* or *inclusa*, whereas Goscelin, writing in England in the same decade, identifies five female recluses living or recently dead and applies reclusive terminology to all of them.[42] Though it is not known that any of the latter held land, Wihtgar at Bury probably subsisted on the rent of Long Melford, and the recluse identified by Herman probably on the rent of Ormesby in Norfolk, as we shall see. Various twelfth-century female recluses were certainly landowners.[43] So it need not be unlikely that one or more of the ten religious land-holding women mentioned in Domesday Book was a recluse. All the evidence suggests that in late Anglo-Saxon England female recluses had yet to possess the label by which their counterparts were known on the Continent. By employing Continental terminology, Goscelin and his contemporaries bring to our attention, for the first time, a vocation already emerging in the realm, but harder to discern in earlier sources, where terminology is ambiguous.

Uncovering the recluses

Here and there in his writings, in ones and twos, Goscelin refers to a total of six recluses resident or lately resident in eleventh-century England. The first two can be found, not surprisingly, in his treatise on the solitary life (the *Liber confortatorius*). Addressing Eve at length from Peterborough abbey during the 1080s, Goscelin wrote, among many other things, of an unidentified female recluse who had been enclosed 'in this place' before Eve herself had fled into isolation, and who had only narrowly escaped when 'this church' burnt down.[44] Peterborough had indeed been burnt some years before he wrote, in 1070, when the army of Hereward the Wake or other raiders fired the monastery and town. Setting the near-incineration of Goscelin's anonymous recluse against this backdrop may explain an idiosyncratic entry in the Peterborough Chronicle, which interests itself sufficiently in a comparable case to note against the year 1087 that when

---

[41] Eadred's charter is S 535. For the Wickhambreux and Canterbury recluses, see below. Wickhambreux was an Anglo-Saxon estate centre on a major trading route: see the map in S. Brookes, 'The Early Anglo-Saxon Framework for Middle Anglo-Saxon Economics: The Case of East Kent', in *Markets*, ed. Pestell and Ulmschneider, 84–96, at 87.

[42] On the ten in *Domesday Book*, see Foot, *Veiled Women I*, 185. For Goscelin's recluses, read on.

[43] For Herman's recluse, see below; for the recluse as estate manager, see *Aelredi Rievallensis, Opera omnia I: opera ascetica*, ed. A. Hoste and C. H. Talbot, CCCM, 1 (1971), 635–82, at 639.

[44] 'Illa autem que ante te, o dulcissima, in hoc loco agonizauerat, hac ecclesia combusta mediis flammis, ut mihi nuper relatum est, intacta superuixit': *LC*, 68; Licence, 'Evidence', 226–7.

King William sacked Mantes, near Paris, two male recluses had burnt to death.[45]
It is not known whether this detail was entered at St Augustine's, in Canterbury,
where the chronicle was originally compiled, or at Peterborough, where it was
copied. Goscelin stayed at both monasteries, at the end of the decade and nearer
its beginning respectively; his presence at either may explain the presence of this
note.

Knowingly or unknowingly, the two recluses who burned to death had
followed in the footsteps of Paternus of Paderborn. Nor were they the only
recluses to re-enact his sacrifice. Brihtric's 'recent example of virtue', Goscelin
wrote, was 'as well known as if it had occurred yesterday'.[46] The comment
suggests that it had occurred at least a year and probably several or many years
earlier. Goscelin heard about it from an eyewitness who was one of those showing
him hospitality: a monk named Æthelsige, given into the monastery as an oblate,
who had spoken with Brihtric as the latter had prepared for his impending
martyrdom. Goscelin's account of events could not have displeased this monk,
for he was present when his amanuensis wrote it down, a fact noted presumably
(as in the next example, below) to authorize the written version.[47]

Having been recently detained on the king's instructions at a fortified settlement less than two miles from Bury St Edmunds, Æthelsige had frequently
visited a recluse named Brihtric, who had lived in a wooden cell attached to the
church.[48] Goscelin presents this recluse as 'a simple and upright man', a rustic
who offered in ceaseless prayer what scraps he had memorized: a Sunday oration,
the first verse of Psalm 50 – one of the seven penitential psalms (its opening begs
God's mercy and forgiveness of sins) – and a doxology, the *Gloria patri*.
Æthelsige would advise him, and the recluse pay attention to his teaching. It
happened one day that pirates attacked the settlement, burning all in their path,
and when the monk begged the recluse to depart his cell for safety Brihtric
refused. The innocent Christ had suffered on his behalf, and he, the guilty one,
would suffer too, presenting himself as a burnt offering to his Lord. He had not
entered his cell on the condition that he should depart in the face of adversity.
Instead he told Æthelsige that his burnt body, shot through with molten lead
from the church roof, would be found cruciform with arms outstretched. (The
lead, we should note, indicates a church of status.) After the flames had raged for
a week, Æthelsige was among those who found the body in that very position,
and he swore that a fragrant aroma befitting a martyr's sacrifice lingered at the
scene as though much incense had been burnt. The vatic recluse was peacefully

[45] *The Peterborough Chronicle, 1070–1154*, ed. C. Clark, 2nd edn. (Oxford, 1970), 11.
A different version of this tale later reached William of Malmesbury: see his *Gesta regum
Anglorum = The History of the English Kings*, ed. and tr. R. A. B. Mynors; completed by R. M.
Thomson and M. Winterbottom, 2 vols (Oxford, 1998–9), I, 511.
[46] *LC*, 67.
[47] 'Testis est presens' ['The witness is present']: *LC*, 67.
[48] I have been unable to identify this settlement.

buried, and Goscelin was clearly moved in recounting the tale. Conscious of his sinfulness to the last, Brihtric had died in a familiar gesture of penance. It could have been a position that recluses customarily adopted, given that Hartker too – as we have seen – was remembered for lying cruciform on the floor, and that thirteenth-century recluses who read *Ancrene Wisse* were instructed to perform penance in this manner.[49] The aroma of incense, commonly associated in hagiography with relics and the bodily remains of saints, was a divine attestation to the acceptability of Brihtric's sacrifice, akin to a burnt offering. Hagiographical trimmings aside, the basic details provide acceptable evidence of a recluse enclosed in England a decade or so after the Conquest; a layman and quite probably an Englishman, apparently at a non-monastic church, who had come to the vocation with rather more ardour than preparation. Like Anmchad, he or his literary reinventors were inspired either by the example of Paternus or, less specifically, by a martyr cult growing up around the rumour of some recluse willingly burnt in a cell.

Eventually, Goscelin arrived in Kent and settled at St Augustine's, Canterbury. There he continued his business of writing *Lives* of the local saints, among them the royal nun St Mildthryth (d. *c*.700), whose relics had been removed to the abbey from her shrine at Minster in Thanet earlier in the century. Three of the recluses whom he mentions surface at the end of his account of her miracles, which he wrote at the abbey during the 1090s.[50] Two appear as subjects of miracles wrought by the saint, the third incidentally; and, although Goscelin's fascination for recluses may have prolonged his treatment of these cases, there is no doubt that each plays a part in his unfolding narrative. Goscelin's first tale involving a recluse, although set at the end of his collection, concerns the *anachorita* Ælfwen, then some eighty years old, who for thirty years had been enclosed (*inclusa*) in a cell at the church of St Stephen the proto-martyr in a suburb of Canterbury.[51] Goscelin's informant, the prior of St Augustine's, was present as he wrote. Like the monk Æthelsige in Brihtric's case, he was a visitor to the recluse. It is even said that he recounted her tale verbatim (it is written down in the first person), although Goscelin suppressed his name to posterity because the prior was self-effacing. Ælfwen still dwelt at St Stephen's at the time of writing, and others who had heard her tale could confirm it, Goscelin averred. The miracles need not detain us: suffice to say that St Mildthryth had twice cured Ælfwen in her youth at Minster-in-Thanet, from different afflictions – a mercy which perhaps eventually inspired her to assume a religious vocation. Goscelin, moreover, sets these cures within a chronological framework (the first had

---

[49] *Ancrene Wisse*, ed. Millett, I, 130. Lying face-down, cruciform, was a posture of penance.

[50] D. W. Rollason, 'Goscelin of Canterbury's Account of the Translation and Miracles of St Mildrith (*BHL* 5961/4): An Edition with Notes', *Mediaeval Studies*, 48 (1986), 139–210.

[51] 'Adhuc in suburbio Cantuarie degit anus fere octogenaria, iamque anachorita trigenaria, inclusa celle in beati protomartyris Stephani basilica, nomine Ælfuuenna': Rollason, 'Translation and Miracles', 197. For the full account, see *ibid.*, 197–201.

occurred about seventy years before he wrote). And given that he wrote during
Ælfwen's lifetime for a community acquainted with her, this chronology may be
secure. Even if his round tally of thirty years is approximate, it is sufficient for us
to posit that she probably entered her cell in the 1060s. The present St Stephen's
church, a mile north of the city at Hackington, dates from *c*.1100. By the time
the church was rebuilt, Ælfwen was probably dead. Afterwards, no recluse is
recorded at that church before the early thirteenth century.[52]

Goscelin's account of Ælfwen introduces another story, with no given source,
concerning an anonymous young woman raised in Essex who ran away to escape
an unwanted betrothal.[53] Initially she passed a few years living as a hermit with a
priest on a nearby island, but someone recognized her, and she was forced to
relocate, at her patron St Mildthryth's direction, to Minster-in-Thanet in Kent.
After spending seven more years as a hermit, she desired a life of enclosure, so she
obtained permission to build a cell for herself against the side of the church. The
minster clergy petitioned the bailiffs on her behalf for licence to enclose, but the
bailiffs (*uillici*) refused. At that point an anchorhold at the nearby estate of
Wickhambreux happened to fall vacant through the death of its unnamed
resident *inclusa*, tempting the postulant to relocate; but St Mildthryth now
intervened by miraculously immobilizing her limbs until she repented her
decision. Impressed, parishioners seized the initiative by recommending her to
the elders of St Augustine's. They targeted this abbey because the jurisdiction of
its saint adjoined their minster and, presumably, in hope of its patronage. Monks
were sent, mass was celebrated, a votive prayer offered, and the postulant recluse
enclosed. That the bailiffs' objections appear to have melted away suggests that
the abbey provided financial backing. Settled at last, she endured a life of spiritual
warfare, living on altar offerings of beans and apples, and in Lent adopting a
penitential diet, eating only three times a week. When she died, she was buried in
her cell. This account is of unique interest because it demonstrates how a recluse,
minster clerics, parishioners, and monks from a local abbey might all play some
part in instituting – and the wardens in obstructing – an anchorhold. The girl's
fugitive circumstances precluded a cenobitic probation (for it is doubtful that
monasteries took runaways), but ten or so years as a hermit was deemed sufficient
qualification to get her a job as a recluse. A comparable case emerges from the
abbey of Saint-Pierre-de-Préaux in Normandy, where the monk Peter became a
recluse in the 1070s after living as a hermit for a number of years.[54] It is possible
to put a date to our events, for Goscelin sets the decisive miracle after the removal
of Mildthryth's remains from Minster *c*.1035, but (we may deduce) before

[52] Clay, *Hermits*, 74, 153, 222–3.

[53] Rollason, 'Translation and Miracles', 207–10.

[54] *Le cartulaire de l'abbaye bénédictine de Saint-Pierre-de-Préaux (1034–1227)*, ed. D. Rouet,
Collection de documents inédits sur l'histoire de France, section d'histoire et philologie des
civilisations médiévales, Ser. in–8, vol. 34 (Paris, 2005), A6 (13–14).

1066 x 1086; for, though the monks held the patronage there, the limits of the abbey's jurisdiction show that the abbot had not yet acquired the church, which he did during these years. It is unlikely that the postulant was enclosed very late within this fifty-year span (1035 x 1086), because by 1086 the community of clerics there had apparently given way to single-priest occupancy.[55] The recluse who died at Wickhambreux must have been enclosed even earlier, perhaps as an heir to the putative anchorhold there, instituted by King Eadred.

The sixth recluse mentioned by Goscelin, again the subject of a miracle, features among his miracles of the apostle to the English, St Augustine, which he assembled at the saint's abbey some years after writing his hagiography of St Mildthryth there.[56] This *anachoreta* was *inclusa* at a church dedicated to St Augustine in Leicester. Blind for fifteen years, her role was not dissimilar to that of Oswen at tenth-century Bury St Edmunds: for she looked after the books and vestments of the priests serving in the church. Eventually, on the vigil of the saint's feast, her sight was miraculously restored as she awaited the celebrant of the mass. The few particulars provided in this account make it difficult to separate the threads of fact, fabrication, and hearsay. The period of fifteen years, for example, could represent a penitential tariff, intended to portray her blindness as a punishment for sin. Goscelin had already used this tariff in his tale of the hermit Alexander, whose hands were miraculously sealed in an oak tree for fifteen years as a punishment for violating and murdering a princess.[57] Blindness too could be interpreted as a penance imposed by heavenly agency. As an insouciant youth, Ælfwen had been struck with it for exactly a year – another conventional tariff – as a divine corrective.[58] The Leicester tale does, nevertheless, present a convincing sketch of a recluse serving the priests at a probable minster, within a substantial town.

This image is similar in certain respects to an arrangement which the historian and hagiographer William of Malmesbury recalled from his childhood, although in his case, contrastingly, in a Somerset village. It appears in his *Life* of St Wulfstan as contextual detail in one of the saint's miracles. William reports that when he was a boy growing up near the village of Bruton he heard tales of the godly priest there and the virtuous *reclusa* who looked after him. This duo is approximately datable because the heavenly vision which they allegedly had of Wulfstan followed shortly after the bishop's death in 1095.[59] It is hard to imagine that either this recluse or the one at Leicester, if fully enclosed, could have cared for the priest in any practical sense other than keeping his liturgical paraphernalia in repair. This sort of work would compare to the work of the

[55] Licence, 'Evidence', 230n.
[56] Goscelin, *Historia, miracula et translatio*, 429F–430A.
[57] *LC*, 104–5.
[58] Rollason, 'Translation and Miracles', 206–7.
[59] *Saints' Lives*, ed. Winterbottom and Thomson, 155.

Somerset recluse Wulfric of Haselbury (*c*.1090–1155), enclosed in 1125, who
made books for use in the church adjoining his cell; and of female recluses who
supplied monastic and secular churches with altar cloths, probably woven in their
cells.[60] Wiborada and Billfrith had bound books too: it was an anchoretic
occupation. Thus the Leicester tale and William's report show recluses in their
typical capacity, performing similar duties in urban and rural churches in
different parts of the country.

Herman of Bury St Edmunds (d. *c*.1098), who had served the East Anglian
bishopric probably as an archdeacon before retiring to St Edmund's abbey, refers
to an aged *reclusa* named Ælfwen, who lived alone somewhere within the
precincts of the abbey of St Benedict at Holme on the east Norfolk coast. He
mentions her in his treatise on St Edmund's miracles, written in the 1090s; but it
is unclear whether she was still alive. Citing her long memory as an authority for
events that had occurred in 1014, Herman may have been remembering testimony he had heard twenty or thirty years earlier, perhaps when visiting her in a
pastoral capacity, or with the bishop. He uses the present participle *uiuens*
('living'), but his ellipsis of any finite verb, which could have attached a tense
to her act of testimony, renders it unknowable whether the participle applied to
her when he wrote.[61] The memories that she allegedly reported were either hers
or tales that her father Thurketel had told her. It is known from his surviving will
that she was set to inherit an estate near Holme at Ormesby, with reversion to the
abbey upon her death.[62] Thurketel, a royal thegn, appears to have served as a
reeve or at least a tax collector for the hundreds of East and West Flegg, from
which he was deputed to collect tribute and bear it to Thetford. The tribute
gathered in 1014 had been returned, his daughter recalled, because of King
Swein Forkbeard's sudden death. It is known that Ormesby passed to the abbey
before 1066, when King Harold II's brother, Earl Gurth, held the lease; and, if
we assume that Ælfwen was still alive at that date, the simplest hypothesis is that
she yielded her inheritance to the monks prematurely to provide for a life of
seclusion.[63] Any such arrangement should have left little room for her to
undertake a cenobitic probation, which would have required some gift to initiate
formal attachment to a suitable house of nuns. Her vocation is better understood
in the looser context of the solitary vowess than as the regulated reclusion
Grimlaïc depicts. If the hypothesis that Ælfwen retired to a cell in the abbey's
precincts as a pensioned recluse is accepted, it might equally apply to another
local noblewoman. For in 1066 x 1070, Earl Ralf I of East Anglia granted Holme

---

[60] *WH*, 45. Two such cloths are recorded in early thirteenth-century church inventories as the
gifts of recluses (of uncertain date): O. Lehmann-Brockhaus, *Lateinische Schriftquellen zur Kunst in
England, Wales und Schottland vom Jahre 901 bis zum Jahre 1307*, 2 vols (Munich, 1955), II,
no. 3764 (401); no. 4249 (537).

[61] *Memorials*, ed. Arnold, I, 38.

[62] *Wills*, ed. Whitelock, no. 25 (S 1528).

[63] *Domesday Book; vol. 33: Norfolk*, ed. P. Brown, 2 vols (Chichester, 1984), I, 1, 59.

his estate at Hoveton along 'with his wife'. Generally Domesday Book uses the latter formula to refer to lands given with a woman upon her entry to a nunnery; but Holme was a house of monks.[64] An explanation for this conundrum, in view of Ælfwen's precedent, is that Ralf's wife, who was of a comparable age and status, withdrew to some dwelling near the abbey, with Hoveton's rent as her corrody.

Herman also reports that a woman named Ælfgyth, from the Winchester region, attached herself to St Edmund and lived a religious life in his presence, in the reign of Abbot Leofstan (1044–65), interceding with him on behalf of suppliants and caring for his relics.[65] Like the recluse of Minster-in-Thanet, she entered a saint's service after receiving his commendation, in the form of a miraculous cure, and Herman believed that her subsequent career – like Oswen's – bore witness to St Edmund's powers.[66] Near the beginning of the twelfth century an anonymous monk rewrote Herman's work and added new miracles, three of which concerned the nun Seitha, who assumed a reclusive or semi-reclusive existence at St Edmund's abbey in the last third of the century. He describes her as an English noblewoman who had left her husband and children to take the veil at Bury at the invitation of Abbot Baldwin (1065–97/8).[67] She dwelt there in a cell or cottage (*tugurium*) in the cemetery and attended festivals in the church with her companion Edith. Like the recluse at St Stephen's, Canterbury, Seitha is cited verbatim. The character of her vocation may be independently attested, for, about the year 1102, Archbishop Anselm wrote a letter to a certain Robert, who had sought his advice with respect to the care of two vowesses, Seitha and Edith.[68] Its contents appear to hint that they were recluses.[69] It is not unlikely that they were the recluses of Bury St Edmunds, under the supervision of either their abbot (Bury possessed abbots named Robert between 1100 and 1107) or a man of the same name. Wihtgar, the recluse in the tower, probably died during Baldwin's abbacy, when the tower was dedicated to St Benedict and became associated with the abbot's chambers. Nevertheless, the abbey was not long without a recluse, for in Abbot Baldwin's era a priest named Albold built a chapel in honour of the martyr St Margaret of Antioch and attached a tower in which a pious virgin named Langlifa was enclosed (*inclusa*) and eventually buried.[70] Albold was probably Ailbold who appears among

---

[64] *Norfolk*, ed. Brown, I, 8, 8; 8, 8n. On Ralf, see Williams, *The English*, 61–2.

[65] *Memorials*, ed. Arnold, I, 51–2: that 'sancto adhærebat sedula' suggests that she was an anchorite.

[66] A comparable tale of a woman cured by a saint (Aldhelm), who became a nun near his shrine in her gratitude, also in the second quarter of the eleventh century, is found in William of Malmesbury: *Gesta pontificum*, ed. Winterbottom and Thomson, ch. 259. These three examples suggest a pattern.

[67] See New York, Pierpont Morgan Library, MS M. 736, from fo. 67r.

[68] *Opera*, ed. Schmitt, IV, no. 230 (134–5); see also no. 414 (others having joined them).

[69] See below, 125.

[70] L, BL, MS Harley 1005, fo. 217v.

witnesses in a charter of the 1090s, in which he is identified as Baldwin's priest.[71] The name Langlifa ('Long-life') is unusual, and sufficiently so to allow the possibility that this individual was *Langliue nunne* (Long-life the nun), whose name was entered into Thorney's Book of Life *c.*1112–13.[72] The date of her death is unknown, but Abbot Anselm of Bury St Edmunds (1121–48) subsequently demolished the chapel and rebuilt it, probably on the same site, where it was dedicated in his abbacy at the north gate of the great cemetery. This would suggest that Langlifa was a cemetery recluse, who may have been charged to pray for the dead. There is reason to suppose that her cell was later reinstated, since there was a recluse in the cemetery in the 1220s or 1230s.[73]

The recluses identified in this chapter are the earliest I can find in the sources, although more may await discovery and many more remain unknown. For the tenth century there is the probable recluse Oswen at Bury St Edmunds and another likely recluse at Wickhambreaux – both the locations of minsters and estate centres – as well as the possibility that SS. Dunstan and Ælfheah chose this vocation. For the eleventh century, there are three recluses at Evesham, at least two of them enclosed before mid-century; a female recluse who may have occupied a cell at a church in Peterborough, possibly before 1070; a female recluse at St Benet's at Holme, possibly before 1066, and another there (or a nun) before 1070; and another in a tower at Bury St Edmunds before the mid-eleventh century, and another, in another tower there, situated in the cemetery before 1098, and a vowess or two living in semi-reclusive withdrawal in the abbey precincts. Eve, the nun who lived as a recluse abroad, adds another to our total; and we must also count several at centres not associated with the cenobitic life. A female recluse at Wickhambreaux in East Kent may have been enclosed before mid-century, as may another, in a cell against the side of the church at Minster-in-Thanet. A male recluse kept vigil alongside a church in a fortified vill or township a few miles from Bury St Edmunds before *c.*1080, and before the mid-1090s a female recluse had a cell at a city church in Leicester and another in a village in rural Somerset. The picture now being assembled shows a land liberally populated by recluses, and we should view it alongside Prior Turgot's impression of the vocation's popularity in Scotland, where, in the reign of Queen Margaret (1046–93), the numerous recluses occupied cells scattered across the realm.[74] Scotland is not well supplied with sources from this era, so this glimpse is invaluable. Although several of our recluses enjoyed monastic patronage, Eve is the only one that is known to have trained in a monastery. Reclusion, even within

---

[71] *Feudal Documents from the Abbey of Bury St. Edmunds*, ed. D. C. Douglas (London, 1932), no. 170 (at 152–3).

[72] L, BL, Additional MS 40,000, fo. 10v; on the date of the entry, see C. Clark, 'The *Liber vitae* of Thorney Abbey and Its "Catchment Area"', in *Words, Names and History*, ed. Jackson, 320–38, at 326.

[73] T. Madox, *Formulare anglicanum* (London, 1702), 423.

[74] '[P]lurimi, per diuersa loca separatis inclusi cellulis . . . uiuebant': Hinde, *Opera*, 247.

a monastic context, was evidently a respectable vocation in its own right. In practice, as the Minster case shows, authority to enclose and ultimate responsibility for the recluse's welfare lay not so much with the bishop as with the owners and wardens of the church concerned. None of these cases suggests a role for the bishop, so it would appear that Grimlaïc's view and the conventions it advocated, which are exemplified in the case of Burchard of Worms's enclosure of the recluse Caritas, were irrelevant to the realities of reclusion in eleventh-century England, where episcopal ceremonies and monastic probation do not appear to be in evidence.

Strictly, these cases show that reclusion in England (and Scotland) can be traced well back into the eleventh century and probably beyond, under a variety of different names and inchoate expressions. The alternative argument, that Goscelin was an early commentator on a vocation newly taking root, is difficult to defend because none of his accounts conveys the impression that recluses were a novelty. Even the felicitous coincidence at Wickhambreux, that when a cell was required a cell fell vacant, passes without comment as though it were an unremarkable occurrence. What may be significant is that virtually all eleventh-century recluses occupied cells at notable minsters or estate centres; even Brihtric's unidentified church possessed a leaded roof. This would suggest that recluses were initially the perquisite of the rich. Soon afterwards, if not already, recluses (as they were coming to be known) were colonizing local churches in urban Leicester and in rural Somerset. John of Ford's portrayal of that county in the second quarter of the twelfth century shows several cells already there. Wulfric's at Haselbury had seen prior occupation, and during Wulfric's lifetime there were recluses at the churches or churchyards of Winterborne, Wareham, Crewkerne, and Sturminster Newton.[75] Their proliferation may be linked to the spread of wealth, for England in the century from *c*.1030 saw unprecedented sums of money invested in rebuilding churches and sponsoring the religious life in all its forms.[76] If reclusion was impressing potential sponsors (as the martyr tales circulating at Peterborough and the actions of the parishioners, clergy, and monks at Minster-in-Thanet suggest), the fact that it did so as parishes emerged may explain why the anchorhold became a focal point of religion in the parish. As the countryside became manorialized, pastoral care became more localized, and recluses would have proliferated.[77] The agents in this process were probably the newly moneyed thegns, busily exploiting their estates, laying out new villages, and founding private churches. Robin Fleming has observed that they were anxious to emulate their social superiors, so it could be that they were copying kings, aristocrats, or monasteries by sponsoring anchorites as a spiritual

[75] *WH*, 15, and pp. xxxvii–xxxviii.

[76] The phenomenon of church-building was no less evident in France and the Empire.

[77] J. Blair, 'Parochial Organization', in *The Blackwell Encyclopaedia of Anglo-Saxon England*, ed. M. Lapidge, J. Blair, S. Keynes, and D. Scragg (Oxford, 1999), 356–8, at 358.

investment and a status symbol.[78] It could also be that East Kent and East Anglia, where the earliest recluses are visible, were rather quicker to respond to spiritual currents within the German Empire. England was always behind Germany and Lotharingia in its understanding of reclusion, for it was not until after the Conquest, and possibly in the writings of the immigrant Goscelin, that reclusion in England was envisaged in the terms that were already familiar and established across the Channel and the North Sea. Even then, the protocol and liturgy were still to be established. Yet the significance of reclusion in eleventh-century England lies in its ad hoc nature. Many people were experimenting with it and trying to accommodate it. That the same was happening on the Continent points to a European phenomenon.

During the eleventh century, the pontifical *ordines* for the consecration of vowed women may have served for female recluses who received episcopal benediction.[79] The twelfth century saw not only the consolidation of the vocation's terminology but also the establishment of ceremonies and procedures of enclosure, although it was still often done on an ad hoc basis in the absence of any bishop.[80] By mid-century, the substantive *inclusus* was being set apart to desig-nate a separate category of religious in the *Life* of the bishop of Hereford, Robert of Bethune (d. 1148), written by one of his companions, an Augustinian canon, in 1148 x 1152. His work refers to the affairs 'of *inclusi* and hermits', as does the *Life* of Christina of Markyate, which mentions '*inclusi*, hermits, and others'.[81] Christina's *Life* is of a roughly similar date. The fact that *inclusus* was the preferred term for the dependent solitaries recorded in official documents, most notably the Pipe Rolls – in which it mixes interchangeably with *reclusus* – implies that its use in this context was well established by the mid-twelfth century. From that date, numerous recluses dotted around the realm received royal pensions, with pensions occasionally being granted to successive occupants of cells. In practice, there was often a series of recluses in succession whose duty was to pray for their sponsors. Early in the 1160s, the Cistercian Aelred of Rievaulx (1110–67), at the request of his reclusive sister, wrote the first guide to the vocation intended for a wide circulation: *De institutione inclusarum* ('First principles of reclusion').[82] This manual subsequently became a steady founda-tion for the many works of guidance that followed. Aelred identified the enclosed as an order (*ordo*) distinct from hermits, a distinction not evident a century

---

[78] R. Fleming, 'The New Wealth, the New Rich and the New Political Style in Late Anglo-Saxon England', *ANS*, 23 (2001), 1–22, at 4; Blair, *The Church*, 498. Landowners were building parish churches through France at the same time, on the profits of newly created wealth.

[79] For these *ordines*, see Foot, *Veiled Women I*, 127–30.

[80] H. A. Wilson, *The Pontifical of Magdalen College*, HBS, 39 (1910), 243–4.

[81] '[I]nclusorum et heremitarum': William of Wycombe, 'Libri II De vita Roberti Betun, episcopi Herefordensis', in *Anglia sacra*, ed. Wharton, II, 295–322, at 308; '[I]nclusis, heremitis, ceterisque': *LCM*, 150.

[82] *Opera omnia I*, ed. Hoste and Talbot. Aelred expected a wide audience (at 682).

before.[83] Throughout his treatise he is consistent in appending the label *inclusi* (f. *inclusae*) to this newly recognized 'order'. His older contemporary Gilbert of Sempringham (1080s–1189), mentor of enclosed women and founder of the Gilbertine order, did likewise.[84] By the 1190s, when the abbot of the Cistercian house of Flaxley wrote of a hermit who wished to upgrade to the 'stricture of the *inclusi*' (*Religionem Inclusi*), a notional hierarchy of vocations was at work.[85] The notion that reclusion was a stricter ascetic calling than eremitism may already be implicit in Goscelin's account of the Essex hermit who became a recluse at Minster-in-Thanet, and perhaps also in the tale of how Gilbert, seeking volunteers to enter cells at Sempringham church in the 1130s, found no man willing to endure such a life. All of this information, together, suggests that in England the vocation of reclusion emerged in the eleventh century and took shape in the twelfth, when it came under the control of bishops keen on extending their control over religious life in their dioceses.

Archaeological insights

Further information can be gleaned from archaeology, which is able to shed light on the dimensions, design, and situation of anchorholds and provide insights into the techniques of their construction. How, then, may it help us account for the popularity of reclusion in our period? Whereas the records often reveal no more than the fact that cells adjoined the outer walls of churches, archaeological remains suggest that the vast majority were lean-to, timber structures rather than the solid domiciles of stone which first come into view in the fourteenth century. The earliest type of cell, which typically adjoined a church, is identified in written records by formulaic descriptions such as 'against the wall' (*sub pariete*); 'against the side' (*sub ala*); 'under the eaves' (*under chirche euesunges*), 'attached to the church' (with a participle of *adhaereo*), or 'adjoining' it (*contiguus*). Brihtric's little wooden cell (*cellula*) was attached to the side of the church (*ecclesie adherenti*).[86] Archaeological traces typically include a squint, window, or door in the wall of the chancel, beam mortises above in its outside, foundations or the remains of an exterior structure associated with these features, and sometimes one or more graves contained in that structure. No universal template for recluses' cells existed, perhaps for the reason that no single authority regulated them. Most were probably designed in accordance with the tastes and specifications of their first occupants or their patrons. Osbern and Goscelin assumed that recluses built

---

[83] 'Huius ordinis': see *Opera omnia I*, ed. Hoste and Talbot, 637–8.

[84] B. Golding, *Gilbert of Sempringham and the Gilbertine Order, c.1130–c.1300* (Oxford, 1995), 20.

[85] *The Cartulary and Historical Notes of the Cistercian Abbey of Flaxley, Otherwise called Dene Abbey, in the County of Gloucester*, ed. A. W. Crawley-Boevey (Exeter, 1887), no. 25.

[86] *LC*, 67.

their own cells;[87] archaeology indicates that doing so would have required very little skill.

To affix a wooden cell to a church of stone, the builder would hollow out mortises in the wall of the chancel and insert the ends of two or three beams. The other ends of the beams could then rest on wooden posts dug into holes in the earth. At East Ham and Chipping Ongar in Essex, twelfth- or thirteenth-century cells required square beam mortises in the external faces of church walls. St Martin's at Chipping Ongar displays two such slots to bear a roof, over an arched recess in the wall, through which a lancet-shaped squint commands a view of the chancel.[88] Bengeo church in Hertfordshire retains three beam slots in the shape of an isosceles triangle over two door-like apertures. These features could be evidence of a twelfth-century cell.[89] The squint (for which the noun 'hagioscope' is a Victorian affectation) was a miniature window cut into the chancel wall so that a recluse could keep a watch on the altar.[90] Squints varied in size and design. St Nicholas's church at Compton in Surrey retains two, one associated with a vanished cell against the northern wall, the other, with a surviving cell against its southern wall. The first is a shaft through the outer wall of the church at an angle aligned with the step that leads into the Norman sanctuary. Before the sanctuary was added *c.*1080, the altar would have stood in the position of the present step. It was in view of this earlier arrangement that the squint was aligned. Seven by eleven inches, it opens into a large coved splay in the outer face of the wall in which the occupant could kneel or prostrate herself towards the altar.[91] A square squint slanting through the chancel's northern wall at St Mary's, Chickney, in Essex likewise served to command a view of the altar. It may date to the eleventh or twelfth century.[92] A twelfth- or thirteenth-century squint at Hardham church in Sussex is similarly aligned and opens into a recess serviceable to a kneeling recluse.[93] The squints or windows at East Ham, Lindsell, and Chipping Ongar in Essex, at Compton in Surrey, and at St Anne's at Lewes in

---

[87] *Memorials*, ed. Stubbs, 83; Rollason, 'Translation and Miracles', 208.

[88] M. O. Hodson, 'East Ham Church: Remains of an Anker-hold', *Transactions of the Essex Archaeological Society*, n.s. 22 (1940 for 1936–9), 345–6; E. S. Deswick, 'On the Discovery of an Ankerhold at the Church of St Martin, Chipping Ongar, Essex', *The Archaeological Journal*, 45 (1888), 284–8.

[89] J. T. Micklethwaite, 'On the Remains of an Ankerhold at Bengeo Church, Hertford', *The Archaeological Journal*, 44 (1888), 26–9. Micklethwaite noticed only two of the three slots. A cell excavated at Letherhead in Surrey (with walls three feet thick and a squint seven feet, nine inches above ground level) was surely a two-storey building, as are the surviving cells at Hartlip in Kent and Chester-le-Street in County Durham. These cells date to the fourteenth century.

[90] See P. M. Johnston, 'Low Side Windows in Churches', in *Transactions of the St Paul's Ecclesiological Society*, 4 (London, 1900), 263–76. Cf. *Ancrene Wisse*, ed. Millett, I, 29, 7.

[91] A. Bott, *A Guide to the Parish Church of Saint Nicholas, Compton, Surrey* (Compton, 2000), 26.

[92] G. M. Benton, 'Discovery of an Anker-hold at Lindsell Church', *Transactions of the Essex Archaeological Society*, n.s. xix (1930), 316–20, at 318.

[93] P. M. Johnston, 'Hardham Church, and Its Early Paintings', *Sussex Archaeological Collections*, 44 (1901), 73–115, at 78–80.

Sussex are rebated on the interior (i.e. the wall's external face) for shutters. At East Ham, hinges and a hole for a bolt survived. There were also three holes in the rebated stone over the top of the hatch, two of which contained the remains of wooden pegs suitable for hanging a cloth.[94] All of these remnants of cells survive only because they scarred stone churches. Before the twelfth century, far fewer churches were built of stone and even fewer have survived. Other cells, labelled 'houses' (*mansiones*) or 'cottages' (*tugurii*), might sometimes have stood alone in cemeteries, so their remains would be difficult to spot or identify.

These sorts of archaeological discoveries add one last important dimension to the picture, because they reveal that cells were cheap and easy to build. A powerful noble such as Ælfric son of Wihtgar, or an abbot's priest such as Albold, could afford to erect a tower to accommodate a recluse, but in general little capital investment was required. Communities of parishioners or thegns who built their own churches could establish recluses at their existing church premises simply by knocking a few holes in the fabric of a wall. Afterwards the recluse could perhaps be supported from the portion of the tithe that the founder was legally entitled to divert from the mother church. The corollary is that anyone willing to earn a living by prayer and asceticism and able to persuade potential sponsors of his or her sincerity in doing so could build a makeshift cell and set up as a recluse. In the case of the recluse at Minster, a saint intervened to prove her credentials, but in most instances earthlier references were probably required before a patron would agree to sponsorship. The Minster tale may hint that endowed cells at churches were oversubscribed at that date (in the mid-eleventh century) as they may have been in mid-tenth-century Lotharingia. Perhaps one or two of them had waiting lists. A cell like the one at Wickham-breux, which probably had a royal endowment, would surely have been a desirable prize for any aspiring recluse. The continuous occupation of some of these cells shows that certain lords, parishes, and monasteries were committed to maintaining recluses and held out secure, salaried, and highly respected positions to suitable future applicants. It is not hard to imagine that eleventh-century England was a land of opportunity for recluses, and in this regard it differed little from the Empire, where their asceticism was prized.

---

[94] Cf. Hodson, 'East Ham', 346; and *Ancrene Wisse*, ed. Millett, I, 20–1, 38.

4

How anchorites made a living

It is now worth shifting the emphasis of the inquiry, by gradual stages, from the rise of hermits and recluses to the function they performed in society, by examining some of the various human interventions, means, and operations by which anchorites were maintained and propagated. For although hermits and recluses interceded for people, gave spiritual advice, and mediated divine grace, they were not economically productive, but remained a luxurious investment even if their presence was held to be a religious necessity. Every one of them had to be supported, either by the gift of a productive plot of land or the provision of food and other necessities, often by the ministrations of servants. Only a prosperous realm could maintain a large number: England's large number reflects its well-documented prosperity in the eleventh and twelfth centuries, when population growth provided a stimulus for the extension of arable cultivation into the wastes, where vast swathes of land were available for the increased production of cereal crops.[1] The surplus wealth that was created sustained thriving secondary and tertiary industries in nascent towns, as well as countless new churches and monasteries and the rebuilding of older ones.[2] Some of the wealth that was generated went on the maintenance of anchorites: indeed, in practical terms, it would go a long way towards explaining their proliferation in a predominantly rural society. In many cases, as we shall see, it was the hermits themselves, while hunting through the wilderness for amenable spots, that grubbed up the trees, tilled virgin soil, and carved out plots in the wasteland. By scrutinizing their activities and the motives or interests of their patrons, we can identify the forces that enabled them to multiply. First we need to ascertain what sort of people sponsored hermits and how they did so, before proceeding to the question, how did these hermits support themselves? Next, we may apply the

---

[1] On England's ability to generate wealth, see P. Sawyer, 'The Wealth of England', *TRHS*, 5th ser., 15 (1965), 145–64; J. Campbell, 'Some Agents and Agencies of the Late Anglo-Saxon State', in *Domesday Studies: Papers read at the Novocentenary Conference of the Royal Historical Society and the Institute of British Geographers, Winchester, 1986*, ed. J. C. Holt (Woodbridge, 1987), 201–18; and R. Fleming, 'Rural Elites and Urban Communities in Late Anglo-Saxon England', *Past and Present*, 141 (1993), 3–37.

[2] Frank Barlow noted the unprecedented, exceptional scale of land transference from the laity to the church in the century *c.*1050–*c.*1150: *idem, The English Church 1066–1154* (London, 1979), 2. On assarting in this period, see E. Miller and J. Hatcher, *Medieval England: Rural Society and Economic Change 1086–1348* (London, 1978), 33–42, 53–7.

same questions to recluses, partly in light of Ann Warren's findings and those of the previous chapter, but also in light of evidence that has not yet been introduced. Without the preconditions of a prosperous agrarian economy it would not have been feasible to populate the landscape with anchorites. The objective of this chapter, accordingly, is to show mainly in practical terms – we shall consider spiritual matters later on – what opportunities were arising, and how anchorites exploited them.

ANCHORITES AND THEIR PATRONS

In the four or five decades after the Norman Conquest, a number of major barons, not least royalty, demonstrated willingness to bestow sizeable tracts of land on hermits and eremitic communities where they could discern some advantage in doing so. Land was at their disposal, and new lords had interests to defend and allies to win.

Ealdwine's community of hermits at Malvern provides a case in point, for its success was bound up with the interests of its patron. It is not known when the hermitage was founded, but the land on which it grew passed by complications of conquest into the hands of King William's sheriff, Urse d'Abetot, who received roughly a third of the manor of Powick, which included the territory of Malvern.[3] Urse soon came into conflict with the local ecclesiastical lordship of Worcester cathedral priory, because the triple hundred of Oswaldslow, which historically fell to the bishop of Worcester, excluded the sheriff's jurisdiction. As a result of this, Urse had virtually no authority in an important area covering three hundred hides (or tens of thousands of acres) in the middle of his shrievalty. Ealdwine's hermitage at Great Malvern lay outside this exempted area, surrounded by territory that was claimed by Westminster abbey. By sponsoring the hermits there, endowing a priory, and conferring it on the royal abbey at Westminster, Urse could have strengthened his authority in the region at the bishop of Worcester's expense. The fact that Westminster prevailed in a subsequent struggle with Worcester over which of them owned the priory upholds the likelihood that Urse favoured its claim; indeed, in his capacity as sheriff he probably sought to advance the king's interests in this matter as well as his own.[4] Whether or not he was an admirer of hermits, there were clear potential advantages in granting them the land at Malvern. Hugh fitzBaldric was another new sheriff who came across a hermitage and elected to sponsor its occupants. Through Hugh's agency, as we have already seen, the fugitive monk Benedict obtained the king's patronage at Selby in North Yorkshire. There too circumstances were conducive to the multiplication of hermits, not only because lots of

---

[3] *Domesday Book; vol. 16: Worcestershire*, ed. F. Thorn and C. Thorn (Chichester, 1982), 8, 10.
[4] On Urse, see J. H. Round, 'Abetot, Urse d' (*c.*1040–1108)', rev. Emma Mason, in *ODNB*.

land had become available in the aftermath of the Conquest (Benedict received
one plough-land), but also because there was a strategic advantage in allocating
some of it to eremitic communities, which could function to heal rifts between
the conquerors and the conquered. These communities provided a point of
contact between incoming lords and the indigenous population. Their asceticism
would have served to win the respect of both. They symbolized peaceful reconstruction in a war-torn region, and in charitable terms their provision might offer
a new start to the destitute and disaffected.

Within a few years three more would-be hermits, Ealdwine of Winchcombe,
Ælfwi, and Reinfrid, came to Hugh fitzBaldric, possibly in search of his
sponsorship after hearing about Selby.[5] He sent them north to a place called
Monkchester (now Newcastle), which lay in the jurisdiction of Earl Waltheof of
Northumbria (1072–6). It is not known whether Waltheof favoured them, but
they soon accepted an invitation from Bishop Walcher of Durham (1071–80) to
restore monastic life at Jarrow, within the bishop's jurisdiction, where he could
afford them help and protection. Walcher, who had the formidable job of
rebuilding religious life in a diocese which was still a war zone, may have
perceived constructive roles for this new eremitic community, for he used it to
accommodate at least one displaced individual, the cleric Turgot, when he
returned to England after a period of exile.[6] Reinfrid meanwhile had another
site in mind and had earmarked an alternative patron, perhaps because Walcher's
vision for Jarrow conflicted with his personal solitary aspirations. The narrative
of Whitby's foundation explains that he had been a soldier in the service of
William de Percy (d. 1096 x 1099), a major baron in the north, who had served
on the Conqueror's Scottish expedition of 1072, probably with Reinfrid in his
company, and rebuilt the castle at York under the direction of Hugh fitzBaldric.[7]
The estates he duly acquired included the ruined monastic site at Streoneshalh
(Whitby), which was supposedly Reinfrid's source of inspiration on the home-
ward journey before he reached Evesham. Leaving Jarrow, the hermit Reinfrid
now headed towards the domain of his former lord, where (according to
Whitby's historian) William granted him the considerable gift of two plough-
lands at Whitby, probably in recognition of past services.[8] Abbot Stephen, later
abbot of York, complicates the picture by intimating that William endowed the
community at Whitby only after Stephen became abbot there, but this claim
served an interest he retained in alienating Whitby's property. When William de
Percy hounded Stephen's party from his estates for some reason, Stephen found a
friend in the king, who granted his colony the site of another seventh-century

---

[5] This suggestion is merely a guess. Simeon says that they sought Hugh to ask for a guide north,
but this could reflect what they got from him, not what they wanted (Simeon, *Historia regum*, II,
201).

[6] *Libellus*, ed. Rollason, 206.

[7] E. Cownie, 'Percy, William de (d. 1096 x 9)', in *ODNB*.

[8] *Cartularium*, ed. Atkinson, I, 1.

monastery at Lastingham in North Yorkshire. Whatever the strategic significance of this gift, it reveals (like the gift at Whitby) that substantial plots of land were available to enterprising anchorites.

Members of the Lacy family of Hereford and Pontefract also sponsored hermits, as well as monasteries and collegiate churches. Ilbert (d. *c.*1093) was probably the first Lacy to allow hermits to settle at Nostell near Wakefield in Yorkshire. He also made gifts to Selby. His son Robert I (d. before 1129) granted or confirmed to the hermits at Nostell the wood surrounding their chapel.[9] In the Hereford branch of the family, Robert's cousin Hugh I (d. 1108 x 1115?) became the patron of a colony of hermits in the Black Mountains on the borders between Wales and Herefordshire at Llanthony. The link between patron and hermit there resembled the link between Reinfrid and William de Percy, in that the leader of the hermits that settled in the Llanthony valley during the 1090s, a man named William, had been one of Hugh's household knights. In 1103, a cleric named Erneis arrived. He had been living as a hermit at a place called Edgarsley near Cannock Forest in Staffordshire; before that he had been a chaplain to Henry I's queen (Edith-) Matilda (1080–1118). William and Erneis built a church, and Matilda herself paid to have it adorned.[10] Like Reinfrid, these hermits appear to have used their influential connexions to secure sponsorship, finding willing patrons in those whom they previously served. Less is known about a monk named Malger and his servants who apparently sought Queen Matilda's help in setting up a hermitage. Matilda responded favourably. In 1116 x 1118, she instructed Vitalis Ingaine (who was probably the forester) and his friend William de Lisures to take these hermits to Luffield in Whittlewood Forest, Northamptonshire, on the king's leave, and afford them protection there.[11] During the 1120s, they found a new patron in Robert, the second earl of Leicester (1104–68), who granted land to Malger for the building of houses and an oratory. A generation later, King Stephen gave land to the hermits of Pheleley in Wychwood Forest (Oxfordshire); to the hermits of Red Moor at Stoneleigh, Warwickshire; and to a hermit in his forest at Writtle near Colchester.[12] By that date, the gifts of land given to hermits were generally much smaller than they had

---

[9] W. E. Wightman, *The Lacy Family in England and Normandy 1066–1194* (Oxford, 1966), 61–3.

[10] F. G. Cowley, *The Monastic Order in South Wales, 1066–1349* (Cardiff, 1977), 29–31; J. E. Burton, *Monastic and Religious Orders in Britain, 1000–1300* (Cambridge, 1994), 50.

[11] *Luffield Priory Charters*, ed. Elvey, I, 15–17. Vitalis probably inherited a forest serjeantry from his father, Richard (d. *c.*1110). At some point, he married William's daughter. See K. S. B. Keats-Rohan, *Domesday Descendants: A Prosopography of Persons Occurring in English Documents 1066–1166. II. Pipe Rolls to Cartae baronum* (Woodbridge, 2002), 533, 1009.

[12] *The Cartulary of the Abbey of Eynsham*, ed. H. E. Salter, Oxford Historical Society, 49, 52, 2 vols (1907–8), I, no. 32, (52); *English Episcopal Acta 14: Coventry and Lichfield, 1072–1159*, ed. M. J. Franklin (Oxford, 1997), 106–9; *Cartularium monasterii sancti Johannis Baptiste de Colecestria*, ed. S. A. Moore, Roxburghe Club, 2 vols (London, 1897), I, 38, 52, 53. On Stephen and his queen Matilda's interest in anchorites, see D. Crouch, *The Reign of King Stephen, 1135–1154* (Harlow, 2000), 316–17.

been in the aftermath of the Conquest, probably for the reason that there was less land available, but perhaps also because some of the early gifts, notably the plough-lands granted at Selby and Whitby, were intended to provide a cenobitic endowment. By comparison, King Stephen only granted seven acres to the hermits at Pheleley in the 1140s, and this was probably land they themselves had reclaimed from the woods.

Kings Henry II and Richard I pensioned numerous recluses, but John (as Ann Warren has shown) appears to have preferred hermits. In 1204 or 1205, he initiated a substantial alms gift of forty shillings per annum to the hermit of St Edwin's chapel in Birchwood in Sherwood Forest. This was a chantry endowment, which meant that a priest – the hermit – was paid to sing masses for the benefactor's soul, in this case for John's soul and those of his ancestors. John also granted half a plough-land in the forest at Knaresborough to the hermit Robert, in 1216.[13] Among his royal servants a notable patron of hermits was the career sheriff and constable William de Stuteville (d. 1203) whose estates lay mostly in the north but also in the south. His involvement with hermits can be traced back to the 1170s or 1180s when he granted to a hermit named Godard and his successors the hermitage of St Leonard on the River Loddon in Berkshire. This gift was not of his own initiative but in confirmation of a grant made by his uncle Nicholas (d. 1177), lord of Stratfield Saye and founder of Valmont abbey in Normandy, who had already granted Godard's hermitage to Valmont.[14] In later years, however, according to a thirteenth-century hagiographer, he sponsored Robert of Knaresborough by granting him alms and his permission to dwell in the forest. A conventional tale reports that his initial response as the king's officer was to expel the hermit, but that the latter eventually won him over.[15] The lesser laity also sponsored hermits at that date. One such sponsor was Robert, son of Walter de Broi of Bletsoe (which is a village several miles north of Bedford). During or before the period 1198 x 1205, he granted possession of the hermitage in the wood at Bletsoe to the hermit Robert Parage and his brethren, to hold from him and his heirs in free and perpetual alms. The gift included the hermitage and a croft abutting a place called Netherehei to the east. Robert also granted the hermits free pasture for five cows, five pigs, forty sheep, and a horse on his demesne in Bletsoe.[16] When set alongside his aristocratic contemporaries, King John and William de Stuteville, Robert, son of Walter, reveals that hermits found sponsors among the laity through all ranks of the landed hierarchy.

Among the ranks of the religious, bishops, abbots, monasteries, and collegiate churches were often generous sponsors. Monasteries, especially, had long

---

[13] On John's support of solitaries, see Warren, *Anchorites*, 151–5.

[14] *English Episcopal Acta 18: Salisbury, 1078–1217*, ed. B. R. Kemp (Oxford, 1999), no. 70 (at 49–50).

[15] VRK, 373.

[16] *English Episcopal Acta III: Canterbury, 1193–1205*, ed. C. R. Cheney and E. John (Oxford, 1986), no. 340 (at 12). For Walter de Broi, see Keats-Rohan, *Domesday Descendants*, 353.

supported members of their own communities who wished to live as anchorites in accordance with the Benedictine Rule, but they also took under their wing self-made ascetics who appealed to them or sought their favour. At the abbey of St Albans in Hertfordshire, for example, hermits captured the imagination of Abbot Geoffrey (1119–46), who developed an enthusiasm for them through his friendship with the hermit Christina of Markyate.[17] On her behalf, he commissioned or adapted a lavish psalter bound with edifying material, and through her influence he was transformed into an upholder of the eremitic profession.[18] Two female hermits pursuing a life of abstinence in a hovel on the abbey's manor of Eywood, which lay alongside Watling Street, benefited from his generosity when he built houses for them.[19] Interest in sponsoring hermits could also be institutional, especially where monasteries that had started off as communities of hermits retained or even cultivated their enthusiasm for eremitism. In the early twelfth century, Whitby, for example, acquired a hermitage at Goathland in the Esk valley, another in the vicinity of Hutton Mulgrave or Dunsley, a third at Westcroft near Hutton Bushel, and a fourth at Hood near Goathland, where a monk of Whitby took up residence.[20] In the early thirteenth century, it acquired yet another hermitage, at Saltburn farther up the coast, by the gift of its lay patron Roger de Argentum.[21] Through these acquisitions the monks maintained a link to their eremitic roots by welcoming hermits into the fold, cultivating their own, and accumulating hermitages.

The monks of Durham cathedral priory sponsored some of their brethren who wished to live as hermits. During the twelfth century, at least five monks of Durham retired to live as hermits on the island of Inner Farne.[22] Aelric is the first on record; one Aelwin was there when the hermit Bartholomew arrived in January 1151, and Prior Thomas (who probably joined him in 1162), and another hermit named William, followed in his footsteps.[23] Arrayed in skins, Bartholomew assumed the likeness of the desert fathers; but the chief model of inspiration for the monks was their patron St Cuthbert, who had withdrawn to live as a hermit upon Inner Farne with his abbot's permission.[24] Durham monks also took an interest in associating with independent hermits such as the venerable Aelric, hermit of Landieu at Wolsingham in Weardale, whom Godric of

---

[17] *Gesta abbatum*, ed. Riley, I, 21–2; *LCM*, 151.

[18] J. Geddes, 'The St Albans Psalter: The Abbot and the Anchoress', in *Christina*, ed. Leyser and Fanous, 197–216, at 207; cf. M. Powell, 'Making the Psalter of Christina of Markyate (the St Albans Psalter)', *Viator*, 36 (2005), 293–335.

[19] *Gesta abbatum*, ed. Riley, I, 80–2, 78.

[20] *Cartularium*, ed. Atkinson, I, 3, 49, 85–6, 161–2; II, 525–7; Burton, 'The Eremitical Tradition', 28.

[21] *Cartularium*, ed. Atkinson, I, 177: 'heremitorium meum de Saltburne'.

[22] On Durham's hermits, see V. M. Tudor, 'Durham Priory and Its Hermits in the Twelfth Century', in *Anglo-Norman Durham*, ed. Rollason et al., 67–78.

[23] Tudor, 'Durham Priory', 67–70; *VB*, 300.

[24] *VB*, 299, says that Cuthbert directed Bartholomew there in a vision.

Finchale encountered during the early years of the twelfth century. Godric's hagiographer Reginald reports that Aelric received his education from the monks of Durham and that when he died representatives of the community arrived to collect his body for burial in the priory cemetery.[25] A comparable example is that of Godric himself, who formed bonds with the priory through the care and support of its members. Durham's sponsorship of hermits is probably reflected in the numbers it sought to commemorate, for among the names enrolled in the Durham necrology, in addition to Godric of Finchale's, are *Columbanus anachorita* (on 18 September), *Godwinus heremita* (5 October), *Æilricus heremita*, and *Wlsin anachoreta* (both 23 x 29 February).[26] The same is probably true of St Albans, where an anchorite named Matilda appeared in a confraternity list, another named Aelward was entered in a necrology, and two more hermits, Roger and Sigar, were buried in the abbey church.[27] It is known that the last two were alive in the time of Abbot Geoffrey, whose enthusiasm for hermits may explain their prominence. The five remembered at Durham can perhaps be identified. Columbanus was probably the Durham monk of that name alive at the beginning of the twelfth century. Godwin may have been Godric's mentor Aelric, who is called Godwin in one manuscript of Godric's *Life*. This is not an error, because care is taken to explain the meaning of *Godwine*, whereas other manuscripts give the meaning of *Æthelric* (i.e. Aelric).[28] The Aelric on the list could be the monk of Durham who retired to Inner Farne. *Wlsin*, which is Latin for Wulfsige, may have been Wulfsige the recluse of Evesham (d. 24 Feb), whose day of death fits the obit.[29] The connexion is plausible because Durham's first prior, Ealdwine, came from Winchcombe, several miles south of Evesham. These various records indicate that Durham, like St Albans, maintained links with numerous hermits, and upheld its tradition of supporting them.

The picture is not dissimilar at monasteries elsewhere. Peterborough abbey, for example, maintained hermitages some miles away at Singleshole and in the

---

[25] *LG*, 45–6, 51–2.

[26] A. J. Piper, 'The Early Lists and Obits of the Durham Monks', in *Symeon of Durham: Historian of Durham and the North*, ed. D. W. Rollason (Stamford, 1998), 161–201, at 199, 191; cf. Durham Cathedral, dean and chapter library, MS. B. IV.24, fo. 17r. The twelfth-century obits entered against 23 February seem to pertain to 23–9 February.

[27] O. Pächt, C. R. Dodwell, and F. Wormald, *The St. Albans Psalter (Albani Psalter)*, Studies of the Warburg Institute, 25 (London, 1960), 29. On Roger and Sigar, see below.

[28] *Libellus*, ed. Rollason, 6–7n; *LG*, 51n; Tudor, 'Durham Priory', 70n. It was not uncommon to have more than one name, or a name in religion (*Godwine* means 'God's friend'): Bartholomew of Farne was christened Tostig and known to his friends as William. Christina of Markyate's baptismal name was Theodora. Both took religious names upon entering religion.

[29] L, BL, MS Lansdowne 427, fo. 22v. A thirteenth-century calendar from Evesham, witnessed by an eighteenth-century transcript in L, BL, MS Lansdowne 427, commemorated 'Wlsinus Monachus et Anachorita istius loci' (fo. 22v). The original, once preserved in L, BL, MS Cotton Vitellius E xvii, was partly destroyed in the fire of 1731. Wulfsige's name would have been in the margin, which has not survived. I am grateful to Peter Jackson for unearthing this snippet of evidence.

marshes of Peakirk and Eye at the end of the eleventh century or beginning of the twelfth.[30] A century later, during the 1190s, Ramsey abbey supervised a hermitage in Norfolk at Downham Market. Its keeper was a monk named Aillet, who had in his charge three brethren (*conversi*).[31] Gloucester abbey possessed woodland chapels, each with an associated hermitage, several miles away at Taynton and Basing. It acquired these hermitages before 1138. The first was apparently a gift bestowed by one Matilda de Watteville, lady of Taynton, which consisted of the hermits' chapel and an adjoining virgate of land (typically some twenty or thirty acres), which the hermits themselves may have assarted from the woods.[32] Worcester cathedral priory also appropriated a hermitage or two. During the 1150s, the bishop and convent reclaimed a hermitage at Packington in Warwickshire by disseising the dead hermit's son, who had taken hold of it on his hereditary claim. The monks subsequently restored it to its proper use.[33] By the 1190s, it was up and running as a hermitage and attracting benefactions in its own right under its principal patron, the local lord William Picot. Among those who joined William in making gifts towards paying for its repair were various relatively minor individuals, such as William's niece Juliana and the parson of Solihull.[34] It is plain from all these cases that plenty of people nurtured an interest in sponsoring and maintaining hermits, from the king and his sheriffs and barons, lesser nobles, and lowlier landowners to the abbots and brethren of the greater Benedictine monasteries and the odd parish priest. In some cases, there were diplomatic and strategic reasons for supporting hermits and eremitic communities, as may be discernible at Malvern and in the north. In others, the personal spirituality of the patrons, or the monastic traditions of sponsoring institutions, appear to have been the main motivating factors.

PIONEERS IN THE WILDERNESS

The availability of land and the willingness of landowners to accommodate and sponsor hermits, particularly in the period *c.*1070–*c.*1120, created ideal conditions for eremitism to thrive. More than ever, in this period, the exploitation of natural resources comes into view, for hermits were taking advantage of the wasteland by carving out farmsteads and erecting new oratories. The decades around 1100 were

---

[30] *Codex diplomaticus aevi Saxonici*, ed. J. M. Kemble, 6 vols (London, 1839–48), no. 984 (cf. S 68). This forgery reveals that there were hermitages at Singleshole and Eye at the time when it was forged.

[31] *Cartularium*, ed. Hart and Lyons, II, 190.

[32] *Historia et cartularium monasterii sancti Petri Gloucestriae*, ed. W. H. Hart, RS 33, 3 vols (1863–7), I, 116, 136–7, 224 (for the *terminus ad quem*), 352; II, 169; *English Episcopal Acta, 7: Hereford, 1079–1234*, ed. J. Barrow (Oxford, 1993), no. 18.

[33] *Cartulary*, ed. Darlington, no. 308.

[34] *Ibid.*, nos 312–16.

the age of the hermit pioneer; the age in which hermits, in a literal sense, lived up to their antique epithet *eremi cultores*: 'cultivators of the wilderness'. Their axes brought down trees and their billhooks cleared the undergrowth; their ploughs and mattocks broke virgin soil; ditches were dug and hedges were laid; enclosures sprang up, timber was cut, and buildings appeared, vegetable plots were planted, and land that had lain abandoned since Roman times was wrested back from nature. By these means and others, the metaphor *eremi cultores* – of cleansing the soul in the desert and bringing harmony to chaos – found practical application in the landscape. Hermits were not the only entrepreneurs to exploit the wastes when the latter were still abundant, but their moral authority won them patrons, and their determination to achieve salvation and escape social sins inspirited their industry. So far the present chapter has examined the contribution of sponsors to the maintenance of hermits, but as our focus shifts to the hermits themselves a fuller picture will begin to appear. For historians still have only a limited understanding of how hermits chose where to settle and how they transformed their patches of wilderness into sustainable, working farmsteads. To gain insights into these processes, it is worth examining the pioneering hermits Godric of Throckenholt (*c.*1060–*c.*1140) and Godric of Finchale (*c.*1070–1170), who both laboured to create their hermitages during the early twelfth century. Theirs are suitable case studies because their *Lives* (written during the last third of the century by authors associated with their hermitages) provide detailed insights into their industry. In their cases, the creation of a farmstead of some twenty or thirty acres took as many years or more, and a lot more labour than a hermit alone could manage. Yet the result at Finchale and Throckenholt, as at hermitages throughout England, was a new type of ideal settlement: a utopian plot, where devotion to God meant reliance upon nature.

Godric of Throckenholt was born in Wisbech, about the year 1060. Wisbech at that time was an island community surrounded by sparsely settled fens at the northern tip of Cambridgeshire, and by The Fens of west Norfolk.[35] The abbot of Ely and later his successor, the bishop, held it as a manor, but sizeable tracts of uncultivated terrain adjoined its borders. At the time of the Domesday survey in 1086 Wisbech could boast the richest fishery in the county, assessed to render some 33,000 eels annually to four abbots and an earl, each of whom had interests there. Twenty tenant fishermen accounted for this total, rendering anything between a few hundred and many thousands of eels each and holding their fisheries for a living in return.[36] Godric may have been one of them, for a decade or so later at the time of his conversion he appears as a man of means in charge of

---

[35] On this landscape, see *The Fenland Project Number 3: Marshland and the Nar Valley, Norfolk*, ed. R. J. Silvester, East Anglian Archaeology, report no. 45 (1988); and also *The Fenland Project Number 10: Cambridgeshire Survey, the Isle of Ely and Wisbech*, ed. D. Hall, East Anglian Archaeology, report no. 79 (1996).

[36] H. C. Darby, *The Domesday Geography of Eastern England* (Cambridge, 1952), 306; *Domesday Book; vol. 18: Cambridgeshire*, ed. A. Rumble (Chichester, 1981), 5, 55–6; 6, 2; 7, 12; 9, 4; 18, 9.

a boat and fishery.[37] For one obscure reason or another, he then disposed of his possessions and went to live as a hermit in a hollow in the woods. A conventional tale claims that he made up his mind to do this after St Andrew appeared to him, while he slept in his boat, and told him to spend the rest of his life performing penance. From the outset, Godric was seldom alone in this enterprise, finding workers to build his hermitage and servants to attend to his needs. He also won the approval of certain rich peasants and others from the neighbouring parishes or villages, who visited or made gifts to his hermitage and, in some instances, joined him there. One of these benefactors added several acres to the hermit's estate, granting that, for as long as he might live, his men should plough and sow the land he had bestowed.[38] With the help of such servants, Godric settled at Throckenholt. The place-name first appears in an eleventh- or twelfth-century charter from Peterborough abbey.[39] As well as the earliest notice of Throckenholt, it also contains the earliest references to nearby hermitages at Singleshole and in the marshes around Eye. These were probably recent assarts, created at the turn of the twelfth century when hermits were carving new abodes out of the wastelands. The hermitage at Throckenholt was one of many such hermitages sprung up at that time in the wastes of the northern fens.

Throckenholt is an Old English name signifying a wood where timber was cut for the ploughshare.[40] Finding abundant building materials and fuel there, Godric never had to return to Wisbech for any necessity; he also found enough iron at Throckenholt to make fittings for his buildings, which would probably have included bindings for timbers, bolts for doors, locks, and nails for attaching these items and for assembling furniture.[41] Before he left Wisbech he went to the smith to procure a spade. An axe and shears also surface among his possessions. Godric trapped red deer and hares, mended his clothes with strips of deerskin, and knelt to pray on a hassock of sedge.[42] For fuel, roofing sheds, and making up balks, he could have used turves; for thatching, reeds or sedge.[43] His hermitage comprised an oratory, raised from ground level as a precaution against flooding or vermin, and several other buildings, including a house or consulting room for receiving visitors and a stable for his cattle. Inside the oratory there was an altar and an image of Mary. Somewhere a cupboard held food. Godric slept sitting upright in a wooden settle, which he had designed with a high cradling back to

---

[37] GT, 23–5.

[38] *Ibid.*, 27, 33, 31.

[39] A version of the Wulfhere charter S 68 appears in *ASC* E, s.a. 656; otherwise, the earliest text of S 68 dates to *s.* xii[med]; cf. *English Episcopal Acta 31: Ely, 1109–1197*, ed. N. Karn (Oxford, 2005), no. 84n.

[40] P. H. Reaney, *The Place-Names of Cambridgeshire and the Isle of Ely*, EPNS, 19 (1943), 278–9.

[41] K. Leahy, *Anglo-Saxon Crafts* (Stroud, 2003), 23, 47, 130.

[42] GT, 31, where 'straps of red-deerskin' corrects my translation 'cords for tying venison'. Oliver Rackham (personal communication) kindly informs me that a hassock is a natural tussock of the sedge *Carex paniculata* or *Carex appropinquata*, which grows big enough to make a seat.

[43] H. S. Bennett, *Life on the English Manor* (Cambridge, 1937), 59.

support his head. Godric's hagiographer emphasizes the hermit's simple faith in God's provision, but he emerges from the narrative as a shrewd pioneer exploiting the resources around him. Summoned by St Andrew from what may well have been a burdensome fishery, Godric, like other hermits liberated from their responsibilities by withdrawal into the wasteland, served only a bountiful deity. Converts were in good supply. Godric, we are told, enlisted 'very many brethren' in his enterprise, some of whom are identified among those who granted land to his new pioneering settlement. Alward of Wisbech gained admission with the gift of two acres. The largest single gift was twelve acres of marsh. Most of the others were an acre or less of arable land, revealing that the hermitage grew through the generosity – and religious conversion – of richer peasants and minor gentry. Alward's case suggests that the hermits held their land in common and that postulants were expected to convey gifts. How much assarting had gone on in clearing the site is unknown, but the gifts of land – which totalled eighteen acres – may not have represented the entirety of its holdings. After Nigel became bishop of Ely (1133–69), he visited the hermitage and approved these gifts in a charter, thereby effectively confirming the hermits' right to settle.[44] From the bishop's vantage point, it was a useful concession. By accepting the hermitage as a *fait accompli*, he affirmed its right to exist while establishing his authority as lord of the manor. By extending its spiritualities and temporalities as diocesan, he enhanced its status while incorporating it into the parochial infrastructure. When Godric died, the settlement he had cultivated for over forty years duly fell to the bishop's disposal.

The outcome was not dissimilar in the case of Godric of Finchale, near Durham: his hermitage too devolved to the bishopric, as did other uncultivated plots farmed out to hermits in Durham diocese.[45] Encouraging hermits to cultivate wasteland could be a lucrative and undemanding policy. The end result in successful cases was at best a profitable farmstead, at worst with some loss of common, grazing, or hunting ground. Labour was volunteered. Moreover, at Throckenholt and Finchale it was expended for several decades. Godric of Finchale was born only a few miles from his Wisbech namesake, and probably within a few years, at Walpole in Norfolk. When he arrived at Durham early in the twelfth century, he had already lived as a hermit in several locations. Two miles outside the city walls in the bishop's forest he earmarked a small piece of dry land, grassy and flat, beside the river Wear where the remains of Finchale priory stand.[46] Experienced in finding sites to support his needs, he could have

---

[44] GT, 32–4.

[45] T. Licence, 'The Benedictines, the Cistercians and the Acquisition of a Hermitage in Twelfth-Century Durham', *JMH*, 29 (2003), 315–29, at 328.

[46] In the 1950s, a local farmer excavated some ruins at a site known as 'St Godric's Garth' about two-thirds of a mile downriver. Rejecting the likely discovery, in the 1920s, of Godric's church beneath the church of Finchale priory, he interpreted the ruins as the original hermitage buildings. In 2007, the author and Dr Gareth Atkins inspected the ruins, now much overgrown. They may be an unidentified hermitage associated with the priory, although not that of Godric himself. See C. R.

discerned that the place was habitable from the evidence of past occupation, not least the bones and foundations of buildings which he discovered there.[47] Since the Roman era, parts of England had tumbled down to woodland. Another location that had done so was part of the Forest of Bloxham in Oxfordshire, which straddled the western boundary of Stonefield parish in Wychwood Forest. Although it had since reverted to woodland, the area had been farmed (a villa has been found there) and may have betrayed its history to the hermits who reclaimed it in the 1120s or 1130s for the foundation of Pheleley hermitage.[48] The woodland cleared for Writtle hermitage near Colchester at roughly the same date lay along a wide track probably marking the remains of a Roman road. Roman tile survives in the ruined buildings there, again allowing the possibility that an assarting hermit chose a spot because it had once proven amenable to settlement. Roger of Markyate, similarly, may have discovered traces of Roman habitation at his woodland abode near Watling Street, as may the female hermits at Eywood. It is reasonable at least to suppose that pioneering hermits sought out sites that had once been inhabited, because land that had been inhabited could be cultivated again. Finchale then may have appealed for this reason.

Godric arrived in the 1110s or 1120s, using some influential friends in Durham to prevail upon the bishop to allow him to settle at Finchale. After securing the bishop's consent, he set to work erecting buildings. First up, under a stout oak, was a crude temporary dwelling, which was soon superseded in the eastern part of his plot by an oratory of the Virgin, attached to a domicile, both of rough timber and branches. Details gradually emerge that the floor of this oratory was strewn with straw, that a cistern for penitential immersions was dug into the earth inside and covered with a hatch, and that its altar to St Mary was raised upon steps. Above the altar, perhaps a little back from it and serving as a crossbeam or tabernacle, was a wooden shelf with a central wooden crucifix, communion vessels, and an image of the Virgin, likewise of wood.[49] Godric may have crafted the images himself, though he did have access to a sculptor and painter of icons, who visited his hermitage and gave him a gilded cross. In the appended domicile, he lived and kept his tools, including an iron-bladed or -edged spade, otherwise of wood but with an iron handle, and an iron-headed mattock. At this date, Godric possessed no other iron tools, although in later years he acquired axes, hatchets, and unspecified utensils. He cut up his food with a sharpened stone or rectangular wooden chopper. His quern was hidden away in

---

Peers, 'Finchale Priory', *Archaeologia Æliana*, 4th ser., 4 (1927), 193–220; cf. J. F. J. Smith, 'The Abridged Life of St. Godric and the Tragedy of Finchale Priory' (a booklet on sale at the Finchale priory shop in January 2007).

[47] *LG*, 69–70. On the Roman remains there, see V. M. Tudor, 'Reginald of Durham and St Godric of Finchale: A Study of a Twelfth-Century Hagiographer and His Major Subject', PhD thesis, University of Reading, 1979, 255.

[48] For the remains there, see O. Rackham, *The History of the Countryside* (London, 1986), 75.

[49] Beams of similar function, not uncommon in churches of this date, preceded the reredos.

a corner in the hope that it should avoid detection, for like any normal peasant Godric was obliged to grind his grain at his lord's mill, presumably on pain of a fine should the bishop's bailiffs discover that he was doing it elsewhere. Milling at home was a perfectly normal form of tax evasion, and Godric did nothing scurrilous in cheating his patron of his dues.[50]

With the passing years came further construction as cottages went up to house servants, visitors, and family members.[51] After they began to arrive, the oratory with its domicile tailored to solitary habitation no longer met the needs of the settlement, which was now a communal hermitage requiring living quarters, guesthouses, and a shared place of worship. New buildings served to meet these requirements, among them a church of St John the Baptist to the south of the oratory, which was joined to it by a thatched, weatherboarded cloister. The cloister and oratory subsequently became Godric's private quarters, and the church, his consulting room. The latter, built in the 1140s from stone broken up by a flood, measured approximately sixteen feet wide by thirty-four feet long.[52] Along its southern wall the hermit erected a storehouse and another consultation chamber. With the exception of these structures and the latrines – also to the south, which carried effluent downriver (and a stink downwind to the church) – construction was focused to the west, because the Wear to the east, arable land, and encircling thickets precluded it elsewhere. Initially Godric's assarting to the west of his church incurred the wrath of the neighbouring villagers, who had long commoned their cattle there, but after making their point by loosing their flock to munch on his ripening corn the villagers gave up.[53] Local resistance of this sort was an occupational hazard for hermits. A charter of *c.*1150 pertaining to Sawtry abbey in Huntingdonshire recounts that a local hermit named Edwin had to protect his hermitage with a double boundary ditch. He had begun the outer ditch in Sawtry marsh as a defence against shepherds who were seeking to burn down his dwelling, but after driving them away he had halted work until his lord, the forester Berengar Ingaine, granted him leave to complete the ditch.[54] More often ditches with fenced or hedged banks served to exclude destructive animals. Twelfth-century examples are recorded at Wiggenhall in Norfolk and Writtle in Essex.[55] At Writtle, King Stephen licensed the hermit to take from the forest any timber he required for his buildings, wood for fencing and fuel, and pasture for livestock. Where such privileges were extended to intrusive hermits, resentment could arise, as it did at Sawtry and Finchale. Hermits who settled without permission could also incur the wrath of landowners and foresters. When William de Stuteville discovered

[50] *LG*, 79, 80; Bennett, *English Manor*, 131.
[51] *LG*, 105, 112; 83 (for the servants).
[52] *Ibid.*, 152–4, 112, 162, 437; Peers, 'Finchale Priory', 199.
[53] *LG*, 341.
[54] *Cartularium*, ed. Hart and Lyons, I, 161.
[55] L, BL, MS Harley 2110, fo. 82v: 'infra circuitum fouearum'; *Cartularium*, ed. Moore, I, 52.

Robert's hermitage in the forest at Knaresborough, he sent his men to demolish it. If the hermit proved stubborn, they were to burn him alive in his hermitage, so the story goes.[56] Godric was fortunate in that he suffered no more than a setback. After the villagers launched their attack on his crops, they left him alone, although deer foraged freely through his orchard and brush. By assarting and land acquisition, Godric would eventually build up an estate of twenty or thirty acres, similar in size to the hermitage farmstead at Throckenholt.[57]

In his hunt through the wood for a suitable spot to settle, Godric had rejected a clearing of marshy, stony ground where barren fruit trees betrayed the poverty of the soil. The pasture he chose proved more fertile, supporting healthy crops of oats and barley. Godric would grind the grain, mixing in water and a half- or third-part ash from burnt roots, before kneading the dough into rolls for baking over the fire. Ash, aside from its penitential significance, served practically to bulk out the flour, just as the retention of these loaves for several months may have been necessitated more by the perishability of grain than any desire on Godric's part to eat bread rock-hard and hairy with mould.[58] At this stage he grew no beans or vegetables, instead collecting roots from the riverbank and woods, which he ground into meal and cooked without salt or fat. He would leave this mixture for weeks until it stank and formed a crusty outer layer. Then he would roll it into small dollops, which he soaked in foetid water. Godric's hagiographer claims that the hermit waited until they were soggy, swollen, and coated with a white-grey film, shaggy with mycelia, before eating them as a tasty substitute for vegetables. But somebody could have been pulling his leg. Godric's servants had seen him prepare these fermenting balls of meal but had never seen him consume them. Their likely function, before they became covered in mycelia, was to provide yeast to leaven the bread which Godric distributed every week to the poor.[59] The hermit also began to cultivate an orchard by clearing deadwood and grafting shoots from stunted fruit trees to healthier specimens near his oratory, trimming them to encourage new growth.[60] At some stage he acquired a cow. The expansion of his workforce and charitable activities prompted him to dig a vegetable garden to produce more food, this husbandry altogether adding apples, milk products, beans, and vegetables to his larder. Later, visitors could expect one of the hermit's servants to lay their table with oatmeal bread, curds, butter or cheese, or even fish fresh from the river: for, although Godric seldom ate fish himself, to feed his clients he had built a fish-weir, with narrow-necked

---

[56] VRK, 373.

[57] Bishop William, probably in the 1140s, granted an additional twenty acres, which the hermit used as pasture. See *LG*, 437, and 346 for his two bovates in Lothian.

[58] *LG*, 74–5, 79–80.

[59] *LG*, 83, 358; on yeast production, see A. Hagen, *A Handbook of Anglo-Saxon Food: Processing and Consumption* (Pinner, 1992), 8.

[60] *LG*, 81, 96.

basketwork traps of osier fixed into the superstructure, for catching salmon, conger eels, and other fish, and for trapping fish in his ponds.[61]

About the year 1130, and on friends' advice, Godric employed a servant whose duties included care of his public affairs. One principal need was for a buffer to preserve his privacy: a receptionist such as the one who assisted Roger of Markyate by receiving his visitors.[62] The servant Godric took on, for a total of eleven years, was the son of his brother William. In the mornings, he had to lead the cow to pasture and by sunset bring it home.[63] Others entering Godric's service from nearby villages may have scented opportunities to advance a career, for, with abbots, monks, gentry, craftsmen, and merchants passing through to consult the hermit, his recommendation could reach a range of potential employers. Friendly Cistercians certainly recruited among his *familia*. Reginald reports that upon Godric's recommendation humble individuals secured posts at one or more of the great northern Cistercian abbeys.[64] During his closing years, Godric probably had numerous labourers. Reginald depicts him at work in the fields with 'very many attendants' (although his claim that they witnessed a miracle gave him a motive for exaggerating the head-count). If such a workforce existed it was probably seasonal rather than permanent. One year, Godric gathered some workers to clear some part of the wood. Another year, when his fields needed ploughing, the aged though not yet bedridden hermit summoned men from the neighbouring village, who brought their oxen.[65] By this stage, as at Throckenholt, some may have owed the hermit labour services. His servants performed errands, bore produce to market on horseback, prepared meals, emptied fish-traps, ran around after their master, complained, neglected their duties, and stole money, cheese, and grain.[66] The grain-thief thought it a plausible lie that he was bearing grain to sell for salt in Newcastle (revealing the sorts of responsibilities that Godric devolved to his subordinates). When the hermit died, in 1170, his hermitage reverted to the bishopric.

Godric of Throckenholt and Godric of Finchale resemble many hermits of their generation in that they sought self-sufficiency to escape reliance on the world. Both spent the first thirty or forty years of their lives at work in the world before retiring dissatisfied with their labours. The wastes promised new opportunities, so long as they could win sponsors and meet the challenge to trust in God's provision. In their hagiography, this challenge resembles the challenge forced upon the Israelites in their desert tabernacles: to survive their journey through the wilderness on manna

---

[61] On his sensitivity towards genteel diets, see *LG*, 206; on his fishponds ('stagna piscarii sui') and weir set-up ('retinaculorum meorum orbiculares semitas, que sunt in ipso fluuii gurgite'): *LG*, 187–8, cf. 123, 125, 240–1. See further, J. M. Stearne and M. Foreman, 'Medieval Fishing Tackle', in *Medieval Fish, Fisheries and Fishponds in England*, ed. M. Aston, BAR British Series, 182 (Oxford, 1988), 137–86.

[62] *LCM*, 87, 97.

[63] *LG*, 121–2.

[64] *Ibid.*, 272.

[65] *Ibid.*, 110, 353, 265.

[66] *LG*, 123 (complaints), 160, 252 (meals, fish-traps), 244 (errands), 195, 244, 345 (theft).

alone. God's provision is a theme in the *Lives* of the two Godrics, although the manna here is the unexpected fish in the fishpond, or a wild animal surrendering to capture, or the barrel of ale inexplicably discovered in the cupboard at Throckenholt. Such instances of divine munificence proved the maxim, God will provide. Normally, however, hermits survived not on manna but by the constant exertions of seasonal labour: by ploughing and sowing, ditch-digging, and hedging in the spring; breaking up fallow land, woodcutting, and hurdling in summer; through reaping, mowing, thatching, and ploughing in the autumn, and through ploughing and woodcutting in winter. Without assistance pioneering was tough, but when a group of like-minded individuals pooled their resources, as at Throckenholt, they could look forward to a future disburdened of duties to lords and the expectations of kinsmen. Proof that pioneering worked lies in the fact that the commonest sort of hermitage in the records is neither the planned foundation, planted and endowed by a patron, nor the isolated dwelling, but rather the organic, spontaneous sort visible at Throckenholt and Finchale and often associated with new hermits. From the perspective of their patrons, such as Bishop Nigel of Ely or the various bishops of Durham who sponsored Godric of Finchale, quitclaiming assarts to these hermits was a convenient form of benefaction, which King Stephen employed in conventional fashion at Writtle and Pheleley. In most cases, the total area under cultivation was approximately a virgate: typically some twenty or thirty acres. Throckenholt held at least eighteen acres; Finchale, well over twenty, and Writtle, by Richard I's reign, twenty-four.[67] The hermitage at Packington in Warwickshire and the hermitage at Taynton in Gloucestershire, when confirmed by the diocesans in the mid-twelfth century to the convents at Worcester and Gloucester respectively, each came with a virgate attached.[68] At all these eremitic farmsteads the tenants-in-chief had worked their way to virgator status by recruiting labour, assarting, and acquiring land. The examples here presented suggest that over a few decades such a hermitage could achieve sufficient acreage to feed between half a dozen and a dozen members. This autarkic existence could hardly have been more different from that of the recluse.

LIVING IN A CELL

If hermits were able to scratch out their livelihood from the soil, recluses were in a different position. The only soil a recluse could scratch (in the absence of a garden) was the dirt dropping into the grave that sometimes yawned in the floor

---

[67] K. C. Newton, *The Manor of Writtle: The Development of a Royal Manor in Essex, c.1086–c.1500* (London, 1970), 8.

[68] *Cartulary*, ed. Darlington, no. 308; *Hereford*, ed. Barrow, no. 18. Note, though, that a virgate on the Gloucester estates could be anything between twenty-eight and sixty-four acres: Miller and Hatcher, *Rural Society*, 140.

of the cell. If recluses needed to work they were obliged to assume sedentary occupations such as the production of books and textiles. The recluse Guy, who wrote to Bishop Herbert of Norwich (d. 1119), had an appetite for spiritual writings. His cell contained many books, although there is no way of knowing whether he was involved in producing them.[69] Wulfric of Haselbury bound and copied books for use in the adjacent church. He must have had a work-surface of some sort and the materials necessary for training a young man of his acquaintance to be a scribe. A female supplicant brought him a piece of precious cloth that was suitable for covering a book.[70] Recluses occupied in the production and decoration of textiles may have kept such items as drop-spindles for spinning, two-beam or horizontal looms for weaving, kit for embroidery, and fabrics and threads. Aelred of Rievaulx cautioned his reclusive sister and recluses generally against making dainty girdles and pouches for youthful monks or clerics. The author of *Ancrene Wisse* added caps and lace to the list of inappropriate objects and encouraged his female recluses to make or mend church vestments instead, and garments for the poor.[71] In the early thirteenth century, at Rochester cathedral, a curtain was hung between the brethren and the high altar during Lent. This curtain, and a cloth for the altar of the Virgin, was the gift of the recluse Sunegifu, who may have woven them in her anchor-house. The church at Sonning in Berkshire kept a casket-cover and girdle, both of red silk, which a recluse named Alice had donated before 1220.[72] Dunstan, according to eleventh-century tradition, had busied himself working gold in his tiny cell. When the devil was foolish enough to assail him, he had dexterously tweaked his nose with his blistering, red-hot tongs.[73] Gold-work required a small hearth, a crucible, moulds, a bench, and a miniature anvil, as well as metalworking tools. The output of a reclusive goldsmith might have included shrines, crucifixes and communion vessels, ornamental covers and decorative mounts for service books, and gold thread for ecclesiastical vestments. A priestly recluse such as Dunstan, of course, might have laboured not to sustain himself but to glorify the Lord.

Most recluses had their meals supplied by standing arrangement. A patron or a pension paid for the food and for the wages of a servant to deliver it. The recluse only had to hand empty dishes back through the window. Wulfric had arranged that the monks of Montacute priory should deliver his food, although they were not always reliable. At other times, he subsisted on loaves, fishes, and other multiplying gifts left by visitors. Richer recluses drew pensions from their own private resources. The aristocratic sisters Loretta, who was enclosed at Hackington outside Canterbury (1219–*c*.1265), and Annora, a recluse at Iffley outside Oxford (1232–*c*.1241), are

---

[69] *Epistolae Herberti de Losinga, primi episcopi Norwicensis, Osberti de Clara et Elmeri, prioris Cantuariensis*, ed. R. Anstruther, Publications of the Caxton Society, 8 (Brussels, 1846), 95.

[70] *WH*, 45.

[71] *Opera omnia I*, ed. Hoste and Talbot, 643; *Ancrene Wisse*, ed. Millett, I, 160.

[72] Lehmann-Brockhaus, *Lateinische Schriftquellen*, II, no. 3764 (401); no. 4249 (537).

[73] *Memorials*, ed. Stubbs, 84–5.

cases in point. Annora planned for her retirement by arranging to retain a hundred shillings per annum, a sum more than double an average recluse's salary. In addition to this annuity, she received occasional gifts of firewood, clothing, and wheat. Loretta received wheat, barley, oats, and bacon from the countess of Eu, probably on top of her own provision.[74] Poorer recluses (or those keener on the ideal of poverty, such as the women addressed by Aelred and the author of *Ancrene Wisse*) tried to pay their way with their handicrafts, but resorted to corrodies or charity when necessary.[75] Vegetarianism was encouraged and parsimony, praised. The recluse at Minster-in-Thanet in the eleventh century survived on a non-Lenten diet of beans, apples, and altar offerings. Aelred advised recluses struggling with abstinence to take two meals a day. For the first, he suggested a pound of bread with a small portion of vegetables or beans (or at least a mixtil), cooked with oil, butter, or milk. For the main meal, a milk- or fish-dish seasoned with apples and raw herbs would have sufficed. Food was to sustain the body, not to appease hunger. In Lent, of course, the diet was supposed to be stricter.[76] The author of *Ancrene Wisse* emphasized only the important point, that recluses should be vegetarians. He wrote more about clothing, which was to be plain, warm, and well made. In winter, the recluse was to put on big cosy shoes; in summer light shoes or bare feet were appropriate. Wimples, warm caps, or veils were decent headgear, but rings, brooches, patterned belts, and gloves were vanities. Aelred recommended thick skins for winter, a tunic for summer, and a pair of padded undergarments. The recluse's veil was not to be made of fine or precious cloth (dark fabric would do), and she was not to hoard boots, shoes, or slippers.[77] A well-wisher once sent Wulfric a wolf- or fox-skin cloak because the recluse was shivering in the cold. Later, in the 1220s or early 1230s, another kind benefactor bequeathed a cloak to the recluse Lucy in the cemetery at Bury St Edmunds abbey.[78]

The average recluse probably employed a single servant to run errands and to collect her food. Wulfric employed only one, a boy from the village, who kept a key to the outer door of his anchor-house. When Wulfric needed a staple for the door on one occasion, he sent his boy to the blacksmith. Gilbert of Sempringham realized that the women enclosed against the wall of his parish church required a body of dedicated servants, so he appointed some poor girls from the neighbour-hood to serve them in secular dress. Later, he raised their status to that of lay sisters, the second branch of his nascent order, although he was reluctant to impose vows on them because they were simple and ignorant. So he taught them how to live devoutly.[79] Aelred advised that a recluse should appoint as her servant an old woman not given to gossiping. 'Seldom can a recluse be found nowadays',

[74] *WH*, 59, 111; Warren, *Anchorites*, 165–6.
[75] *Opera omnia I*, ed. Hoste and Talbot, 639; *Ancrene Wisse*, ed. Millett, I, 160.
[76] Rollason, 'Translation and Miracles', 210; *Opera omnia I*, ed. Hoste and Talbot, 648–9.
[77] *Ancrene Wisse*, ed. Millett, I, 158–60; *Opera omnia I*, ed. Hoste and Talbot, 649.
[78] *WH*, 44; Madox, *Formulare anglicanum*, 423.
[79] *WH*, 37–8; and *The Book of St Gilbert*, ed. R. Foreville and G. Keir (Oxford, 1987), 35, 37.

he complained, 'without some wittering old woman or gossiping wife at her window'. Once appointed, the discreet old lady was to guard the door of the anchorhold (probably the door of an outer parlour), admitting worthy visitors and turning away others. This must have been a full time job. It was also this woman's responsibility to receive and keep safe the recluse's supplies, and to delegate onerous duties to a second, more junior servant – a girl, whose offices were to bring water and firewood and cook the recluse's meals. The recluse also needed a confessor. Aelred recommended that she should find a wise, respectable old priest from a nearby monastery or church.[80] Any sensible recluse would have done so instinctively. At Bury St Edmunds, Seitha habitually confided in the pious sacrist Toli (d. 1096) seventy years before Aelred wrote.[81] Yet the author of *Ancrene Wisse* was distrustful of secular priests and even less trusting of monks. Writing to recluses possessed of two rooms, the cell and the parlour, he located the maid or maids in the latter. His instruction was that recluses should address their maids through the cell window and talk to visitors through the parlour window. Such an arrangement possessed the advantage that the maids might act as witnesses to what was said and done, thus warding off any slander from disgruntled clients. *Ancrene Wisse* enlarged upon Aelred's complaint against the ubiquitous crone who fed the recluse every titbit of gossip: a cackling magpie. The phenomenon had resulted in a saying: 'You can hear the news from a mill or market, a smithy, or an anchor-hold.'[82]

Set at the heart of the community at the parish church, it was an unwise recluse that entered her cell to achieve peace and quiet. In such a position, pursuing such a profession, the recluse was a captive audience to whoever wished to bend her ear. The *Life* of Wulfric of Haselbury shows all sorts of requests and complaints being voiced at Wulfric's window, but these were the significant matters which its author thought fit to mention. Mundane, trivial, and repetitive approaches are not equally represented. Always, priests have certain parishioners who make inordinate demands on their time. The average recluse too must have had hangers-on: already we have noted the ubiquitous gossip-monger loitering at the window, but attention-seekers, inquisitive children, and obsessive personalities could scarcely have been unfamiliar. Those that gave the recluse gifts would have expected her attention in return. The recluse, moreover, would have had her own special clients whose needs occupied her interests (a subject discussed in a later chapter). There is no way of gauging the amount of traffic to any anchor-house; the more famous its occupant, the wider her appeal would have been. No doubt it was possible to live as a recluse and engage more in temporal matters than in spiritual ones, and many recluses appear to have found various ways of

---

[80] *Opera omnia I*, ed. Hoste and Talbot, 638–40.

[81] T. Licence, 'History and Hagiography in the Late Eleventh Century: The Life and Work of Herman the Archdeacon, Monk of Bury St Edmunds', *EHR*, 124 (2009), 516–44, at 529.

[82] *Ancrene Wisse*, ed. Millett, I, 28, 27, 29, 36.

making a living. Manuals such as Aelred's or *Ancrene Wisse*, with their devotional recommendations, may mislead us into thinking that a recluse did nothing but pray and occupy her time with psalms. The stereotypes of the recluse as an estate manager, schoolmistress, gossip-monger, or weaver of dainty garments for handsome young clerics, however, may be closer to the common reality than the image of the saintly ascetic. The suggestion in these manuals is that the anchorhouse had become an institution and that recluses could undertake all sorts of practical roles.

Recluses, like hermits, found sponsors throughout the social hierarchy, from the king, his barons and bishops down to the lowliest parishioners in towns and villages. During the eleventh century, it was normal to sustain a recluse on the income derived from some manor. Ælfwen of St Benet's probably lived on the rent from Ormesby, Wihtgar at Bury St Edmunds on that of Southwold, and Mantat probably on the rent of Twywell and Conington. From the twelfth century, the Pipe Rolls reveal that the king's officers paid for recluses from the income of the Exchequer. Bishops paid for them out of their episcopal revenues. Nigel of Ely (1133–69), at the time of his death, was supporting six recluses. The bishop of London, *c.*1160, supported only one.[83] In 1176, Peterborough abbey supported two in the town or abbey of Peterborough itself and a third recluse at Oundle in Northamptonshire.[84] The lay baron Judhael of Totnes (d. 1123 x 1129) retained one on his estate at Barnstaple in Devon, in the years around 1113, much like the nobleman Sigefyrth a hundred years earlier.[85] The hermitage at Ardland, in the Forest of Dean in Gloucestershire, passed with the hermit's consent to the Cistercian abbey of Flaxley, in the 1190s, after its occupant became a recluse in order to devote himself to prayer. To support him in this, and in response to petitions from many people, the abbot and convent of Flaxley agreed to make provision for a priest to say the office in his chapel, for all his food and clothing, and for the needs of those dwelling there with him. They promised to make these provisions for the rest of his life.[86] In the 1220s and 1230s, the recluse Vitalis lived at a chapel at Thornham in Suffolk. During these decades, he acquired more than twenty acres and various rents through the generosity of over a dozen benefactors from Thornham and its environs. The meagreness of their gifts hints at a contingent of peasantry among them. Gila of Rishangles, the daughter of Peter of Winderville, gave two pieces of land in the fields of a nearby village. Hawise, the daughter of Alexander of Mellis, gave two acres in the fields of Thornham, saving certain rents. Bartholomew de Breche granted an acre.

[83] PR, 16 Henry II (1169–70), 96; cf. Warren, *Anchorites*, 57 (who counts seven at Ely), and see *Ely*, ed. Karn, 34.

[84] PR, 23 Henry II (1176–7), 105.

[85] Herman of Tournai, *De miraculis s. Mariae Laudunensis*, PL 156: 961–1018, at col. 984. This account must be treated with great care because it is full of errors. On Judhael, see J. B. Williams, 'Judhael of Totnes: The Life and Times of a Post-Conquest Baron', *ANS*, 16 (1994), 271–89.

[86] *The Cartulary... of Flaxley*, ed. Crawley-Boevey, no. 25. Warren, *Anchorites*, 16–17.

Ascelin Breton of Yaxley granted a rent of three quarters of a penny, and William, son of Nigel of Thornham Parva, bestowed half an acre in front of the recluse's chapel. The greatest benefactor, Robert of Cranley, granted one and a half acres adjoining the chapel, half an acre in Blakelond, one rood in Langelond, three roods in Osegotescroft, a piece of meadow in Nortcroftmedwe, and the rent of twelve pence paid by his tenant Walkelin.[87] This roll call of support indicates that recluses owed as much to the small-scale generosity of laypeople in the thirteenth century as they did in the eleventh, when the parishioners of Minster offered apples and beans to Ælfwen.

---

[87] *Eye Priory Cartulary and Charters*, ed. V. Brown, Suffolk Charters, 12, 13, 2 vols (1992–4), nos. 182–3, 185–97, 200, 202.

5

Eradicating sin, in theory

The purpose of this book so far has been to identify a plausible context in which the rise of hermits and recluses may be explained as a historical phenomenon; and it has been argued up to this point that an idea which began to grow during the Anglo-Saxon period, when anchorites developed a reputation as individuals who won God's approval, flourished in the favourable conditions of the eleventh century, when they emerged across Western Europe as champions of renunciation, who stood for a purer, holier life patterned on the life of the desert fathers. Recluses, unlike hermits, chose white martyrdom in the form of self-imprisonment, but all anchorites ideally were united in their rejection of worldly self-interest and sin. In the eleventh and twelfth centuries, they flourished by supporting themselves and by winning sponsorship at all levels of society. To some extent, the Norman Conquest could have worked as a catalyst in the rise of anchorites at Great Malvern and in the North, or because anachoresis was a profession admired by the conquerors and the conquered alike, but it now appears more doubtful that the rise of anchorites should be viewed as 'a post-Conquest conservative response to a changing world'.[1] Anchorites were making an impact in England and in Normandy before the invaders came, as a current of ascetic spirituality, which was exerting its influence through large parts of Western Europe, rekindled latent interest in them. Moreover, although hermits and recluses looked to the desert fathers, their new form of monasticism could hardly be called conservative: rather, it rehearsed the old paradox whereby radical innovation masquerades as a return to first principles – that blend of conservatism and radicalism which characterizes revolutions. Nor is it any more apparent, after four chapters spent investigating anchorites, that they attained their influence by bridging gaps between conquerors and conquered, or by acting as arbiters in the resolution of disputes. The possibility remains that their aim was to find freer outlets for their religious fervour, as Leclercq and, more recently, Jestice suggested – or indeed to free themselves from the constricting bonds of society. But there is still plenty of terrain to explore before any of these hypotheses can be validated, or another hypothesis inserted in their stead.

[1] Warren, *Anchorites*, 287.

The second part of this book (which has its roots in the previous chapter) sets out to investigate why so many different people chose to become, and chose to sponsor, hermits and recluses. What could they have hoped to achieve by this? And what was the useful function of these individuals in relation to the society that sponsored them? It is clear now that any broad answer to these questions must to some extent relate to other parts of Europe; for the phenomenon was not confined to England, even if its particular English manifestations betray the influence of Anglo-Saxon ascetic ideals and English patterns of monasticism, lordship, and parochial organization. Yet to find answers to these questions is not an easy business. Most sources touching the subject of anachoresis were not written by anchorites but by their critics or admirers, so we cannot readily attempt to rethink the thoughts of the anchorites themselves without playing into the hands of commentators who sought to present them in a certain light. This problem need not impede our inquiry so long as we are aware of it, because the ways in which medieval people interpreted, or misinterpreted, anchorites tell us just as much about the place of those figures in society as their own thoughts on the matter would do if we had them. A promising way to approach the initial question 'why did people become or sponsor anchorites?' is to start by examining how those who wrote about them modelled them in their imaginations; for these models should reveal what anachoresis stood for in the minds of self-selecting commentators, mostly monastic hagiographers, who, by the twelfth century, generally approved of anchorites, as we have seen. In the case of Goscelin and numerous other monks, it has also been seen that these writers were well placed to comment on anachoresis, because they stopped to talk with anchorites and listen to what they had to say. Anchorites of course (in the sense that they were a category of vowed religious with otherworldly objectives) had more in common with the monks who wrote about them than with almost anyone else.

During the eleventh century, as we have already seen, the anchoretic life came to be regarded as a model of spiritual perfection: in particular, monks began to regard it, almost unthinkingly, as a career-enhancing attribute in the hagiography of any saint. If this reveals anything, it reveals a desire at work within society to establish some standard of holiness. The present chapter aims to identify the qualities of that nascent ideal by asking what it meant to become a model of spiritual perfection – a question which can only be considered properly in relation to the performance of penance; for penance was prerequisite to the process of improving or perfecting sinful humanity. Spiritual perfection and penance are both ideas which relate to the eradication of sin, in that the former conjures up the image of a sinless or near-sinless condition – to the extent that any human might achieve this – whereas penance was the means by which a sinner's debt to God could be written off. Sin, of course, was the inevitable human failing: the tendency towards wickedness which corrupted Adam and Eve and tainted their countless descendents. Combating its devastating effects and saving damnable humanity from punishments due in the afterlife was the pastoral role of the church, and the penitential system was its essential saving mechanism. To perform penance meant to undertake prescribed actions such as reciting the psalms or fasting, either in public or in private, often for a fixed period of time, to atone for sin and make reparation to God.[2] The drive to create a model of spiritual perfection in eleventh-century Europe coincided with much renewed interest in penance, which in certain cases was fuelled by friends of the eremitic movement such as the emperor Otto III and Peter Damian, although other proponents of penance were far less interested in anachoresis, notably Ælfric and his co-reformers in England.[3] Their example shows that interest in penance and enthusiasm for anachoresis did not necessarily go hand in hand. Nevertheless, over the course of the eleventh century anchorites did manage to persuade many people, including influential monks in England, that their particular vocation was a path to spiritual perfection. Now one way of explaining this renewed interest in penance, the rise of anachoresis, and the unprecedented scale of conversion to monastic life in the period 1050–1150 is to see these phenomena as symptoms of a widespread anxiety about sin: about its stranglehold upon humanity and its threat to the welfare of souls. Heightened anxiety about sin could explain these parallel trends.

In recent years, the debate on sin has shied away from monks and hermits (whose penances are of less interest to social historians bent on reconstructing the experiences of the laity), to focus instead on the effectiveness of the penitential system. It has asked, how willing were would-be penitents to perform recommended penances, and did the system provide assurance that their debts to God had been paid? Historians disagree on whether penance was popular or infrequent, but a point relevant to our inquiry has come forth from the debate, in that prominent bishops, monks, and other clergy of the eleventh century were eager that more penance should be performed, both inside and outside the monasteries.[4] Their thirst for penance suggests that those who were setting high standards of religious conduct (reforming bishops, agents of Cluny, and new hermits among them) expected more from sinners than sinners were willing or able to undertake. It may have been largely as a result of their expectations that

---

[2] For an introduction, see S. Hamilton, *The Practice of Penance, 900–1050* (London, 2001). On penance in its European context, see R. Meens, 'Introduction, Penitential Questions: Sin, Satisfaction and Reconciliation in the Tenth and Eleventh Centuries'; and *idem*, 'Penitentials and the Practice of Penance in the Tenth and Eleventh Centuries', in *Early Medieval Europe*, 14 (2006), 1–6 and 7–21.

[3] For Otto, see Hamilton, 'Otto III's Penance'. On the penitential interests of the reformers, see *idem*, 'Rites for Public Penance in Late Anglo-Saxon England', in *The Liturgy of the Anglo-Saxon Church*, ed. H. Gittos and M. B. Bedingfield, HBS Subsidia, 5 (2005), 65–103, at 65–89; and C. Cubitt, 'Bishops, Priests and Penance in Late Saxon England', *Early Medieval Europe*, 14 (2006), 41–63.

[4] Cluny advertised itself to the laity as a haven for would-be penitents, where they should hurry to wash away their sins: Cowdrey, *The Cluniacs*, 128. Wulfstan (d. 1023), bishop of London 996–1002 and York 1002–23, thought that public penance was too little observed in his era: see the discussion in Hamilton, 'Rites for Public Penance', starting at 65.

the eleventh and early twelfth centuries developed an almost palpable anxiety about sin, which is manifest in the writings of reformist popes and monks and in the charters of monastic benefactors. Jonathan Riley-Smith, David Crouch, Christopher Harper-Bill, and Marcus Bull among others have noted the many expressions of fear and gloom. Riley-Smith attributed this fearfulness to the inadequacy of the resources available by which the laity could meet the demands or aspirations of the religious, while Bull ventured the observation that the popularity of the monasteries seems to indicate widespread dissatisfaction with the lay condition.[5] C. N. L. Brooke has observed that senior monk-bishops of the late eleventh century would sometimes doubt that anybody could be saved outside the walls of a monastery, reserving their greatest admiration for ascetics who took on impossibly harsh penances.[6] Although Sarah Hamilton has revealed that the practice of penance in various forms was widespread and popular through the period 900–1050, this need not mean that the penitents, religious converts, and pilgrims who undertook to eradicate the stain of sin were satisfied that the job had been done, or that it could ever be done completely.[7] If the real problem, as monks and hermits were intimating, was the stranglehold of sin upon human beings and the world, the penitential exertions of people who lived in the world might not have possessed any lasting value. In view of this objection, the ideal solution to sin would have combined renunciation of the world with the rigours of the penitential system, to generate a trustworthy formula for purification. Hermits and recluses, more than anyone else, advocated this formula and followed it in their lives. In a sin-troubled age, anachoresis was set to become a new gold standard for holiness.

What defined this new gold standard for holiness? What did it mean in practice to be a model of spiritual perfection? These are not straightforward questions because ideas of what the model entailed – that is, allegories for interpreting anachoresis – may have arisen or fallen from favour in accordance with developments in the eremitic and reclusive vocations, as outlined in the first three chapters, and in perceptions of how sin was to be tackled. There is not space here to analyse every last allegory that won acceptance during these centuries. So we shall limit our attention to three important interpretations of anachoresis, which were apparently subject to fashion. The first – interpretation number

---

[5] E.g. J. Riley-Smith, *The First Crusaders, 1095–1131* (Cambridge, 1997), 27–8. Bull also comments, 'it would be unwise to underestimate the capacity of laymen to become burdened by a long sequence of individually private, and often relatively minor, sins': *Knightly Piety and the Lay Response to the First Crusade: The Limousin and Gascony, c.970–c.1130* (Oxford, 1993), 166, 173. Cf. D. Crouch, 'The Troubled Deathbeds of Henry I's Servants: Death, Confession, and Secular Conduct in the Twelfth Century', *Albion*, 34 (2002), 24–36; and C. Harper-Bill, 'Searching for Salvation in Anglo-Norman East Anglia', in *East Anglia's History: Studies in Honour of Norman Scarfe*, ed. C. Harper-Bill, C. Rawcliffe, and R. G. Wilson (Woodbridge, 2002), 19–40, at 22.

[6] C. N. L. Brooke, *Popular Religion in the Middle Ages: Western Europe 1000–1300* (London, 1984), 147, emphasizes the pessimism of the monk-bishops Peter Damian and Anselm.

[7] Hamilton, *Practice of Penance*, 7, 15, 209.

one – viewed the solitary life as a self-imposed exile from sin, which counted as a satisfactory penitential or ascetic exercise. It was satisfactory in the sense that it eradicated all sin, thereby restoring humanity's pristine condition. The second interpretation presented anachoresis as the preliminary phase, only, of a longer penitential process that ran on into the afterlife. The third interpreted it more as the imitation of Christ and as a response to his call to renounce worldly things and follow in his footsteps. Hagiography appears to suggest that monastic writers before the end of the eleventh century, generally, preferred the first of these interpretations, whereas twelfth-century hagiographers inclined towards the second and the third. Somewhere in the middle, there was a transition through which the three vied for primacy. Afterwards the exile interpretation remained, but only in as much as old ideas sometimes linger after novel ideas have already begun to supplant them. The rise of the second interpretation could be attributed to a growing conviction that sin could not be eradicated solely through pious living or penance on earth. The third interpretation rose in tandem with developments in the eremitic movement, which were clearest in its latest phase (i.e. after *c*.1090). This chapter examines these three interpretations and asks what the relative popularity of each at different times may reveal about how anachoresis was perceived and how perceptions of it developed in the era 1050–1200.

MODEL 1: EXILE AS A SATISFACTORY PENANCE

The belief that exile, as a penitential or simply an ascetic exercise, could cleanse the soul from sin took hold in England as early as the seventh century, through the influence of Irish missionaries and holy men (*peregrini*).[8] God was a jealous lover. 'White martyrdom' (to the Irish, *bán martre*) 'meant that for the sake of God a man would separate himself from all that he loved', and commit his life to God.[9] In her study of voluntary exile in Anglo-Saxon England, Dorothy White-lock reinterpreted the Old English poem *The seafarer* as 'the monologue of a religious ascetic who had chosen exile on and beyond the sea for the love of God'.[10] His pilgrimage was one from death to life; the world behind him was 'dead'. Although his body was made of heavy and earthy matter, his soul was light and aerial. Like a bird it left his body and soared over land and sea to return

---

[8] For a detailed survey of the early period, see J. Leclercq, *Aux sources de la spiritualité Occidentale: Étapes et constantes*, Les Éditions du Cerf, 21 (Paris, 1964), 35–77.

[9] C. A. Ireland, 'Some Analogues of the OE "Seafarer" from Hiberno-Latin Sources', *Neuphilologische Mitteilungen*, 92 (1991), 1–14, at 2.

[10] On the hermit as exile, see Leclercq, '"Eremus" et "eremita"', 13; and Clayton, 'Hermits', 152; and references. D. Whitelock, 'The Interpretation of *The Seafarer*', in *The Early Cultures of North-West Europe: H. M. Chadwick Memorial Studies*, ed. C. Fox and B. Dickins (Cambridge, 1950), 261–72. See also J. C. Pope, 'Second Thoughts on the Interpretation of *The Seafarer*', *ASE*, 3 (1974), 75–86, at 75. I have cited or adapted translations from *Anglo-Saxon Poetry*, tr. and ed. S. A. J. Bradley (London, 1982), 329–35; and *The Seafarer*, ed. I. L. Gordon (London, 1960).

filled with an insatiable desire for what it had seen: 'those ultimate and eternal joys'.[11]

My thought roams beyond the confines of my heart; my mind roams widely with the ocean tide over the whale's home, over earth's expanses, and comes back to me avid and covetous; the lone flier calls and urges the spirit irresistibly along the whale-path over the waters of oceans, because for me the pleasures of the Lord are more enkindling than this dead life.[12]

So the soul's yearning for heaven guided the exile's journey. In F. N. M. Diekstra's words, 'just as the exile feels the persistent urge to travel back to his homeland, the soul, constantly mindful of its origin, attempts to escape from the prison of the body and fly to heaven'. The eponymous seafarer can therefore be seen as a *peregrinus*, whose voyage to another land is an allegory for a hermit's flight from sin. This is the idea behind the exile interpretation of anachoresis. *Contemptus mundi* (contempt for worldly things), *gloria in tribulationibus* (conquering by suffering), and *peregrinatio* (passing through life as a stranger, as a citizen of heaven) are associated themes.[13] Scholars pursuing Whitelock's rationale interpreted voluntary exile as a penitential journey and categorized poems that address this theme (*The seafarer, The wanderer, Resignation*) as 'penitential poetry'. Yet critics objected that neither *The wanderer* nor *The seafarer* expresses remorse for sin.[14] Although it could readily be argued in Whitelock's defence that remorse was no doubt implicit in the very action of casting oneself into exile, Colin Ireland rightly observes that exile was considered to be an ascetic exercise in its own right, whether compelled by sin or not.[15] We should also remember that penance and asceticism were closely, sometimes inextricably, linked. For these reasons, it will not much help to ask whether exile was primarily penitential or ascetic. The important point is this: that it was a recognized way of eradicating sin.

In the eleventh century, it was virtually axiomatic that perfect penance meant the renunciation of sin. Adam's sin had estranged mankind from God; only by turning back to God could his exiled race reclaim Eden.[16] The ecclesiastical and temporal authorities of Anglo-Saxon England prescribed exile as penance and as a punishment respectively for the gravest misdemeanours. Those that volunteered for it took this path in order to eradicate their sins. In this light, the seafarer's exile or

---

[11] Pope, 'Second Thoughts', 83–4, imagines it as an eagle. For the popularity of this theme, see F. N. M. Diekstra, 'The Flight of the Exile's Soul to Its Fatherland', *Neophilologus*, 55 (1971), 433–46.

[12] *Anglo-Saxon Poetry*, ed. Bradley, 333.

[13] Diekstra, 'The Flight', 435. See also M. Brito-Martins, 'The Concept of *Peregrinatio* in Saint Augustine and Its Influences', in *Exile in the Middle Ages: Selected Proceedings from the International Medieval Congress, University of Leeds, 8–11 July 2002*, ed. L. Napran and E. van Houts (Turnhout, 2004), 83–94.

[14] For a summary of this debate, see A. J. Frantzen, *The Literature of Penance in Anglo-Saxon England* (New Brunswick, NJ, 1983), 181.

[15] Ireland, 'Some Analogues', 3.

[16] S. B. Greenfield, *Hero and Exile: The Art of Old English Poetry*, ed. G. H. Brown (London, 1989), 197–204; Pope, 'Second Thoughts', 80.

peregrinatio may be seen as an emblem of his purpose. The symbolism of his voyage denotes the rejection of transient pleasures (the home he leaves behind), so that his soul may ascend to heaven. Instances of anchorites depicted in this guise – as exiles for God's love – abound. The hermit or recluse Mantat, for one, twice describes himself as an exile (*wræcca*), and once as 'God's exile'.[17] Thancred, Torhtred, and Tova, whose anachoresis Folcard likens to a lifelong (white) martyrdom, were 'exiles (*exulati*) from the deeds of this world'.[18] In hagiography, the penitential or ascetic nature of voluntary exile is usually signalled by some formulaic reference to the conventional penitential or ascetic exercises of fasting, vigils, and prayer. Occasionally, clues to its nature are more explicit, as in the tale of the hermit Suneman. A tag from the Aeneid sends him in the wake of his classical predecessors, the exiled Trojans, to find a new fatherland across the seas. That Suneman's voyage was thought to have inaugurated a penitential career is evident from the statement that others joined him 'to do penance' after he arrived on the fen island of Cowholm, where he founded St Benet's abbey.[19] In the hagiography of Eadwold of Cerne, Goscelin develops the same theme – of the wanderer in foreign lands – by representing Eadwold as God's 'pilgrim' or 'exile' (*advena*). The young prince longs to escape the sins that beset him and exchange luxury for a desert, so he breaks his metaphorical chains and quests after his spiritual homeland. Later, Goscelin hints at unfulfilled penance and the convert's desire to make amends by revealing that, as a latecomer to religion, Eadwold was conscious of the need to make up for lost time. He dies only after he has completed his 'labours'. This remark may hint at a suggestion that he has fulfilled some scheduled tariff of penance. His penance is evidently adjudged satisfactory in the story, because angels subsequently arrive and bear his soul to heaven (for the role of the angels, read on).[20]

Eve, by 'seeking her true home far from home', had become a double exile – a point not lost on Goscelin. Her loneliness as a foreigner (*advena*) in exile (*in exilium*) from her homeland (*patria*) was amplified by her anachoresis. She was, as Goscelin put it, in her exile 'all the more an exile' (*exulatius*) and commensurately closer to God. Her vocation assisted her salvation because it freed her from the sinful world and facilitated the expulsion of her sin, which Goscelin encouraged her to purge.[21] Throughout his book of encouragement, as in his account of Eadwold, the world is identified as a place of bondage, as Egypt, as Babylon, as St Augustine's *civitas terrena*, an antitype to the City of God.[22] Eve had

---

[17] *Wills*, ed. Whitelock, no. 23 (S 1523).

[18] Birch, *Liber vitae*, 285.

[19] Suneman wanders 'per diuersa tunc deserta', a reference to Verg. *Aen.* III.4 ('diuersa exsilia et desertas quaerere terras'). Cf. Licence, 'Suneman and Wulfric', 363–4, 370.

[20] Eadwold, 204.

[21] *LC*, 26, 38; and 29, 41. '[P]urgans attentius intima tua': *ibid.*, 106.

[22] *Ibid.*, 77, and see 32, and 37 for the description of the *civitas Dei* and the *ciuitas terrena*. Cf. Osbert of Clare's images: B. Briggs, 'Expulsio, proscriptio, exilium: Exile and Friendship in the Writings of Osbert of Clare', in *Exile*, ed. Napran and van Houts, 131–44, at 135.

escaped its servitude by becoming one of 'God's pilgrims and paupers', 'a foreigner and a pilgrim' who had 'fled into solitude', and by 'renouncing worldly luxury' in a 'spirit of poverty'. Her cell was a haven (*asilum*) from the 'tempestuous world', a 'safe-house of refuge' from the 'maelstrom of evil'.[23] The recluse of Thanet likewise fled her home to seek 'asylum': the term used by eleventh-century Cluny to advertise itself as a refuge for would-be penitents.[24] Eve, at the Lord's instruction, had forgotten the home of her fathers. In the manner of Abraham, she had left her native land to seek the land of milk and honey to which God had appointed her. Benedict of Selby was another type of Abraham. Ordered to leave his homeland with the very words that God had spoken to the patriarch, he became *aduena* and *peregrinus*. Abraham was a suitable exemplar because in Hebrews 11 he was presented as God's virtuous exile.[25] Goscelin also made reference to the Trojans, as a *locus classicus* of exiled homecoming, and as an antitype, in that their mission to found a city on earth was at odds with the objective of inheriting the heavenly city.[26] When Eve found her final place of rest in Latium, 'requies ea certa laborum' (Verg. *Aen*. III.393), it was a spiritual Latium. Eadwold embarks on the same quest.[27] As he nears his destination, a reference to the sceptre on which Aeneas had sworn provides a classical analogue for his pilgrim's staff as it bursts propitiously into leaf (Verg. *Aen*. XII.208). But whereas Aeneas had sworn on the certainty that his sceptre could no longer bud, Eadwold's staff blossoms and roots in the hillside to betoken the end of his wanderings (*finita peregrinatione*). When a layman set down his staff, he signalled that he entered into penance.[28] The earthly Latium, for which Aeneas had sworn on a dried-up stick, was as nothing to the land of promise that lies ahead of Eadwold. Rome's glorious citadels (*Romanis arcibus*) he spurns, just as he had spurned the throne, so that he may inherit the heavenly city.[29]

Goscelin's favourite scripture for expressing the longing of the bird-soul to fly from its bodily prison came from Psalm 54.7: 'Oh for the wings of a dove'. Through Jerome's *Letter* 22, it has been suggested, the hagiographer came to associate this scripture with a soul's yearning for heaven. In his *Life* of St Mildthryth, one of the characters, Domne Eafe, sets sail into exile, 'ardent

[23] *LC*, 69, 37, 38, 78.

[24] 'Exi de terra tua et de cognatione tua…uelut in asylum salutis Dei perfuga': Rollason, 'Miracles of St Mildrith', 208; cf. Cluny, as the 'asylum poenitentium': Cowdrey, *The Cluniacs*, 128.

[25] *LC*, 37–8, 115; Burton, 'Selby Abbey', 56. Cf. Heb 11.8–10, 13–16. On Abraham as the model exile, see also Ireland, 'Some Analogues', 2.

[26] R. Hayward and S. Hollis, 'The Anchorite's Progress: Structure and Motif in the *Liber confortatorius*', in *Writing the Wilton Women: Goscelin's Legend of Edith and Liber confortatorius*, ed. S. Hollis (Turnhout, 2004), 369–83, at 377–8.

[27] 'Hic ad certum locum deduxit te Dominus': *LC*, 72. The Virgilian theme is introduced, with references to the exiled Trojans and the same tag, at 47; cf. Eadwold, 196–7.

[28] S. Hamilton, 'The Unique Favour of Penance: The Church and the People, *c.*800–1100', in *The Medieval World*, ed. P. Linehan and J. L. Nelson (London, 2001), 229–45, at 239.

[29] Eadwold, 202.

to fly with the wings of a dove to Christ her certain rest'.[30] The passage in which
her soul's scouting flight draws her onwards over the waves is somewhat remi-
niscent of *The seafarer*. 'The sail-winged vessel cut a wake through the sluggish
heaving ocean, and the zephyr-sped sails hastened her course, but the girl's deep
sighs and holy desires flew before the feathers of the winds.'[31] Eadwold, longing
to escape the captivity of court, is also made to sigh, climactically: 'Oh for the
wings of a dove . . . that I may fly far away to the wilderness.' He too would seek
his rest across land and sea. The Sussex anchorite Cuthman's eleventh- or
twelfth-century *Life* presents him as a questing pilgrim. When his resources ran
out, 'he left his own household gods and homeland', wheeling his sick mother on
a cart.[32] He then vowed no rest until he should reach whatever place God had
assigned to him. When this place had at last been identified by a predetermined
sign, he thanked his heavenly guide and, like Eadwold, established a hermitage at
the terminal point of his wandering pilgrimage (*Hic est finis uagationis mee*).[33]
The soul in exile could also be represented as a lost sheep seeking its shepherd.
Hagiographers often introduce this idea by their use of bucolic allegory.
Nearing his fold, the wanderer Suneman is led homewards by shepherds and
cowherds.[34] Eadwold's wanderings conclude when a shepherd directs him to
his destination, and shepherds appear in the *Life* of St Godric of Finchale,
pointing the way to Finchale.[35] All these symbols – the yearning sigh, the bird-
soul, the wanderer, the sheep seeking its shepherd, even the Trojans questing
after Latium – stood for the soul's return to God. To summarize: interpretation number one with its multifarious trappings began with a penitent spirit,
thirsting for reunion with God, and finished on the completion of a satisfactory penance in exile, by a purified soul bound for heaven.

MODEL 2: EXILE AS THE PRELIMINARY
PHASE OF PURGATION

Folcard and Goscelin (and, if we hazard a guess at when their legends took shape,
the depictions of hermits like Suneman and Cuthman) give some impression of
how the eremitic life was perceived during the late eleventh century. As well as
counting as satisfactory, a hermit's penitential exile was viewed as a sort of
earthly purgation. The idea that penance and purgation were two names for a

[30] *Ibid.*, 194; Diekstra, 'The Flight', 440. D. W. Rollason, *The Mildrith Legend: A Study in Early Medieval Hagiography in England* (Leicester, 1982), 108–43, at 120.
[31] Translated from Rollason, *The Mildrith Legend*, 120.
[32] J. Blair, 'Saint Cuthman, Steyning and Bosham', *Sussex Archaeological Collections*, 135 (1997), 173–92, at 189 (the *lares* were presumably figurative).
[33] *Ibid.*, 190.
[34] Licence, 'Suneman and Wulfric', 370.
[35] Eadwold, 202; *LG*, 62.

continuum by which the soul was restored to perfection, the first being usually the name of the process in life, the second its name after death, went back to St Augustine (354–430).[36] Goscelin took it to mean that souls were cleansed either 'here, through the fire of their labours [on earth] or there [in the other-world] through purgatorial fire'.[37] In a similar scheme, Peter Damian, who saw the anchorite's life as the path to perfect penance, used the substantive *purgatorium* to describe it as a purgatorial vocation. This 'purgatory' was not an other-world state, of course, but rather a state of penance on earth. In later years, Peter's coinage entered the vocabulary of the Cistercian abbot, saint, and statesman Bernard of Clairvaux (*c.*1090–1153), who wrote that the eremitic vocation was a 'purgatory'.[38] Some similar idea is expressed in the *Life* of Bartholomew of Farne, written *c.*1200, which describes the hermitage on Inner Farne Island as 'a sort of purgatory on earth, established for the wholesome healing of bodies and souls'.[39] As ideas about purgation took shape, hagiographers took less interest in exile and more in the purificatory exercises, paraphernalia, and strictures that cleansed anchorites of sin. Earlier accounts have their vigils and immersions or typically non-specific references to fasting, vigils, and prayer, but in the twelfth century more is said of hairshirts, hauberks, and flagellation. These trademarks of the penitent had gained prominence among the followers of Romuald and Peter Damian, and were sometimes thought to recreate fearsome purificatory feats undertaken by the desert fathers. In their spirit, Godric of Finchale tormented his flesh by chopping wood, in an abrasive hairshirt (*cilicium*) and mail vest (*lorica*), or by hurling his naked body among brambles, after the example of St Benedict.[40] His namesake at Throckenholt vowed to wear a *lorica* until God should forgive his sins. Wulfric of Haselbury, Godric's sister Burchwen, and St Bartholomew of Farne all used hairshirts. Wulfric and the hermit William at Llanthony also used mail vests.[41] Christina of Markyate self-flagellated after being tempted by lust; her mentor Roger 'mortified his flesh'.[42] Wulfric would scourge himself until the blood flowed freely, saying the *Miserere* for forgiveness and begging God to keep him from temptation. His wet dreams so upset him that on Easter Day, after he had lost his Lenten battle to contain his semen, he went out from his cell and confessed his crime before the entire Easter congregation in the adjoining church.[43]

[36] G. R. Edwards, 'Purgatory: "Birth" or Evolution?' *JEH*, 36 (1985), 634–46, at 645.

[37] '[S]aluabuntur aut hic per ignem laborum [aut] ibi per ignem purgatorium': *LC*, 111.

[38] See below, 149. On exile as a purgative fire, see also Diekstra, 'The Flight', at 437.

[39] *VB*, 312.

[40] *LG*, 76–7.

[41] *WH*, 19; *LG*, 140; *VB*, 300; *MA*, VI, 129. William was a hermit who helped to establish the community of canons at Llanthony.

[42] *LCM*, 115, 117, for her disgust with her sinful passions; for Roger, see 81, 83.

[43] *WH*, pp. lii, 41–3. On wet dreams in the monastic tradition, see C. Leyser, 'Masculinity in Flux: Nocturnal Emission and the Limits of Celibacy in the Early Middle Ages', in *Masculinity in Medieval Europe*, ed. D. M. Hadley (London, 1999), 103–20.

This sort of intimate detail, sporadic in hagiography of the eleventh century, more common in the twelfth, had as much to do with the scrutiny then being paid to the realities of the human condition (which historians have called 'the discovery of the individual') as it did with growing interest in penance and purgation. The scrutiny of the individual saw an outpouring of realistic biographies, within the hagiographical genre, by authors commonly acquainted with their subjects at first or second hand.[44] Christina of Markyate, the two Godrics, Bartholomew of Farne, and Wulfric of Haselbury could all still be remembered when their *Lives* were written. All that had been left of Eadwold, Wihtburh, Suneman, and Cuthman when their portraits were penned was their sanctity. For twelfth-century hagiographers, not only of anchorites but also of abbots and bishops, their subjects were real men and women with real inner struggles; and this must account in part for the detail they have to offer. At the same time, these twelfth-century hagiographers had another reason for paying close attention to ascetic and penitential practices, in that an idea was beginning to form, that no amount of purging on earth could cleanse the soul of sin. Exile was no longer seen as a once-and-for-all cure for sin. Rather, it was at best only a beginning. What mattered more in the twelfth century was the hermit's battle for salvation along a long purgatorial road that often extended into the afterlife. This road, of course, was not a newly laid route. Mantat had feared for the fate of his soul no less in Cnut's reign, ordaining in his will that two hundred psalters and masses be said annually on his behalf. Yet the message became clear in the twelfth century, that anachoresis did not necessarily constitute a satisfactory penance. Indeed, according to those who wrote about them, Godric of Throckenholt and Godric of Finchale's sister Burchwen were unable to complete their penance on earth and were duly appointed to suffer beyond the grave.[45] In short, interpretation number two attached less significance to exile and more to the processes whereby souls were cleansed of sin. These processes on earth could take place in any suitable setting, whether hermitage, monastery, or episcopal residence. Even so, the hermitage was the only purpose-built factory for purging sin.

MODEL 3: ANACHORESIS AS THE *IMITATIO CHRISTI*

Interpretation number three, which saw anachoresis as the imitation of Christ's poverty and an answer to his summons to renunciation, also came to the fore in this century, through the impact of the hermit preachers of north-west France. The model was nothing new. Simeon of Trier, according to his hagiographer,

[44] See Morris, *Discovery of the Individual*; C. W. Bynum, *Jesus as Mother: Studies in the Spirituality of the High Middle Ages* (London, 1982), 82–109.
[45] GT, 36; *LG*, 143.

who wrote in 1035, desired to follow the pauper Christ in poverty. The monk Reginald of Canterbury, *c.*1100, depicted the desert father Malchus as a naked follower of the naked Christ.[46] But when twelfth-century hagiographers took on the motif they were consciously or unconsciously echoing the clarion call of the mendicant hermit preachers of Brittany. Renunciation had been the answer to their question, 'what must I do to be saved' (Mt 19.16, 21, 29) just as it had been Christ's answer to the rich man. It had become the latest allegory of redemption. New hermit preachers like Robert of Arbrissel were lifestyle evangelists to whom exile would have seemed inappropriate and whose vision of their vocation was grander than interpretation number two would allow. Their renunciatory imitation of Christ had to be seen by others that it might win souls. An attitude of imitation better suited them. After this message sunk in, whatever the particulars of a hermit's career, few hagiographers could resist the new interpretation. The hagiographer of the hermit Congar claimed that he had become a hermit to fulfil Christ's precept: 'he is not worthy of me who will not for my sake leave father and mother, sisters, wife, children, and lands' (Mt 10.37; 19.21).[47] Godric of Finchale's conversion supposedly came through Mt 19.21: 'if you would be perfect, go, sell all you have and give to the poor, and come, follow me'.[48] Godric of Throckenholt was believed to have sold his possessions and distributed the proceeds among the poor. Christina of Markyate's hagiographer, a monk of St Albans, claimed that she had set out to follow Christ in response to his summons in Mt 19.29. A thirteenth-century canon of Dale abbey in Derbyshire suggested that Mt 19.21 had inspired the man who founded a hermitage there in the mid-twelfth century. The verse appears in a similar context in the *Life* of the sometime anchorite Gilbert of Sempringham, which was written *c.*1200.[49] Examples could be multiplied, but the essential message was that people no longer became hermits or were thought to have become hermits to perform a satisfactory penance which was consummated in exile (or even to perform as much penance as they could), but in response to Christ's injunction: do as I do and be saved. This made sense, for whereas the efficacy of penitential exile was not guaranteed, Christ's promises could scarcely be gainsaid. The twelfth-century saw the growth of the cult of Christ, so a compelling, Christocentric model would have been appealing.

---

[46] 'De sancto Symeone', 89C; *The Vita sancti Malchi of Reginald of Canterbury*, ed. L. R. Lind, *Illinois Studies in Language and Literature*, 27, nos. 3–4 (Urbana, 1942), 143.

[47] *NL*, I, 249.

[48] *LG*, 41 (where Mt 19.21 is cited). At 218, acting like Christ, he advises a rich man to do likewise.

[49] *LCM*, 63; A. Saltman, 'The History of the Foundation of Dale Abbey or the So-called Chronicle of Dale: A New Edition', *Derbyshire Archaeological Journal*, 87 (1968 for 1967), 18–38, at 25; Golding, *Gilbert*, 16.

MODELLING RECLUSION

These three interpretations were applicable to eremitism and reclusion alike. Recluses, however, had their own, distinctive allegory, which cast the recluse's cell as a sepulchre and the act of entering it as a descent into the tomb. Metaphorical death symbolized the recluse's passage from everyday life on earth. She left the world of men to perform penance in the purgatory of her cell and to live the life of angels in an antechamber to heaven (two ideas which co-existed). She became a white martyr, a willing, sacrificial lamb. Chapter 3 showed how this imagery of death influenced the epitaphs of the recluses at Saint Gall in the tenth and eleventh centuries. In the diocese of Worms, Caritas entered her cell during the office of the dead, which was probably a conventional part of the enclosure ceremony by that date (*c*.1010), at least in Germany and Lotharingia. The earliest extant depictions of the reclusive vocation from England show that their authors were not only aware of this model but that they also turned to it when thinking about the vocation. The devil, Goscelin wrote, would tempt Eve to leave her cell. When this happened, she should remember the words of St Augustine: 'Let me die, Lord, lest I die – that is: let me die to the world, and to sin, and live for the Lord of life.' She should also recall St Paul, etc: 'For you are dead; your life is hidden with Christ in God (Col. 3.3) . . . dying for the Lord I do not die, but I live. For blessed are the dead who die in the Lord (Rev. 14.13).'[50] Osbern of Canterbury's brief description of Dunstan's cell at Glastonbury shows his familiarity with the same theme, in that he twice likens the cell to a tomb in its dimensions.[51] Among our surviving twelfth-century sources, the earliest liturgy concerned with recluses (an enclosure ceremony copied into a bishop's book of ceremonies) shows the extent to which the vocation had appropriated this symbolism to define its ritual. The postulant recluse was conducted to her cell, to the chanting of antiphons and psalms from the office of the dead.[52] The officiant then proceeded with the office of extreme unction before saying prayers for the dying. After the recluse entered her cell, she was sprinkled with dust and the cell, sealed. This ritual appears to have been similar to the one that Burchard had performed. When the celebrated Cistercian abbot Aelred of Rievaulx (*c*.1110–67) wrote the first enduring manual of instruction for recluses in the early 1160s, he reminded his audience that 'whoever renounces the world and chooses solitary enclosure, desiring not to be seen but to be hidden, and, as if dead to the world, co-entombed in a cave with Christ', should be 'dead and buried to the world'.[53] His words could readily have passed as an exposition of the liturgy.

---

[50] *LC*, 70; cf. *ibid.*, 79, 89.
[51] *Memorials*, ed. Stubbs, 83.
[52] Wilson, *Pontifical*, 243–4, cf. 197–8.
[53] *Opera omnia I*, ed. Hoste and Talbot, 649, 660 ('seculo mortua et sepulta'), 677; and see P. L'Hermite-Leclercq, 'Aelred of Rievaulx: The Recluse and Death according to the Vita inclusarum', *Cistercian Studies Quarterly*, 34 (1999), 183–201.

Having 'died', the recluse entered a realm both purgatorial and paradisiacal, in which penitential exertions alternated with foretastes of heavenly consolations. Like the older ritual of the public expulsion of penitents from the community of the faithful in Lent, the drama of dying to the world marked a formal exodus from sin, which was duly to be followed by penance.[54] In constituting a one-off, lifelong, and hopefully satisfactory penance, the reclusive vocation in the eleventh century performed the same function as the hermit's voluntary exile. Such was the opinion of Burchard's hagiographer, who believed that when Caritas died after only three years in her cell she yielded to God a soul fully purged.[55] Recluses who were fortunate enough to be martyred achieved this end sooner than they would otherwise have expected. While awaiting death or martyrdom, recluses would approach it as best they could. Hartker of Saint Gall and Brihtric near Bury St Edmunds lay face down on the ground in their anchorholds with their arms outstretched to form a cross, in what was a recognized gesture of penance.[56] Brihtric uttered again and again the first verse of Psalm 50, one of the seven penitential psalms. Its opening begs God's mercy and the forgiveness of sins. The fragrance that lingered after his death proved that his steadfastness had made full reparation for his sins. Wulfric self-flagellated and repeated the *Miserere* – that is, the penitential Psalm 50.[57] There could also be a penitential explanation for why some recluses entered cells or were forced into them on account of illness or disability. Ælfwen of Canterbury interpreted a year of blindness that she had suffered in her adolescence as punishment for her youthful insouciance. Twice St Mildthryth had cured her, and so her decision, in later years, to be sealed inside a cell may have stemmed from an awareness of her past transgressions. A blind recluse is recorded at Leicester, a lame recluse at Barnstaple, and a sickly or disabled recluse at Bury St Edmunds, who was apparently put into the tower there on account of his infirmity. Archaeologists digging at Sedgeford in north Norfolk unearthed a possible recluse with a congenital hip and leg malformation, which caused severe curvature of her spine.[58] Practicalities aside, if recluses saw these disabilities as divine punishments for their sinfulness these individuals might have been career penitents. Alternatively, sickness or disability could have been interpreted as a graciously given opportunity to live a salutary life of endurance – another form of earthly purgatory, we may suppose.

The paradisiacal quality of the anchorhold obtained in its function as a waiting room or antechamber to heaven. Goscelin alludes to this with his rhetoric of asylum and description of Eve's cell as a secure place of rest. The twelfth-century

---

[54] On inclusion as a penitential activity, see Jestice, *Wayward Monks*, 108, 111–12.

[55] *Vita Burchardi*, ed. Waitz, 839: 'ad ultimum animam pleniter expurgatam suo reddidit creatori'.

[56] L. Gougaud, *Devotional and Ascetic Practices in the Middle Ages* (English edition prepared by G. C. Bateman) (London, 1927), 3–12.

[57] *LC*, 67. *WH*, p. lii.

[58] Licence, 'Evidence', 232.

enclosure ceremony is explicit, likening a recluse's cell to paradise, 'my place of rest' (*requies mea*).[59] Many cells were set within cemeteries, causing their occupants to live among the dead. The significance of their location may have taken account of the fact that cemeteries were places of rest and waiting, where the dead awaited God's kingdom. The intention perhaps was that the recluse should wait among and as one of the dead at the threshold of heaven. There she would live a life in communion with the angels: a variant of the *vita angelica*. The *vita angelica* was a model of monastic life that set monks in the company of angels because they joined in the prayers and praises of the celestial hosts. (Eventually, the elect would make up the number of fallen angels.)[60] When applied to the life of the recluse, the *vita angelica* developed a special meaning, in that recluses invited angels to be their companions and ministers not so much by joining in their praises, though they did this, but by putting themselves in their care. Grimlaïc wrote that the earliest solitaries knew that the farther they fled the world's pleasures the more they should receive angelic visitors. He advised recluses to follow their example.[61] The epitaph of St Wiborada expresses this idea in its observation that after she had been removed from human interaction she was sustained through the ministrations of angels.[62] This special relationship between recluses and angels was unique. The same idea may inhere in the statement that Caritas 'lived the life of angels' and Turgot of Durham's claim that recluses in eleventh-century Scotland lived the life of angels on earth, because both statements hint at something more than the *vita angelica* of monks. When Anselm wrote to a mentor of female recluses, *c.*1102, he advised that the women in his charge should imitate the angels in heaven and live as though angels ministered to their every need, even as though they were in their company, in the presence of God. This was to be their one rule ('sit regula uestra').[63] Bishop Herbert Losinga of Norwich (1091–1119) wrote to a recluse named Guy in a similar vein, on the oddity that he should have sought his bishop's counsel when he, the importunate, was a citizen of heaven, freely versant with the angels (for he spoke 'in the tongues of angels', after 1 Cor. 13.1).[64] Here too the belief is discernible that recluses received angelic ministrations and dwelt in angelic company. This all served to draw attention to the reclusive vocation's

[59] Wilson, *Pontifical*, 244 (and note, 'In paradisum deducant te angeli').

[60] On the monastic model, see McLaughlin, *Consorting*, 228–9 and references. See also Morris, *Discovery of the Individual*, 31. In view of the fact that anchorites often embraced silence, it should not be thought that silence was part of the *vita angelica*. Angels were (loqacious) messengers. Monks put a guard on their lips not to imitate angels but to do away with small talk: cf. S. Bruce, *Silence and Sign Language in Medieval Monasticism: The Cluniac Tradition c.900–1200* (Cambridge, 2007), 2–3.

[61] *Grimlaici . . . regula*, 591B.

[62] *Vita s. Wiboradae*, ed. Pertz, 457: 'Affatu angelico pascitur atque cibo'.

[63] *Vita Burchardi*, ed. Waitz, 838. Hinde, *Opera*, 247. *Opera*, ed. Schmitt, IV, no. 230 (134–5).

[64] 'Ex abundanti quaeris nostrarum colloquia . . . cum tua conuersatio in coelis sit, et linguis angelorum loquens, humanis minime consolationibus indigeas': *Epistolae*, ed. Anstruther, 95.

paradisiacal dimensions. Holy, hidden recluses were so very close to heaven that they communicated with the heavenly host.

MODELS OUTSIDE THE MONASTERIES

These, then, were the main interpretations, put about by monastic authors, of the purpose of anachoresis – that prolonged rite of passage, whereby a soul would reach perfection by eradicating sin. Yet it would be sensible to query whether this passage to perfection was similarly perceived outside the monasteries. Vernacular writings, intended for lay audiences, provide one or two clues that the image of the anchorite familiar outside the cloister was not dissimilar to the image imagined within. A case in point is the Anglo-Norman poem on the *Voyage of St Brendan*, written during the first quarter of the twelfth century and dedicated to Henry I's queen.[65] Amid many wonderful adventures over the course of his voyage, the protagonist Brendan and his companions arrive at an island where they discover the aged hermit Paul. Paul then reveals all the proofs of his asceticism before informing the visitors that his reason for coming to the island was to await – and apparently prepare for – Judgement Day.[66] His aim in this was to avoid sin, lead as blameless a life as possible, and entrust himself to God. Here, a well-known vernacular tale links anachoresis to the quest to purify the soul. The collection of *Fables* assembled and rendered in Anglo-Norman by Marie de France, probably in the late twelfth century, tells the story of a recluse and a peasant which reinforces the idea that lay perceptions of anchorites were similar to monastic ones. In the fable, the peasant bothers the recluse with a difficult question, asking him again and again why Adam ate the apple and caused the fall of humanity. The recluse eventually finds a way to answer his question by secretly placing a mouse under an upturned bowl and instructing him not to look to see what is underneath. He departs leaving the peasant in charge of the bowl, but the peasant cannot control himself: he lifts the lid, and the mouse escapes. The recluse then reprimands him and teaches him the moral of the story: that no one should criticize another person's sins because each of us is sinful, and each should accuse himself by paying attention to his own sins.[67] In this fable, the recluse assumes the typical anchoretic role of an individual ascetic who possesses a heightened awareness of sin which gives rise to a penitent mentality. Its underlying assumptions strengthen the argument that, in tales circulating beyond the cloister, anachoresis was linked to the problem of sin and the search for a solution.

---

[65] Benedeit, *The Anglo-Norman Voyage of St Brendan*, ed. I. Short and B. Merrilees (Manchester, 1979), 1–5.

[66] *Ibid.*, 72, lines 1558–9.

[67] Marie de France, *Fables*, ed. and tr. H. Spiegel (Toronto, 1987), no. 53.

We may also approach the question (whether anachoresis was associated, outside monasteries, with overcoming sin) by investigating whether the predominantly extra-claustral genre of Romance, which emerged in the late twelfth century, employed the same motifs as monastic writers or viewed anachoresis in a completely different light. There is no need to trawl the literature itself because there is already a quantity of helpful scholarship touching the subject. Although it reveals that Romance was more interested in heroes than saints, it tends to uphold the argument that lay audiences and monks thought about anachoresis in compatible ways. Angus Kennedy has observed that in this vernacular genre – as in hagiography – the hermit is typically represented:

as a venerable old man endowed with wisdom and moral authority, called upon to act as a guide, counsellor, and interpreter of God's will, rewarded for his spiritual endeavours with the divine gifts of prophecy and healing, enjoying a privileged relationship with the animal world and, above all, having direct access to the company of God and his angels who reveal themselves to him in visible, tangible form.[68]

To an extent, this stock figure was remoulded in Romance to emphasize qualities that would have appealed to a lay aristocratic and courtly audience.[69] Hagiographers, in contrast, stressed those qualities that would have appealed to monks. Nevertheless, after account has been made for such differences, it is evident that Romance saw the anchoretic life as a quest for spiritual perfection, to the extent that very many knights were shown concluding their chivalric quest – much as any monk might conclude his spiritual quest – by retiring to the hermitage to adopt its higher warfare. Lancelot (for example) and any number of others become penitents and dwell in oases in the forests where their souls are cleansed of sin.[70] Their 'privileged relationship with the animal world' and their 'access to the company of God and his angels' betoken their quasi-restoration of man's prelapsarian state, where all things had been ordered in Eden, with creation in submission to man, and man obedient to God. These motifs imply that hermits in Romance eradicated their sins. The comparison between Romance and hagiography reveals that, by the end of the twelfth century, different audiences were viewing anachoresis as a crowning glory for any career, be it religious or of the world.

This suggests that anchorites had many admirers. Yet it would be misleading to end the chapter without returning briefly to their critics. For just as Ælfric, in

---

[68] A. Kennedy, 'The Portrayal of the Hermit-Saint in French Arthurian Romance: The Remoulding of a Stock-Character', in *An Arthurian Tapestry: Essays in Memory of Lewis Thorpe*, ed. K. Varty (Glasgow, 1981), 69–82, at 70. Tales of hermits' interactions with animals have recently been assessed in D. Alexander, *Saints and Animals in the Middle Ages* (Woodbridge, 2008).

[69] Kennedy, 'The Portrayal', 78.

[70] *Ibid.*, 73–5; F. Romanelli, '*Le chevalier au barisel*. L'acculturazione dei cavalieri tra lo spazio dell'*aventure* e il tempo della confessione', *Medioevo Romanzo*, 11 (1986), 27–54, at 40–2, 51; J.-C. Huchet, 'Les déserts du roman médiéval: le personnage de l'ermite dans le romans de XIIᵉ et XIIIᵉ siècles', *Littérature*, 60 (1985), 89–108, at 93.

the late tenth century, tried to puncture their inflated reputation, so tales and songs circulating in England in the eleventh and twelfth centuries chipped away at the anchoretic ideal. Often these tales derived from cautionary stories in the accounts of the desert fathers. Some were humorously subversive, others more serious, but most had the same sort of underlying message: that the trials of anachoresis were dangerous, even unrealistic. In his treatise on the solitary life, which he wrote for the edification of Eve, Goscelin recounts a tale that was known to him only from songs, about the hermit Alexander whom the devil tempted to seduce and murder a king's daughter.[71] The tale has many elements – Alexander is forced to perform penance and later becomes a monk – but it begins by showing how a hermit went astray. A similar tale, from the *Vitas patrum*, which circulated independently, describes how the devil tricked a hermit into killing his father.[72] Some of these critical or cautionary tales, including the one recounted by Ælfric, suggested that anchorites were particularly susceptible to pride, the temptation naturally being that, in the zeal of solitary asceticism, they might overestimate their own virtue. During the eleventh century, a story from the *Vitas patrum* conveying a similar message formed the basis of a satirical song. A hermit named John the Dwarf told his companion that he was going into the desert to live like an angel, without any food or clothing. When hunger forced him to come begging eight days later, his friend mockingly inquired who the caller might be, for John 'has become an angel . . . he's no longer interested in *people*'. Suitably chastened, John conceded that his ambition to become an angel was beyond him, so 'he learnt to become a good *man*'.[73] The fact that this tale and similar ones circulated as songs in the eleventh and twelfth centuries implies that the messages they conveyed resonated with the sentiments of people at that time. Anachoresis, they intimated, tempted vain men who considered themselves better than everyone else, even though the pious efforts of others were perfectly valid. Those that aspired to perfection, moreover, were in for a shock, when the difficulty of their proposition, or diabolical temptations, proved that their ambition was unrealistic.

It could be said in conclusion that during the eleventh century, and on into the twelfth, a vocation concerned with the eradication of sin won great respect and some pointed criticism. Earlier, Chapter 1 argued that the new hermits who proliferated in Italy, Normandy, and France summoned sinners to repentance and a life of ascetic rigour patterned on the example of the desert fathers. The present chapter has argued that the movement's hallmarks, in the thinking of various writers addressing assorted audiences, were a heightened awareness of sin,

---

[71] 'Quod refero, cantu et relatione, non lectione didici': *LC*, 104.

[72] S. Thompson, *Motif-Index of Folk-Literature*, 6 vols (Copenhagen, 1955–8), K943.

[73] *Carmina Cantabrigiensia: Die Cambridger Lieder*, ed. K. Strecker, *MGH SRG*, 40 (Berlin, 1926), no. 42 (97–101); *The Cambridge Songs (Carmina Cantabrigiensia)*, ed. J. M. Ziolkowski (London, 1994), no. 42 (118–21, 292–6). Italics mine.

a commitment to performing penance, and the desire to purify the soul. This argument fits the comments of Jonathan Riley-Smith, Christopher Brooke, Marcus Bull, and others, who see the century 1050–1150 as an age preoccupied with penitence and remission of sins. For a while, historians linked this anxiety to the inefficacy of the penitential system, after H. E. J. Cowdrey argued that it provided 'perilously few resources for the sinner to meet his needs . . . in face of the overmastering prospect of the Last Judgment'.[74] Since then, however, it has increasingly come to light that the penitential system could be adapted to sinners' needs. This raises the question: if the anxiety about sin was not the result of its failings, where might it have come from? Chapter 1 has already traced the eremitic movement back to the generation before the millennium, which exhibited heightened anticipation of God's impending Judgement and the need to prepare for it. This was the context in which Romuald effectively upped the stakes for salvation by emulating the asceticism of the fathers – a move that apparently surprised his contemporaries, as if it had caught them off-guard. As the idea spread, that anyone concerned about the prospect of salvation had to embrace a life of radical asceticism, it bred dissatisfaction with existing mechanisms for eradicating sin. The penitential system, which was the widest-reaching of these mechanisms, may not have changed in any significant way, but it may now have fallen subject to two suspicions: that its rigours were insufficient and that there was a better method of cleansing the soul in withdrawal to a monastery or a hermitage. The burgeoning interest in penance and the growth of recruitment to different forms of the religious life – one might also add the increasing popularity of pilgrimage and instant success of crusading – could be regarded, accordingly, as the products of a new mood: as the ameliorative, placatory efforts of a society, which had learned to fear the consequences of its sins, to make its reparation to a demanding God.

There is a precedent of sorts in Peter Brown's assessment of the situation in late antiquity: 'Christian holy persons', he wrote, 'had been shot into prominence, at this time, by an exceptionally stern and world-denying streak in late antique Christianity'. Elsewhere, he suggested that sin was a driving concern in generating this atmosphere. Another driving concern was a perceived need to prepare for the coming Judgement.[75] These insights also apply to eleventh-century Europe, allowing parallels to be drawn between the rise of the holy man in the Near East in late antiquity and the rise of the anchorites (who patterned themselves on those earlier holy men) in the era covered by this book. The earlier phenomenon was able to undergo this form of renewal, albeit in an alien context, because the memory of asceticism and reverence for the life of the fathers endured in the Christian ascetical tradition. Like the recluse who surfaces in the fable set down by Marie de France, the exemplary ascetic, whether

---

[74] Cowdrey, *The Cluniacs*, 134.
[75] Brown, *Authority*, 77; on sin, see *ibid.*, 57–8.

he lived in late antiquity or in eleventh-century Worcester, pursued the twin ideals of purifying his soul and alerting society to its sins by setting a gold standard of holiness. His feats of asceticism intimated that effective, cutting-edge techniques for beating sin were most probably to be found inside the ascetic monastery, anchorhold, or hermitage. And this would explain why so many people, concerned for the welfare of their souls, chose to withdraw to these earthly purgatories. As I noted earlier, their recourse to anachoresis is sometimes interpreted as a rebellion of the individual against social strictures (whether in the world or the established monasteries).[76] Yet this hypothesis rests on questionable premises, for it assumes a new degree of self-awareness or the discovery of individuality. Conversely, if we view the resurgence of anachoresis as a result of increased sensitivity towards sin, no such assumptions are necessary; for it was not awareness of individuality but of their common fallen humanity and the brokenness of their relations with God that inspired men and women to leave the world and become anchorites. Their point of departure – desire to be rid of sin – was no less communal than individual. The next chapter will examine how they strived to achieve their goal.

[76] See above, 8.

6

Eradicating sin, in practice

So far I have argued that anachoresis became popular as a solution to the problem of sin, which loomed large in the eleventh century and lingered into the twelfth. But why might this have been the case, and what were the practical implications? To put the question differently: why was anachoresis, above other vocations, thought to be an effective solution to depravity? Lester K. Little linked the rise of anachoresis in these centuries to a new and growing perception that greed (*radix malorum*) was corrupting Christian society. This would account in part for the appeal of renunciation and the rhetoric of poverty – of selling one's possessions and of leaving behind the world's false wealth and ensnaring riches; clearly this link is important and helps to explain the phenomenon. Yet it cannot explain the entirety of the phenomenon, for, if greed was the only problem, anchorites – one might assume – would have opted for a life of simplicity and poverty without nurturing further desires to embrace harsh penitential or ascetic practices. Some no doubt did, but many did not, and whatever explanation scholars may arrive at must take the latter into account. In light of our new question, touching the relationship between anachoresis and sin, the most obvious reason that the former would have been perceived to be a solution to the latter is that anachoresis was, by definition, the art of spiritual warfare, developed through the ages precisely for the purpose of purifying its practitioners by ridding them of evil. This was true of no other religious vocation, whether it was the regimen of the cenobium (which was predicated on the apostolic life and obedience to a rule as patterns of Christian living) or the episcopacy, or the priesthood. Anachoresis, by its nature, was uniquely adapted to repairing the damnable soul. When it came to fighting sin, whether abstracted in temptations or incarnate in demonic attacks, the sum total of its wisdom knew every trick of the trade and every tested tactic. Every strange or seemingly inconsequential action that pertained to anachoresis (like immersion, flagellation, and self-ostracism) was the functioning product of accumulated wisdom and application. An anchorite's actions in afflicting her flesh would be no less rational than a blacksmith's in working his forge. The present chapter, in pursuing our new question, explores this rationale by inter-preting the anchorite's life of spiritual warfare as a battle-plan for beating sin.

From the days of St Antony (251–356), whom Jerome (we may recall) saw as the exemplar for all anchorites to come, spiritual warfare was the essence of anachoresis. The Benedictine Rule defined anchorites as solitary monks who battled the devil, and many stories were told which illustrated the ensuing trial of wits. The tale of a hermit who captured a devil; the legend of the hermit Alexander, whom the devil tempted to seduce and murder a princess, and the story of St Dunstan tweaking the devil's nose with his tongs drew upon this tradition.[1] To the question, 'what did hermits do all day', the ideal answer was that they waged spiritual warfare. This is not to say that they were constantly engaged in combat (no soldier ever is), but rather that they were constantly building up their defences, preparing against attack, and anticipating the movements of the enemy. The enemy, in the abstract sense, was temptation, by which I mean anything that threatened to lead them away from good and holy living. Much like a grand master in chess who learns to anticipate, many moves ahead, scenarios that could land him in trouble, so anchorites learned, through constant practice, what they had to avoid. Temptation can be the hardest thing to recognize, for what at first seems like a good idea can turn out to be quite the opposite. It can launch assaults on many different fronts, hence the old adage: 'the devil is not always at one door'. To discover its ways is to set about achieving some difficult goal such as a life of virtue and prayer. As far as temptation (the enemy) was concerned this was tantamount to a declaration of war. Anchorites, then, were those who declared war upon or escalated hostilities with the enemy. Many of the stories that concerned them represented the skills they learned, as practised professional warriors, in detecting and destroying that enemy; in others they themselves were overcome, so dangerous was their vocation. Three sources of temptation were recognized by the church: the world, the flesh, and the devil. The present chapter examines the anchorite's warfare with each in turn. It concludes on the theme of forbearance, for the length of time spent engaging in this struggle was the measure of an anchorite's success, just as successive seasons on the battlefield proved the mettle of any soldier. Traditionally, as we have seen, the arena of solitary warfare was regarded as a tougher spiritual battlefield than the cenobium. If there were heroic tales of single combat to be told, this was their most likely setting.

ESCAPING THE WORLD

The world of sin-ridden humanity was the first of the anchorite's three foes. St Augustine of Hippo famously called it the *civitas terrena* (the 'Earthly City'): that is, the world built by men for and according to their interests. More often

---

[1] For the vision of the hermit who captured a devil, see C. D. Wright, *The Irish Tradition in Old English Literature* (New York, 1992), 175–9. For the text, see F. C. Robinson, 'The Devil's Account of the Next World: An Anecdote from Old English Homiletic Literature', *Neuphilologische Mitteilungen*, 73 (1972), 362–71; and *The Vercelli Homilies and Related Texts*, ed. D. G. Scragg, EETS, o.s. 300 (1992), no. ix. In late Anglo-Saxon England, this was one of the most popular religious tales in circulation. For the tale of the hermit Alexander, see *LC*, 104.

than not this city was at odds with God's scheme for the salvation of mankind (the 'City of God'). Anchorites therefore renounced it, in order to realize the latter. In effect, this meant that their foe was defeated as soon as the would-be anchorite joined battle. Flight, paradoxically, was the method of despatch, because to flee the world or shut it outside one's cell was to break its power to corrupt good intentions. Monasticism's premise indeed was that human society was so infected with original sin, playing out its sinful consequences day-in, day-out in ordinary interaction, that to gossip, trade, and make merry was to embroil oneself in the fatal problem. None of these things pertained to building God's kingdom, and everything that was no help was a distraction. Worse, there were evils on all sides: the boastfulness of empty words, the vanity of fashion and human pursuits, the covetousness aroused through the ownership of possessions, the quick-fix pleasure of sex, the folly of erudition. Those who wished to be perfect: to see no evil, hear no evil, and speak no evil, could scarcely attain their goal in such surroundings. Their immediate foe – the world – was overwhelming; so their battle had to begin with flight. Hagiographers and other spiritual writers represented this action with rhetoric and symbols of exile or renunciation, which were studied in the last chapter. The recluse at Leicester 'had shut herself away from worldly desires', and Eadwold, having 'walked free from the fetters of worldly captivity', 'preferred to avoid and banish himself from the fury and vainglory of worldly dalliance'.[2] Godric of Finchale shuddered at the thought of human company, preferring to make his home among wild beasts.[3] (They threatened only his body.) Flight from the world was the surest way of precluding external temptation. The principal concern of the warfare thereafter was to combat temptations of mind and body, as well as diabolical assaults.

PURIFYING THE MIND AND OVERCOMING THE FLESH

Having fled into solitude or withdrawn inside a cell, the anchorite began the task of training both mind and body to relinquish old desires. The mind was vulnerable to temptation in as much as it entertained evil thoughts or retained fond memories of the world it had left behind. These had to be quenched, purged, and replaced with holy longings. To assist himself in this end, St Cuthbert constructed his oratory in such a way that he could see nothing but the sky, 'thus restraining both the lust of the eyes and of the thoughts, and lifting the whole bent of his mind to higher things'.[4] In Grimlaïc's mind, prayer was effective in purging evil thoughts, for, when an

---

[2] *Acta SS, Maii* VI, 430A; Eadwold, 206.
[3] *LG*, 67–9, 71; Ridyard, 'Functions', 238.
[4] *Cuthbert*, ed. Colgrave, 217. The beehive cells on Skellig Michael, a Celtic monastic site off the west coast of Ireland, command a view of the sea and the sky.

anchorite prayed, impurities were purged through the confession of sins and chased away by the contemplation of God's goodness. Smaragdus too perceived that prayer cleansed the soul.[5] At the simplest level it involved emptying one's mind of bad things and filling it with good. Anselm advised some recluses: 'Let your conversation always be pure and godly'; that way evil thoughts should never get a foothold. Likewise, Goscelin wrote to Eve: 'Diligently purge your innermost being until you strike the artery of God's living waters, so that longing for heaven wells up from the insatiable abyss of your heart.'[6] This image of digging a well – of shifting sin's accumulated dirt to strike pure water – is a metaphor of how solitary purgation was believed to operate. To adapt it, one might say that the morbid deposits of original sin always threatened to clog the artery, and the way to keep it healthy was to purge them, like an anchorite.

Devotional prayer cleansed the mind by edifying the spirit, focusing the mind on God, and maintaining the anchorite's dialogue with heaven. In the Bible and the works of the fathers, it took various forms: the recitation of psalms and sacred texts, silent receptive expectation, meditative reflection during *lectio divina* (i.e. while reading sacred writings), the prayerful dedication of manual labour to God, or the mechanical utterance of blessings. The blend of these components in any anchorite's devotion depended on his education and outlook. Brihtric, Goscelin narrates, was 'a simple and upright man', a rustic 'who knew nothing except Christ crucified' (1 Cor. 2.2). Lacking a clerical education, he could only offer in prayer what few scraps he knew: a Sunday oration, the first verse of Psalm 50, and the *Gloria patri*. Scraps they were, but he offered them ceaselessly.[7] Christina, being sufficiently educated to read the psalter, entered the first of her cells with broader devotional horizons. From the first day of her enclosure, she consoled herself by choosing psalms appropriate to her circumstances, which fired her enthusiasm for heaven, bewailed her persecution, and cried out for deliverance.[8] Wulfric entered seclusion as an experienced parish priest. His devotions consisted mostly in reciting the psalter, once by day and once by night; other devotions included 'hymns, prayers, and frequent genuflexions'.[9] Godric of Finchale recited his psalter, which he memorized, but was also prone to spontaneous outpourings of the soul such as 'Sweet Jesus have pity on your wretched servant'; 'O loving Christ, how long must we be apart', and 'Have mercy Lord, remember not my sins'. Other prayers took the form of short hymns he had learned or composed.[10] Tears, a

---

[5] *Grimlaici . . . regula*, 619–21; Smaragdus of Saint-Mihiel, *Diadema monachorum*, PL, 102: 593–690, at 597.

[6] *Opera*, ed. Schmitt, IV, no. 230 (134–5, 135); *LC*, 106 (summary translation).

[7] *LC*, 67.

[8] Her first choice was Psalm 37: *LCM*, 93, 99.

[9] *WH*, 37, 19.

[10] Reginald puts a few prayers of this sort into Godric's mouth: *LG*, 72, 158, 203; and see 41–2, 201 for his psalter. For Godric's hymns, see *ibid.*, 119, 144; also H. Deeming, 'The Songs of St Godric: A Neglected Context', *Music and Letters*, 86 (2005), 169–85.

symbol of cleansing, often accompanied these pleas to heaven. According to Grimlaïc, weeping and groaning served to remind anchorites of the gravity of their sins and renew their fears of the torments of hell.[11] A trickle of monks from Durham said masses for Godric or sung psalms while he kept silence. With their assistance, the hermit constructed his own horarium from the psalmody and prayers he knew.[12] Aelred of Rievaulx recommended short prayer, but he also encouraged his sister, in keeping with the meditations of St Bernard of Clairvaux, to embark upon prolonged meditation on Christ. The recluse was to imagine herself as an intimate participant in her saviour's life from birth to death, living through him and with him, considering how she would react to each scene of his unfolding drama. She should contemplate his divine conception and picture herself as Mary nurturing the baby in her womb, or washing Christ's feet, or standing with his mother at the foot of the cross. Pursuing her contemplative journey she should enter the house of the Pharisees and meditate on her redeemer, before at last anticipating the joys of heaven.[13] In Aelred's Cistercian logic, when the mind was filled with such thoughts it could scarcely contemplate evil.

Whereas the mind was vulnerable to evil thoughts, the body was prey to unruly, insatiable appetites for food, sleep, comfort, and sexual stimulation. The flesh – 'this rotten corpse' – hung heavily around every anchorite, hampering the agility of his soul with its corpulence and sluggishness.[14] When the flesh was disburdened through fasting and affliction, it became easier for the aerial soul to ascend heavenwards in contemplation (a theme noted in the previous chapter). Abstinence with this objective was a way of offloading ballast to lighten the soul's ascent and enliven the spirit to battle. Grimlaïc wrote, timelessly: 'We cannot well stay vigilant when the stomach is laden with rich food; ... for, as a warrior heavy-laden is weighed down and impeded in battle, so too the recluse is encumbered at vigils when hot-swollen with a bellyful of meats.'[15] Excess baggage portended death both spiritual and physical. 'How fitting he should sit on a tomb', muttered Godric of Finchale to Aelred, eyeing a fat monk's repose, 'for soon he'll be laid in the ground. See how he warms with sluggish-ness ... he has stuffed the rotten putrefaction of his flesh with all sorts of delicacies. Now he can barely walk without a stick, nor mount his horse without help.' After muttering these remarks (according to his hagiographer), Godric contrasted the monk's malaise with his own abstemious condition: 'I on the other hand, having served Christ these many years as an indigent pauper, and having arrested and punished my miserable spirit with toilsome hardship, do not need such supports, but sweat incessantly with vigorous labour.'[16] In the ascetic

---

[11] *Grimlaici ... regula*, 620.
[12] *LG*, 136–8, 204, 211, 110–11.
[13] *Opera omnia I*, ed. Hoste and Talbot, *passim*.
[14] Hart, *Charters*, 166.
[15] *Grimlaici ... regula*, 635.
[16] *LG*, 176.

tradition, the sin of gluttony pandered to the body at the soul's expense. The man that pampered his flesh, it was thought, made a corpse of himself to die in, whereas the spiritual man attended to the best interests of his soul.

Anchorites warred against the flesh by torturing it into submission, extinguishing its lusts with pain, until the only appetite it could contrive was the desire for physical relief. Knowing that a hermit's objectives were a mind dedicated to prayer and the flesh in submission to it, Godric set about taming both.[17] His strategy was to combine his devotions with mortifications in two-pronged assaults that purged his mind and afflicted his body simultaneously, blocking off both avenues of temptation at once. To prepare the ground, he would fast for two or three days at a time, or six if this was what it took to weaken his fleshly appetite. Throughout the day he agonized in prayer to be rid of sin; then, rising with the moon, he tormented his body by chopping wood, dressed all the while in his abrasive hairshirt and hauberk. Returning to his oratory, dripping with sweat, he would assail heaven once more with a crescendo of tearful prayers. If sin still loitered Godric would engulf it in torment by hurling his naked body among brambles, after the example of St Benedict.[18] He averted hunger with stale bread and mouldy roots, and he repulsed fatigue by sleeping on sack-cloth with a stone for his pillow.[19] Allied to the two-pronged attack was a stratagem of variation. For while hauberks and hairshirts functioned to inflict continual punishment, varying the attack by adding immersions or flagellations, during which these garments were removed (before being inflicted once again upon his duly weakened flesh), lessened the risk that the flesh might harden to them. It also provided respite. On nights when snow covered the ground, Godric chose to immerse his naked body in the River Wear, presenting himself as a living sacrifice by raising his hands heavenward while pouring forth tearful prayers, and steeling his resolve with the thought that these trials were as nothing when compared with hell.[20] Wulfric passed his nights immersed in a cistern. Overwhelming bodily appetites with the icy water, this 'executioner of his flesh' recited the psalter to supplant sinful thoughts with praise.[21] Godric of Throckenholt's preferred blitzkrieg, intended as much as a respite (*refrigerium*), was a scourge of reeds. Whenever his chafed flesh formed a scabrous crust under his hairshirt and hauberk, he removed them and bade a confidant scrub his back with his scourge until the blood ran dripping to the floor.[22] His flesh thus softened, he would dress it once

---

[17] *LG*, 68, 77.

[18] *Ibid.*, 77–8, 76.

[19] *Ibid.*, 81–4.

[20] *Ibid.*, 85–6. This was an old Irish penitential practice. See C. Ireland, 'Penance and Prayer in Water: An Irish Practice in Northumbrian Hagiography', *Cambrian Medieval Celtic Studies*, 34 (1998 for 1997), 51–66.

[21] *WH*, 17–19; cf. Grimlaïc's tactics, *Grimlaici . . . regula*, 621, 635. Walter Daniel explains that Aelred of Rievaulx immersed himself in icy water 'to quench the heat in himself of every vice': Walter Daniel, *The Life of Ailred of Rievaulx*, ed. F. M. Powicke (London, 1978), 25.

[22] *GT*, 30.

more in the torments of those garments, just as Wulfric and Godric habitually did after their nocturnal immersions. The rotation of torments replicated, and perhaps reminded anchorites of, the rota of pains inflicted on sinners in hell (often represented by extremes of heat and cold), to stop their bodies from acclimatizing to suffering.[23]

Anchorites also quenched their appetites by restricting their consumption of food. 'The belly and the genitals are neighbours' it was said. Fuel the one, and the two are swiftly ablaze.[24] Fasting and abstinence were practical strategies for starving their unruly conflagrations, without which no spiritual warrior could survive. Eadwold of Cerne was remembered for having lived on bread and water; the recluse Eve won fame for her abstinence, and St Albans revered the anchorite Wulf partly on account of his Spartan intake.[25] Many of the saintly anchorites who were emulated in this era had their diets recorded in detail, which later suggested regimes for their followers. Jerome's *Life* of St Paul spoke of a hermit who had lived thirty years on barley bread and muddy water. Guthlac (or his hagiographer) responded to this tale, for his daily repast was said to have consisted of a scrap of barley bread and a cup of muddy water, taken after sunset.[26] Eadwold had his barley bread from a local shepherd. Godric of Finchale preferred to pattern his diet on that of his patron, St John the Baptist.[27] The dietary regimes devised by anchorites were often in line with prevailing peniten-tial practices, which may have been intended to serve the practical function of averting fleshly appetites. Godric of Throckenholt fasted on the penitential staples of bread and water. Goscelin depicts Eadwold adhering to a similar penitential or ascetic regime: three times a week, on Sundays, Tuesdays, and Thursdays, his servant brings bread, occasionally with milk. Other anchorites restricted their intake to roots, herbs, and perhaps fruit and vegetables grown in gardens adjoining their hermitages. Godric of Finchale grew beans and apples; the recluse of Thanet was likewise content with apples and beans. During Lent, she adopted a penitential regime in which, according to Goscelin (and adhering to usual strictures set out in penitentials), 'she ate this sort of food three days a week'. Whenever she was urged to moderate her abstinence lest she suffer for lack of sustenance, she told of a friend – perhaps another recluse – who habitually ate nothing between Wednesday and Sunday, and felt none the worse.[28] This was all part of her warfare – in seizing every initiative from her enemy, the flesh.

---

[23] For hell's rotating torments, see J. Le Goff, *The Birth of Purgatory*, tr. A. Goldhammer (London, 1984), 9, 36, 126 (here too the alternation of hot with cold was sometimes a respite: see *ibid.*, 120).

[24] *Ancrene Wisse*, ed. Millett, I, 139 and 139n.

[25] *Chronicle*, ed. Darlington and McGurk, II, 538; Elkins, *Holy Women*, 25–6; *Gesta abbatum monasterii sancti Albani*, ed. H. T. Riley, RS, 28, 3 vols (1867–9) I, 21.

[26] *Guthlac*, ed. Colgrave, 95.

[27] *LG*, 42–3.

[28] Rollason, 'Miracles of St Mildrith', 210.

WARRING WITH DEMONS

Anchoretic warfare also involved relentless attacks by evil spirits, which inflamed the lusts of the flesh or planted wicked thoughts in the mind. These were the beings cast out of the lofty regions of the higher heavens for their rebellion under Lucifer. They were animal in genus, rational like humans but aerial in body and eternal in time. 'Spirits fanatically bent on doing harm, completely at odds with justice, swollen with pride, green with envy, and well versed in deceit', their objective by any means at their disposal was to divert souls – especially the pious – from the narrow path and plunge them into hell.[29] Traditionally, demons mustered in lonely places. St Antony had gone to battle with them on their own terrain. Some nights when he was alone at prayer on the inner mountain his followers heard tumults, voices, and a clash of arms, or saw the mountainside swarming with strange beasts, or caught sight of the hermit struggling as with invisible entities. Ever since Antony had driven the demons from the desert, hermits following in his footsteps had advanced the frontiers of God's kingdom, in England from Inner Farne to Crowland, expelling Satan's minions and establishing outposts along the haunted border regions. Maintaining such bastions required unceasing ascetic struggle. Bede described the hermit Felgild, Cuthbert's successor-but-one, as 'the third heir of that dwelling and of that spiritual warfare', implying that without a steady reinforcement of hermits the devils might return.[30] Sometimes the demons wept at being driven from their haunts, complaining that they could make no impact on God's saints; but Bede's *Life* of Cuthbert decries them as usurpers.[31] Taking Christ's fight to the devil in the wilderness was the anchorite's prerogative, enshrined within the Benedictine and eremitic traditions. Godric duly set out 'to do battle with the ancient enemy'; Finchale was 'the arena of his combat with the ancient serpent'.[32] It was acknowledged that anchorites could become so wise to the devil that they might qualify as expert demonologists. Cuthbert 'had learned how to lay bare before tempted men the manifold wiles of the ancient foe'.[33] Romuald battled demons so successfully that he decided to write a guide for those who wished to fight them.[34] Eleventh-century monks thought it plausible that a hermit could trap a devil and force from it secrets about the otherworld, or that St Dunstan could catch Satan's nose in his tongs. The recluse Ælfwine of Evesham was held to possess a special faculty for seeing the demons that swarmed all over his

---

[29] Augustine, *De civitate Dei*, VIII.14, 22.
[30] *Cuthbert*, ed. Colgrave, 303.
[31] *Ibid.*, 215–7.
[32] '[L]ocum certaminis sui' (cf. 'loco huius certaminis': *Cuthbert*, ed Colgrave, 228): *LG*, 41, 225.
[33] *Cuthbert*, ed. Colgrave, 229
[34] *Vita*, ed. Tabacco, 70. His book is not known to survive.

monastery.[35] Goscelin rejoiced that Satan, who 'once had not been content to rule over the stars and even the angels', was forced to battle the recluse of Thanet, 'a feeble little girl'.[36] Henry of Coquet was such a successful exorcist that, after his death, the saint saved a sick priest's soul from a troupe of demons and drove them retreating into the ether.[37]

The sheer logistical scale of the diabolical campaigns mounted against anchorites was a great proof of their sanctity, for the devil desired above all to corrupt the purest of God's saints. His armoury was amply equipped for physical and mental warfare, so that over the course of a single anchorite's career hundreds if not thousands of demons skilled in all forms of temptation could be mobilized in every conceivable disguise, and countless plots hatched or traps sprung, all for the purpose of claiming one soul (or of stopping anchorites from leading others to heaven). First there were the bludgeoning weapons of violence and intimidation designed to inflict pain, shock, confusion, and terror upon the would-be ascetic. Wicked spirits arrived at Finchale to beat the hermit, smash his possessions, and toss him from his bed. One entered his oratory and started to attack him while he prayed. With all the strength it could muster it hurled the pyx at him, then the horn of communion wine, then the vessel containing the wafers, before ripping down a shelf and its contents and pelting him with these projectiles from the far wall. Tusked demons vomiting flame tormented him. One appeared with a burning spear and threatened to carve him up the middle; others took the forms of wolves, bears, bulls, lions, 'poisonous' toads, and ravens.[38] At dusk they invaded the shadowy corners of his cell, like pitch-black pygmies, growing indignant when Godric ignored them and approaching him with hammers, clubs, pincers, burning splinters, and bloodthirsty hissing. In the dark, they would rise from the floor or burst through the cobbles.[39] Devils plagued the recluse of Thanet in the guise of bears, roaring lions, howling wolves, toads, frogs, hissing venomous water snakes, and monstrous reptiles.[40] At Haselbury a troupe of demons assembled to conceive an attack upon Wulfric before dragging him from his oratory through the church; another devil 'gazed at him with terrible eyes' and struck him with a stick.[41] At Markyate one of these spirits set fire to Roger's cowl during his devotions; others invaded Christina's cell in the likeness of toads: 'Their sudden appearance, with their big and terrible eyes, was most frightening.'[42] On the lonely island of Inner Farne, a demon seized Bartholomew by the throat and throttled him; another grabbed him by the hood as he prayed and flung him far

---

[35] *Chronicon abbatiae de Evesham*, ed. Macray, 322.
[36] Rollason, 'Miracles of St Mildrith', 208.
[37] *NL*, II, 26.
[38] *LG*, 88, 93, 231, 94, 87, 199, 63, 196, 76. Toads had a reputation for being poisonous animals.
[39] *Ibid.*, 104, 164–5, 107, 275; and 197, cf. 277.
[40] Rollason, 'Miracles of St Mildrith', 208, 209.
[41] *WH*, 39–40.
[42] *LCM*, 105, 99.

across the room. Shaggy black demons riding goats assaulted his hermitage with lances.[43] But there was a theological case to be made that God allowed such evils to befall the saints in order that they might be proven and strengthened like Job. For the devil could do nothing without permission.

When violence and intimidation proved ineffective, devils turned their attention to distracting anchorites from their devotions or to discouraging them. Godric of Finchale stood praying in the river one night when a hideously deformed demon appeared on the bank, spewing flame and gnashing its teeth. Seeking to interrupt the hermit's prayers by luring him from the water, it made a show of stealing his clothes, which he had left on the riverbank. The knot of toads that invaded Christina's cell intended 'to distract her attention from God's beauty by all kinds of ugliness'.[44] More often, demons sought to dismay anchorites, sometimes by mocking them, sometimes by defiling sacred objects, and occasionally by demonstrating resilience to normal techniques for expelling them. Typically they resorted to facetious obloquy. One devil accused Ælfwine of Evesham of violating his vow of poverty by accepting a gift: 'O what a great monk you are, tossing aside your vocation for the sake of a halfpenny! Ha! Truly now your hypocrisy is openly proven!' 'You're no true hermit you fat peasant', jeered a demon at the hermit of Finchale. '*Godric* indeed! *Pile of shit* would be a better name for you; . . . this Godric's the vilest peasant, the filthiest pigsty cleaner . . . You pretend to be a saint when everyone detests you!' Another taunted his psalmody: 'Ahoy decrepit bumpkin, rustic shit-heap! I know as well how psalms *should* be sung as you know how to croak them out with hisses!'[45] Many demonic jibes like this one focus on Godric's lack of education and may have echoed the critical sentiments of certain high-minded monks of Durham. Placing them in the mouths of devils served a clear polemical purpose, but it may also show what sort of remarks stung the hermit. The devil's tendency to mock Godric for being a 'mad rustic', coupled with defensive tirades from his hagiographer asserting that God could still work his wonders through an 'ignorant layman', may betray his sensitivities.[46] Writing about Godric in the 1190s, the chronicler William of Newburgh picked up the same theme, claiming that God had used this man 'to the confusion of the noble and great'.[47] Rejoicing in the scandal of simplicity with words echoing those Goscelin had used to describe the recluse Brihtric, William characterized Godric as the simplest rustic who knew nothing but Christ crucified.[48] In Bede's *Life* of St Cuthbert, the attribution of rustic simplicity implied that the subject was incapable of inventing an untruth;

---

[43] *VB*, 305, 314.

[44] *LG*, 87; *LCM*, 99.

[45] *Chronicon abbatiae de Evesham*, ed. Macray, 323; *LG*, 234, 93.

[46] *LG*, 93, 95, 314, and see 192.

[47] *Chronicles of the Reigns of Stephen, Henry II, and Richard I*, ed. R. Howlett, RS, 82, 4 vols (1884–9), I, 149.

[48] *Ibid.*, 149 (1 Cor. 2.2).

but it could also suggest vulnerability, and both Goscelin and William recorded of their respective anchorites that the devil had turned simplicity to his advantage.[49] Battle lines may well have been drawn between those who shared the Cistercian contempt for learning (Godric's hagiographer and William wrote partly for Cistercians) and those suspicious of Godric's lack of it. The latter camp may have been seen to be fuelling the devil's campaign to plant self-doubt in the hermit's mind.

Devils also sought to instil doubt and dismay by defiling sacred objects as though sacred things held no power over them. Christina's demonic toads squatted on the pages of her psalter; other demons tore pages from Godric's, shouted blasphemies, or farted in his oratories and flung his Holy Communion vessels to the floor.[50] On one occasion, his devotions cast a warped reflection when the devil put on a comparable show of piety to ridicule his. Bursting through the northerly corner of the church, he divided himself into four homunculi, which aped the hermit by genuflecting and beating their breasts before the altar. Turning to him with a show of reverence, they bowed their heads mockingly as though acknowledging his sanctity, before returning their attention to the altar in pretence of prayer.[51] Even devils could pray – so what if Godric did? At crucial moments of the hermit's career when anxieties ran high and much was at stake, his adversary drew on hidden reserves of strength to overcome his embattled resolve. These efforts apparently peaked over the long period when Godric was bedridden during his final illness, the devil thinking that at last he might get the better of him. Godric lay ill; physically, he was at his weakest, when a young servant noticed devils crouching at his bedside. The youth sprinkled holy water on them but they refused to budge. Again he tried, this time drenching them, and still they sat there, grinning at him. In an earlier encounter with a demon, Godric had expressed some astonishment at its ability to withstand the blessing of holy water. Now, this device, usually efficacious for dispelling phantasms, no longer seemed to work.[52] The intermittent deactivation of apotropaic mechanisms served to remind anchorites where their power source lay: without grace such gestures were nugatory, redundant. God was permitting the devil to play on Godric's fears, that he might be tested. On a separate occasion, two demons appeared at his sickbed declaring: 'Behold, we have come here to cart you off to hell because you're a crazy old man who's gone in the head.'[53] Whenever devils appeared that no other person could see, Godric would bellow loudly, roll back his eyelids, and fix his gaze on where they stood, until others could see them.[54] Through all these manifestations the devil tried to

---

[49] *Cuthbert*, ed. Colgrave, 165; *Chronicles*, ed. Howlett, I, 150.
[50] *LCM*, 99; *LG*, 364, 354, 252, 94.
[51] *LG*, 277.
[52] *Ibid.*, 196–7, 251, 166.
[53] *Ibid.*, 311.
[54] *Ibid.*, 249.

persuade the hermit that his piety was a sham, that he was unqualified for sanctity, that he was a hypocrite, that the armoury of heaven was no match for his superior foe, and that he certainly should be damned. His overarching objective was to entice Godric into the sin of despair, the first sin that tempted the penitent freebooter Guthlac when the devil reminded him how far from salvation he stood, having perpetrated so many crimes.[55] If fear and despair made no inroads on the anchorite, the tempter used craftier tactics.

One ruse was to interrupt or end some laudable activity by tricking the anchorite into thinking that what he was doing was misguided. So unbearable did the devil find Brihtric's ceaseless prayer that he criticized his importunity as offensive to God, cunningly citing scripture to deter him: 'do not pile up words in prayer'.[56] 'Bruised by these tricks the simple man imposed silence on his lips.' The devil's mischief was exposed the next day when Brihtric related this incident to the wise monk Æthelsige. Another ploy, first unmasked in the *Life* of St Antony, was to make an anchorite feel inadequate by urging Sisyphean feats of asceticism on him until he should despair of fulfilling his proposition.[57] Bent on such purposes, one devil, dressed as a pilgrim, went to Finchale pretending to be a hermit. Drawing back his cloak to reveal putrid, ulcerous flesh almost dissolving on account of his punishing mortifications, he asked his appalled host to inspect his miserable condition. If Godric were a genuine hermit, boasted the impostor, he would be following his example. To belittle and entice him by pretended achievements, the demon recounted tales of how he had been rapt up to heaven before God and his angels. On a separate occasion, a devil in disguise put Godric's labours to shame by digging his entire vegetable garden in a moment.[58] Yet another fiendish stratagem was to lull the victim into a sense of complacency before catching him off-guard. Even Wulfric was unable to win every battle, and the enemy – it was supposed – timed his every victory to inflict the maximum misery. Wulfric confessed to a Cistercian abbot that for eighteen years he had been tempted to masturbate on the toilet. One Easter, after his vigils had been making some headway through Lent, the foe disarmed him with sleep before stealing upon him on the night before Easter Day and effecting a wet dream.[59] Wulfric was thus overcome. Some demonic attacks aimed to dupe anchorites into committing specific sins. A traditional tale circulating in our period told of how the devil, robed as an angel, appeared before an anchorite to warn him that the day thereafter Satan should arrive disguised as the anchorite's father. When his father appeared, he axed him to death.[60] Murder was Satan's goal in the tale of Alexander too, again successfully accomplished. Among the

---

[55] *Guthlac*, ed. Colgrave, 97.
[56] 'Verbum in oratione ne repetas' (cf. Eccl. 7.15): *LC*, 67.
[57] *Guthlac*, ed. Colgrave, 184.
[58] *LG*, 164–5, 107–8.
[59] *WH*, 41–3.
[60] Thompson, *Motif-index*, K943.

malevolent, shape-shifting spirits that plagued Godric of Finchale were demons of avarice, one of which sent him digging for treasure, another of which, dressed as a goldsmith, tempted him with his wares. Some assailed his chastity in the guise of pretty girls. Two claimed to specialize respectively in goading others to wrongdoing and polluting the flesh with lust. One demon even tried to make him drink poison.[61]

Although the devil remained a wily, chimerical opponent, experienced anchorites learned to recognize and repel his attacks. Patristic texts, particularly the *Life* of St Antony and *Moralia in Job* ('A moral exegesis of Job') by Pope St Gregory the Great (c.540–604), contained a wealth of expertise on how to discern and overcome the tempter's machinations. Goscelin advised Eve to read the *Life* of St Antony because it would 'safeguard her against the devil's plots'.[62] He also offered advice of his own. Prior Roger of Durham (d. 1149) taught Godric of Finchale so many things about spiritual warfare that the devil blamed the monk for briefing the hermit against his illusions and punished Roger by filling his nostrils with a suffocating stench. After the monk Æthelsige had exposed the devil's trickery to Brihtric, the recluse returned to his routine of perpetual prayer, fortified with greater fervour.[63] Sometimes God would grant his warriors special powers, so although demons were normally invisible some anchorites acquired the ability to see them. This was of great assistance because their plots could then be laid bare. Ælfwine of Evesham 'saw the enemies of the human race so clearly that he could discern their speech and actions as though they were men'. Godric of Finchale 'was accustomed to see the trickery and traps of demons which duped other men; he would often describe their countless molestations in the dead of night. Thus enlightened, many were plucked from their snares'. Two monks singing nocturns for the hermit once fell into an argument, one accusing the other of fluffing the notes and nodding off. Godric then revealed that a tiny tonsured demon had been running between them, inciting the first to anger while rendering his companion drowsy and full of mistakes.[64] As soon as devils were detected, attempts could be made to overcome them. Godric fought back with staunch indifference or resistance, by making the sign of the cross, bidding them depart in the divine name, confronting them with images of the saints from his psalter, pouring holy water on them, and even by attacking them with axes. Holy water and the sign of the cross were effective in Bartholomew's duels with the demons of Inner Farne; Brihtric too dismissed a devil by making the sign of the cross. Other devils proved more resilient. Some nine hours of spiritual exertion were needed to defeat a self-proclaimed 'prince of

---

[61] *LG*, 275, 276, 242, 254, 356, 248.

[62] *LC*, 80.

[63] *LG*, 95; *LC*, 67.

[64] T. Licence, 'The Gift of Seeing Demons in Early Cistercian Spirituality', *Cistercian Studies Quarterly*, 39 (2004), 49–65; *Chronicon abbatiae de Evesham*, ed. Macray, 322; *LG*, 104n, 256–7.

demons' which arrived threatening to slice Godric in half and which made three assaults on him during the ensuing battle. Godric retaliated by denouncing it, making the sign of the cross, and invoking Christ 'the Victor and Judge'. Frightening noises bellowed from his oratory (a servant who ran in was terrified by what he saw), but at last the fiend was overthrown and expelled.[65] When Godric overcame evil spirits, they frequently punished him by leaving tempting thoughts, nausea, or putrid odours.

Some attacks were so dangerous that only intervention from heaven could stop them. In the context of spiritual warfare, heavenly agents could be pitted against diabolical potentates after a principle that operated throughout medieval society: that the man whose liege-lord was mightier than his opponent's might hope to prevail. In a crisis, the absolute power of God and his saints over devils could be wielded as a trump. So when the devil tried to strangle Bartholomew of Farne the hermit cried out loudly, ceaselessly, and, as it happened, successfully for the Virgin to come to his aid. In other instances, saints intervened of their own volition to save anchorites, affirming that anchorites were of their own company. Mary's sudden appearance dispelled the demons that had been dragging Wulfric brutally through the church and cemetery. St Bartholomew's timely arrival prevented an air-borne troupe of demons, which had kidnapped Guthlac, from dropping him into the maw of hell.[66] Like the devils that appeared at Godric's bedside, they claimed God's authorization to hurl him in, but St Bartholomew's authority compelled them to carry the hermit back to Crowland 'with the utmost gentleness'. The next morning, Guthlac saw two of these spirits weeping beside him, and when he asked why they wept they answered: 'We mourn for our strength which has been everywhere broken by you, and we bewail our lack of power against your strength; for we dare not touch you nor even approach you'; having said these words, they vanished.[67] The innate power of scripture could be equal proof against devils. When a company of marching soldiers besieged Guthlac's barrow, he dispelled the phantasm by chanting the first verse of Psalm 67: 'Let God arise, let his enemies be scattered; let his foes flee before him'. St Antony had used this verse to the same effect.[68] When the recluse of Thanet perceived that the army of reptiles invading her cell was no more than a phantasm, with a flash of inspiration she began reciting the first fourteen verses of St John. 'Speaking the gospel, she hurled flaming darts of the Lord's Word into that whole pestiferous crew.' When she had finished, her cell was utterly purged. The demons had fled, 'like night struck by the sun'.[69] Grimlaïc recommended prayer as a means of repelling the devil, advising recluses to persist in this tactic

---

[65] *LG*, 199–200.
[66] *VB*, 305; *WH*, 40; *Guthlac*, ed. Colgrave, 107.
[67] *Guthlac*, ed. Colgrave, 109.
[68] *Ibid.*, 111, 186. Guthlac's action is modelled on Antony's.
[69] Rollason, 'Miracles of St Mildrith', 209.

notwithstanding the devil's attempts to interrupt or even harm them.[70] All these apotropaic devices, whether prayer, symbols of the faith, appeals to saints, or the citation of scripture ultimately reminded a solitary of her dependence on God: every time one weapon failed she was forced to return afresh to the divine armoury. Her constant raging warfare clarified her spiritual insight and sharpened her faculty of discerning conflicts between good and evil in everyday affairs. At the same time, her power over the lethal spirits which ensnared ordinary women and men with invisible subterfuge set her above her fellow beings, as a figure they could look up to.

FORBEARANCE IN THE VOCATION

An anchorite's life of spiritual warfare required strength of character and staunch determination. Renouncing the world was only the first hurdle. Afterwards a lifetime had to be spent besieging the rebellious flesh and pitting the resolve against hordes of malevolent enemies. These trials could make the world all the more enticing. Like its allies, the flesh and the devil, it would never lie down and die, but lingered in the realm of memory, where it tempted its exiles to return. Certain anchorites, having entered solitude under compulsion or with insufficient resolution, abandoned their proposition when the storm clouds had passed or because it all proved too much for them. When King Richard, his persecutor, died, the fugitive knight who was living with Robert of Knaresborough went back to his wife and children, 'like a dog to its vomit'.[71] The hermits Ealdwine and Guy considered abandoning their hermitage at Malvern to go on pilgrimage. The Carthusians Andrew and Alexander grew so bored of their cells, 'having only the walls which shut us in to look at', that they hurried home.[72] Knowledge that many abandoned the solitary life roused greater admiration for anchorites who endured in its travails. Often this found an outlet of expression in recounting the tally of years any anchorite had racked up in isolation. So impressed was Dominic of Evesham that Wulfsige and Basing had lived in seclusion for seventy-five and seventy-two years respectively that he noted only this about them.[73] Godric's obit recorded that he had lived as a hermit at Finchale for sixty; Godric of Throckenholt's hagiographer, that he had lived in the wilderness for forty; John of Worcester wrote that in 1062 Wulfsige had been a recluse for over forty years; and Goscelin noted that Ælfwen had been enclosed at St Stephen's, Canterbury, for thirty. A lead plaque unearthed in the abbey church of Saint-

---

[70] *Grimlaici . . . regula*, 620, 622.
[71] VRK, 368–9 (Prv 26.11).
[72] *Gesta pontificum*, ed. Winterbottom and Thomson, I, 434–5; *St Hugh of Lincoln*, ed. Douie and Farmer, I, 81.
[73] *Chronicon abbatiae de Evesham*, ed. Macray, 322.

Amand in Nord in northern France recorded that Emma (d. 1124) had lived there as a recluse for thirty-six years. Louis Gougaud, searching medieval sources, found five recluses enclosed for over twenty years, three for more than thirty, five for more than forty, one for fifty-six, and one for eighty. Bartholomew of Farne, so it was recorded, had dwelt (in his earthly purgatory) for forty-two years, six months, and nineteen days.[74] Every day was made to count. Longevity too could be interpreted as a mark of sanctity. The ascetics Paul, Antony, and Romuald were thought to have passed a hundred, and it was noted that Godric of Throckenholt and Ælfwen of Canterbury had reached eighty. If the figures are trustworthy, Wulfsige, Basing, Godric of Finchale, and Gilbert of Sempringham lived to be nonagenarians or centenarians. Their restricted diet may have prolonged their lives. In these sorts of cases, however, their longevity impressed contemporaries rather less than the length of time the ascetics had devoted to the anchoretic vocation.

Forbearance in the vocation was both physical and psychological. Christina spent four years concealed in a cramped cupboard in Roger's cell: 'O what trials she had to bear of cold and heat, hunger and thirst, daily fasting', her hagiographer exclaimed, before detailing the adverse physiological consequences of her confinement.[75] Sickness, fasting, and lack of comforts probably weakened hermits and recluses, rendering them vulnerable to bitter winters. Records from Saint Gall reveal that nine of the thirteen recluses whose deaths were recorded during the tenth and eleventh centuries died in the period from late November to the middle of March. Seven died during the three months December, January, and February alone. Writing in 1018, the chronicler Thietmar of Merseburg remarked that many winters passed in which the recluse Sisu of his diocese almost froze to death.[76] Other monastic writers imagined the hardships suffered by anchorites in late antiquity. Goscelin in his discourse to Eve eulogized their endurance, describing feats for which they were often praised. Paul, the first hermit, had dwelt in solitude for sixty years in perfect isolation, with only palm trees to feed and clothe him and a pool in a concave rock to drink from. Mary of Egypt had withstood the seasonal extremes of forty-six winters and summers in the desert, neither home nor shelter nor coat nor cave to cover her, waiting on heaven in nakedness. Nakedness and endurance were themes in the rhetoric of imitating Christ. Such hardships were generally seen as proof of uncompromising commitment to God.

[74] *LG*, 331; GT, 38; *Chronicle*, ed. Darlington and McGurk, II, 591; Rollason, 'Miracles of St Mildrith', 197; Serbat, 'Inscriptions; Gougaud', *Ermites*, 93; *VB*, 322.

[75] *LCM*, 103.

[76] Schlumpf, *Quellen*, 6; *Chronik*, ed. Holtzmann, 502–4. This pattern of death may not have been exceptional. Seasonal mortality in a pre-industrial population is assessed in E. A. Wrigley, R. S. Davies, J. E. Oeppen, and R. S. Schofield, *English Population History from Family Reconstitution 1580–1837* (Cambridge, 1997), 332–3. In that sample, winter deaths clump between January and April and are noticeably higher among the elderly. I am grateful to Peter Kitson for pointing me to this reference.

The show of psychological forbearance was just as impressive as the physical. Monks such as Goscelin appreciated that the besetting sin of their vocation known as accidie – the loss of motivation through ennui – for obvious reasons loomed larger in the solitary life. Eve, 'a little girl', would have to sit in her cell until her fiftieth or hundredth year while the devil whispered boredom, recalling the bright, sunlit world outside.[77] Aelred believed that accidie was the deadliest temptation a recluse had to face. (As was noted earlier, the tedium of confinement could defeat even avowed Carthusians.) His sibling should nevertheless prevail, he wrote, if she alternated her activities, so when she tired of one she tried another.[78] The recluse who importuned his bishop for fresh reading material, despite dwelling in a cell already full of biblical, patristic, and contemporary books, craved new stimuli, as did those recluses who in boredom took to gossiping.[79] Other solitaries devised routines to relieve the long days and nights. Godric of Throckenholt, who usually conducted his devotions sitting on a wooden chair, sometimes prayed kneeling on a hassock inside his oratory. 'So effective was this arrangement of switching between the two that by a secret regimen he could avoid accidie during his prayers.' Bartholomew of Farne staved off listlessness by alternating between writing, reading, singing psalms, praying, and undertaking long vigils; he also caught lumpfish. Godric of Finchale apportioned his time to prayer, meditation, and manual labour, dividing his devotions between his two oratories. 'Alternating between them often proved a great reinvigorating comfort to him', wrote his hagiographer Reginald.[80] These anchorites probably learned how to combat tedium through trial and error, for however loudly prevailing wisdoms may or may not have proclaimed a formula the solution depended upon the individual. For Godric and Godric, the alternation of activities on its own was not enough: they also felt an urge to vary their location, posture, and the saint addressed in prayer. Accidie was capable of destroying anchorites on its own without any additional onslaughts of devil and flesh. Simply to last in the vocation therefore was a hallmark of dedication.

Forbearance showed that an anchorite had sacrificed his or her destiny to God. In the hagiographical tradition, when someone opted for the solitary life a representative of heaven would appear and send the would-be anchorite to a place divinely allotted, there to live out her days in God's service. In this place, having yielded her life to God, the anchorite acted out a future no longer her own but set according to heaven's design. When Ealdwine thought about leaving his hermitage at Malvern to go on a pilgrimage, Bishop Wulfstan, foreseeing God's plans for him there, bade him stay.[81] When the recluse of Thanet tried to remove herself to an empty cell in a neighbouring village, a furious St Mildthryth, who

---

[77] *LC*, 75, 70.
[78] *Opera omnia I*, ed. Hoste and Talbot, 645.
[79] *Epistolae*, ed. Anstruther, 95.
[80] GT, 28; *VB*, 300; *LG*, 153.
[81] *Gesta pontificum*, ed. Winterbottom and Thomson, I, 434–5.

had sent her there forever, froze her to the spot; so too a debilitating illness from heaven quelled Henry's misguided compunction to leave Coquet, when sad family members were tempting him to return to Denmark.[82] Some writers, as we have seen, thought that an anchorite's stay on earth was limited by a providential timescale ordained as much for the anchorite's purgation as for the unfolding of the Lord's magisterial design. Earlier, it was argued that Eadwold's anachoresis is represented as a satisfactory penance. Likewise the recluse of Thanet only died when she had 'completed her objective'.[83] In exile-model hagiographies, the significance of the divinely allotted spot lay partly in its function as an ordained *locus purgatorius*, whereby it replicated on earth the notion that imperfect souls at death were assigned set places of punishment or purification in the otherworld. The *Liber confortatorius* concludes its discussion of long-suffering anchorites accordingly with the bold claim that any ascetic of this calibre 'should die so pure as never to encounter the all-consuming purgatorial fire'.[84] Godric of Throckenholt's hauberk, donned with the prayer that it should endure until his sins be forgiven, fell apart after seven years: the time it took him to be purged.[85] The same process is implicit in Wulfric's oracle to the girl Matilda, for whom God had ordained fifteen years in an anchorhold before her removal in the sixteenth to a mansion prepared in heaven.[86] In her case, fifteen years as a recluse was a satisfactory penance, just as fifteen years of blindness afflicted the recluse at Leicester.[87] Geoffrey of Coldingham's description of Inner Farne, as 'a sort of purgatory on earth, established for the wholesome cleansing of bodies and souls', bears on his concluding statement that Bartholomew died after spending forty-two years, six months, and nineteen days there.[88] This, it appears, was the tariff for his sin. Those who counted the years that anchorites spent in solitude would have measured in these totals their souls' purification. For the tally of years spent in solitary warfare could be seen to reflect penance fulfilled and sins cleansed through a system of purgation overcoming the world, the flesh, and the devil.

There is a case to be made in conclusion that the art of spiritual warfare was the art of purification; that fasting, vigils, and flagellation served to lessen bodily desires, and that prayers, psalms, and spiritual exertions drove away evil thoughts. We tend to think of these practices as penitential practices, which served to punish sinners and display their remorse to God; but to label them 'penitential'

---

[82] Rollason, 'Miracles of St Mildrith', 208–9; *NL*, II, 23.
[83] Rollason, 'Miracles of St Mildrith', 210.
[84] *LC*, 77.
[85] *GT*, 32.
[86] *WH*, 82.
[87] *Acta SS, Maii* VI, 429F; cf. the year of blindness inflicted on the recluse of Thanet for her sins. In Goscelin's *Life* of Ivo, a thegn is crippled for fifteen years for mocking the saint: *Chronicon abbatiae Rameseiensis*, ed. Macray, p. xxxiii.
[88] *VB*, 312, 322.

might not do justice to their practical purpose or explain why they took the shape they did. In his study of prayer in water in early medieval Ireland, Colin Ireland argues that it is misleading to think of immersion as a penance, because its function was to control carnal desires.[89] This argument can be extended to encompass fasting, vigils, the use of garments such as hauberks and hairshirts, and the act of flagellation. These were no mere tokens of repentance but practical mechanisms for suppressing fleshly appetites, just as prayers and psalms were recognized prophylactics for the soul. Penitents and their priests may sometimes have interpreted fasting, flagellation, and the recitation of the psalter as fundamentally retributive, but those familiar with anachoresis and its art of spiritual warfare understood that they were restorative. 'O hermit's life', wrote Peter Damian, in an apostrophe to that vocation, 'bathtub of souls, annihilation of sins, purgatory of the soiled, you purify secret thoughts, wash away the filth of wicked deeds, and lead souls to the brilliance of angelic cleanness.' Anachoresis was a furnace 'wherein the vessels of the supernal king are forged and beaten to an everlasting lustre with the hammer of penance'. An anchorite's cell was 'a workshop of astonishing spiritual exercise in which the human soul surely restores in itself the image of its creator and returns to the purity of its source'.[90] What happened in the anchoretic movement of the eleventh and twelfth centuries was that people like Peter discovered the cleansing power of anachoresis and proclaimed its ability to restore fallen humanity. To convey this idea, he employed the noun 'purgatory' (*purgatorium*), as cited above, in relation to anachoresis. Borrowing it in a letter praising the solitary life, Bernard of Clairvaux wrote: 'through this brief purgatory [i.e. a hermit's sojourn on Earth] heaven's eternal banquet is secured'.[91] In this monastic context, the noun *purgatorium* referred to a cleansing life of penance: the anchorite's existence of constant spiritual warfare.[92] These anchorites were battling for salvation by creating a working purgatory on earth.

---

[89] Ireland, 'Penance', 54.

[90] *Die Briefe*, ed. Reindel, 273–6.

[91] '[A]nimarum purgatorium sordidarum' (from Damian); 'hoc per breue purgatorium comparatur eternum et celeste conuiuium': J. Leclercq, 'Deux opuscules médiévaux sur la vie solitaire', *Studia monastica*, 4 (1962), 93–109, at 99.

[92] Cf. Le Goff, *The Birth of Purgatory*, 3, 157, 165–8.

7

How anchorites helped others

So far we have focused on the objectives of the anchorites themselves. We now come to the paradox observed in the Introduction: that society supported and revered these seemingly antisocial figures. It is hard to imagine today a more misanthropic gesture than the active rejection of society, and yet women and men of the eleventh and twelfth centuries appear to have believed that anchorites nurtured an abiding love of humanity. According to Mayr-Harting's analysis, the anchorite was an arbitrator who was ideally positioned, by severing all social bonds, to resolve the tensions that arose in an age of social and economic upheaval. He also acted as a 'hinge-man' (the concept is Mayr-Harting's) between the community and the wider world. In addition, he was a healer and a repository: a sort of primitive banker, who was given charge of people's valuables.[1] All these hypotheses are plausible, and there is little reason to overturn them. Nevertheless, we may wonder, in light of our findings, whether these were his most important functions, given that eradication of sin was apparently the most significant concern in the efflorescence of anachoresis. We may also doubt that society would have venerated bankers, arbitrators, and hinge-men *per se*. Brown's emphasis may rest more squarely on the issue, for he saw anchorites as intercessors for mankind whose ascetic labours earned them a place in God's throne room, where they would intercede for sinners. To adapt the metaphor of the bridge: the anchorite could stand across the chasm opened up by sin, which separated human beings from God. In his role as heavenly intercessor and a preacher of repentance on earth, he reconciled humanity to God in heaven by working to annul the consequences of sin.[2] Ridyard substantiates this hypothesis in her article on Godric of Finchale, showing, by several examples, that 'the essence of his ministry' was 'to reveal and correct . . . sin, thus supporting his acquaintances in their somewhat shaky steps towards salvation'.[3] Watkins reiterates her findings, noting that the hermit ministered to afflictions of the soul by prescribing pilgrimages and penances as remedies for laypeople's sins.[4] Might this special function explain the appeal of anchorites to patrons and suppliants?

---

[1] Mayr-Harting, 'Functions', 341–3.
[2] Brown, *Authority*, 58, 74–5.
[3] Ridyard, 'Functions', 248. For instances of Godric recommending penance, see 239–43.
[4] C. S. Watkins, 'Sin, Penance and Purgatory in the Anglo-Norman Realm: The Evidence of Visions and Ghost Stories', *Past and Present*, 175 (2002), 3–33, at 30–1.

We could look at this problem from a different angle by asking whether hermits and recluses arose to meet a need where the ordinary clergy were failing to meet the demands of sin and penance. First we might ask, how equipped were the eleventh-century clergy to deal with the problem of sin? Catherine Cubitt has shown that in the decades around 1000 Ælfric and the two archbishops, Wulfstan of York and Sigeric of Canterbury, took an interest in pastoral care. Ælfric and Wulfstan even appear to imply that lay confession to priests, and the priestly administration of penance, was commonplace.[5] Old English terminology and literature for confession and penance was sophisticated; and recent research by scholars such as Victoria Thompson and Tracey-Anne Cooper shows that, by the mid-eleventh century, there was a demand in some quarters for pastoral and confessional texts suitable for training all sorts of laypeople in the basic requirements of the faith.[6] Whether Ælfric, Wulfstan, and the compilers of these texts had minster clergy in mind or the clergy from local churches or noble households is an unanswered question, but we should at least consider the possibility that the clergy in the minsters (including monks) were more active in the sphere of pastoral care. John Blair reminds us that the proliferation and establishment of local churches over the course of the long eleventh century would have led to the multiplication of priests, many of whom probably lacked the education in religious learning and discipline that was available to clergy trained in minsters. Many of these priests were drawn from, or indistinguishable from, the peasantry, so even the most optimistic estimation of their quality would have to concede that it was variable.[7] It is also worth remembering that the multiplication of priests (not forgetting the many priests who were privately retained) made it increasingly more difficult for bishops to exercise disciplinary control within their dioceses. In 1086, the diocese of Thetford, comprising Norfolk and Suffolk, contained at least 700 churches. This caused Julia Barrow to wonder 'how bishops in eastern England in the eleventh century coped before the introduction of archdeacons'.[8] Blair comments: 'the striking lack of any focused interest in the supervision of local clergy or parish life in early eleventh-century tracts on the episcopal office raises doubts about how often bishops were in a position to confront such problems'.[9] One outcome of these changes during the eleventh

---

[5] Cubitt, 'Bishops, Priests and Penance'. See also Crouch, 'Troubled Deathbeds', 30n.

[6] V. Thompson, 'The Pastoral Contract in Late Anglo-Saxon England: Priest and Parishioner in Oxford, Bodleian Library, MS Laud Miscellaneous 482', in *Pastoral Care in Late Anglo-Saxon England*, ed. F. Tinti (Woodbridge, 2005), 106–20; and T.-A. Cooper, 'Lay Piety, Confessional Directives and the Compiler's Method in Late Anglo-Saxon England', *The Haskins Society Journal*, 16 (2005), 47–61. On the preponderance of Old English pastoral texts in mid-eleventh-century Worcester, see R. Gameson, 'St Wulfstan, the Library of Worcester and the Spirituality of the Medieval Book', in *St Wulfstan and His World*, ed. J. S. Barrow and N. P. Brooks (Aldershot, 2005), 59–91, at 63.

[7] Blair, *The Church*, 491–2.

[8] J. Barrow, 'The Clergy in English Dioceses c.900–c.1066', in *Pastoral Care*, ed. Tinti, 17–26, at 25.

[9] Blair, *The Church*, 495.

century could well have been the proliferation of unimpressive, unregulated, and undisciplined priests in the old devotional hinterlands of the minsters; and where impressive clergy were lacking, anchorites may have arisen as authoritative oracles and expert opponents of sin, not only in England but also in France and the Empire. If so, their authority presumably had a basis quite unlike a priest's sacramental power.

Earlier, I favoured the claim made by Cowdrey, Brooke, Riley-Smith, and others, that the eleventh and twelfth centuries nurtured anxiety about the consequences of sin, which manifested itself in profuse conversion to religion (cenobitic and anchoretic), pilgrimage, crusading, and the popularity, according to Hamilton, of traditional forms of penance. If this much is accepted then it stands to reason that people alive in those centuries to whom such solutions were neither optional nor obvious might have turned for help to a fixer or expert. In theory, they could always have turned to a local priest, but the priesthood at this date, in so far as it was trained at all, was not trained in the art of combating sin, at least not to the extent that anchorites were through the practice of their vocation. To some extent, priests would have learned how to handle sin by the process of trial and error in the course of their ministry or by reading manuals on the subject where manuals were available and where priests could read. Even so, because it was not the priest's occupation to conquer his own sins night and day, and because the anchorite's struggle to do so seemed to set her closer to God, there would have been sufficient reason to prefer the anchorite to the priest when seeking advice on sin. A considerable body of scholarly research now shows that in French Romance of the late twelfth and thirteenth centuries a stock role of the hermit was to administer penance, after urging visitors to repent and hearing them confess their sins.[10] Ridyard found the hermit Godric performing a similar role in Latin hagiography written in England in the late twelfth century. Together, these discoveries suggest that French lay audiences and English monastic ones shared an understanding of what anchorites did, perceiving that their function was to eradicate sin. Perhaps the ordinary clergy were indeed failing in this respect. Yet the role of inculcating penitence was only half the anchorite's function. The other half involved reconciling penitents to God. At the outset of her book Warren stated that, in return for the resources that were invested in solitary religion, anchorites 'were asked only for their prayers'. 'To understand why people supported the solitary movements', she continued, 'is to comprehend the awe that the asceticism of the recluse engendered . . . and to acknowledge the perceived value of the ascetic's intercessory powers. Anchorites, holy men and

---

[10] E.g. Huchet, 'Les déserts'; Romanelli, '*Le chevalier*', 34, 40–2, 51–2; P. Bretel, *Les ermites et les moines dans la littérature française du Moyen Age (1150–1250)* (Paris, 1995), 237–48, 444–6; J. Baldwin, 'From the Ordeal to Confession: In Search of Lay Religion in Early Thirteenth-Century France', in *Handling Sin: Confession in the Middle Ages*, ed. P. Biller and A. J. Minnis (Woodbridge, 1998), 191–209 at 199–208.

women, repaid their patrons through prayer.'[11] Warren treated the appeal of intercession as though axiomatic, although she was the first modern historian to highlight this particular role. Investigating her idea, the present chapter examines the anchorite's function in these conjoined capacities: as a spiritual advocate or intercessor and one who dealt with sin.

INSPIRING REPENTANCE

It has become conventional for historians to approach sin within the context of the penitential system operated by the church. We search for evidence of penitence, leading to a formal act of confession, followed by an undertaking to perform penance or comparable good actions in its stead. To claim that anchorites might have acted as confessors is to introduce them into this framework so as to bear on the contentious debate, whether the laity made regular confession before the Fourth Lateran Council enjoined it in 1215. Murray has argued that before this date confession mattered only where an influential prelate was studiously interested in pastoral theology, or within regulated religious communities; but Hamilton reserves judgement: she says that we cannot know how often confession was made, while Crouch, Cubitt, and Thompson contend that lay confession was probably widespread.[12] Murray searched for it within hagiography, a literary genre mostly preoccupied with monasteries and exemplary bishops, which probably explains why he found it chiefly in pastorally precocious dioceses and penitent gatherings of monks. Still, it is doubtful whether hagiography commonly reflected lay piety in the average parish or within the average noble household. With regard to the latter, we scarcely know what duties hired- and client-priests performed on behalf of their patrons except for saying prayers and masses; yet there is a suggestion in Turgot's *Life* of Queen Margaret of Scotland that the queen confessed her sins during her spiritual conversations with him and before taking the Eucharist.[13] When we study the parishes, we have no means of discovering how often priests had similar conversations with their parishioners. The Fourth Lateran Council defined confession as the regular, sacramental admission of sins to one's parish priest. However, practice before 1215 was sufficiently varied for Peter the Chanter's circle, in the Parisian schools of theology during the late twelfth century, to debate whether confession should

---

[11] Warren, *Anchorites*, 7, 16, cf. 127. I have substituted 'intercessory' for Warren's 'intercessionary'.

[12] A. Murray, 'Confession before 1215', *TRHS*, 6th ser., 3 (1993), 51–81; Hamilton, 'Unique Favour', 242; D. Crouch, 'Troubled Deathbeds', 25–30; Cubitt, 'Bishops, Priests and Penance'; V. Thompson, *Dying and Death in Later Anglo-Saxon England* (Woodbridge, 2004), 58–9.

[13] For these priests, see Barrow, 'The Clergy'. For Margaret, see Hinde, *Opera*, 244–6. Margaret may be compared to Stephen's Queen Matilda, who also made regular confession: Crouch, *Stephen*, 316.

be made to priests, monks, or hermits.[14] Anchorites would have appealed because in the meeting of minds which occurred in confession the moral stature of the confessor mattered, prompting 'a popular drift... away from confessors qualified by law, to those qualified by wisdom and holiness' – a drift detected by Murray, when he researched the thirteenth century.[15] Eleventh- and twelfth-century priests should hardly have been any wiser or holier than their thirteenth-century counterparts, so it is reasonable to expect that penitents would have drifted towards anchorites in the eleventh and twelfth centuries. In the late eleventh century, friends and supporters of the reform party of the papacy, as well as Gregory VII himself (1073–85), were urging the laity to boycott clergy who were either married or guilty of simony. Their influence in England was limited, but doubts about the clergy were not confined to Rome and may have enhanced the growing appeal of ascetic religious.

What evidence is there to contend for such a drift? Little can be found surviving from the eleventh century. Mantat's aside to Cnut and Emma – 'God knows that no tonsured man has been more useful to you both than I, and that shall be known to you in the future life' – is frustratingly cryptic.[16] It is not inconceivable that he had served as their confessor, but his comment may simply refer to innumerable masses or prayers said on their behalf. The history of the deeds of Evesham's abbots seems to claim that the recluse Wulfsige was confessor to Earl Leofric (d. 1057) and Lady Godgifu, but it exists only in a thirteenth-century recension, so the legend may be late.[17] Of the ninth-century hermit Wulf, the St Albans *gesta abbatum* (i.e. the history of the deeds of the abbots) reports that 'bishops and men of substance came to him that they might merit expiation from their various sins through confession and be commended to his prayers'.[18] Yet the relevant section of the *gesta* is unlikely to pre-date the mid-twelfth-century account by the monk Adam the Cellarer, which a later continuator incorporated. We should also allow for the possibility that the image of anchorites acting as confessors to powerful men was a topos employed to magnify their authority. None of this evidence is satisfactory, but there is better evidence from the twelfth century. Ridyard began to assemble it, noting three instances in which Godric of Finchale enjoined penance as a solution to sin, and two additional instances in which he identified people's sins and urged them to make amends.[19] It is seldom apparent whether a voluntary act of confession

---

[14] Baldwin, 'From the Ordeal', 203.

[15] A. Murray, 'Counselling in Medieval Confession', in *Handling Sin*, ed. Biller and Minnis, 63–77, at 68, 70.

[16] *Wills*, ed. Whitelock, no. 23.

[17] *History*, ed. Sayers and Watkiss, 152. Note, though, the Latin is unclear. It may be saying that their confessor was Wulfsige's brother, Prior Æfic of Evesham, who is the main subject of the passage.

[18] My paraphrase: *Gesta abbatum*, ed. Riley, I, 21.

[19] Ridyard, 'Functions', 239–43.

actually occurred, but these stories clearly do assume that the sinner, usually a layperson, had been forced to confront his or her sins. We can augment Ridyard's catalogue with some further cases, such as the case of King Stephen: for, as Crouch has observed, Stephen was said to have visited Wulfric at Haselbury both before and after becoming king and confessed his sins to him.[20] Although this story was reported in the 1180s, thirty years after the deaths of its protagonists, the idea that Stephen might have visited an anchorite gains credence from a writ he issued to the hermit Robert, dwelling in the royal forest at Writtle near Colchester, because the writ was issued at Writtle itself, hinting that the king visited Robert.[21] Given that the king entrusted this hermit with intercession for his soul, some discussion of his sins with him might have assisted the intercessor. Nor was the king Wulfric's only client. On another occasion, so it was said, three penitent priests went to Wulfric in search of forgiveness and advice on how best to improve their conduct.[22] One wonders whether they had first despaired of confessing to each other.

In the case of an old man who went to see Godric of Finchale, 'asking on account of his sins that [the hermit] by his holy prayers should make him acceptable to God', it is unclear whether confession and a penitential undertaking were made.[23] The situation required it, but Godric's hagiographer either took it for granted or chose not to mention that the hermit, who was not ordained, assumed the role of a confessor. Wulfric, who was a priest, was qualified in this respect and is shown insisting that sins be acknowledged and penance performed before he expends intercession on a noblewoman called Agnes. When she seeks his prayers, he proves unresponsive. To her persistence, he answers, 'I'll pray for you if am permitted'. Later, when Agnes returns with her petition, he announces that he is forbidden to fulfil her request on account of her sins, for she neither keeps holy days in her grand halls nor respects God's saints. To this, she confesses, promising to make amends, and so he agrees to pray for her, albeit with the warning that she has little time left on earth. She ends her days a penitent.[24] Wulfric's functions of revealing and censuring sin in this story appear to be more anchoretic than priestly, not least because the lay hermit Godric of Throckenholt performs them too. His niece Wulfgifu, a brewer in Wisbech, had not been serving customers their due measure. After she comes to

---

[20] *WH*, 117–18; and see Crouch's discussion in 'Troubled Deathbeds', 32–3; and *idem, Stephen*, 316–17.

[21] Christopher Harper-Bill identified Robert as Robert de Sackville who became a monk at Colchester towards the end of Stephen's reign, but his basis seems to be the juxtaposition of the two Roberts in the cartulary: *English Episcopal Acta VI: Norwich, 1070–1214*, ed. C. Harper-Bill (Oxford, 1990), no. 81n. The idea that Robert was Robert de Sackville came from A. Christy, 'The Hermitage in the High Woods, Writtle: Some Facts and Fancies', *Essex Review*, 18 (1909), 129–36, at 134–5.

[22] *WH*, 113.

[23] *LG*, 274.

[24] *WH*, 115–16.

him with a troubled conscience, he learns (through prayer) that God has forgiven her, so he summons her in order to recommend suitable amends, 'instructing her right away to increase the measurement of brew that she was accustomed to serve, and making other secret injunctions'.[25] Wulfgifu's case is akin to the previous one in which the old man went to Finchale, where the expected acts of confession and penance are nowhere explicit. Again the hagiographer may have omitted them. Alternatively, we may be looking at an informal setting in which the whole uncomfortable business was put to one side in favour of pastoral negotiations whereby suppliants got the prayers they sought and anchorites weeded out sins while extracting promises of reparation and future good behaviour. Hagiographers had an interest in omitting reference to these discussions not only to disguise the possibility that lay hermits functioned as confessors but also in so far as it undermined their intimations that anchorites found out sins primarily by their prophetic powers. It is also worth noting that, if anchorites knew all the gossip, confession should scarcely have been necessary. Where prophetic powers came into play, a reminder of imminent death was an effective goad. Wulfric used it on Agnes, and Godric of Finchale and Roger of Markyate supposedly employed it to underline the urgent need for atonement.[26] Such were the different ways by which anchorites compelled those who sought their prayers to confront their sins and amend their ways.

The cases of Agnes and Wulfgifu, from the *Lives* of Wulfric of Haselbury and Godric of Throckenholt, support Ridyard's argument, that anchorites functioned to 'reveal and correct . . . sin', thus supporting their acquaintances 'in their somewhat shaky steps towards salvation', by extending the range of evidence for this function beyond the *Life* she studied. Godric of Finchale's role was nothing unusual: hermits and recluses helped people to eradicate their sins. What, now, of the hypothesis that anchorites may have arisen as greater authorities in such matters than the ordinary clergy? We may, if we wish, accept it as inherently likely for the reasons already given, but there may also be evidence betraying this perception in the *Life* of Godric of Throckenholt. Godric, we are told, chose to wear a hauberk (a mail vest), praying that this penitential garment might endure as long as his debt of sin. It then took on a life of its own, suffering the sympathy pains of his sins as they were slowly expunged. After six years, it burst in two, but a wicked woman arrived at his oratory, and the hauberk miraculously restored itself in response. On another occasion, a portion of it crumbled, and, although his priest discerned a favourable verdict in its disintegration and took it as a sign that his penance was complete, Godric nevertheless repaired it. A year later it burst into pieces during midnight mass, thus providing the sign that he desired.[27] This story in which priest and anchorite disagree on what constitutes an effective penance

[25] GT, 36.
[26] Ridyard, 'Functions', 241; *Gesta pontificum*, ed. Winterbottom and Thomson, I, 476–7.
[27] GT, 28–32.

implies that the priest's judgement in the matter fell short of God's and Godric's. It also implies that Godric was more able to determine God's intention. Of course, it is only one story. Suggestive though it may be, it does not establish any general point (and saints like Godric were exceptional cases: they, no doubt, could be wiser than village priests in matters where ordinary anchorites might not have been). Perhaps the underlying assumption is that an anchorite's sustained asceticism better equipped him to know God's will. In so far as this assumption was at work, penitents wary of priests may have preferred to consult anchorites, conscious, in doing so, that the informal confessional negotiations described in the previous paragraph, whereby an anchorite's clients would promise to perform penance in return for his valuable prayers, would spare them the discomfort of formal penitential procedures while offering them an attractive incentive to deal frankly with their sins. Kings and nobles paid good money for the intercession of anchorites, so there was something to be said for bartering for it with an acknowledgement of sins, and penance promised on credit.

In reality, such calculations may have been nugatory in comparison with the impact on the average sinner's conscience of coming face to face with an anchorite; of encountering this figure whose very existence and success undermined so much that society took for granted, with the effect of holding its norms in constant check, as if under a holy spell. For the anchorite not only abandoned the comforts and ambitions of society but in doing so escaped its thraldom, prompting observers to worry: what form of mastery is this, what form of power, that one not so different from us might escape the world? From this perspective, the anchorite became a locus of the sacred whose authority lay in a singular feat of renunciation.[28] Here we may recall what the Italian nobleman Rainer had allegedly said about Romuald: 'Not the emperor, not any other man, is able to strike great fear into me in the way that the appearance of Romuald terrifies me – before his face I do not know what to say, nor can I find any excuses by which I could defend myself.' Peter Damian continues: 'In truth, the holy man possessed by divine gift the grace that whatever sinners, especially powerful men of the world, would come into his presence would soon be struck with inner trembling, as if in the presence of the majesty of God.'[29] Before them was the living proof that this ideal of human perfection could be realized – and, by prompting such feelings in sinners, anchorites could bring them to repentance. Just as Romuald struck fear into the mind of his earthly lord, so Robert of Knaresborough was said to have 'unnerved dread despots' and 'fearlessly admonished King John'.[30] One could easily imagine that many people, like Agnes, might not have gone to anchorites

---

[28] This idea is explored in Howe, 'The Awesome Hermit'.

[29] From Howe's translation, 'Awesome Hermit', 106; *Vita*, ed. Tabacco, 83. Cf. *Vita quinque fratrum*, ed. Kade, 738 (citing Romuald): 'pone te ante omnia in presentia Dei cum timore et tremore, quasi qui stat in conspectu imperatoris'.

[30] F. Bottomley, *St. Robert of Knaresborough* (Ruddington, Notts., 1993), 16.

with the intention of acknowledging their sins but were nevertheless made to do so in the course of the encounter, discovering simultaneously that the act of confronting sin alleviated fears which weighed upon their consciences. Such sinners may have gone along importunate and come back penitent, transformed by their terror of the anchorite. One of an anchorite's functions therefore was to bring impressionable sinners to book.

INTERCESSION

If inspiring repentance was one of an anchorite's functions – but let us drop that utilitarian term and refer to their 'ministry' – another role was to intercede for people, not only so that God might respond to sundry petitions to forgive their sins, but also in matters pertaining to their general well being. Ridyard cast light upon the one role, Brown and Warren identified the other. These two roles should be seen as mutually supportive, because both aimed at the salvation of sinners, even if the second also took account of people's temporal needs. Warren explained the appeal of anchorites to their sponsors by linking it to the demand for anchoretic intercession. 'Patrons', she wrote, 'earned heavenly credits with their support of recluses'.[31] This image may conjure up a picture of pious benefactors accruing credits in order to clear penitential debts, unit by unit, in an imaginary heavenly account book. It is more appropriate for the period 1100–1500, which Warren covered, than for our period, because pious people of the later Middle Ages were more inclined to count suffrages for the soul like credits. Prior to this tendency, in the period 800–1100, Megan McLaughlin has argued that the nobility thought of prayer more as a defining action of the virtuous religious with whom they wished to associate than as some commodity to be accumulated.[32] During the eleventh and twelfth centuries, however, associative and accumulative notions of intercession mingled.[33] This transition has barely been studied: the problem is not simply that anchoretic intercession lacks a historiography; the historiography of intercession itself is inchoate. Attention paid to anchorites is a useful tool for shaping it because their zeal singled them out amid the multitude clamouring at heaven's gates. Their impressiveness was the main reason for turning to them, as was the recommendation of hagiographical tradition, in which the anchoretic vocation was a byword for the life of prayer. Two tasks, accordingly, fall to the remainder of this chapter. The first is to examine the notion that anchoretic prayers were desirable. The second is to discover who benefited from them, and how.

---

[31] Warren, *Anchorites*, 16.
[32] McLaughlin, *Consorting*, 13–14, 130, 153, 177.
[33] *Ibid.*, 129, 153–4, 247–9, 256.

Intercession can be defined as prayerful entreaty in the role of an intermediary on behalf of another. In hagiography, it is often depicted in accordance with an idealized perception of how it should be undertaken: heartfelt, incessant, and accompanied by vigils, fasting, tears, and groans. The intercession of anchorites was thought to be a powerful form of intervention. Henry III (1039–56), emperor of Germany (and also Edward the Confessor's brother-in-law), wrote that the farther an intercessor was from the world the purer his prayers were.[34] Goscelin believed that those concealed inside cells shone through all the more brightly.[35] By achieving perfection on earth, anchorites established intimacy and influence with the saints, becoming their co-heirs and compatriots. They also learned how to intercede. The hagiographer Reginald of Canterbury (*fl.* 1100) wrote a *Life* of the desert monk Malchus: 'from his lips he hurls a spear, with his prayer he pierces heaven's apex'.[36] Wulfric's hagiographer observed that his prayers were believed to penetrate every cloud and fly straight to the heavens like arrows fired by a strong man's hand.[37] By night, he prayed for himself; during the day he interceded for his clients.[38] Roger's commitment to prayer was such, reports the St Albans *gesta abbatum*, 'that when the devil, enraged, once tried to interrupt him by setting fire to his cowl, even this proved unable to distract his attention or curtail his orations'.[39] Christina of Markyate's hagiographer remarked of this same wonder: 'how great the fire which burned inwardly in his spirit, to have rendered his body insensible to the material fire which burned without'. The gloss here alludes to proto-eremitic prayer. Roger's inner conflagration recalled the great contemplatives of fourth-century Egypt, the fathers to whom he was likened. The eighteenth book of the *Verba seniorum*, on contemplation, told that when a brother went to the cell of the anchorite Arsenius in Scete he looked in and saw the old man on his knees, aflame with spiritual fire.[40] In the twelfth book, on prayer, one hermit advises another: 'if you will, you shall be made wholly a flame'.[41] Christina, who witnessed the devil ape this wonder in Roger, 'was no less on fire when she stood by his side in prayer'.[42]

Intercession was requested and expected of anchorites perhaps above all else. 'Prayer comes before everything', Goscelin told Eve, adding 'above all things always seek God's face'.[43] The recluse, he wrote, should divide her time between

---

[34] 'Epistolae diuersorum ad s. Hugonem, s. Petri Damiani', PL, 159: 931–46, no. VI (931–2), at 932B.

[35] Eadwold, 206.

[36] *Vita sancti Malchi*, ed. Lind, 148.

[37] WH, 67; cf. the 'arrows of psalmody': *Guthlac*, ed. Colgrave, 91. Aelred of Rievaulx's prayers also pierced the heavens, according to Walter Daniel: *Life of Ailred*, ed. Powicke, 20.

[38] WH, p. li, 48; cf. Mayr-Harting, 'Functions', 338.

[39] *Gesta abbatum*, ed. Riley, I, 98; cf. *LCM*, 104.

[40] *Verba sen.* XVIII.1; cf. Smaragdus, *Diadema monachorum*, 620A.

[41] *Verba sen.* XII.8.

[42] *LCM*, 104–6 (adapted from Talbot's translation).

[43] *LC*, 79.

prayer and devotional reading, but prayer was emphatically her priority. Having taken the part of Mary (i.e. the contemplative life), she 'owed intercession to everyone', not least her comforter who requested it.[44] Eighty years later, Aelred reminded his sister that she too had chosen Mary's part over Martha's, reminding her 'what is more useful than prayer?' Aelred enjoined her intercession upon the wretched poor, groaning orphans, desolate widows, the downcast, needy pilgrims, virgin vowesses, those in peril at sea, tempted monks, troubled prelates, and strenuous soldiers. For all these, he told her, 'open up your heart in love, expend your tears, and pour out your many prayers'.[45] Bartholomew of Farne was said to have prayed constantly.[46] When the recluse Guy petitioned the bishop Herbert Losinga (d. 1119) for yet more edificatory reading material, he met with a stark reminder from the bishop that his 'one law' was prayer. Guy was in danger of distraction. Warning him to guard his treasures of purity and simplicity, Herbert concluded his letter by asking for Guy's prayers.[47] Anselm, who himself considered becoming a hermit, as we saw earlier, sought the prayers of his correspondents in only a small handful of his letters. Seldom did he request prayers from bishops and monks, but when he wrote to recluses, once before 1078 as a monk of Bec and once as archbishop of Canterbury *c*.1102, he ended his letters 'pray for me' and 'pray for me, I pray'.[48] Gerald of Wales (d. *c*.1220) trusted the anchorite dwelling at Newgale beach in Pembrokeshire to be his 'intercessor to the Lord day and night'.[49] Those who came knocking at Wulfric's door in search of intercession included the illustrious noblewoman Bence of Lincoln and the aforementioned Agnes who was sister-in-law to the earl of Gloucester. The famous recluse consented to pray ceaselessly for their souls.[50] Robert of Writtle's principal sponsor was King Stephen, who granted him his hermitage for the benefit of his soul and the souls of his uncle King Henry and wife Matilda. When Henry II inherited it, he confirmed the Writtle hermitage to Colchester abbey on the condition that two monk-priests should remain there always to pray for his soul and for the souls of his royal predecessors.[51] When King John set up a hermitage chantry at Birchwood in Sherwood Forest, adding an annual grant of forty shillings, its salaried hermit was to sing masses in the chapel for his soul and the souls of his ancestors.[52] Clearly the prayers of anchorites were not only sought by pious ecclesiastics but also bought by successive generations of kings.

[44] *LC*, 103–4, 117.
[45] *Opera omnia I*, ed. Hoste and Talbot, 661–2.
[46] *VB*, 305.
[47] *Epistolae*, ed. Anstruther, 96.
[48] *Opera*, ed. Schmitt, III, no. 112; IV, no. 230; cf. Warren, *Anchorites*, 56, 104–5.
[49] *Giraldi Cambrensis opera*, ed. J. S. Brewer, J. F. Dimock, and G. F. Warner, RS, 21, 8 vols (1861–91) I, 178. My identification of Niuegall as Newgale is not certain.
[50] *WH*, 115–16.
[51] *Cartularium*, ed. Moore, I, 52, 38.
[52] Warren, *Anchorites*, 152.

Although monks were expected to intercede for souls themselves, and looked above all to the saints, they also entrusted their welfare to the prayers of anchorites. While they prayed for others they recruited anchorites to pray for them. A twelfth-century monk once wrote to a friend, lamenting the death of his beloved abbot and expressing the opinion that it was his alms to the poor and the prayers of the many anchorites he had sponsored that had cleansed the dead prelate of his sins. This abbot may have been Geoffrey of St Albans (1119–46).[53] Whoever he was, if he existed, he maintained from his revenues a princely total of twenty-four anchorites. If it was Geoffrey, it is striking that the saving efficacy of the St Albans liturgy and the prayers of the brethren were not mentioned as factors in cleansing him of his sins. Were these benefits too obvious or were they less consequential? The community of monks at Westminster also trusted in anchoretic intercession. When, in the spring of 1134, Abbot Herbert, Prior Osbert, and the monks, with the assent of the diocesan, granted the hermitage of a hermit named Godwin, at Kilburn on the outskirts of London, to the three young anchorites Emma, Gunhilda, and Christina, they did so in order that the souls of the whole Westminster convent and those of their friends, the monks of Fécamp, alive or dead, might be redeemed. (Fécamp, as noted in a previous chapter, sponsored hermits of its own.) Of course, the agreement between Westminster and Fécamp reminds us that communities of monks also sought each other's prayers, and it should be remembered that their primary concern was usually to secure the prayers of the saints. Nevertheless, whether for purposes of practicality or perceived spiritual value, monks did not pay to retain communities of monks specially to pray for them, as they paid to retain hermits. The monks of Westminster granted land in Southwark worth two shillings a year to the priestly hermit Aelmer, along with a corrody of bread, ale, wine, mead, and pittances, in return for God's protection from plague and pestilence.[54] It appears that his prayers were meant to ward off these evils. If at Kilburn they sponsored anchorites to pray for their souls, at Southwark they funded a hermit to pray for their temporal protection. This reliance of monks on anchorites in the 1130s and 1140s is further proof that their intercession was valued in monasteries.

Some monks who entrusted themselves to the intercession of anchorites did so because they believed that anchorites, or perhaps one particular anchorite, stood closer to God. In a psalter made at St Albans in the early twelfth century, the recluse Christina of Markyate is portrayed in an illuminated initial leading a small flock of monks in the guise of an advocate, extending her hand through a dividing line between the earthly realm and the stars to touch Christ's hand in heaven.[55]

---

[53] *Analecta Dvblinensia: Three Medieval Latin Texts in the Library of Trinity College, Dublin*, ed. M. L. Colker (Cambridge, MA, 1975), 107; cf. *LCM*, 150.

[54] *Westminster Abbey Charters 1066–c.1214*, ed. E. Mason, assisted by J. Bray; continuing the work of D. J. Murphy, London Record Society, 25 (1988), nos. 264, 249.

[55] Pächt, Dodwell, and Wormald, *The St Albans Psalter*, pl. 72b.

She alone has authority to reach across the divide and introduce the monks to Christ. Abbot Geoffrey of St Albans believed that Christina would present him to Christ when she was rapt in contemplation. 'Great is my glory in this', he used to say, 'that though for the moment you are forgetful of me, you present me to him'.[56] Once when Christina was praying anxiously for his salvation she saw herself standing in a heavenly chamber with two venerable figures robed in white. On their shoulders reposed a dove, and it seems very likely that the trio symbolized Father, Son, and Holy Spirit. Geoffrey was seeking entry to the chamber to no avail and begging her to introduce him to them. So 'with all the love she could pour out, with all the devotion she knew, she pleaded with the Lord to have mercy on her beloved'. No sooner had she done so than she saw the dove glide through the chamber 'and delight the eyes of the onlooker with its innocent gaze'.[57] The Holy Spirit had alighted upon Geoffrey, and the vital introduction that he sought had been made. This story evokes Peter Brown's idea of the anchorite as a patron or intercessor in God's heavenly throne room, which the chamber appears to signify.[58] Christina is authorized to enter. Geoffrey is obliged to remain outside but, through Christina's mediation, has at least the opportunity of an introduction to the Godhead within. In this powerful allegory, winning a place in heaven, like winning a place at court, began with special commendation to the king. To Abbot Geoffrey, the hermit Christina was an elite courtier who could provide this.

CLIENTS AND CONFRATERNITIES

It should now be plain that kings, nobles, ecclesiastics, and peasants sought the prayers of anchorites. What, now, can be said of the relationship between anchorites and their clientele? In the scattering of accounts from the several hagiographies of our period in which anchorites are shown interceding for the souls of named individuals, seven of the recipients are relatives: two mothers, three brothers, a sister, and a niece.[59] The others, like Abbot Geoffrey, appear mostly to have been close friends. Anchorites prayed for all sorts of people, but the several visions reported as responses to intercession for these named individuals imply that the fate of their souls mattered to the intercessor more than the fate of the majority. (We will examine these visions when examining the nature of anchoretic intercession.) The impression that anchorites cared most for those closest to them is reinforced by the names listed for commemoration in what may have been Christina of Markyate's prayer book: the St Albans psalter. Although

---

[56] *LCM*, 155.

[57] *Ibid.*, 157.

[58] Brown, *Authority and the Sacred*, 74.

[59] I include in this tally a case from the *Life* of Robert of Knaresborough in which the hermit prays his mother out of 'torments' and into eternal rest: VRK, 381–2. For the other cases, read on.

these obits were added after Christina's death, there is little doubt that they represent her own, albeit posthumously augmented, collection; and given that the average anchoretic career is likely to have precipitated prayer requests from tens if not hundreds of clients it is difficult to imagine that anchorites could have fulfilled their intercessory duties without keeping such lists, or necrologies, or *libri vitae*. Among the obits in the St Albans psalter are the names of Christina's mother and father, two brothers, a putative aunt, Abbot Geoffrey, and various friends.[60] Familial interests are just as prominent in the *Life* of Godric of Throckenholt, which mentions eight of his relatives, four by name: his parents, his sister, an anonymous relation, her husband Godric, Richard, Wulfgifu his niece, and his nephew Peter the chaplain. Familial bonds play equally prominent roles in the *Lives* of Thancred, Torhtred, and Tova; Christina, one of whose sisters joined her hermitage; Godric of Finchale, also joined by family members, and Henry of Coquet, torn between remaining on his island and returning to his kindred in Denmark. The idea that anchorites targeted their intercession at the salvation of their loved ones may seem unremarkable, but it reveals an inner circle of clients with special claims upon them. Members of this circle could turn to an anchorite in confidence through the bond of blood or established trust. Strangers and occasional visitors occupied what may be termed an anchorite's outer circle. Such visitors were unlikely to have felt any entitlement to the anchorite's prayers unless they brought gifts. McLaughlin has noted, in reference to monastic benefaction, that 'members of the laity apparently felt obligated to make a gift in return for the prayers they enjoyed'.[61] Where anchorites accepted gifts, spiritual bonds could be established and benefits expected by the giver.

It is useful to think of an anchorite's inner circle in combination with her outer circle of clients as the anchorite's confraternity, similar to a monastic confraternity. Entry to the latter was undertaken so that the entrant might become a dweller in the monks' prayers and share in their spiritual advantages.[62] These societies offered the soul hope by association: members hoped to enter heaven, as it were, on the coat tails of the religious. Between the reigns of Cnut and Henry II, some 3,200 names ranging from kings to peasants, lay and religious, were entered into Thorney's *liber vitae*: the abbey's 'book of life'.[63] The proem to the *liber vitae* of Hyde abbey in Winchester explains how each day at mass the sub-deacon presented the register before the high altar, reciting from it as many entries as time permitted, and then, to symbolize the participation in the office of all enrolled

[60] Pächt, Dodwell, Wormald, *The St Albans Psalter*, 27–9; R. Koopmans, 'Dining at Markyate with Lady Christina', in *Christina*, ed. Fanous and Leyser, 143–59, at 149–50.

[61] McLaughlin, *Consorting*, 146, and on this topic, see 139–46, 153.

[62] *Ibid.*, 86–90, 102–32; see also A. Angenendt, 'How Was a Confraternity Made? The Evidence of Charters', in *The Durham Liber vitae*, ed. Rollason et al., 207–19.

[63] C. Clark, 'Additional MS. 40,000', 'The *Liber vitae* of Thorney Abbey and Its "Catchment Area"', and 'A Witness to Post-Conquest English Cultural Patterns: the *Liber vitae* of Thorney Abbey', in *Words, Names and History*, ed. Jackson, 339–47.

therein, laid it beside the sacred vessels.[64] At Thorney abbey, extended family groups were enrolled, including the monks' relatives. One early twelfth-century entry lists 'Laurence, father of master Benedict the monk, Osilia his mother, and his brothers Pagan and Hugh'.[65] Kindred like these may have been enrolled gratis. Strangers, even of status, were probably expected to make some donation.[66] 'Here died our sister Queen Emma', records an Ely necrology, 'who purchased the confraternity of this church with a multiplicity of gifts'.[67] The monks, in return, would promise to aid donors' souls and sometimes the souls of living or departed kindred with masses, psalters, prayers, and other religious services. Abbot Baldwin of Bury (1065–97/8) decreed that on the anniversary of King Edward's death the monks should receive an allowance of fish on the condition that they accord their benefactor more frequent remembrance in their prayers.[68] In this case, the monks were expected to add private remembrance of an individual benefactor to their daily collective commemoration of benefactors in the liturgy and the regular celebration of their anniversaries. This injection of spontaneity into monastic liturgical protocol holds a clue as to how anchorites could have fulfilled their intercessory obligations to sizeable confraternities without rendering their suffrages impersonal. For collective prayers could be uttered on behalf of listed names, but specific prayers could be said for individuals or situations pressing on the anchorite's mind. Members of anchoretic confraternities may have hoped for salvation by their association with holy anchorites. Wulfric's hagiographer thought that the knight who gave Wulfric his hauberk did so expecting to share the benefits of that spiritual warfare which his gift had equipped.[69] The hauberk itself could serve to remind Wulfric to remember the knight's generosity.

The most detailed depiction of an outsider's admission to the heart of a hermit's confraternity is the case of Abbot Geoffrey. Half of Christina's *Life* is preoccupied with the subject of her burgeoning obsession with him.[70] Christina first came to hear of Geoffrey, a wayward abbot, when a dead monk appeared before her to complain about his refusal to take advice. After careful thought, she sent word to the abbot to dissuade him from a rash plan that he had contrived. The haughty man grew angry, returning the message not to trust in dreams. Privately however he was alarmed that she could know something otherwise unknown outside his head. That night the same dead monk invaded his own

    [64] Clark, 'Additional MS. 40,000', 307.

    [65] L, BL, MS Add. 40,000, fo. 3r; see also Clark, 'Additional MS. 40,000', 306; and, generally, J. S. Moore, 'Family-Entries in English *Libri vitae, c.*1050 to *c.*1350, Part 1', *Nomina*, 16 (1992–3), 99–128; 'Part 2', *Nomina*, 18 (1995), 77–117. See also H. Tsurushima, 'The Fraternity of Rochester Cathedral Priory about 1100', *ANS*, 14 (1991), 313–37.

    [66] McLaughlin, *Consorting*, 139–46, 153.

    [67] *Katalog*, ed. Gerchow, 287.

    [68] *Anglo-Saxon Charters*, ed. A. J. Robertson, 2nd edn. (Cambridge, 1956), 196. On private commemoration at feasts, and anniversary meals, see McLaughlin, *Consorting*, 75, 151.

    [69] *WH*, 19.

    [70] *LCM*, 135–93.

dreams with 'several black and terrifying figures' that attacked and suffocated him. In terror, he vowed from then on to obey Christina's injunctions and hurried to apologize to her. Christina began to cherish and watch over him, inspired by her own humble part in his reformation, and they grew ever closer. Geoffrey for his part 'promised to avoid everything unlawful, to fulfil her commands, and to help her convent in the future: all he asked was her intercession with God'. The nature of the relationship is subsequently reiterated: 'He supported her in worldly matters: she commended him to God more earnestly in her prayers', and later still: 'Whilst he centred his attention on providing... material assistance, she strove to enrich the man in virtue, pleading for him... earnestly.' It was not his gifts that won her love but his struggle for purity: 'For as she became aware that he was making every effort to become more spiritual, she was so zealous on his account that she prayed for him tearfully almost all the time and in God's presence considered him more than herself.' She admitted, moreover, 'that there was none of those who were dear to her for whom she could plead to God with such devotion and instant prayer'.[71] Here, as with Wulfric and Agnes, a soul first reproved by an anchorite won at length the latter's commendation. Christina's hagiographer even claims that 'there were several who wished to reach the same holiness of life and to gain the same affection from her as did the abbot. But, falling out of favour, they veiled their disappointment by speaking ill of her.'[72] If this claim goes deeper than polemic it shows that access to the anchorite could arouse envy among those not so favoured. Christina's hagiographer was anxious to point out that Geoffrey had won a rare prize.

Where anchorites had acquired reputations or were sparsely distributed, demand to enter into confraternity with them may have been considerable. Faced with such a demand the anchorite had three options. She could allow her lamp to burn openly, as it were, by embracing a ministry to sinners; she could hide elsewhere, or she could somehow stem the flow of supplicants. Ministering could become very burdensome. Many accounts of anchorites discouraging or refusing gifts supposedly because of their piety but also, one suspects, because of implicit obligations to the giver suggest that anchorites were well aware of this. When rumours spread of a hermit living in the forest at Finchale, the pious and curious alike began hunting him, bearing gifts of food and drink. Typically, upon sensing someone approach, Godric would hide in the thickets. If cornered, he would refuse gifts, but visitors nevertheless left them at his oratory. One woman so desired to see him that she could find no rest until she did so. Having at last taken her gift of bread and cheese, Godric knelt down and prayed for her.[73] The dilemma previously confronting him was possibly the same dilemma that had confronted the recluse Ælfwine at Evesham when a visitor begged him

---

[71] *Ibid.*, 135–9, 139–41, 155, 143–5.
[72] *Ibid.*, 149–51.
[73] *LG*, 72–3; Ridyard, 'Functions', 239.

to accept a halfpenny. To take it was to accept an obligation. Wulfric told a cleric who offered him two pennies to leave them by his window: 'someone will come and take them'; but when Ælfwine accepted the halfpenny, the devil taunted him for breaking his vows.[74] (Presumably, he had sworn to renounce property.) The second option was to run away: the hermit's so-called 'flight from responsibility'.[75] We have already examined the tale of how Reinfrid left Jarrow for Whitby to escape the unsummoned crowds and would-be disciples. At other hermitages, rules were devised to limit the flow of visitors. No one was to enter Bedemansberg without the consent of the abbot of Colchester; applicants to see Godric at Finchale had to apply through the prior of Durham, and Roger's visitors had to get past his servants.[76] Roger's inaccessibility to random visitors is captured in his alleged interchange with one of his servants about a visitor who had been and gone. '[Servant] That fellow... didn't know you very well. [Roger] Who was it? [Servant] I don't know, but he came from Huntingdon looking for some girl.'[77] From the other side of the divide – from a stranger's perspective – comes a tale in the *Life* of St Wulfric. Wulfric had just said mass in the church when he added a special collect for an unnamed person there present. A sinful man named Henry was visiting. 'O happy man', he thought, 'for whom that saint now deigns to say a collect'.[78] When he later discovered that the collect was for him, he was so humbled that the anchorite had spared a care for his soul that he converted to religion.

For those lucky enough to find a place in an anchorite's inner circle of clients the prospects of salvation were propitious. Seldom do we find that anchorites shouldered the penitential burdens of clients, but when death had dissolved the power of some loved one to fulfil due penance this transference of penance is seen in action. In the Christian religion, the idea that one person's suffering might spare the punishment of another originated with Christ's sacrifice on the cross. The idea sometimes evident in hagiography is that an anchorite might pay the penitential debt of a dead relative to free that person from torment in the afterlife. Godric of Finchale's hagiographer, the monk Reginald of Durham, recounts such a tale, which he claims to have heard from Godric.[79] Godric's mother Eadwen had died and been led to 'places of punishment'. Praying tearfully, the hermit 'hurried to redeem her soul from its infernal prison, and, after purchasing it with pious deeds, eagerly set about paying the price for her sins'.[80] The penance he undertook included nocturnal immersions in the River Wear. When snow covered the ground, he entered the icy water 'gladly to undergo such grievous torments ... to restore his mother's soul to safety and to

---

[74] *WH*, p. liv; *Chronicon abbatiae de Evesham*, ed. Macray, 323.
[75] Golding, *Gilbert*, 26.
[76] *Cartularium*, ed. Moore, I, 38; *LG*, 136.
[77] Adapted from *LCM*, 95. The visitor was Christina's husband.
[78] *WH*, 69.
[79] *LG*, 125–7.
[80] *Ibid.*, 125, 125n.

obtain her expiation'.[81] In response to his accumulated prayers – and there is a sense that the prayers were counted ('toties pro anima matris [suae] preces') – he was eventually assured of her salvation by seeing her in a vision. Reginald's emphasis on the accumulated prayers and his statement that Godric set out to pay the price for Eadwen's sins imply that, in the monk's opinion at least, Godric was empowered to write off sinners' debts in the afterlife. Many tales show anchorites praying for the dead, even prayerfully assisting their release from torments, but besides what surfaces in Reginald only one further instance of a hermit expressly undertaking substitutive penance can be found, in the *Life* of St Henry of Coquet. Henry, so the story goes, was divinely notified of his brother's sudden death as a special grace, because God conceded that he might do penance for his brother's soul. The hermit promptly instructed the island's custodian, a monk, to inform both religious and laypeople, so that 'assisted by their alms and prayers' his brother's soul 'might be freed from the noose of suffering and sin'.[82] In this account, the opportunity to undertake another's penance is regarded as an unusual heavenly dispensation, awarded to the hermit, no doubt, in recognition of his virtue. God briefly allows him to become a scapegoat for his brother's sins. It is a reflection of how anchorites might have been thought to help the souls of people closest to them.

MEDIATING GOD'S POWER

Godric of Finchale's different hagiographers reflected his ministry differently. Reginald, through prolonged exposure to the hermit, attained a very high estimation of his power. Walter, a near contemporary who abridged Reginald's work, was more guarded.[83] His restraint may attest an embryonic stage in the formation of Reginald's own ideas (the abridgement, it has been argued, probably derives from a lost earlier recension of Reginald's work). In any case, his treatment of certain stories in which Godric assists the salvation of souls suggests a variance of opinion as to the sort of claims that might be advanced. We can see this variance in three stories in particular, the first of which concerns Godric's sister Burchwen. In Reginald's version, Godric pours out ceaseless tearful prayers in sack-cloth, cinders, and ashes for Burchwen's departed soul. The prayers are for absolution; the penance is expiatory. His aims are to assist her salvation and discover God's judgement upon her.[84] Until he does so he vows to remain watchful and accord himself no rest; he also begs the aid of the Virgin. The

---

[81] *Ibid.*, 125.

[82] *NL*, II, 24.

[83] Tudor, 'Reginald', 335–9. Reginald's work was thought to be tedious, unstructured, and inelegant.

[84] *LG*, 143.

outcome is a mystical dream in which two angels enter Mary's oratory and lay Burchwen's soul upon the altar. From this, Godric understands that she has inherited eternal joy with the heavenly choirs.[85] Walter's version is far less assuming. It omits Godric's quest for a verdict, along with all reference to expiatory penance, maintaining simply that Godric prayed for Burchwen's absolution and that Mary heeded him. Instead of being established in heaven his sister is simply 'freed from torments'.[86] Godric's power to secure a verdict is diluted by the omission of any stated intention on his part to do so, and the hermit himself interprets the vision more guardedly: his sister has been freed but there is no given assurance of her salvation. Walter's account gels more readily with tales supplied by Christina's hagiographer, whose tone is similarly unassuming.[87] One of these tales concerns Christina's brother Gregory, who was a monk of St Albans. When Gregory falls ill, she 'pleaded with God to reveal to her in his mercy what plans he had in mind' for him. Growing sadder as his health worsens, with no answer forthcoming, Christina 'for the sake of her brother moved Christ with floods of tears until she heard a voice from heaven saying these words: "You may be sure his lady loves him"'. Convinced that his death is imminent, she goes to Gregory and tells him that Mary will summon him. Accordingly, he 'fortified himself with the sacraments of Christ so much the more composedly as he felt the more certain that he would die', and then he dies 'full of hope'.[88] As in Walter's account of Burchwen, the anchorite's prayers seem effective; however, again their efficacy hinges on grace, mediated through the Virgin, and the ultimate verdict is uncertain. Gregory shall die – that much can be ascertained; Mary will intercede for him – this too can be deduced; but there is no promise of salvation.

The second tale concerns an anonymous woman, the object of Godric's prayers. According to Walter's abridgement, Godric was labouring in his field in the early afternoon when he saw a man's figure floating through the air towards him. Then it greeted him with a blessing. 'Amen' he replied. Nothing more was said; then Godric realized that the figure was the spirit of a woman formerly devoted to him, to whose repose he in turn had devoted prayers. The ghost floated away into Burchwen's cell and vanished, seen neither by his sister nor the shepherds. 'He therefore understood that [the woman] had been freed from her torments, and he entered his oratory and thanked God.'[89] In Reginald's version, the eccentric claim that the ghostly figure of a man was in fact the spirit of this woman remains unresolved (Reginald adds 'as he says himself' to assure

---

[85] *LG*, 144–5.
[86] *Ibid.*, 145n.
[87] Talbot sensed a rough quality to it. Although Fanous has challenged this view (S. Fanous, 'Christina of Markyate and the Double Crown', in *Christina*, ed. Fanous and Leyser, 53–78, at 53), Christina's hagiographer certainly wove in less theology than Godric's.
[88] *LCM*, 159–61.
[89] *LG*, 143n.

his audience that the reported testimony is accurate). This time, however, the conclusion claims that Godric 'immediately understood what God had desired to show him by such a vision: that he had heard his prayers for her, and that, plucked from places of torment, he had granted her a share in eternal joy'.[90] Reginald's version, thus recounted, differs from Walter's in two respects. First, he had processed his raw material to cement the link between Godric's intercession and the woman's salvation. Second, as in his account of Burchwen, he seems to envisage the possibility of a soul passing through purgatorial torments in the otherworld so successfully as to resolve any uncertainty over its salvation prior to Judgement Day. Walter's version again finds closer parallels in a similar account from Christina's *Life*. Christina, her mentor Ælfwen, and their friends had been praying for the safety of the youth who had helped her escape. That night as she lay barely awake, his figure stood shining beside her and told her to trust in God. In the morning, on learning of his death, she understood that he had joined the elect.[91] Here, as before, the tale of the youth and Walter's tale share a simple design in which visions reveal the favourable conditions of souls dwelling in the anchorites' prayers. Neither case explicitly claims that the prayers secured those conditions, but the visions effect closure and enable the anchorites concerned to draw a line under a particular, special chapter of intercession.

The third and final story concerns the soul of Godric's departed brother. In Walter's version, he is described as 'illustrious', but Reginald's heightens the tension and the impressiveness of Godric's impending feat by making him 'wholly given over to worldly things'.[92] Godric's brother suddenly drowns in the River Wear when a storm engulfs his dinghy. The hermit is inconsolable. He fears all the more – the drama intensifies – because his brother's spirit has been snatched away 'by so horrid a death' (without the chance to repent and receive the viaticum). Surely, says the audience, his soul is lost. After some time, Godric eventually decides to undertake the harshest penance for a number of years, treating this burden as a substitutive sacrifice 'as though he undertook to blot out all his brother's sins'.[93] As well as according his brother the customary vigils and prayers, he puts on a new hauberk and a viler hairshirt, upping his penance a notch in proportion to his brother's desperate situation. His efforts pay off when God resolves to console his servant. One night, as Godric prays for his brother, the latter suddenly appears. The spirit declares that until recently he had 'sustained many punishments and run the fearful risk of enduring torments to their full'. Now, assisted by Godric's prayers, he dwells in the heavenly Jerusalem, where Godric

---

[90] *Ibid.*, 142.

[91] *LCM*, 96. I translate 'join the elect' in the sense that he had been appointed to join the souls in heaven or the souls awaiting heaven in paradise ('electorum adiunctus est con[sorcio]').

[92] '[V]ite preclaris erat' vs. 'operibus secularibus omni erat tempore deditus': *LG*, 147n, 145.

[93] *Ibid.*, 146.

shall one day join him.[94] Later that day the elated hermit reported his vision to Prior Germanus of Durham (1163–89), with an indication of the timescale of his vicarious penance, adding that his brother had died sixteen years ago.

This third and last of our tales, concerning Godric's brother, is Reginald's most polished performance. Having worked out the theology of this genus of *miraculum*, he introduces drama: the worldliness of the object, his 'horrid death', Godric's initial despair, his eventual resolution, the upping of his penance, and his brother's near destruction. Reginald's final message is that Godric's intercession for a soul and vicarious penance could in tandem secure a happy result, even though greater sins might mean a greater burden. The message is strongly substitutive, but throughout Reginald's glossed accounts runs a subtext antagonistic to his glosses. This dialectic appears as an interaction of two monologues, through which the hermit, speaking suffrages, and God, speaking grace, somehow reach agreement. In every glossed tale, it is anticipated but never a *de facto* certainty that the saint's prayers and penance should prove efficacious. The prayers are tallied ('*toties... preces*'), the penance tailored to the sinner, but the divine action is invariably prompted by grace as though neither substantially matters. Superficially, Reginald's reckoning of prayers and penances plays up the effectiveness of suffrages, but Godric's real power lies in God's love for him. Christina's hagiographer, in contrast, who also juxtaposes two tales concerning the fate of souls, plays down the power of suffrages. The dove fixes its gaze on Geoffrey, the Virgin promises to come for Gregory, the young man appears in brilliant light, but nowhere is Christina's intercession explicitly made instrumental in securing a soul's salvation. Salvation is not guaranteed for any of these souls, nor is there any hint of vicarious penance. Each vision merely closes a chapter of wishful prayer, and does so in such a way that the impact of that prayer in the otherworld, and the nature of the otherworld itself, is left uncertain. God's love for Christina and the ability of her tears to move his humanity – both explicit elements in the narrative – consequently rise to the surface. Their advantage outstrips any that vicarious penance could confer. This more mysterious dialogue between prayers and their responses is the subtext undermining Reginald's gloss. Its implication, reinforced by the restraint observable in Walter's account and that of Christina's hagiographer, is that anchorites may have been more guarded about their powers than Reginald's final saint-creating portrait of Godric suggests. Much might depend upon grace. Heavenly visitations, if they came, functioned more in a consolatory capacity to close chapters of intercession than to prove that intercession had secured a result. Although they afforded comfort, uncertainty could remain: the power of the anchorite was in the mind of each believer.

[94] *LG*, 146.

Reginald believed that the holy hermit Godric could pray a soul into heaven and receive confirmation of the fact. But his belief was atypically bold. Reginald's fingerprints show him getting a grip on a difficult phenomenon, but from beneath them Godric emerges as a humbler personality who interceded through the saints he venerated, namely the dedicatees of his two chapels: Mary and the Baptist. His vision of Eadwen takes place in the Baptist's chapel where the Baptist appears and reveals Eadwen's soul safe in his keeping. It was he who had snatched her from her torments and brought her to show him before bearing her onwards to eternal bliss.[95] Godric's vision of Burchwen occurs in Mary's oratory. This time the Virgin is the agent. Two angels enter the oratory with Burchwen's soul and lay it upon the altar. She then sings: 'Crist and Seinte Marie, sio on scamel me iledde, þæt ic on this hi-herthe ne sculde uuit mine bare fot itreide', at which the angels return the *Kyrie*.[96] It is essential to the message of each story that the resultant visitation takes place in its proper oratory, through the respective saints' agency. Godric encouraged his clients to think of themselves as participating not in his own merits but in the saving merits of those saints. When the old man went to see him asking for Godric's 'holy prayers' to make him acceptable to God, Godric received him in his consultation chamber and began to comfort him as he sat at his feet. 'Do you know which saint's church this is?' he asked him. 'No master' he replied. 'It is dedicated in honour of St John the Baptist by whose merits here the sins of many are made null and void.'[97] He then told him to look upon and revere the crucifix. The day before, he said, he had seen a dove fly out of it. At this the man grew pale and trembled. After Godric's death, he repeated this tale to Reginald and many others. The relevant point to be drawn from it lies in the opening interchange on the Baptist, which is superfluous contextual material for the miracle concerning the dove. Reginald appears to have reported it for the sake of completeness (a tidier storyteller might have stripped it away). For this reason, it is likely to reconstruct a real conversation, in which the hermit redirected a supplicant seeking his prayers to the intercession of a trusted saint. Such glimpses of the real Godric, if that is what they are, show his ministry to souls in its own distinctive light. Whereas Reginald promoted Godric's merits, the hermit himself pointed to the saints.

The purpose of this chapter was to identify the functions of anchorites and reveal how their ministry might have differed from the ministry of the ordinary clergy. The arguments may be summarized as follows. The proper ministry of an anchorite united several different roles, one of which was to force people to confront and remedy their sins. The latter could be discovered through local gossip, prophetic insight, judicious questioning, or a penitent's confession. Appropriate penance or reparations could be agreed informally, with the valuable

---

[95] *LG*, 126.
[96] *Ibid.*, 144; and see Deeming, 'Songs'.
[97] *LG*, 274, 154 (the Baptist's chapel was his consulting room).

offer of the anchorite's intercession, an incentive. Another part of an anchorite's ministry was to intercede for souls and for the welfare of clients generally. In exceptional cases, he might pay debts of penance on behalf of the dead. His unique vocation for eradicating his own sin enabled him to break down the barrier which human iniquity had erected between man and God (or bridge the gulf opened by sin) and approach God authoritatively as a petitioner and intercessor; having earned God's favour through his obedience, he won influence in God's court. The anchorite's success in this vital intercessory role depended on the perpetuation of a constant prayer-dialogue with heaven, through which he honed his communication skills, learned to discern God's will, and in learning the latter realized his own deepest desire to see the fulfilment of God's providential design and the salvation of souls. Sometimes anchorites conducted this dialogue with particular, favoured saints. This dialogue at the same time, or perhaps the ability to bridge the gulf between God and man, gave rise to another duty of the anchorite's ministry, which was to communicate God's messages to people on earth. Her hard-won role was that of the go-between. As such, she could satisfy the curiosity of her clients concerning the wefare of souls in the otherworld. If we now begin to wonder whether the ministry of the ordinary clergy differed from the ministry of the anchorite, we might reflect that only prolonged ascetic endeavour frightened sinners into repentance and that only a life spent purging sin empowered intercession. Pious women and men of the eleventh and twelfth centuries reacted to being shocked into contrition: perhaps all the more so if that era – as previously suggested – was particularly fearful of the consequences of sin. They wanted expert intercession and advice on the status of souls. Hermits and recluses could meet these wants. Most priests may not have been able to do so, although they were empowered to dispense the sacraments. This being so, it is very likely that anchorites functioned to provide a ministry different from the priest's. The more they proliferated, the more the need for their ministry would have been perceived and the more this perception would have perpetuated their appeal.

8

How anchorites became saints

The argument, now, is drawing to a conclusion: that anchorites gained influence during the eleventh century in seeking to attain perfection by purging themselves of sin; that their purification qualified them to function as mediators between God and humanity, and that this marked them out as potential saints because it demonstrated their sanctity on earth. They were not the only pious individuals who became saints, of course. Nevertheless, as Chapter 2 has argued, by the time that old saints were beginning to be refashioned in the late eleventh century, anachoresis was a virtually indispensable hallmark of sanctity. The esteem it had come to enjoy, moreover, may have ignited interest in proclaiming the sanctity of contemporary anchorites, for ten anchorites alive in the twelfth century became subjects of hagiography before the middle of the thirteenth. A question worth asking in relation to this phenomenon is whether the success of these anchorite cults was related to changes in the nature of religious benefaction. During the eleventh century, the hagiography of contemporary saints was sporadic and attended mostly to monastic bishops, who were the spiritual luminaries of the century. Typically these bishops enriched, revived, or championed monastic communities, but in the competitive monastic market place of the twelfth century older monasteries were forced to devise new stratagems for attracting new benefactions. As the century wore on, endowments began to dry up, maintenance of property and personnel became more expensive, and reformed forms of the religious life challenged the old Benedictine hegemony. Monasteries could no longer dictate the agenda; the arrival of choice had empowered the consumer. To keep benefactors interested, houses founded during the Benedictine revival took pains to market their assets. Anglo-Saxon saints were reinvented so that their careers suited the times, or translated to grander shrines to promote their reputations; Continental saints popular with the Normans were embraced, and modern saints were recruited – saints whose appeal extended beyond the cloister. Anchoretic saints were suitable for this purpose because the rise of anchorites across Europe stood as proof of their credentials and because their cults enabled those who promoted them to keep apace of the new renunciatory trend in religion, or even to promote their own renunciatory spirituality. Monks were just as taken as laypeople with this model of perfection, so it would be a mistake to think that their motives in promoting anchorite cults were always strategic.

It would also be a mistake to see monasteries, always, as the instigators of these cults. Sometimes, as we shall see, the impetus came from a bishop; in other cases it came from a nexus of local people who were inspired by the anchorite and hopeful of his continued wonder-working presence among them. Monks sometimes only got on board and produced the hagiography by which such cults are known to us when the cults were already up and running. The cult at Throckenholt began with Godric's relatives tending his tomb and venerating his relics, before gathering momentum as new rumours of miracles were noised through the neighbourhood. This last chapter examines how such rumours spread: how stories were told in Wisbech at the house of Godric's nephew Peter the chaplain; how Wulfsige's reputation travelled on the back of rumoured miracles flying between monasteries such as Evesham, Worcester, and Westminster. In the cloisters of late eleventh-century Peterborough, there was talk of fanatical recluses who had burnt in their cells. In most cases, the point to stress is the spontaneity of the cult in question: that cultic developments were very often rapid, although monastic enthusiasm usually fanned the flames. Typically these cults were grounded in the perceived sanctity of the living individuals as manifested to and remembered by those who had encountered them. Indeed, there is no reason that medievalists should regard sanctity as the preserve of anchorites who were physically deceased. Anchorites, symbolically dead to the world, could be saints in their own lifetimes. In one or two instances, their contemporaries were so confidant of this that hagiography commenced while their subjects were still alive, and it was claimed that brawls broke out when they died, over which interested party had rights to the body. Yet their hagiography could be tinged with nostalgia. The cell at Haselbury and the Throckenholt hermitage were fallen to ruin; memories had dimmed; Roger, Wulfric, and Godric of Finchale were seen as bastions of a bygone era, and it would appear, in view of the evidence, that the anchoretic saints of the twelfth century were the last England produced.[1] This chapter asks how and why their cults came into being: how those who emulated the saints became saints (*aemulatio aemulationem parit* – from emulator to exemplar). Starting at Peterborough in the 1080s and concluding in the 1250s at Knaresborough, it follows the concatenation of anchorite cults as it unfolded.

The earliest indication of stirring interest in the sanctity of contemporary recluses in England may be found in Goscelin's short account of the Suffolk recluse Brihtric, who appears in no other source known to me, and who differs from other anchorites examined in this chapter in as much as there is no evidence that he attracted a cult. He belongs here rather because the story of his death illustrates the process whereby the transmission of oral testimony might, as it did in other instances, inculcate a cult. Given the circumstances of his death – we may recall that he wilfully perished in a blaze – it should be surprising if no pious

---

[1] Later anchorite cults were isolated exceptions. Never again were so many culted within a century.

contemporary invoked his saintly assistance. But seldom are private prayers articulated in the sources. The story 'so well known' was surely well disseminated: indeed, one of the eyewitnesses was Goscelin's source. In such favourable circumstances, Brihtric could and perhaps should have attracted a cult: that is all that can be said. The odour of sanctity that accompanied the discovery of his body spoke for itself, and Goscelin's intention in recounting the tale was to show that virtuous anchorites were not the preserve of the distant past or the distant deserts of Egypt, but alive in the eleventh century. We may compare Brihtric's case to that of the female recluse, apparently enclosed at Peterborough, who narrowly escaped immolation.[2] A few years after Goscelin heard these stories, other burnt anchorites surfaced in the chronicle compiled at St Augustine's, which noted against the year 1087 that when William I sacked Mantes two male recluses were burnt to death. The link may have been Goscelin himself, who had settled at St Augustine's. When the historian William of Malmesbury picked up this tale from some different source in or before the 1120s, he maintained that only a single recluse had died – a woman at that – after refusing to leave her cell at St Mary's church.[3] Another burnt recluse surfaces in the annals of the recluse Marianus, in John of Worcester's early twelfth-century chronicle: namely Paternus who died at Paderborn in 1058. A couple of weeks later Marianus prayed on the mat on which Paternus had died. Inspired, he sought to be enclosed at Fulda the next year.[4] These tales of recluses burning or willingly embracing that possibility appear to be peculiar to those several decades. It may be that in the last decades of the eleventh century and early in the twelfth there was a craze for such stories, symbolizing the martyr-mentality of the ascetic recluse. If this was so, it is easy to see why ecclesiastical authorities might not have approved and why cults of burnt recluses might not have got any further than a subversive idea.

Moving forward a generation we find that monastic interest in the saintliness of contemporary anchorites went much further in the case of Wulfsige of Evesham, a recluse whose reputation certainly did inspire a cult. Wulfsige seems to have received an early notice for commemoration in a list of obits kept at Durham, his memory probably borne to the north by Ealdwine, some-time prior of Winchcombe, new hermit, and first prior of Durham cathedral priory.[5] His next appearance is in Dominic of Evesham's account of the abbey's illustrious men, written during the first third of the twelfth century, which states simply that a recluse of Evesham named Wulfsige had lived the solitary life for seventy-five years. Wulfsige may still have been alive when Dominic entered Evesham, but Dominic nowhere reveals whether they knew each other. As we have already seen, Wulfsige was also remembered at Worcester as an influential

---

[2] See above, 77–9.
[3] *Peterborough Chronicle*, ed. Clark, 11; *Gesta regum*, ed. Mynors et al., I, 511.
[4] *Chronicle*, ed. Darlington and McGurk, II, 585.
[5] See above, 96.

figure in the career of Bishop Wulfstan. John of Worcester, writing in the 1120s, claimed that the recluse had successfully persuaded Wulfstan to accept the bishopric after many had failed. Yet William of Malmesbury's account of the episode in his Latin adaptation of Coleman's *Life* never mentions the recluse.[6] Although Malmesbury applied a liberal editorial hand, he had no obvious motive to delete this detail, so it may be that John derived it from a source other than Coleman. John also notes the detail that in 1062 Wulfsige had lived in seclusion for over forty years.[7] Rumours about the recluse were certainly circulating, for during the next decade word of him reached Westminster. Osbert of Clare, prior of that abbey, when composing a *Life* of Edward the Confessor in the 1130s, wrote that St Peter had appeared to a holy recluse named Wulfsige, bidding him send to the king, that he should re-found his ancient monastery in London. At the same time the pope himself sent to Edward that he should found or re-found a monastery in honour of St Peter; thus, by a providential coincidence of signs, Westminster was refounded.[8] Osbert probably had the same Wulfsige in mind, for he had ties to Worcester and had heard other miracle tales from monks of that priory. He had learned of a vision witnessed by Earl Leofric of Mercia, for example, from the lips of his Westminster contemporary, the former Worcester monk Maurice.[9] Like John of Worcester, he presents the recluse playing a pivotal role in a great and providential event, and it appears that John and Osbert alike were eager to involve Wulfsige in the memories of their own respective saints, Wulfstan and Edward, as though the mere association could enhance their auras of sanctity. If a cult was forming around the recluse in the 1120s and 1130s these tales suggest that its impetus came not from his stark cameo in Dominic's work but from a babble of imaginative hearsay that was starting to attract wider interest among monastic writers.

If John of Worcester and Dominic of Evesham can be conflated, Wulfsige should have died in or before 1097 (one set of annals may date his death to 1104).[10] The fact that Dominic afforded Wulfsige the briefest of notices suggests that at the time of writing no coordinated attempt was underway at his abbey to promote the recluse's sanctity, even if it was being rumoured in the locality. If a cult of rumours was developing, it is the earliest of the many known to have attached to contemporary anchorites in that century. Whatever its origins, during the two or three generations after Dominic wrote, Wulfsige's cult at

---

[6] *Saints' Lives*, ed. Winterbottom and Thomson, 49.

[7] *Chronicle*, ed. Darlington and McGurk, II, 591.

[8] 'La vie de s. Édouard le Confesseur par Osbert de Clare', ed. M. Bloch, *AB*, 41 (1923), 5–131, at 80–1.

[9] P. Jackson, 'Osbert of Clare and the *Vision of Leofric*: The Transformation of an Old English Narrative', in *Latin Learning*, ed. O'Keeffe and Orchard, II, 275–92, at 279.

[10] London, Royal College of Arms, MS Arundel 10, against the year 1104: 'Willelmus heremita apud Evesham' obit. Hic Baddebi Croiland primo dederat.' *Willelmus* is presumably an error for *Wlsinus*, whom Crowland remembered for the gift of the manor of Badby (which was later given to Evesham). Cf. *Historiae Anglicanae scriptores varii*, ed. J. Sparke, 2 vols (London, 1723), I, 59.

Evesham must have flourished, for, according to a fourteenth-century chronicle written at Peterborough abbey, the Evesham monk Thomas of Northwich (d. 1207) found enough miracles associated with the saintly anchorite to fill three volumes, perhaps while acting as the custodian of his shrine. Northwich had a reputation both for wisdom and for his knowledge of medicine.[11] The reference to these lost volumes betrays substantial cultic activity with a generous flow of supplicants. If Evesham produced a *Life* of St Wulfsige to accompany the collected miracles it has been lost, but perhaps visitors were informed of his deeds by notices set above his shrine, like those above the joint shrine of the saintly hermits Roger and Sigar in the abbey church of St Albans.[12] During the thirteenth century, Evesham was referring to Wulfsige as a saint. Thomas of Marlborough wrote that, until a new lectern was purchased in 1217, lessons had been read 'by the tomb of St Wulfsige'.[13] A thirteenth-century Evesham calendar, describing Wulfsige as a 'monk and anchorite of this place', commemorated his death against 24 February.[14] An Evesham necrology recorded Wulfsige's obit, also against 24 February, in red ink, which it reserved for abbots, priors, and major benefactors. About this time the convent was instructed to commemorate the anchorite in albs, denoting his status as a lesser saint (greater saints merited copes).[15] Wulfsige's tomb was to be censed during vespers on feast days and sprinkled with holy water when the abbot was present at Sunday procession.[16] Later the monks commemorated Wulfsige's anniversary with wastel bread: bread made from the finest flour.[17] These clues suggest that Evesham commemorated him gratefully as a benefactor and venerated him as a miracle-worker.

In the mid-south-west, stories of the saintly Wulfsige were only beginning to circulate when on 12 September 1122 (perhaps) the hermit Roger of Markyate died in Hertfordshire. Such was Roger's reputation that tongues were wagging in barely two years. William of Malmesbury heard from the monks of Eynsham that Roger had foreseen the death of Bishop Robert Bloet of Lincoln, on 10 January 1123, and had issued the bishop with a foreboding oracle. Roger had

---

[11] The chronicle is that attributed to John of Peterborough, a mid-fourteenth-century abbot. For Thomas of Northwich, see *Scriptores*, ed. Sparke, I, 59; *History*, ed. Sayers and Watkiss, 199, 417.

[12] *Annales monasterii s. Albani*, ed. H. T. Riley, RS, 28, 2 vols (1870–1), I, 433.

[13] *History*, ed. Sayers and Watkiss, 489.

[14] L, BL, MS Lansdowne 427, fo. 22v. The entry commemorates 'Wlsinus Monachus et Anachorita istius loci'. This manuscript is an early eighteenth-century transcript. The original, once preserved in L, BL, MS Cotton Vitellius E xvii, was partly destroyed in the fire of 1731. Wulfsige's name would have been written in the margin, which has not survived. A note states 'Conuentus in Allus' (*sic* for *Albis*). I am grateful to Peter Jackson for unearthing these details.

[15] Lansdowne 427, fo. 4r. The entry commemorates 'Willelmus Monachus et Anachorica [*sic*] istius loci'. Like the copyist of the annals in College, Arundel 10, the copyist has mistakenly given or expanded *Willelmus* for *Wlsinus*.

[16] *Officium ecclesiasticum abbatum secundum usum Eveshamensis monasterii*, ed. H. A. Wilson, HBS, 6 (1893), cols. 3, 11, and at 174.

[17] *History*, ed. Sayers and Watkiss, 489 (for a reference to Wulfsige's tomb), 559.

supposedly warned Bloet that one day he would regret not becoming a monk, but regret this too late, as events proved.[18] This story shows how rapidly hermits of repute could accrue legends and catch the attention of chroniclers. William must have heard it in or before 1125, and before that it had already reached Eynsham, borne there possibly by some member of the bishop's entourage; for Bloet, who had died suddenly at nearby Woodstock, was embalmed at Eynsham where his entrails were buried before his body was carted back to Lincoln. Memories of Roger were also being forged at St Albans. Roger's obit was entered in the St Albans psalter, identifying the hermit as a monk of the abbey. Christina's hagiographer claimed likewise that Roger 'was a monk of ours, but [he] lived in a hermitage, though even here he kept obedience to his abbot'.[19] Roger's link to the abbey may have been invented or exaggerated to boost its reputation by the recruitment of a new saint, or to claim some proprietary interest in his hermitage. All Christina's hagiographer reports about his past is that, after returning from Jerusalem (whether on crusade or as a pilgrim), Roger was met by angels and guided to his future hermitage. Such an itinerary leaves little room for a career at St Albans. The land he settled, at Caddington next to Watling Street, lay central to the network of St Alban's estates but actually belonged to the canons of St Paul's in London.[20] If the Jerusalem tale and his tenure of this estate are to be reconciled with Roger's supposed status as a monk, his subordination to the abbot of St Albans is more likely to have occurred after he became a hermit. His previous connexions were probably with St Paul's. This may explain why he never looked to St Albans to be Christina's patron, but to Archbishop Thurstan of York.[21] Thurstan had been a canon of St Paul's, and the fact that Roger knew him early in his episcopate before he had gained a reputation for sponsoring small religious houses reinforces the hypothetical St Paul's connexion. Roger may have enjoyed confraternity with St Albans in his later years, but his links lay elsewhere. Perhaps he came from St Paul's or was related to one of the canons.[22]

Hermits normally sought burial in their hermitages. Roger's body was, at some juncture, entombed at St Albans, possibly against his wishes, if the contests that are alleged to have erupted over the bodies of other saintly anchorites during the century offer any points of comparison.[23] Hagiographers sometimes maintained that when a famous anchorite died rival parties competed for the relics. Although the stories of subsequent struggles may be pure invention to show how valuable such relics were, there is an element of truth in them, in that pious

---

[18] *Gesta pontificum*, ed. Winterbottom and Thomson, I, 476–7.

[19] *LCM*, 81.

[20] *Charters of St Albans*, ed. J. Crick, Anglo-Saxon Charters, XII (Oxford, 2007), 213–14.

[21] *LCM*, 111.

[22] St Paul's looked after its own and their relatives: see C. N. L. Brooke, 'The Composition of the Chapter of St. Paul's, 1086–1163', *Cambridge Historical Journal*, 10 (1951), 111–32.

[23] *LCM*, 126.

people did indeed seize upon relics. Mayhem supposedly followed the deaths of Wulfric of Haselbury and Robert of Knaresborough when troops of monks from Montacute and Fountains respectively, in the teeth of local resistance, attempted to clothe the dead holy men in their habits and cart them away for burial. In 1127 or 1128, only five years after Roger's death, the monks of Tynemouth in Northumberland removed Henry of Coquet's corpse from his island hermitage to enshrine it with the relics of their patron St Oswald, king and martyr. The day Henry died a portentous thunderclap sent a monk hurrying to his oratory where he found the dead hermit sitting on a stone, his candle still burning. A crowd of islanders wishing to revere his body on Coquet soon assembled to protect their 'treasure', but the monks made away with the corpse under the cover of a fog.[24] Stories of relic-theft are not uncommon, but, if the tale is to be believed, the monks' hasty manoeuvre suggests that they as much as the locals had anticipated acquiring a saintly patron. Roger of Markyate presents a similar case, in which it is conceivable that the monks of St Albans seized their quarry not long after life left his body. Tynemouth priory was a daughter house of St Albans, staffed by the abbey. Had the parent house set a precedent by appropriating Roger's body shortly beforehand, Tynemouth's acquisition of Henry's remains *c.*1128 could be viewed in this context. If so, it might indicate that the precedent proved lucrative, with a burgeoning cult – a hypothesis reinforced by the abbey's promotion, soon afterwards, of a second saintly hermit, Sigar. Such was the interest in these anchorites during their lifetimes that it would be unwise to dismiss tales of rivalry over their relics as a mere hagiographer's topos. Whatever really occurred, it can at least be said that, as Wulfsige gained cultic status at Evesham during the twelfth century, cults were also growing around 'the tomb of St Roger the hermit' at St Albans and the shrine of St Henry at Tynemouth.[25]

Other cults of hermits were flourishing in Wales under the aegis of new bishops. One such was Urban of Glamorgan (d. 1134), a Welshman who became bishop in 1104. Some years afterwards, with building work underway on his new cathedral at Llandaf, he turned his mind to the matter of providing it with relics.[26] After a short space of time, he settled on two hermits buried amid a multitude of other saints within the holy confines of Bardsey Island (Ynys Enlli). St Dyfrig had retired to the island in the sixth century; St Ælgar, by birth a Devonshire man, had lived there in the 1090s. In May 1120, with the consent of Archbishop Ralph d'Escures of Canterbury, Bishop David of Bangor, and Gruffudd, 'king' of Gwynedd, Urban removed them both to his new cathedral. For some reason, the only bits of Ælgar he took were his teeth (perhaps relic hunters

---

[24] *NL*, II, 25–6.

[25] *Gesta abbatum*, ed. Riley, I, 101, 184; *Annales*, ed. Riley, I, 433.

[26] On Welsh hermits, see R. R. Davies, *The Age of Conquest: Wales, 1063–1415* (Oxford, 2000), 178–9; on Urban and the Llandaf saints, J. R. Davies, *The Book of Llandaf and the Norman Church in Wales* (Woodbridge, 2003).

had already been busy at the grave).[27] Ælgar's translation set the agenda, for soon afterwards as part of the power struggle between the two sees another contemporary hermit was culted at St David's.[28] Bishop Bernard (1115–48), a Norman and formerly the queen's chancellor, may have seized upon the local hermit Caradog in response to the popularity contemporary saintly anchorites were enjoying in England. Equally he may have acted in light of the spirituality he discovered at St Davids. During the previous generation, at least one notable member of St David's community, a bishop, had retired into solitude: Bishop Sulien to Llanbadarn Fawr in 1085.[29] Caradog himself, who retired some twenty years after Sulien to live as a hermit at Haroldston East near Haverfordwest, was later said to have been a priest of St Davids, though because the claim emanates from the community that promulgated his cult it must be treated with care. Its source, Gerald of Wales, writing in or after 1188, held one of the four arch-deaconries of that diocese.[30] According to Gerald, after Caradog died, on 13 April 1124, a controversy arose (as usual) as to who should take possession of his body. At first it fell into the hands of Tancred, the castellan of Haverford-west, but after suffering repeated bouts of illness as a result of the saint's displeasure he relinquished the body to the canons, who enshrined it with the bones of St David and St Andrew in their cathedral. William of Malmesbury was said to have visited the shrine and, in his devotion to the incorrupt saint, tried to slice off one of Caradog's fingers. The saint clenched his fist and the terrified historian withdrew, seeking forgiveness.[31] Caradog was allegedly still working miracles in Gerald's day.

Wulfric of Haselbury is the next anchorite known to have acquired a saintly reputation, of such stature that the historian Henry of Huntingdon (*c.*1088–*c.*1157) could in effect proclaim him a living saint. Henry's account of Wulfric appears at the very end of his 'Miracles of the English' (*De miraculis Anglorum*), composed *c.*1135 as the ninth book of his 'History of the English' (*Historia Anglorum*) and intended to be the last part. The book comprises a series of pen-portraits of England's saints: over twenty listed by Bede and some twenty more recent saints whose churches Henry encouraged his readers to visit, to discover 'the miraculous deeds of these miraculous men'. Finally, he considered whether there were still saints in the modern day and concluded that although 'our age . . . is greatly injured and sadly overshadowed by the gloom of sin', yet it is not 'utterly forsaken by God', and 'although miracles in our times are very rare, whenever they are done they are most glorious'. These comments introduce his

---

[27] *The Text of the Book of Llan Dâv: Reproduced from the Gwysaney Manuscript*, ed. J. G. Evans and J. Rhys (Oxford, 1893), 1–5.

[28] Davies, *Age of Conquest*, 183–4.

[29] J. W. Evans, 'St David and St Davids and the Coming of the Normans', *Transactions of the Honourable Society of Cymmrodorion*, n.s. 11 (2005 for 2004), 5–18, at 9.

[30] *Opera*, ed. Brewer et al., VI, 85–7.

[31] *NL*, I, 176.

account of Wulfric of Haselbury, written twenty years before the saint's death.[32] Henry states his intention, 'to make public the glorious record of a man whose living spirit still survives today'. He then tells of Wulfric, a priestly recluse in the county of Dorset (*recte* Somerset), who always wore a hauberk next to his flesh 'to subdue his turbulent passions'. When it was almost worn out, he requested a new one from his temporal lord, but enraged by its length, which was visible below his garment, he snatched up shears 'and cut the soldered iron rings at the bottom and in the openings of the sleeves, as if it were linen cloth'. Upon seeing this, his joyful lord 'sank down at the holy man's feet'. Wulfric swore him not to tell anyone, but 'it could not be kept secret'; for 'many religious rejoiced to have rings from the holy hauberk, and the famous story has travelled everywhere through all parts of the kingdom'. The story, Henry averred, 'is attested by those who have seen parts of the hauberk, or visited his delightful presence, or heard his desirable speech . . . and it is also spread among all the people and is commonly known everywhere'.[33] Ranking Wulfric as a modern miracle-worker alongside such great saints of old as Æthelthryth, Guthlac, and Dunstan, the historian intended to proclaim his sanctity while the recluse was still alive, barely ten years inside his cell. His statement that 'miracles are rare in our times' recalls William of Malmesbury's description of Roger as one 'who lived a strict life too seldom practised these days'. William recalled another saintly recluse as a figure from his childhood.[34] To these two historians, holy anchorites were nostalgic figures, and when one such as Roger or Wulfric arose people were quick to take note.

During these years, when the names of Wulfsige of Evesham, Roger of Markyate, maybe Henry of Coquet, and Wulfric of Haselbury, being bantered to and fro, were fast acquiring cultic status, the venerable hermit Godric died at Throckenholt. At first his settlement fell to ruin, but while it languished in ruinous state whisperings of Godric's sanctity began to spread. His nephew Peter the chaplain, inheritor of the circular settle in which the hermit had prayed and slept, held his relic in great veneration. By and by, a knight riding through Wisbech stabled there one evening and told a small audience at Peter's home that when he was a boy he had seen the hermit miraculously cut his hauberk with shears. The knight's name was Thomas de Gyney. Godric had received the hauberk from Thomas's father, William, and cut it in his presence. Many were listening as Thomas recounted this tale, and pious folk later passing near Throckenholt visited the deserted hermitage out of reverence. Rooting around inside the ruined oratory, they found fragments of mail, which subsequently displayed thaumaturgic properties. One of the rings came into the hands of a wise woman, but when some invalids were led to her she decided to place her

---

[32] Henry, Archdeacon of Huntingdon, *Historia Anglorum: The History of the English People, 1000–1154*, ed. and tr. D. E. Greenway (Oxford, 1996), pp. lxv–lxvi.

[33] *Ibid.*, 695–7.

[34] *Saints' Lives*, ed. Winterbottom and Thomson, 153–5.

trust in Godric, St Andrew, and her new relic. She put the relic in water, gave this to the sick to drink, and their fever soon lifted. On another occasion, a gang of scavengers, camping out at Throckenholt to strip whatever they could from the ruins, left in marked haste, dropping Godric's image of the Virgin along the way. Rumour soon spread that God had dimmed their wits, causing them to forsake their plunder. Later some of the hermit's surviving kindred kept cockerels there, only to be surprised by yet another miracle. For every rooster brought to the place refused to crow until a stoat's burrow in the side of Godric's tomb was filled in, to an instant cacophony of cock-a-doodle-doos.[35] These were the sorts of stories circulating among Godric's friends and relatives in the 1130s and 1140s that gave rise to Godric's cult, and they illustrate a process, possibly operational in the tenth and eleventh centuries but obscured by lack of documentation, by which a hermit could impact sufficiently upon his locality to inspire reverence in life and posthumous veneration. The reappearance of the hauberk legend is evidence of rumour in motion, showing that through the fluidity of orality a story told at Huntingdon about one anchorite could be associated with another by the time it reached Wisbech, and that fragments of an anchorite's hauberk could prove equally desirable to relic hunters in Cambridgeshire or Somerset.

If a notable article is correct, then within a decade or so of Godric's death an anonymous monk of St Albans went a step further than Henry of Huntingdon by preparing the hagiography of a living hermit. Such a development need not have been revolutionary in an era when a reputable archdeacon had already lauded the sanctity of a living recluse; and at a monastery such as St Albans, which may already have anticipated the posthumous cults of Roger and (perhaps, by proxy) Henry of Coquet. The opinion of Rachel Koopmans is that Christina of Markyate was accredited all the attributes of sanctity while she still lived and breathed, her biographer betraying no qualms about proclaiming her prophetic prowess and conversations with saints. His far-sighted project, Koopmans suggests, was undertaken to please a specific patron and intimate of Christina, namely Abbot Geoffrey. And whereas the first half maps Christina's unfolding spiritual journey the second intertwines it with his in a contrived literary embrace. As it happened, Geoffrey pre-deceased Christina, who may never have inspired posthumous veneration either at St Albans or at Markyate. Koopmans accounts for the failure of her cult by arguing that the project fell apart through factionalism among the monks, which erupted after Geoffrey's death in response to the late abbot's burdensome liberality to anchorites. This is the hypothetical scenario by which Christina's supposedly unfinished *Life* may be dated to the mid-1140s and so dated to her lifetime. On internal evidence, such a date merits consideration, for the terms in which the hagiographer presents Christina's affection for Geoffrey make it hard to imagine that the unnamed

---

[35] GT, 38–42.

pastor he at one point addresses as her 'beloved' was any other man than Geoffrey himself. A date before 1146 (when Geoffrey died) may be defensible on this evidence regardless of whether one accepts Koopmans' broader hypothesis. With regard to the latter, her idea that some monks considered Christina a 'liability' is plausible, but it could equally have been the case that as the years passed and her admirers passed away Christina lost the aura of sanctity once so promising and died little more than an old prioress.[36] Far from being quashed as a divisive embarrassment, Christina's projected cult may simply have come to nothing.

This parsimonious hypothesis might be preferable if one accepts that the *Life* was composed before 1146, yet there is also good reason to query that date. Koopmans' proposed version of events rests on her claim that the project was aborted and the *Life* never finished. Her argument runs that the hagiographer Nicholas Roscarrock (d. 1633/4), who saw and described a version of the *Life*, must have seen a manuscript that differed from the extant manuscripts and that broke off after an extra page or two. Whether one accepts this claim depends on how one reads Roscarrock, but I see no reason to doubt that his description of the ending of the manuscript he saw accords with that of the extant, incomplete one (which may lack a quire or more). Even if he did see a fuller, albeit incomplete, manuscript, the missing portion could have been destroyed at any conceivable stage and in any circumstances. Koopmans found some extracts from a lost, fuller version of the *Life* interpolated into the St Albans *gesta abbatum*, noting that they never mention Christina's death and inferring from this that the version known to the interpolator was unfinished.[37] However, the interpolator or editor of the *gesta abbatum* was not primarily concerned with Christina's career; the circumstances of her death were not relevant to his narrative. One statement in the extant *Life* seems to suggest that Christina was alive at the time of writing, but the meaning is not altogether clear: there is more than one way of reading it.[38] Several other passages hint that Christina was dead. Two of them can perhaps be discounted: a statement concerning her scars, 'which could never be expunged in her lifetime', is primarily intended to communicate the idea that the scars were indelible; similarly, the statement 'nor would such a lofty place have awaited them [Roger and Christina] in heaven' need only intimate that a place had been prepared, not that it was

---

[36] R. M. Koopmans, 'The Conclusion of Christina of Markyate's *Vita*', *JEH*, 51 (2000), 663–98, at 686.

[37] *Ibid.*, 667, 674.

[38] 'Quomodo autem hanc uisionem uiderit, cum ipsa bene sciret, ab ea usque presens nullo modo potuimus elicere', for which Talbot gives 'How she saw this vision (though she herself well knows) we have never been able to elicit from her up to the present': *LCM*, 150–1. 'Potuimus', however, is the perfect tense, implying that the action was over. And it is doubtful whether imperfect *sciret*, although required, should be rendered in the present. The sentence could read: 'How she saw this vision, though she knew well, we were in no way able to elicit from her up to now.' 'Up to now' may signal that the issue remained unknown, not that Christina was still available for questioning, but this remains unclear.

taken.[39] But the claim that Roger and Christina 'reign [with God] in the highest glory' and the recounting of a miracle, the beneficiary of which had been sworn to secrecy during Christina's lifetime, make a forceful case that she was dead at the time of writing.[40] This dates the *Life* (or at least its final touches) to some point after 1155, which is the last year when Christina was evidently still alive. The author speaks as though he was a regular visitor to her hermitage, perhaps collecting notes in preparation for his work. If Geoffrey's prominence argues that it was written for him, an alternative candidate could be Geoffrey's nephew, Abbot Robert de Gorron (1151–66), as Talbot suggested.

If there is little evidence that Christina was regarded as a saint during her lifetime, there is better evidence that a cult grew at Throckenholt in the 1140s. Miracles were multiplying, rumour winged its way through the neighbourhood, and still no regular custodians had laid claim to Godric's makeshift shrine. Against this backdrop Bishop Nigel's neglect of his property coupled with Thorney's eremitical interests provided the abbey not only with a motive but also a powerful case to petition the diocesan in a bid for a takeover. The monks may have joined forces in this with Godric's former supporters, for about the middle of the century the d'Oyrys and their knightly tenants at Walsoken in Norfolk, who were benefactors of Godric's hermitage, were recruited to the abbey's confraternity and their names entered in its *Liber vitae*.[41] A slightly earlier entry lists the names *Agga* and *Gudrun*, separated only by *Lefsius presbiter*. These men are probably to be identified as Hagg of Leverington and Guthrum son of Aelweard, who appear side by side as co-witnesses to the charter that was issued at the dedication of Godric's church. Perhaps these men were hermits formerly of his community and still dwelling thereabouts. In the minds of those who had joined or sponsored Godric, a takeover by Thorney, renowned for preserving the memory of hermit saints, could have augured the survival of his legacy and tapped, in the monks, a source of intercession for their souls. Abbot Robert of Thorney (d. 1151) was a man of famed eloquence, who may have used his gift in petitioning for Throckenholt.[42] In 1151, shortly before the abbot's death, the abbey acquired the site from Bishop Nigel, apparently upon the undertaking that brethren should retire to it under the abbot's supervision, and for use as a cemetery. The original objective of this takeover may be reflected in the fact that, unlike many hermitages annexed by monastic communities, Throckenholt in later years never claimed to have developed into a priory. The distinction could well be important, for although the house readily conforms to

---

[39] '[Q]ue nunquam potuerunt ipsa superstite deleri'; '[N]ec maneret eis in celis tanta celsitudo': *LCM*, 74, 102. In the second citation, Talbot proposes *eis* for *eos*, which is given in the manuscript.

[40] '[I]n summa gloria cum ipso simul regnant': *LCM*, 102; for the miracle, 121. It should be noted, in Koopman's defence, in reference to the miracle, that others witnessed and may have reported the cure.

[41] GT, 16–17.

[42] 'Translatio s. Guthlaci. Ex MSS. Anglicanis' (*BHL*, 3731–2), *Acta SS, Apr.* II, 54–60, at 56B.

Martin Heale's criteria for identifying priories it lacked a prior, and the monks defined it as a hermitage. During the twelfth century, a warden kept it. At the turn of the fourteenth century Thorney's abbot stipulated that the 'hermitage' be served by two or three monks 'as before'; and as late as 1441, when Thorney's pittancer Richard Dodyngton compiled his account roll, it was still being labelled a *heremitarium*.[43] Throckenholt had retained a strong eremitic identity: a legacy of its founder (and perhaps also his patrons and surviving members of his community) that the monks wished to preserve.

About these years, perhaps during the 1150s, the monks of St Albans added another saintly hermit to their collection: Sigar of Northaw. Some time after the mid-thirteenth century, when the account of Roger and Christina from the lost version of the latter's *Life* was interpolated into the abbey's *gesta abbatum*, whoever entered it introduced a unique cameo portrait of Sigar. Sigar was reputed to have been a monk of St Albans living in the woods at Northaw, whose holiness shone forth in the days of Abbot Geoffrey. Every night he had walked to the abbey for matins, until at last he died, was interred in the same tomb as Roger, and boards were put over it recounting the wondrous deeds of these holy hermits.[44] Such modes of advertisement were not uncommon. Visitors to Throckenholt might recall Godric's travails by memorizing the metrical epitaph on his tomb, while Robert's miracles at Knaresborough were proclaimed on placards hung round his.[45] There is no reason to suppose that Sigar was a fictional creation, unlike certain of the abbey's saints (notably St Amphibalus), but the account of him is so stylized that little can be salvaged save the location of his hermitage. This may prove illuminating, for Sigar, unlike Roger, resided on one of St Alban's estates, confirmed to the martyr and his community by Archbishop Lanfranc. Throughout the 1150s the resident tenants, the Valognes family, contested ownership of Northaw until an appeal to the king in 1159 resolved the dispute in the monks' favour.[46] The Lanfranc charter seems to have availed them little during the course of this dispute, and it could be that in these years the monks promoted the cult of Sigar as an additional and spiritual claim upon the land. Their links to Roger may already have fostered some design on Caddington, and it is worth recalling that the monks of Durham used Godric's long tenure of Finchale, allegedly as one of their monks, as a lever to wrest the land from the bishopric. In light of David Rollason's argument that cults and land claims went hand in hand, it seems a likely hypothesis that the abbey's dispute with the Valognes family ignited Sigar's cult, as fuel for its claim to Northaw.

[43] GT, 15–16.

[44] *Gesta abbatum*, ed. Riley, I, 105–6; *Annales*, ed. Riley, I, 433.

[45] GT, 42; for Robert, see below.

[46] *English Episcopal Acta 28: Canterbury, 1070–1136*, ed. M. Brett and J. A. Gribbin (Oxford, 2004), no. 10.

Haselbury's fabled holy man was, in the meantime, approaching death. Over the previous generation, Wulfric had assumed such status as a living relic that a Cistercian monk from the abbey of Waverley came hankering after a ring from his hauberk.[47] Tension mounted as rival claimants hatched plans to secure Wulfric's remains, and as soon as the celebrated recluse died on 20 February 1155 a battalion of monks from Montacute priory, Wulfric's material patron, supposedly arrived to collect his body. Osbern the village priest was waiting at the church with assembled villagers to prevent them, but, ignoring his protestations, they set about dressing the corpse for removal to their priory. The priest responded by locking them inside the church and hurrying off to gather a larger mob from nearby Crewkerne. Then, as the monks tried to escape with the body by smashing through the wall of Wulfric's cell, some of the villagers in the church engaged them in a bloody scuffle. When Osbern returned with his new display of force, the brethren were at last obliged to withdraw to Montacute, sad and empty-handed. The bishop later settled the matter in Osbern's favour, and Wulfric's wish to be buried in his cell was fulfilled. However, some time after 1170, fearing another raid, Osbern removed Wulfric's body to a secret location inside the church.[48] These events and the comparable struggle that followed the death of Henry of Coquet suggest that a local community could be no less desirous of an anchorite's enduring presence than a monastery, and that feelings in both camps could run high. Despite this purported display of interest in Wulfric, no miracles were reported at his tomb for the next fifteen years. Even in the 1180s, few were occurring, and only the momentum of a hagiographer's enthusiasm propelled the subsequent cult.[49] It is possible that people lost interest in Wulfric because there was neither any shrine to attract their attention nor any devoted acolytes to retain it by recording miracles. As at Throckenholt, the cell lay in ruins for many years before a wonder or two began to be witnessed there. In contrast to Throckenholt and Haselbury, where a rapid drive to cult an anchorite was sustained, as was the case at Finchale, the results could be quite different: at Finchale only two years elapsed after Godric's death before miracles were reported, and during the next decade the energetic hermit exceeded two hundred.

In the north, Godric's fame was spreading and attracting a wide variety of visitors, including a party of nuns from Galloway.[50] Like Wulfric, he was treated as a living saint. A Cistercian monk, arriving with his abbot, went so far as to pluck hairs from his beard; another, after requesting some memento, gratefully received a loaf of the hermit's bread.[51] Within a year the first monk fell seriously ill. Despairing of earthly medicine, he remembered the hairs that he had kept.

---

[47] *WH*, 100.

[48] *Ibid.*, pp. xxxi–iii, 127–30: note that Wulfric died in Henry II's first year, 1155, not 1154 as Bell thought. (John of Ford, who was a Cistercian, reckoned his years from Lady Day.)

[49] *Ibid.*, p. lxxvi.

[50] *LG*, 185, and, for the nuns, 258–9.

[51] *Ibid.*, 263, 186.

When he put them in water and drank it, he fell into a sleep in which Godric appeared to him and promised that God would cure him. Cured, the monk later told Reginald and assured the hagiographer that the dream had occurred when Godric's was still alive. When the second monk, an abbot, returned home with Godric's oatmeal bread, a group of invalids spied him and sought his aid. He distributed the bread, and fifteen were cured, of all sorts of afflictions. Among the Cistercians, who cultivated an eremitic identity themselves, Godric, like Wulfric, attracted devotion. With his reputation, it was not long before there was talk of hagiography. The hermit's earliest *Life* was the work of the Durham hagiographer Reginald, who names Prior Thomas of Durham and Aelred of Rievaulx as the most prominent of those who urged his pen. This dates the conception of his work to 1158 x 1163, although Godric's opposition to the project delayed it for some years. To start a *Life* and gather materials before the subject's death was no mere foresight: it was to recognize a living saint. At this, Godric protested, but at last he conceded, coaxed by Reginald, if we are to believe the latter.[52] It is not unlikely that Godric's *Life* was proposed in the expectation that his death was imminent. Already a nonagenarian, from *c*.1162 the ailing hermit was bedridden, and there may have been a concern that memories of his manifold wonders should scarcely outlive him. Many of Godric's closer acquaintances, including Prior Roger of Durham (d. 1149), Abbot Robert of Newminster (d. 1159), and three bishops of the diocese who had taken care of him, were already in their graves. It was a mark of Godric's greatness that such preparations were made in his lifetime and that they involved major figures in the different monasteries. The task fell to Reginald because, as an acquaintance of both Thomas and Aelred, he proved acceptable to the two men, of different monastic orders, interested in Godric's hagiography. He may also have been a relative of the hermit (adding a personal dimension and another qualification) if the relative of that name and the Reginald who lived at Finchale in 1170 x 1174 are one and the same.[53]

Saint-making of a sort was a topic of the day, with high-profile efforts being made in the early 1160s to secure the papal canonization of Edward the Confessor and Anselm. Aelred was involved in the Edward campaign, but he shared with Thomas and Reginald a more than passing interest in anachoresis. It was in these years that he wrote his formative treatise on enclosure for his anchorite sister. Thomas became a hermit on Inner Farne in 1163, and Reginald may have stayed at Finchale during the 1170s. It is doubtful whether these men aimed at securing the papal canonization of Godric, for, although this form of recognition tempted the king and archbishop as the highest stamp of authority the cults of their predecessors Edward and Anselm could obtain, the old method

---

[52] I expand Tudor's date of 1161 x 1163: cf. Tudor, 'Reginald', 83. Thomas may have attained office as early as 1158 (he was deposed in 1163): *HRH*, 43. See *LG*, 269–70.

[53] *LG*, 243; *English Episcopal Acta 24: Durham, 1153–1195*, ed. M. G. Snape (Oxford, 2002), no. 33.

of saint-making by popular acclaim and episcopal sanction was still very much the norm. Reginald accordingly dedicated his work to the diocesan, Bishop Hugh Puiset, in the hope that Godric's cult might merit his approval. At the same time, matters were complicated by the problem of Godric's exact status qua the Durham convent. On 21 May 1170, after the hermit had breathed his last, the monks lingering at his hermitage dressed his body in the monastic habit, arguing

> ... that he had certainly once been a monk of the church of Durham ... and although, living at his hermitage, he had not dwelt within the monastery as a cloistered monk, he had nonetheless served the Lord in obedience to their commands, worn their habit for many years, and been bound to them in confraternity by a common decree in chapter.[54]

After claiming the saint as their own, the monks then buried him with great ceremony at Finchale in the presence of a huge crowd. His obit was first set down as 'Godricus heremita' then amended to read 'Godricus heremita et monachus' ('Godric, hermit and monk'), as if the monks wished to reinforce his credentials as one of their own.[55]

With news of his death, those who loved the hermit and regarded him as a saint sought to acquire mementoes in the hope that miracles would confirm his sanctity.[56] Godfrey, the almoner of Kelso on the Scottish borders, had already visited Finchale and received rings from Godric's hauberk. Later, when he was distributing alms, an invalid asked him whether the monks had any relics. Remembering the pieces of mail he bade her put them in water and drink, and she was cured. This was Godric's first posthumous miracle, but though a few similar miracles were worked 'in other parts' no wonders were witnessed at the shrine for two full years.[57] When miracles began in 1172, it was on the feast of the nativity of Godric's patron John the Baptist (24 June). The timing of their inception was interpreted as a sign that the Baptist's imitator had at last been found worthy of becoming his co-miracle-worker, and the belief spread that the two saintly hermits wrought miracles together.[58] After this breakthrough, it became customary on the Baptist's vigil for a crowd to gather at the hermitage and pass the night in prayer. With anticipation reaching fever pitch, miracles occurred. Of 225 itemized by Reginald, ten are explicitly associated with the Baptist's June feast while a further eight involve the saint as agent or spectral visitor who directs the sick to Godric's shrine. From this, it appears that each year on this festival at least one, and probably more, of those assembled at the hermitage claimed a cure, for the only dated or datable miracles fall in 1172,

---

[54] *LG*, 325–6.
[55] *Durham Episcopal Charters, 1071–1152*, ed. H. S. Offler, SS, 179 (1968), 68–72.
[56] *LG*, 368–9.
[57] *Ibid.*, 371.
[58] *Ibid.*, 371–2. The next cure was attributed to the merits of the saints (plural): see 373.

1175, and 1177, and there is no suggestion that miracles continued to be recorded beyond the 1170s. The total number of pilgrims to Finchale in that decade presumably exceeded a thousand. Most were local. Nine tenths of those whose abode is named journeyed from within a forty-mile radius, and over two-thirds of those identified were women – a statistic which may reflect the misogyny of St Cuthbert, whose sanctuary barred female pilgrims.[59] One woman, whom Cuthbert struck mad because she had entered his cathedral, found Godric more sympathetic, being cured of her madness at Finchale.[60] Visitors to Godric's shrine were typically of low or middling status: the daughter of a Durham burgess, a craftsman's wife, a priest's daughter, an artisan's son with a tumour, a lord's retainer, a two-year-old girl with her parents, a former servant of the hermit, shepherds, priests, the occasional monk, a steward, a reeve, an old blind man named Gamel, and even a crippled lamb. Restored by the saint's powers, the lamb was purchased by the local lord and donated to the shrine at Finchale, to be tended there in the saint's honour.[61]

Godric's cult, in all likelihood, should have fared even better had it not been for Thomas Becket's headline-grabbing martyrdom seven months after his death. From then on, pilgrims flocked to Canterbury. Finchale, away to the north, could to some extent compete by carving out its own northern constituency. It is a testimony to Godric's authority and popularity as a miracle-worker that it was able to do so despite Cuthbert's cult at Durham. Becket's influence on Finchale's fortunes is palpable. Godric's hagiographer could not decide whether to recruit the saintly archbishop to his cause or slight his miracle-working credentials. Friendly competition between the saints was a trope in hagiography, but Reginald's response is interesting because it put St Godric on a par with established saints. There are nine stories in total in which Becket, like the Baptist, participates in cures at Finchale. One Finchale pilgrim saw the Baptist, Becket, and Godric as three white birds circling her head and curing her concomitantly; elsewhere in the *Miracula* they appear side by side; in another vision, Becket is described as Godric's 'companion in the heavens'.[62] Reginald tried various tricks to divert towards Finchale the flow of northern pilgrims to Canterbury. Agnes, a villager of Carlton in Durham, was determined to visit Becket in spite of her debilitating malady, but her mistress advised her to try St Godric, who healed her.[63] One severely disabled man from Northumbria went all the way to Canterbury only for Becket to upbraid him in a dream: 'Why do you Northumbrians come here to me when in your own region you have St Cuthbert, a saint of far greater worth, and my colleague St Godric?' The pilgrim neither honoured nor

---

[59] This statistic is based upon a sample of about 200: R. C. Finucane, *Miracles and Pilgrims: Popular Beliefs in Medieval England* (London, 1995), 166–7, 127.

[60] *LG*, 403.

[61] *Ibid.*, 419–20.

[62] *Ibid.*, 377, 382, 384, 387, 390, 410.

[63] *Ibid.*, 412.

trusted his local saints. And he sent the wretch back home to the north.[64] No fewer than nine invalids cured at Finchale had failed or enjoyed only partial success in earlier petitions at Canterbury. Some of these failures are unexplained or attributed to 'God's inscrutable decree'. In other instances, Reginald speculates that Becket had passed over a cure so that Godric might be glorified. Near the end of the *Miracula* he affirms that Becket 'used to proclaim St Godric to be his fellow brother in the Lord by transferring a great number of sickly folk to him'.[65] Cuthbert likewise sent petitioners to Godric, on one occasion reserving a cure for 'his devoted servant' (i.e. the hermit), and he twice appeared at Finchale with other saints associated with that shrine.[66] Godric also cured pilgrims who had been disappointed by St James, at Compostella, and St Andrew, in Scotland.

The publication of Godric's *Life* – at least in its more popular abridgements (for Reginald's was rewritten twice within a generation) – preceded similar enterprises at Thorney and the Cistercian abbey of Ford in Dorset. Godric of Throckenholt had been dead for thirty or forty years when Thorney immortalized him. Wulfric had been dead almost thirty when his *Life* was commissioned, shortly before 1184, by Bishop Bartholomew of Exeter and completed soon after by the monk John of Ford. In all that time, the two holy men had worked barely ten posthumous miracles between them. John was rather anxious to revive Wulfric's cult. It troubled him that the cell was 'destitute'; that its occupant had 'almost perished from the memory of man', and that no one celebrated his anniversary.[67] To the extent that John's abbey had no discernible designs upon Wulfric's relics, his purposes in writing were 'purely moral and academic'.[68] Yet he knew and plied the subtleties of Cistercian saint-making. Benedictine hagiographers apparently felt obliged to cast saintly outsiders like Godric of Finchale and Roger of Markyate as members of their own convents. Cistercians, perhaps more conscious of their unity as an international order and unpractised in promoting house saints, tended to reinvent them more as saints sympathetic to their cause. Outsiders whose cults they propagated, such as Bishop Malachy of Armagh, Godric, and – in this instance – Wulfric, were regarded as Cistercians in spirit if not in cowl. For this reason, John emphasized aspects of Wulfric's spirituality that would have appealed to Cistercians, such as his *simplicitas*; he drew many key narratives from Cistercian monks and lay brothers, and he claimed that Wulfric favoured the Cistercians over other religious. None of this is very surprising, but it is worth noting that his stance prompted John to deal unfairly with the Cluniac monks of Montacute. Montacute had materially sustained Wulfric during his career as a recluse, yet it hardly features in John's

[64] *LG*, 459–60.
[65] *Ibid.*, 473.
[66] *Ibid.*, 379, 381, 387, 392.
[67] *WH*, pp. lxxvi, 123.
[68] Mayr-Harting, 'Functions', 338.

account. When it does, it appears not as the hand that feeds but as a bugbear. The Montacute cellarer decides to cut off Wulfric's food supply and instantly drowns, accursed by the holy man; the monks, trying reasonably enough to claim Wulfric's body, are cast as the aggressors. John's heroes are the unworldly Cistercians and the embattled villagers fighting the might of Montacute to retain the body of their holy man while the Cluniacs unceremoniously smash a hole through his cell. In John's mind, only the Cistercians, humble village priests, and simple layfolk appreciated Wulfric. From his account, the monks of Montacute emerge as the losers.

John consulted a large number of witnesses when he collected his tales, usually crediting each by name. They fall into three rough categories. The first includes Walter, son of Wulfric's temporal lord William fitzWalter and later a monk of Glastonbury, a man John trusted for conventional reasons because of his age, his religious profession, and his honest *simplicitas*. This Walter was prepared to give an account of Wulfric to all that asked. William, a lay brother of Ford who 'despised the pomp of the world', had been a more intimate acquaintance; the recluse had even discussed heavenly mysteries with him. Richard, son of a local village priest, had trained as Wulfric's scribe before becoming a monk at Ford. Henry, abbot of Tintern, another Cistercian, owed his conversion to the anchorite.[69] All these men were valuable sources who had known Wulfric well. Other witnesses had not been so close or had simply picked up the odd story. This second category includes a couple of anchorites, John of Winterborne and Odolina of Crewkerne, who afford a fleeting glimpse of a Dorset-Somerset reclusive grapevine similar to that in operation in the *Life* of Christina.[70] The last group to supply material for John's hagiography were those connected to the holy man in so far as God had cured them through his agency. Between these three categories, thirty years after Wulfric's death, enough people remembered him to enable a discerning hagiographer, even excluding the doubtful and repetitious, to assemble a substantial account comprising over a hundred stories. As ever, it is well to remember that as time passes memories fail or are embroidered, and discomfiting doubt distils itself into disbelief or conviction. John added his own glosses and exegeses, drawing biblical parallels and proclaiming Wulfric's virtues. Silently he interpreted, repackaged, edited, and interpolated his sources to present a plausible saint. The interest he stirred duly re-ignited Wulfric's cult, so that by the mid-1230s the historian Roger of Wendover could remark that 'innumerable miracles are being performed there [at Haselbury] even up to this day'.[71] It is not immediately clear how such momentum was sustained, but John's eagerness that Wulfric's feast should be commemorated ('there is no one who comes to the solemn feast', he wrote), and the role of the Baptist's feast in

---

[69] *WH*, pp. xx–ii, xxii–vi, xxxiii, xxiv–v, xxxiv–vii.
[70] *Ibid.*, pp. xxxvii–viii, 81, 90–1.
[71] *Rogeri de Wendover, liber qui dicitur flores historiarum*, ed. H. G. Hewlett, RS, 84, 3 vols (1886–9), I, 9.

galvanizing enthusiasm at Finchale, suggests that it may have been sustained by the annual gathering of invalids on a designated day. For, as long as the electric atmosphere of an apprehensive crowd keeping vigil at the shrine continued to generate miracles year in year out, a cult would retain its potency.

Spurred on by the success of Godric's cult and possibly aware of the interest Wulfric's was enjoying, the monks of Durham turned their attention to Bartholomew of Farne. Forty-two years spent as a hermit on the island had earned their brother a saintly reputation among the many who visited him or learned of his austerities. When he died in 1193, the task of composing his *Life* fell to the hagiographer Geoffrey, who also seems to have assembled an abridged *Life* of Godric (he is the only hagiographer on record as having written about two of his eremitic contemporaries). Durham had never been a house to delay such projects, and Geoffrey's stated concern to record Bartholomew's deeds 'while memories were still fresh' suggests that the hagiography followed swiftly after the hermit's death. The cult, conversely, got off to a less than equal start. By the time Geoffrey presented his completed work to Prior Bertram of Durham (1189–1213), Farne's new saint had only three modest miracles to his name. One man had poured forth prayers at the shrine for four whole days before his goitre disappeared.[72] Getting miracles from St Bartholomew was like drawing blood from a stone. This aside, several factors conspired against the cult from its inception. Chief of these was that Bartholomew lacked the stature of his neighbour at Finchale. The late twelfth-century chroniclers of the region, William of Newburgh and Roger of Hovedon, emphasize this by noting Godric's death but ignoring Bartholomew's.[73] Godric and Wulfric found their way into various chronicles from different parts of England; Bartholomew found his way into none. Another likely factor in stifling his cult was the unhappy coincidence that his anniversary fell on 24 June, the Baptist's day: the day on which it was already customary for sick folk to gather at Finchale. This forced the hapless Bartholomew to compete with both Godric and the Baptist, who diverted attention away from his shrine on the one day when invalids might otherwise have converged upon it to create the sort of atmosphere that generated miracles at Godric's. Finally, Inner Farne was already a shrine to Cuthbert. The knowledge that any miracles wrought there were potentially attributable to Durham's first patron provided a powerful counter-incentive for the monks to attribute them to Bartholomew. With the odds stacked against him it is hardly surprising that no more miracles were added to his meagre output. In the 1230s, Roger of Wendover reported that Godric's shrine at Finchale was still working miracles.[74] His relics had spread to Lichfield, Meaux, and St Albans.[75] Caradog's shrine was thriving to

---

[72] *VB*, 323–4.
[73] *Chronicles*, ed. Howlett, I, 149–50; *Chronica magistri Rogeri de Houedene*, ed. W. Stubbs, RS, 51, 4 vols (1868–71), I, 276.
[74] *Flores historiarum*, ed. Hewlett, I, 78.
[75] Thomas, 'Cult of Saints' Relics', 82.

the extent that in 1200 his hagiographer Gerald of Wales petitioned Pope Innocent III – but failed – to procure his canonization.[76] Bartholomew's cult in contrast had sunk without trace.[77]

With the death of Bartholomew, anchorite spotters, had there been any in twelfth-century England, might as well have retired their notebooks. After 1193, no anchorite was notable in the way that Wulfsige, Caradog, Wulfric, Godric, and Godric had been. This remained the case for twenty-five years. When a hermit cult did emerge, it was to be the last of the famous cults in England.[78] Robert of Knaresborough died on 24 September, probably in 1218.[79] Among the anchorites discussed in this chapter, he is intriguing not only for achieving cult status so much later than all the others, alone of the anchorites of his generation, but also for the complexity of his hagiography. After Robert died, his hermitage passed to a clerk before coming into the possession of his former companion Ivo, in 1227. King Henry III confirmed to that recipient the forty acres King John had given Robert. Ivo conveyed his estate to Coverham abbey, then the cell fell into disuse, before being appropriated *c.*1250 for the foundation of a Trinitarian priory.[80] A *Life* in Latin prose proclaiming Robert's devotion to the Trinity, speaking proudly of 'our patron', can be ascribed with confidence to the Trinitarians: it is a typical in-house hagiography of an adoptive founder.[81] Another Latin prose *Life*, this one incomplete, reveals an earlier stage in the development of Robert's cult.[82] Nothing is known of it beyond the appended name, Richard of Studley (this author is unidentified). However, its origins could well be Cistercian. Studley's *Life* opens with a surprising and prolonged broadside against scholastic learning, an attack not unlikely to have emanated from a Cistercian monk. Having discredited such vain pursuits as geometry and astronomy, the author introduces his oral source: an aged servant of Robert recently become a lay brother at Fountains abbey, a simple rustic (assuredly) whose truthful narration the author's pen has faithfully transmitted. The link to Fountains abbey strengthens with his use of the classic Cistercian topos from Deuteronomy (*in loco horroris et uaste solitudinis*) to

[76] Gerald read his *Life* to the pope in person. Although he had received favourable letters from three Welsh abbots to accompany this petition, Innocent wrote back in May 1200 declining the canonization: *Opera*, ed. Brewer et al., III, 63, 90, 182.

[77] His *Life*, however, continued to be copied at Durham in the thirteenth and fourteenth centuries.

[78] I know of only one later hermit who attracted a *Life*: the fifteenth-century 'Saint' John Warton, in Durham: M. Harvey, *Lay Religious Life in Late Medieval Durham* (Woodbridge, 2006), 64–7.

[79] On Robert, see B. Golding, 'The Hermit and the Hunter', in *The Cloister and the World: Essays in Medieval History in Honour of Barbara Harvey*, ed. J. Blair and B. Golding (Oxford, 1996), 95–117.

[80] *The Metrical Life of St. Robert of Knaresborough, together with the other Middle English pieces in British Museum MS. Egerton 3143*, ed. J. Bazire, EETS, o.s. 228 (1953 for 1947), 20.

[81] Bottomley, *Robert of Knaresborough*, 29, 31.

[82] These *Lives* (*VRK*) are edited as 'Vitae s. Roberti', ed. Grosjean, *passim*.

describe Robert's hermitage at Knaresborough.[83] First used in the *Life* of St Bernard to describe the terrain chosen for the foundation of Clairvaux, the topos famously resurfaces in the Fountains abbey foundation narrative written for the abbot of that monastery *c.*1207.[84] It is doubtful that such a loaded topos would have dropped from the lips of a rustic lay brother. Fountains again surfaces in a story from the later *Life*, that after Robert's death the monks of that monastery tried to remove his body, 'by force of arms', for burial at their abbey.[85] There is also a role, as Robert's protector, for the prominent benefactor of Fountains, William de Stuteville, who was buried at the abbey. Such was Fountains' interest in the hermit Godric of Finchale that after his death it sent to Durham for an exemplar of his *Life*, which the brethren copied with lavish illustration.[86] So it could be that Robert's first *Life* was compiled at Fountains.

The case for a Cistercian initiative in culting St Robert fits with what is known of Cistercian devotion to anchorites in late twelfth-century England. Reginald wrote his *Life* of Godric partly on behalf of the Cistercians and at their instigation, and monks of Meaux abbey acquired relics of Godric along with hairs from the beard of 'H', an unidentified recluse (a cult apparently unknown).[87] John of Ford compiled Wulfric's *Life* without designs to profit by it, and Robert's first *Life* appears to have been written in the same spirit, for although its author observed early on that miracles had occurred at Knaresborough since Robert's death he pointedly refused to report them for lack of an authoritative witness. By drawing attention away from the miracles to the virtues of the man, he reassures his audience that he has no vested interest in the cult. Like John of Ford his purpose is edificatory; the proof of Robert's sanctity lies less in his posthumous miracles than in his humble piety. The Trinitarians in contrast had a keen interest in promoting Robert's material cult: not only did they want a patron capable of flexing some muscle; they were eager to capitalize on a lucrative shrine. Even as Robert's unburied body lay in the chapel, their hagiographer claimed, pilgrims trooped past to kiss the bier, leaving gifts of gold and silver. In the fullness of time, the blind, lame, deaf, and dumb were restored their faculties, and, through the powers of their saintly anchorite, lepers were cleansed, paralytics cured, untreatable ailments alleviated, demoniacs exorcized, and the dead restored to life. St Robert, it seems, had become the medieval equivalent of a Victorian patent medicine. Soon the saint's tomb was ornamented round about

---

[83] VRK, 365–7, 369.

[84] (Deut. 32.10) *Memorials of the Abbey of St. Mary of Fountains*, ed. J. R. Walbran and J. T. Fowler, SS, 42, 67, 130, 3 vols (1863–1918), I, 2, and 128 for the date of the narrative.

[85] VRK, 398. It is not known whether this story derives from the missing portion of the earlier *Life*, but it is conceivable that a Fountains monk should have opposed such an action by his brethren.

[86] LG, 466.

[87] A fourteenth-century relic list includes hairs, bones, mail, clothing, and portions of Godric's hairshirt. Twice Godric is named; twice 'sancti G. heremite' is given, more likely Godric than Guthlac (cf. Thomas); and 'et barba H. inclusi': Thomas, 'Cult of Saints' Relics', 517, 523.

with inscriptions and paintings proclaiming Robert's miracles.[88] The historian Matthew Paris (d. 1259) noted that his fame shone forth in 1238 when the tomb emitted a bountiful supply of medicinal oil.[89] St Albans, where Paris wrote, possessed the tomb of Roger and Sigar, which was still attracting gifts. King Henry III, visiting the abbey in the 1250s, left an offering of rich cloths at their shrine.[90] Robert's cult continued to prosper throughout the Middle Ages, with the composition of additional *Lives*, in Latin and English verse, so that in later years the last of the greatest anchoretic saints also proved to be one of the most enduring. Even so, from the 1120s up to the 1220s, scarcely a decade had passed without a new cult of a saintly hermit or recluse, alive or dead, manifesting somewhere in the realm.

In conclusion, although the twelfth-century flowering of anchoretic hagiography may not, at first, seem to reflect the ascendency of anchorites (when we consider that saints' *Lives* and miracle collections multiplied over that century and that anchoretic cults had probably come and gone in the past without written memorials) it remains true, nevertheless, that no piece of hagiography celebrating any contemporary hermit or recluse survives from the period between the eighth century and the twelfth. The idea that a person alive in the present day might become a saint by following in the footsteps of the desert fathers and becoming an anchorite is present in Felix's *Life* of Guthlac (written *c.*740), and it is there again suddenly in the twelfth-century *Lives*. In Henry of Huntingdon's account of Wulfric, the recluse is portrayed as a living saint and included in the company of the greatest saints of the realm (who had all been dead for hundreds of years), while Reginald's miracle collection presumes to rank Godric of Finchale alongside John the Baptist and St Cuthbert, the greatest saint of the North, just as Goscelin had flattered Eve as a worthy new member of the Baptist's *familia*. The papal canonization of anchorites in eleventh-century Europe had sanctioned the idea that anachoresis was a path to sanctity. In England, from the eleventh century, hagiographers paid tribute to this idea by investing saints with anchoretic credentials. In the twelfth century, they proclaimed the sanctity of contemporary anchorites. This, it appears, was the next logical step, in view of the presence of saintly anchorites who were the products of the ascetic movement that had spread through Western Europe in the century 1040–1140. Once again, as in the eighth century, religious commentators were ready to declare that anachoresis was an effective path to sanctity in the modern age. Whether the impetus for their cults came from the laity, parish clergy, monks, or bishops – and we have examined cults in which each of these parties played some sort of

[88] VRK, 398–9.

[89] *Matthaei Parisiensis, monachi sancti Albani, chronica majora*, ed. H. R. Luard, RS, 57, 7 vols (1872–83), III, 521; *Matthaei Parisiensis, monachi sancti Albani, historia Anglorum, sive, ut vulgo dicitur, historia minor*, ed. F. Madden, RS, 44, 3 vols (1866–9), II, 415.

[90] Clay, *Hermits*, 113.

formative role (and some in which they worked together) – anchorites had become fully functional saints, whose eradication of sin brought miracles and healing. By rejecting their society's worldly aspirations and reviving the radical alternative of uncompromising asceticism, they had forced the guardians of religion to reassess their standards of holiness and acknowledge the extent to which they fell short of an ideal.

Conclusion

The aims of this book, set out in the Introduction, were to explain how and why anchorites gained influence in medieval society and to discover their social functions. These two aims were chosen on the assumption of a logical connexion between them: that the anchorite's social function would explain why this figure rose to prominence in that age, or that the context in which this figure rose would betray whatever need the anchorite was supposed to meet. Peter Brown pioneered this approach by asking a similar set of questions of the holy man in late antiquity, and his ideas, and the ideas of other scholars, have shaped this inquiry. Several hypotheses have been offered to explain that strange phenomenon whereby society in the central Middle Ages turned with no little alacrity to an antique template of asceticism which repudiated worldly ambition: that these anchorites arose to heal the rifts of the Norman Conquest; that they arose as a result of dissatisfaction with and within the monasteries (the 'crisis of cenobitism'); that they arose as a result of a broader crisis of conscience related to economic change and the growth of materialistic ambition; that their vocation became popular as a route for escaping the bonds of society, or of freer religious expression. By offering such solutions, historians of spirituality and social historians have sought to impart historical meaning to this phenomenon according to their terms of reference. Yet with each of these hypotheses something has been found wanting. Scholars who linked the rise of anachoresis to the Norman Conquest paid little attention to the Anglo-Saxon inheritance and the broader European context. Those who looked to the monasteries under-rated the fact that the movement defined itself, not in opposition to contemporary cenobitism, but by its own points of reference, from the accounts of the desert fathers and the Bible. If the movement was a criticism, it was not a criticism of cenobitism but of the perceived tepidity of numerous monks. The putative crisis of conscience in society is hard to substantiate and reliant on the theory that particular ages develop particular mentalities. Anxiety about greed does appear to have been growing in the eleventh century, but it did so in tandem with the ascetic movement and could be interpreted as a consequence of it rather than a cause. With respect to the last of the hypotheses, anchorites, by definition, wanted to break free from society to find God, but their proliferation in our period is more likely to reflect new sensitivity towards humanity's common imperfection than any novel individualism. In view of these objections, the historian might wonder whether there really is any overarching explanation. Is it not explanation in itself to trace the movement from its beginnings through the subtle transformations of its thinking, as this book has endeavoured to do?

The question remains, do we need a big explanation? Might we not account for the movement simply as the reawakening of a dormant idea? The idea that reawoke was that religion should be uncompromising, making no concessions to sin or to the sinful world. The fact that generations of Christians had been trained to revere any number of uncompromising martyrs and ascetics invested this idea with innate power. When confronted by men like Romuald, what else would they do but admire them? Novelty may have been an important factor, for if no one in the West was living like the fathers, the impact of those who now did so should indeed have been powerful. Among the Greeks, lavriote monasticism, although enjoying a revival, was nothing particularly new. In Italy, among the Latins, its old ideal of solitary asceticism was a summons to revive the purity of the early church. One need not posit any crisis in cenobitism or society to argue that, once this ideal had come alive again in the West, radical asceticism could have made an impact very quickly in a favourable climate. It is reasonable to speculate that fears linked to the millennium and the coming Judgement, contemporary concerns to discover purer, uncontaminated expressions of religion, and anxiety about the consequences of sin would have made people more receptive to its influence. Nevertheless, the point should be reiterated that Christian society, despite occasional scepticism and distaste, had been conditioned to admire anachoresis. If its way of allaying its fears about the consequences of human behaviour and incurring Christ's imminent wrath was to wage a war on sin, religious tradition identified the hermitage as the ideal arena. If, simultaneously, it was learning to appreciate Christ's humanity, the consequent deepening and strengthening of its empathetic love of God commended anachoresis.[1] The next question of concern is whether there really was a causal link between the rise of the anchorite and the function she came to perform. Peter Brown argued that there was, in late antiquity, and Mayr-Harting built on his example, arguing that the anchorite arose as a mediator to heal rifts in a changing world. But anchorites arose before they began to perform social functions, ostensibly for the reason that an idea was starting to spread, that anachoresis was the most dependable pathway to the heavens. People subsequently began turning to anchorites because they wanted some share in their merits and because anchorites were not only influential with God and the saints, on account of their asceticism, but also trained in the art of overcoming sin. Anchorites, in short, did not rise to meet a need in society: rather, they stimulated

---

[1] Fulton, *From Judgment to Passion, passim.* On the growth of (universal) devotion to the crucified Christ in late Anglo-Saxon England, see B. C. Raw, *Anglo-Saxon Crucifixion Iconography and the Art of the Monastic Revival* (Cambridge, 1990); and M. B. Bedingfield, *The Dramatic Liturgy of Anglo-Saxon England* (Woodbridge, 2002).

a want by attending to their souls. This then fostered a concern in the heads of many conscientious or anxious observers that they should do the same.

Glancing backwards at the first ascetic revolution, we can look for parallels in the fourth century when Christian asceticism emerged. Why did hermits – later known as the desert fathers – attain their powerful influence then? In 312, the Roman emperor Constantine embraced Christianity. Later, the slow, nominal *en masse* conversion of his subjects so swelled the ranks of the faithful that it was difficult to identify sincere believers. Those within this category who recalled the persecutions instigated by the tetrarchs, and the numerous martyrdoms which had ensued during the first decade of the century, could now look back at that period almost with nostalgia, as a time when martyrdom had proven genuine faith. What opportunity was there now for the sheep to distinguish themselves from all the goats? The great church father St Augustine of Hippo (354–430) argued that the ascetic movement of the fourth century, which gave rise to Christian monasticism, was a protest against a blurring of the distinction between the church and the world – a way for the elect to distinguish themselves from the rabble. The church was allegorically portrayed in St Peter's boat taking in such a catch of fish that it began to sink.[2] Asceticism was an ark against the inundation of nominal believers. Might this also have been the case in the eleventh century? The late Frank Barlow, noting the unprecedented, exceptional scale of land transference from the laity to the church during the century *c.*1050–*c.*1150, ventured that it 'was perhaps one of the most religious periods of all time'.[3] Did this new mass market for shares in heaven persuade those who believed that they were investing the most that they needed to up the price? Such a pattern of thought certainly surfaces as a theme in the writings of eleventh-century anchorites and their sympathizers: in Robert of Tombelaine's image of a hidden church of the pure (for example); in the idea that the established monasteries provided no credible outlet for excellence, and in the fear of succumbing to the tepidity of lukewarm brethren. Even so, it is hard, once again, to determine whether any measure of anxiety about salvation was a cause of the ascetic movement or a reaction to its high standards. After all, Romuald had impressed the German emperor and his nobles long before Barlow's century of religiosity began. If a context is needed for the brilliant idea of reviving the lifestyle of the desert fathers, we must look to southern Italy in the late tenth century. From there, it appears that a new form of eremitism spread across the Empire to France, Normandy, and England.

Recluses also proliferated, inspired in some cases by accounts of martyrs such as Wiborada, Paternus, and Brihtric, or outbursts of reclusive enthusiasm such as that which generated three at eleventh-century Evesham. During that century,

[2] H. Chadwick, 'The Ascetic Ideal in the History of the Church', in *Monks, Hermits and the Ascetic Tradition*, ed. Sheils, 1–23, at 7–8, with references.
[3] Barlow, *English Church 1066–1154*, 2.

they spread imperceptibly as churches were constructed and founders or parishioners sponsored recluses to watch over them. By the time Christina of Markyate was a young woman, their networks were dotted across the country, covertly building the *Civitas dei* in the midst of the *Civitas terrena*. Today, we think of parish religion in terms of the parish priest, but medieval parishioners often looked to the parish priest and parish recluse. Both were desirable because each performed a separate function. The latter was an expert intercessor and spiritual warrior accustomed to beating off the devil; she could also be an oracle, communicating God's will. The rise of the recluse may have been slower than that of the hermit, beginning perhaps as early as the mid-tenth century and peaking in the thirteenth. There were certainly charismatic recluses such as Wulfsige and Wulfric, but there was no revolutionary idea like the Romualdian revival of desert asceticism, which catapulted hermits into prominence. This notwithstanding, recluses retained their niche in the landscape long after the eremitic movement was subsumed into mainstream monasticism through the conversion of communities of new hermits to various cenobitic regimes. In England in the period 1070–1110, when Benedictine cenobitism was the dominant incarnation of monasticism, most of these communities became Benedictine, including those at Great Malvern, Selby, and Whitby. Through the period 1110–1220 the majority adopted a different rule attributed to St Augustine. Augustine's rule for communal life was shorter and simpler than St Benedict's rule, allowing its adherents greater freedom to determine the character of their devotions. Rediscovered at the end of the eleventh century and becoming popular in Europe, it was suitable for clerical communities, charitable religious, and hermits alike because it bound its followers by monastic vows without inhibiting either the performance of active duties or the contemplative pursuit of prayer. Augustinian priories founded on hermitages included Llanthony and Nostell, Barnwell in Cambridgeshire, Dale in Derbyshire, Healaugh Park in West Yorkshire, Bicknacre in Essex, Bushmead in Bedfordshire, Norman's Burrow in Norfolk, and Penmon Priory on Anglesey, near the well of the sixth-century hermit St Seiriol.[4] In the 1130s, the Cistercians began to win admirers by enshrining eremitic principles of simplicity and austerity in their new cenobitism, thereby combining the virtues of eremitism with the regulated life in common. From the 1140s, they too began to found abbeys on the sites of hermitages, such as Pipewell in Northamptonshire, Sawtry in Huntingdonshire, Beaulieu in Hampshire, Kirkstall in West Yorkshire, and Stoneleigh in Warwickshire.[5] Eventually, in this way, cenobitism dissolved the

---

[4] D. Knowles and R. N. Hadcock, *Medieval Religious Houses, England and Wales* (London, 1953), 144, 148, 126, 135, 139, 127, 131, 147, 149. See J. Herbert, 'The Transformation of Hermitages into Augustinian Priories in Twelfth-Century England', in *Monks, Hermits and the Ascetic Tradition*, ed. Sheils, 131–45.

[5] Knowles and Hadcock, *Religious Houses*, 113, 114, 105, 110, 115.

short-lived eremitic congregations. Still, individual hermits remained, as they always had done, dotted over the landscape.

Although they emerged by different routes in different parts of Europe, recluses, hermits, and asceticism all attained new influence as manifestations of the search for a purer, more spiritual life opposed to the world and its evils. Pious men and women of the eleventh and twelfth centuries in particular grew sensitive to the gap between God and humanity as the ascetic movement gained momentum. Some of them converted to anchoresis, or patronized, cultivated bonds with, or consulted anchorites in order to bridge the chasm between heaven and earth. Others entered religious communities or embarked on pilgrimages or crusades, or associated themselves with monasteries in the hope of pleasing God, or performed penance, or transferred wealth and property to the church, nurturing similar hopes. The extent to which we see these centuries as a gloomy age overshadowed by sin depends on our appraisal of the effectiveness of these remedies in providing peace of mind and in pacifying troubled consciences. Anchorites offered hope by mediating between heaven and humanity; they indicated how the latter might find peace and fulfilment in service of divine love; yet they also compounded and created fearfulness by setting uncompromising standards in their austerities, alerting people to sins that might not otherwise have troubled them, and sharpening the perception that heaven was for the few. As a stern, difficult solution, anachoresis may not have suited the majority of religious people; indeed it remained the preserve of a spiritual elite. Yet the fact that this elite won applause points to a conflict between society's ideals and its normative aspirations. Western Europe, by the eleventh and twelfth centuries, had been thoroughly Christianized; the centuries of conversion were over; it possessed innumerable saints and was brimful with churches and clergy, yet the otherworldly ends of its faith sat uncomfortably amid the welter of opportunities for worldly enrichment and the cultivation of social status.[6] Many who did not articulate the idea may still have entertained the notion that God's plans for man and man's own ambitions were parting company. The result of this appears to have been that Western European society during the long eleventh century developed introspective tendencies such as spiritual anxiety and critical self-examination. Those who renounced this society held a mirror to its conscience and filled its members with unease at departing from their ideals. Society responded by lavishing admiration on them and by seeking their prayers and approval, but for the most part it was reluctant to imitate their example. As a gulf was perceived to open up between God's domain and man's, some jumped one

---

[6] As Murray argues, new opportunities in these centuries created a new appetite for wealth and status: *Reason and Society*, 59, 81. He sees the period as an age of rapid change (see *ibid.*, 25–6). This notion can be traced back to M. Bloch, *La société féodale*, 2 vols (Paris, 1939–40): *Feudal Society*, tr. L. A. Manyon, 2 vols (2nd edn., London, 1962), i, 69–71, 103–8.

way or the other, but many wanted a foothold in both. Those torn two ways may have worried the most because of their precarious situation.

The dialectic between religious ideals and human ambitions, which invested the eleventh and twelfth centuries with its uneasy ambivalence, was eventually resolved. Giles Constable noted that, in the twelfth century, although 'examples of extravagant asceticism were still frequent and were admired by many people' there emerged 'a growing distrust of conspicuous signs of holiness'.[7] Priors of Durham urged Godric to moderate his asceticism, and prelates in France, Flanders, and Normandy urged anchorites to do the same.[8] Wise pastors and satirical songs had long recognized that outlandish asceticism was a Phaetonic course that could crash and burn the reckless. In any case, asceticism was burning itself out. In England, after the wave of eremitic monastic foundations in the north, and the rise of the Augustinian canons and the Cistercians, much of its regenerative energy was spent. Newly founded monasteries settled into regimes. When the abbey of Newminster in Northumberland was founded *c*.1138, it was as austere as any other new Cistercian abbey in the north. But when Robert of Knaresborough became a monk there some forty years later, his asceticism was said to have astonished the brethren.[9] The story does smack of hagiographical hyperbole; yet the declining appeal of excess is also evident in the changing rhetoric of reclusion. To the Flemish Cistercian William of Saint-Thierry (d. 1148), the recluse's cell was not so much a purgatory as a womb in which a monk, 'cherished, nourished, and enfolded', might reach the fullness of perfection.[10] In later years, when manuals of advice began to appear, moderation was urged and excessive penance discouraged. A priest who wrote a letter of advice to a recluse in the late twelfth or early thirteenth century warned him not to heed those anchorites who deemed fasting and uncomfortable garments prerequisite to salvation.[11] The author of *Ancrene Wisse*, whose advice was to prove so influential, discouraged a whole gamut of practices to which anchorites a century beforehand had entrusted their purification. They included the wearing of hauberks, haircloth, and hedgehog-skins, beatings with leaded or leather-thonged scourges, rolling in holly or brambles, and any excesses in vigils, fasting, suffering cold, or in similar asperities.[12] The vocation of the recluse retained its imagery of death, but the themes of penance and purgation ceded ground to the themes of spiritual development and contemplation. (The imagery of the *locus*

---

[7] G. Constable, 'Moderation and Restraint in Ascetic Practices in the Middle Ages', in *Culture and Spirituality in Medieval Europe* (Aldershot, 1996), 315–27, at 318.

[8] *LG*, 135–7; Constable, 'Moderation and Restraint', 319–20.

[9] *VRK*, 378–9.

[10] H. Leyser, 'Hugh the Carthusian', in *St Hugh of Lincoln: Lectures Delivered at Oxford and Lincoln to Celebrate the Eighth Centenary of St Hugh's Consecration as Bishop of Lincoln*, ed. H. Mayr-Harting (Oxford, 1987), 1–18, at 3. William was referring to a Carthusian's cell.

[11] P. L. Oliger, 'Regulae tres reclusorum et eremitarum Angliae saec. xiii–xiv', *Antonianum*, 3 (1928), 151–90, 299–320, at 184 (the letter is late twelfth or early thirteenth century).

[12] The point is made by Clay, *Hermits*, 120.

amoenus won ground from the imagery of the *locus poenalis.*) Even so, penance and purgation were essential. Robert of Knaresborough's first hagiographer wrote of how the hermit 'afflicted . . . and tortured his flesh with continual penance'. And Roger of Wendover cited a remark attributed to Godric of Finchale: 'here I do penance for my sins'.[13] The author of *Ancrene Wisse* expected the recluse to embrace a penitential life. The anchor-house was her prison, which she entered to weep for her sins and for the sins of others. It was also her grave, which she occupied like one of the dead.[14]

Those who reacted against ascetic excess were seeking a middle path, a golden mean in religious devotion. Society too, for its own peace of mind, had to reach a compromise between renunciation, on the one hand, and earthly ambition, on the other. Few were willing to sacrifice the latter for the hope of heaven, as anchorites did, but no one wanted to be damned, so ways had to be found by which the laity could work out their salvation without relinquishing their lay status. The situation in which men and women had to rely on a few extraordinary holy people to bridge the gap between earth and heaven was a temporary solution at best, which would hardly have been tolerable in the long run; other bridges had to be thrown up over the gap to meet the demand for passage across. It had always been taught that laypeople could help their souls through almsgiving, charity, the avoidance of sin, and the pursuit of virtue, but over the course of the twelfth century, and more so in the thirteenth, a consensus began to develop, that these good things were quite sufficient to prepare the soul for heaven. This consensus was facilitated by the proliferation of resources for overcoming sin. Two of the most important were indulgences, which began to multiply in the twelfth century as a system for paying off penitential debts and investing that payment in good works; and the sacrifice of Christ recreated in the mass, which was increasingly credited with aiding the souls, alive or dead, for whom masses were said.[15] These mechanisms for aiding souls worked automatically, as it were, so that laypeople no longer had to rely so much on holy men and women to make them acceptable to God. The thirteenth century saw an improvement in the quality of pastoral care after a new papal and episcopal drive to educate parish clergy and extend their influence over the conduct of the laity. English bishops reacted positively to the decrees of the Fourth Lateran Council of 1215 by implementing, in diocesan synods, statutes concerning the morals and training of the clergy and by circulating manuals to instruct priests in their dioceses. The laity was supposed to make confession at least once a year to the parish priest, who could thereby examine the health of souls and eradicate the canker of sin. The friars, who arrived in the 1220s and rapidly multiplied thereafter, combined

---

[13] VRK, 369; *Flores historiarum*, ed. Hewlett, I, 168.
[14] *Ancrene Wisse*, ed. Millett, I, 42, 43, 21.
[15] N. Vincent, 'Some Pardoners' Tales: The Earliest English Indulgences', *TRHS*, 6th ser., 12 (2002), 23–58.

the virtues of religious renunciation with a pastoral mission to the laity, and as the quality of the clergy improved and its ministry attended more to revealing and correcting laypeople's sins, it operated more effectively in the role that had once fallen to anchorites.

Early in the thirteenth century, a Wiltshire Cistercian put into Latin a legend he had heard told in English songs.[16] Set during the reign of the saintly king Oswald of Northumbria (d. 642), the story is a palimpsest on chapter sixteen of the *Historia monachorum*, in which the monk Paphnutius searches to discover souls equal to his in virtue; but whereas Paphnutius sets out humbly to communicate to the unsuspecting their worth in the eyes of God, the protagonist in the palimpsest, a hermit named Godeman, after forty years of solitary asceticism succumbs to vainglory. Thinking himself peerless in holiness he is shocked to discover, through a vision, that Oswald's merits surpass his own. Determined to investigate, he abandons his solitude, petitions the obliging monarch, whom he finds touring his realm, and is given leave to spend a day in the life of the king. The king gives Godeman his signet; the hermit departs for Bamburgh and upon arriving at the palace shows the ring to Oswald's queen, who dutifully sets him on the throne, before a lavish banquet. The hermit is very hungry, but as soon as he tastes the delicacies they are snatched away and distributed to the poor. Barley bread, water, and a dish of beans are brought instead. Chapel follows, before Godeman is led into the royal chamber, where, under silken sheets, he is made to bed down naked with the naked queen. This proves too much for the old man, but when the queen detects his excitement a maid is summoned who drags him from bed, plunges him into a cistern of icy water, and forces him to recite the seven penitential psalms and a litany. With chattering teeth, stiff with cold, he is eventually lifted out, dried with clean linen, and tucked back into bed, only to suffer another erection when the queen embraces him. Again, he is hauled out and plunged into the cistern. After a third failure, he is forced to lie on a bed of cinders and sacking, starved of sleep, until summoned at last to matins, at cockcrow. The queen tells him that this is the king's daily routine even outside Lent, for since the birth of their heir they have preserved a regime of chastity. Duly chastened, the crestfallen hermit bewails his vainglory and repents. Whatever the tale's pedigree, by the time it was put into Latin, its moral was gaining force: that anchorites who thought themselves superior had a lesson to learn from the virtuous laity.[17]

---

[16] Oxford, Bodleian Library, MS Digby 11, fos. 146r–147v. The tale also surfaces in Middle English: 'Die Evangelien-Geschichten der Homiliensammlung des Ms. Vernon', ed. C. Horstmann, *Archiv für das Studium der neueren Sprachen und Literaturen*, 57 (1877), 241–316, at 289–90.

[17] Reginald, in his *Vita Oswaldi* of the 1160s, commented that bawdy tales about the king circulated at Bardney: see D. Rollason, 'St Oswald in Post-Conquest England', in *Oswald: Northumbrian King to European Saint*, ed. C. Stancliffe and E. Cambridge (Stanford, 1995), 164–77, at 167.

For how could any holy anchorite claim to have overcome sin without surviving the constant test of sharing silken sheets with a soft naked body, or of hungering for the delicacies of a kingly banquet? A king living virtuously in the world could be purer than any hermit. So the ordinary laity could aspire to virtue too.

Glossary

anachoresis: the act or state of withdrawal from human company

anchorhold: a cell inhabited by a *recluse*

anchorite: one withdrawn from human company

apotropaic: possessing the power to repel evil

ascetic: *n.* one who resists bodily desires; *adj.* pertaining to bodily self-denial

asceticism: the practice or principle of resisting bodily desires

cell: a small building, usually locked or sealed, inhabited by a *recluse* or *recluses*

Christomimesis: the imitation of Christ, or likeness to Christ

Civitas dei: the 'City of God'; God's people and projects, known only in heaven

Civitas terrena: the 'Earthly City'; worldly people, projects, and power structures

confraternity: a formal, beneficial bond between religious devotees and their spiritual clients

demons: fallen angels, bent on harming people or leading them into temptation

devils: see *demons*

eremitic: pertaining to the life of the *hermit*

eremitism: the state or practice of withdrawal to achieve the solitude of the desert

flagellation: physical assault upon the flesh, to punish it or quell its desires

hairshirt: a coarse garment of woven animal hair, fibres, or sack-cloth

hauberk: a long coat of mail

hermit: one who strives to achieve the solitude of the desert

hermitage: the abode of a *hermit* or *hermits*

imitatio Christi: see *Christomimesis*

immersion: submerging the body in water, to punish it or quell its desires

Life: a biography, styled as hagiography

monasticism: withdrawal from ordinary human society in pursuit of God

penance: action undertaken before God in compensation for injury caused by sin

peregrinatio: exile (typically wandering) for love of God and in search of God

proto-eremitic: of or relating to the first hermits

purgatory: a condition in which the soul is cleansed

recluse: an *anchorite* committed to a *cell*

reclusion: the vocation of *anchorites* committed to remain in *cells*

red martyrdom: suffering violent death in consequence of one's faith

solitary: *n.* an *anchorite*

thaumaturgic: able to heal

vigil(s): the religious exercise of staying awake and alert, to watch and pray

vita angelica: the 'angelic life'; participating in the praises of the angels, or in their missions and communications, or living a life sustained by their ministry

white martyrdom: suffering a life of *ascetic* hardship in consequence of one's faith

Select bibliography

REFERENCE WORKS

Blair, J., 'A Handlist of Anglo-Saxon Saints', in *Local Saints and Local Churches in the Early Medieval West*, ed. A. T. Thacker and R. Sharpe (Oxford, 2002), 495–565

Butler, L. A. S., 'Two Twelfth-Century Lists of Saints' Resting-Places', *AB*, 105 (1987), 87–103

Lapidge, M. (ed.), *Anglo-Saxon Litanies of the Saints*, HBS, 106 (1991)

—— *The Anglo-Saxon Library* (Oxford, 2006)

Rollason, D., 'Lists of Saints' Resting-Places in Anglo-Saxon England', *ASE*, 7 (1978), 61–93

Rushforth, R. J., *Saints in English Kalendars before 1100 AD*, HBS, 117 (2008)

Sharpe, R., *A Handlist of the Latin Writers of Great Britain and Ireland before 1540*, with additions and corrections, new edn. (Turnhout, 2001)

——(ed.), *English Benedictine Libraries: The Shorter Catalogues*, Corpus of British Medieval Library Catalogues, 4 (London, 1996)

Thomson, R. M., *A Descriptive Catalogue of the Medieval Manuscripts in Worcester Cathedral Library* (Cambridge, 2001)

Wormald, F. (ed.), *English Kalendars after AD 1100*, HBS, 77, 81, 2 vols (1939–46)

MANUSCRIPTS

CCCC, MS 389

CUL, Peterborough dean and chapter MS 1

CUL, Peterborough dean and chapter MS 5

Cambridgeshire County Record Office, MS 588DR/Z3

Durham Cathedral, dean and chapter library, MS B.IV.24

L, BL, MS Add. 40,000

L, BL, MS Cotton Vitellius E xvii

L, BL, MS Cotton Vespasian B xi

L, BL, MS Cotton Vespasian B xxiv

L, BL, MS Harley 1005

L, BL, MS Harley 2110

L, BL, MS Lansdowne 427

London, College of Arms, MS Arundel 10

New York, Pierpont Morgan Library, MS M. 736

Oxford, Bodleian Library, MS Digby 11

Petworth House Archive 11,601

THESES AND UNPUBLISHED PAPERS

Alexander, D. D., 'Hermits, Hagiography, and Popular Culture: A Comparative Study of Durham Cathedral Priory's Hermits in the Twelfth Century', PhD thesis, University of London, 2000

Brett, M., 'The Rise and Fall of Throckenholt', with responses from James Holt, Dorothy Owen, Cecily Clark, and David Rollason, unpublished paper, 1979

Jackson, P., 'Wulsy of Evesham: The Invention of an Eleventh-Century Hermit', unpublished paper, 1992

Lavery, S. P. J., 'A Study of the English Lives of St Mary of Egypt in their Literary Context', PhD thesis, University of Cambridge, 1993

McKee, H. A., 'St Augustine's Abbey, Canterbury: Book Production in the Tenth and Eleventh Centuries', PhD thesis, University of Cambridge, 1997

Ortenberg, V. N., 'Aspects of Monastic Devotions to the Saints in England ca. 950 to ca. 1100: The Liturgical and Iconographical Evidence', PhD thesis, University of Cambridge, 1987

Parkinson, B. J., 'The Life of Robert of Bethune by William of Wycombe: Translation with Introduction and Notes', BLitt. dissertation, University of Oxford, 1958

SHARP (Sedgeford Historical and Archaeological Research Project): the report on skeleton no. 5001, 'S5001' (1999–2000)

Thomas, I. G., 'The Cult of Saints' Relics in Medieval England', PhD thesis, University of London, 1975

Tudor, V. M., 'Reginald of Durham and St Godric of Finchale: A Study of a Twelfth-Century Hagiographer and His Major Subject', PhD thesis, University of Reading, 1979

PRIMARY SOURCES

Abbo of Fleury: 'Passio s. Eadmundi', in *Three Lives of English Saints*, ed. M. Winterbottom (Toronto, 1972), 67–87

Adam of Eynsham: *Magna vita sancti Hugonis = The Life of St Hugh of Lincoln*, ed. and tr. D. L. Douie and D. H. Farmer, 2 vols (Oxford, 1985)

Ælfric: *Homilies of Ælfric: A Supplementary Collection*, ed. J. C. Pope, EETS o.s., 259–60, 2 vols (1967–8)

——'Life of St. Ethelwold', in *Three Lives*, ed. Winterbottom, 17–29

——M. Godden, *Ælfric's Catholic Homilies: Introduction, Commentary and Glossary*, EETS n.s., 18 (2000)

Aelred of Rievaulx: *Aelredi Rievallensis, Opera omnia I: opera ascetica*, ed. A. Hoste and C. H. Talbot, CCCM, 1 (1971)

Alcuin: 'Vita Willibrordi archiepiscopi Traiectensis', in *MGH, scriptorum rerum Merovingicarum*, VII, ed. W. Levison (Hannover, 1920), 81–141

—— *The Bishops, Kings and Saints of York*, ed. P. Godman (Oxford, 1982)

Anselm: *S. Anselmi Cantuariensis archiepiscopi opera omnia*, ed. F. S. Schmitt, 6 vols (Edinburgh, 1946–61)

Arnold, T. (ed.), *Memorials of St. Edmund's Abbey*, RS, 96, 3 vols (1890–6)

Assman, B. (ed.), *Angelsächsische Homilien und Heiligenleben*, Bibliothek der angelsächsischen Prosa, 3 (Kassel, 1889)

Atkinson, J. C., *Cartularium abbathiæ de Whiteby, ordinis s. Benedicti fundatae anno MLXXVIII*, SS, 69, 72, 2 vols (1879–81)

Bates, E. H., *Two Cartularies of the Benedictine Abbeys of Muchelney and Athelney in the County of Somerset*, Somerset Record Society, 14 (London, 1899)

Bazire, J. (ed.), *The Metrical Life of St. Robert of Knaresborough, together with the other Middle English pieces in British museum MS*, Egerton 3143, EETS o.s., 228 (1953 for 1947)

Bede: *Bede's Ecclesiastical History of the English People*, ed. B. Colgrave and R. A. B. Mynors (Oxford, 1969)

—— 'Vita s. Cuthberti', in *Two Lives*, ed. Colgrave

Bell, M. (ed.), *Wulfric of Haselbury by John, Abbot of Ford*, Somerset Record Society, 47 (Frome, 1933)

Benedeit, *The Anglo-Norman Voyage of St Brendan*, ed. I. Short and B. Merrilees (Manchester, 1979)

Blair, J. (ed.), 'St Frideswide reconsidered', Oxoniensia, 52 (1987), 71–127

Blake, E. O. (ed.), *Liber Eliensis*, CSer. 3rd ser., 92 (1962)

Bottomley, F., *St. Robert of Knaresborough* (Ruddington, Notts., 1993)

Bradley, S. A. J. (tr.), *Anglo-Saxon Poetry* (London, 1982)

Bruno of Querfurt, *Vita quinque fratrum*, ed. R. Kade, in *MGH SS*, 15, ed. G. Waitz, 2 vols (Hannover, 1887–8), II, 709–38

Burchard of Worms (subject): *Vita Burchardi episcopi Wormatiensis*, ed. D. G. Waitz, in *MGH SS* 4, ed. G. H. Pertz (Hannover, 1841)

Byrhtferth of Ramsey, *The Lives of St Oswald and St Egwine*, ed. and tr. M. Lapidge (Oxford, 2009)

Clark, C. (ed.), *The Peterborough Chronicle, 1070–1154*, 2nd edn. (Oxford, 1970)

Colgrave, B. (ed. and tr.), *Two Lives of Saint Cuthbert: A Life by an Anonymous Monk of Lindisfarne and Bede's Prose Life* (Cambridge, 1940)

—— (ed. and tr.), *Felix's Life of Saint Guthlac: Introduction, Text, Translation and Notes* (Cambridge, 1956)

Colker, M. L., *Analecta Dvblinensia: Three Medieval Latin Texts in the Library of Trinity College, Dublin* (Cambridge, MA, 1975)

Constable, G. and Smith, B. S. (eds.), *Libellus de diversis ordinibus et professionibus qui sunt in aecclesia*, new edn. (Oxford, 2003)

Darlington, R. R. (ed.), *The Cartulary of Worcester Cathedral Priory, Register I*, Publications of the Pipe Roll Society, 76, n.s. 38 (London, 1968 for 1962/3)

Doble, G. H., *The Life of St Nectan*, translated from the manuscript recently discovered in the ducal library at Gotha, Cornish Saints Series, 45 (Torquay, 1940)

Domesday Book: *Domesday Book; vol. 16: Worcestershire*, ed. F. Thorn and C. Thorn (Chichester, 1982)

—— *Domesday Book; vol. 1: Kent*, ed. P. Morgan (Chichester, 1983)

Dominic of Evesham, *Acta proborum uirorum*, in *Chronicon abbatiae de Evesham, ad annum 1418*, ed. W. D. Macray, RS, 29 (London, 1863), 320–5

Dumville, D. and Keynes, S. (general editors), *The Anglo-Saxon Chronicle: A Collaborative Edition*, vol. 17, *The Annals of St Neots, with Vita prima sancti Neoti*, ed. D. Dumville and M. Lapidge (Cambridge, 1985)

Dunning, T. P. and Bliss, A. J. (eds.), *The Wanderer* (London, 1969)

Eadmer: *The Life of St Anselm, Archbishop of Canterbury, by Eadmer*, ed. and tr. R. W. Southern (Oxford, 1972)

Eberwin: 'De sancto Symeone, recluso in porta Trevirensi', *Acta SS, Jun.* I, 89A–101E

Elvey, G. R. (ed.), *Luffield Priory Charters*, Buckinghamshire Record Society, 15, 18; Northamptonshire Record Society, 22, 26, 2 vols (Welwyn Garden City, 1968–75)

Episcopal acta: *English Episcopal Acta, 1: Lincoln, 1067–1185*, ed. D. M. Smith (London, 1980)

——*English Episcopal Acta 3: Canterbury, 1193–1205*, ed. C. R. Cheney and E. John (Oxford, 1986)

——*English Episcopal Acta 6: Norwich, 1070–1214*, ed. C. Harper-Bill (Oxford, 1990)

——*English Episcopal Acta 7: Hereford, 1079–1234*, ed. J. Barrow (Oxford, 1993)

——*English Episcopal Acta 14: Coventry and Lichfield, 1072–1159*, ed. M. J. Franklin (Oxford, 1997)

——*English Episcopal Acta 18: Salisbury, 1078–1217*, ed. B. R. Kemp (Oxford, 1999)

——*English Episcopal Acta 24: Durham, 1153–1195*, ed. M. G. Snape (Oxford, 2002)

——*English Episcopal Acta 28: Canterbury, 1070–1136*, ed. M. Brett and J. A. Gribbin (Oxford, 2004)

——*English Episcopal Acta 31: Ely, 1109–1197*, ed. N. Karn (Oxford, 2005)

Evans, J. G. and Rhys, J. (eds.), *The Text of the Book of Llan Dâv: Reproduced from the Gwysaney Manuscript* (Oxford, 1893)

Folcard of Saint-Bertin: *Vitae*, in *Historians*, ed. Raine, and *Liber vitae: Register and Martyrology of New Minster and Hyde Abbey, Winchester*, ed. W. de G. Birch, Hampshire Record Society (London, 1892)

Foreville, R. and Keir, G. (eds.), *The Book of St Gilbert* (Oxford, 1987)

Fowler, J. T. and Hodges, C. C. (eds.), *The Coucher Book of Selby*, The Yorkshire Archaeological and Topographical Association, Record Series, 10, 13, 2 vols (1891–3)

Geoffrey of Burton: *Life and Miracles of St. Modwenna*, ed. and tr. R. Bartlett (Oxford, 2002)

Geoffrey of Coldingham: *Vita Bartholomaei Farnensis*, in *Symeonis monachi opera omnia*, ed. T. Arnold, RS, 75, 2 vols (1882–5) I, 295–325

Gerald of Wales: *Giraldi Cambrensis opera*, ed. J. S. Brewer, J. F. Dimock, and G. F. Warner, RS, 21, 8 vols (1861–91)

Gilbert Crispin: *Vita Herluini*, in *The Works of Gilbert Crispin*, ed. A. S. Abulafia and G. R. Evans, *Auctores Britannici medii aevi*, 8 (Oxford, 1986), 183–212

Gordon, I. L. (ed.), *The Seafarer* (London, 1960)

Goscelin of Saint-Bertin: *Historia, miracula et translatio s. Augustini*, Acta SS, Maii VI, 375–443

——'La légende de ste Édith en prose et vers par le moine Goscelin', ed. A. Wilmart, *AB*, 56 (1938), 5–101, 265–307

——'The Liber confortatorius of Goscelin of Saint-Bertin', ed. C. H. Talbot, *Analecta monastica, textes et études sur la vie des moines au moyen age, troisième série, Studia Anselmiana*, 37 (Rome, 1955), 1–117

—— 'The Life of Saint Wulsin of Sherborne by Goscelin', ed. C. H. Talbot, *RB*, 69 (1959), 68–85

—— Goscelin of Canterbury's account of the translation and miracles of St Mildrith (*BHL*, 5961/4): an edition with notes, ed. D. W. Rollason (1986), 139–210

—— *The Hagiography of the Female Saints of Ely*, ed. and tr. R. C. Love (Oxford, 2004)

—— 'The Life of St Wulfsige of Sherborne by Goscelin of Saint-Bertin', tr. R. Love, in *St Wulfsige and Sherborne: Essays to Celebrate the Millennium of the Benedictine Abbey 998–1998*, ed. K. Barker, D. A. Hinton, and A. Hunt (Oxford, 2005), 98–123

—— 'Goscelin of Saint-Bertin and the Hagiography of St Eadwold of Cerne', ed. T. Licence, *Journal of Medieval Latin*, 16 (2007), 182–207

Gregory of Tours: *Historia Francorum* in *S. Georgii Florentini Gregorii Turonensis episcopi opera omnia*, ed. J.-P. Migne (Paris, 1849), PL, 71: 161–604

Greenway, D. and Watkiss, L. (eds. and trs.), *The Book of the Foundation of Walden Monastery* (Oxford, 1999)

Greenwell, W., *Feodarium prioratus Dunelmensis: A Survey of the Estates of the Prior and Convent of Durham Compiled in the Fifteenth Century*, SS, 58 (1871)

Grimlaïc: *Regula solitariorum*, PL, 103: 574–663

Grosjean, P. (ed.), 'Vitae s. Roberti Knaresburgensis', *AB*, 57 (1939), 364–400

—— (ed.), 'Vie de S. Rumon; Vie, Invention et Miracles de S. Nectan', *AB*, 71 (1953), 359–414

Hart, C. R., *The Early Charters of Eastern England* (Leicester, 1966)

Hart, W. H. (ed.), *Historia et cartularium monasterii sancti Petri Gloucestriae*, RS, 33, 3 vols (1863–7)

—— and Lyons, P. A. (eds.), *Cartularium monasterii de Rameseia*, RS, 79, 3 vols (1884–93)

Henry of Huntingdon: *The History of the English People, 1000–1154*, ed. D. E. Greenway (Oxford, 1996)

Herbert Losinga: *Epistolae Herberti de Losinga, primi episcopi Norwicensis, Osberti de Clara et Elmeri, prioris Cantuariensis*, ed. R. Anstruther, Publications of the Caxton Society, 8 (Brussels, 1846)

—— *The Life, Letters and Sermons of Bishop Herbert de Losinga*, ed. E. M. Goulburn and H. Symonds, 2 vols (Oxford, 1878)

Howlett, R. (ed.), *Chronicles of the Reigns of Stephen, Henry II, and Richard I*, RS, 82, 4 vols (1884–9)

Hugh Candidus (att.): *The Chronicle of Hugh Candidus: A Monk of Peterborough*, ed. W. T. Mellows (London, 1949)

Isidore of Seville: *Sancti Isidori episcopi Hispalensis de ecclesiasticis officiis*, ed. C. M. Lawson, CCSL, 113 (1989)

Ivo of Chartres: *Epistolae*, PL, 162: 11–290

James, M. R. (ed.), 'Two Lives of St. Ethelbert, King and Martyr', *EHR*, 32 (1917), 214–44

Jerome: *Sancti Eusebii Hieronymi epistulae*, ed. I. Hilberg, CSEL, 54–6, 3 vols, 2nd edn. (1996)

John of Fécamp: *Un maître de la vie spirituelle au XIᵉ siècle: Jean de Fécamp*, ed. J. Leclercq and J.-P. Bonnes (Paris, 1946)

John of Tynemouth: *Nova legenda Anglie*, ed. C. Horstmann, 2 vols (Oxford, 1901)

Jotsald of Cluny: *De uita et uirtutibus sancti Odilonis abbatis*, PL, 142: 897–940

Kelly, S. E. (ed.), *Charters of St Augustine's Abbey Canterbury and Minster-in-Thanet* (Oxford, 1995)

Kotzor, G. (ed.), *Das altenglische Martyrologium*, Abhandlungen (Bayerische Akademie der Wissenschaften. Philosophisch-Historische Klasse), *Neue Folge*, 88, 2 vols (Munich, 1981)

Krapp, G. P. and Dobbie, E. van K. (eds.), *The Exeter Book* (London, 1936)

Leclercq, J. (ed.), 'Deux opuscules médiévaux sur la vie solitaire', *Studia monastica*, 4 (1962), 93–109

Lehmann-Brockhaus, O., *Lateinische Schriftquellen zur Kunst in England, Wales und Schottland vom Jahre 901 bis zum Jahre 1307*, 2 vols (Munich, 1955)

L'Hermite-Leclercq, P. and Legras, A.-M. (eds.), *Vie de Christina de Markyate*, 2 vols (Paris, 2007)

Licence, T. (ed.), 'The Life and Miracles of Godric of Throckenholt', *AB*, 124 (2006), 15–43

Liebermann, F., *Die Heiligen Englands, angelsächsisch und lateinisch* (Hannover, 1889)

Love, R. C. (ed.), *Three Eleventh-Century Anglo-Latin Saints' Lives: Vita s. Birini, Vita et miracula s. Kenelmi and Vita s. Rumwoldi* (Oxford, 1996)

Luard, H. R. (ed.), *Annales monastici*, RS, 36, 5 vols (1864–9)

Macray, W. D. (ed.), *Chronicon abbatiae de Evesham, ad annum 1418*, RS, 29 (1863)

——(ed.), *Chronicon abbatiae Rameseiensis*, RS, 83 (1886)

Magennis, H. (ed.), *The Old English Life of St Mary of Egypt* (Exeter, 2002)

Marbod of Rennes: *Marbodo di Rennes, Vita beati Roberti*, ed. A. Degl'Innocenti, Biblioteca del Medioevo Latino (Florence, 1995)

Marie de France: *Fables*, ed. and tr. H. Spiegel (Toronto, 1987)

Mason, E. (ed.), assisted by Bray, J., continuing the work of D. J. Murphy, *Westminster Abbey Charters 1066–c.1214*, London Record Society, 25 (1988)

Matthew Paris: *Matthaei Parisiensis, monachi sancti Albani, historia Anglorum, sive, ut vulgo dicitur, historia minor*, ed. F. Madden, RS, 44, 3 vols (1866–9)

——*Matthaei Parisiensis, monachi sancti Albani, chronica majora*, ed. H. R. Luard, RS, 57, 7 vols (1872–83)

Milfull, I. B. (ed.), *The Hymns of the Anglo-Saxon Church: A Study and Edition of the Durham Hymnal* (Cambridge, 1996)

Miller, S. (ed.), *Charters of the New Minster, Winchester* (Oxford, 2001)

Moore, S. A. (ed.), *Cartularium monasterii sancti Johannis Baptiste de Colecestria*, Roxburghe Club, 2 vols (London, 1897)

Offler, H. S. (ed.), *Durham Episcopal Charters, 1071–1152*, SS, 179 (1968)

Oliger, P. L., 'Regulae tres reclusorum et eremitarum Angliae saec. xiii–xiv', *Antonianum*, 3 (1928), 151–90, 299–320

Orderic Vitalis: *The Ecclesiastical History of Orderic Vitalis*, ed. and tr. M. Chibnall, 6 vols (Oxford, 1969–80)

Osbern of Canterbury: *Vita s. Elphegi, in Anglia sacra siue collectio historiarum antiquitus scriptarum de archiepiscopis et episcopis Angliae, a prima fidei Christianae susceptione ad annum MDXL*, ed. H. Wharton, 2 vols (London, 1691), II, 122–42

——*Vita s. Dunstani*, in *Memorials*, ed. Stubbs

Osbert of Clare: 'La vie de s. Édouard le Confesseur par Osbert de Clare', ed. M. Bloch, *AB*, 41 (1923), 5–131

Pächt, O., Dodwell, C. R., and Wormald, F., *The St Albans Psalter (Albani psalter)* (London, 1960)

Peter Damian: 'Vita beati Romualdi', ed. G. Tabacco, *Fonti per la storia d'Italia*, 94 (Rome, 1957)

——'Vita sancti Rodulphi episcopi Eugubini et s. Dominici Loricati', PL, 144: 1007–24

——'Opusculum undecimum: liber qui appellatur, *Dominus uobiscum*, ad Leonem eremitam', PL, 145: 231–52

——'Opusculum duodecimum: apologeticum de contemptu saeculi, ad Albizonem eremitam et Petrum monachum', PL, 145: 251–92

——'Opusculum decimum quartum. De ordine eremitarum, et facultatibus eremi Fontis Avellani', PL, 145: 327–36

——'Opusculum quinquagesimum primum. De uita eremitica, et probatis eremitis', PL, 145: 749–64

——*Die Briefe des Petrus Damiani*, ed. K. Reindel, *MGH*, 4 vols (Munich, 1983–93)

Peter the Venerable: *The Letters of Peter the Venerable*, ed. G. Constable, 2 vols (Cambridge, MA, 1967)

Pseudo Ingulf: *The Chronicle of Croyland Abbey by Ingulph*, ed. W. de G. Birch (Wisbech, 1883)

Pseudo Peter of Blois: 'Ingulfi Croylandensis historia, Petri Blesensis continuatio', in *Rerum anglicarum scriptorum veterum: tom. I*, ed. W. Fulman (Oxford, 1684)

Raine, J. (Sr, ed.), *Miscellanea biographica*, SS, 8 (1838)

Raine, J. (Jr, ed.), *The Historians of the Church of York and Its Archbishops*, RS, 71, 3 vols (1879–94)

Reginald of Canterbury: *The Vita sancti Malchi of Reginald of Canterbury*, ed. L. R. Lind, *Illinois Studies in Language and Literature*, 27, nos. 3–4 (Urbana, 1942)

Reginald of Durham: *Libellus de vita et miraculis s. Godrici, heremitae de Finchale, auctore Reginaldo monacho Dunelmensi*, ed. J. Stevenson, SS, 20 (1847 for 1845)

——*Libellus de admirandis Beati Cuthberti, virtutibus quae novellus patratae sunt temporibus*, ed. J. Raine, Sr, SS, 1 (1835)

Riley, H. T. (ed.), *Chronica monasterii s. Albani: Gesta abbatum monasterii sancti Albani, a Thoma Walsingham, regnante Ricardo secundo, ejusdem ecclesie precentore, compilata*, RS, 28, 3 vols (1867–9)

——*Annales monasterii s. Albani*, RS, 28, 2 vols (1870–1)

Robinson, F. C. (tr.), 'The Devil's Account of the Next World: An Anecdote from Old English Homiletic Literature', *Neuphilologische Mitteilungen*, 73 (1972), 362–71

Rodulfus Glaber: *Opera*, ed. and tr. J. France, N. Bulst, and P. Reynolds (Oxford, 1989)

Roger of Hoveden: *Chronica Rogeri de Houedene*, ed. W. Stubbs, RS, 51, 4 vols (1868–71)

Roger of Wendover: *Rogeri de Wendover, liber qui dicitur flores historiarum*, ed. H. G. Hewlett, RS, 84, 3 vols (1886–9)

Ruotger: *Vita Brunonis archiepiscopi Coloniensis*, in *MGH SRG*, n.s. 10, ed. I. Ott (Weimar, 1951), 1–50

Salter, H. E. (ed.), *The Cartulary of the Abbey of Eynsham*, Oxford Historical Society, 49, 52, 2 vols (1907–8)

Saltman, A., 'The History of the Foundation of Dale Abbey or the So-called Chronicle of Dale: A New Edition', *Derbyshire Archaeological Journal*, 87 (1968 for 1967), 18–38

Schlumpf, E., *Quellen zur Geschicte der Inklusen in der Stadt St. Gallen*, Mitteilungen zur vaterländischen Geschichte. Herausgegeben vom historischen Verein des Kantons St. Gallen, 41 (St Gallen, 1953)

Scragg, D. G. (ed.), *The Vercelli Homilies and Related Texts*, EETS o.s., 300 (1992)

Serbat, L., 'Inscriptions funéraires de recluses a l'abbaye de Saint-Amand (Nord)', *Mémoires de la sociéte nationale des antiquaires de France*, 71, 8th ser., 1 (1912), 193–224

Smaragdus of Saint-Mihiel: *Diadema monachorum*, PL, 102: 593–690

Sparke, J. (ed.), *Historiae Anglicanae scriptores varii*, 2 vols (London, 1723)

Stevenson, J. (ed.), *Liber uitae ecclesiae Dunelmensis: nec non obituaria duo ejusdem ecclesiae*, SS, 13 (1841)

Strecker, K., *Carmina Cantabrigiensia: die Cambridger Lieder*, MGH SRG, 40 (Berlin, 1926)

Stubbs, W. (ed.), *Memorials of St Dunstan, Archbishop of Canterbury*, RS, 63 (1874)

Sulpicius Severus: *Vie de Saint Martin*, ed. J. Fontaine, SC, 133–5, 3 vols (1967–9)

Symeon of Durham: *Libellus de exordio atque procursu istius, hoc est Dunelmensis, ecclesie = Tract on the Origins and Progress of This the Church of Durham*, ed. and tr. D. W. Rollason (Oxford, 2000)

Talbot, C. H. (ed. and tr.), *The Life of Christina of Markyate: A Twelfth-Century Recluse*, new edn. (Oxford, 1987)

—— *The Life of Christina of Markyate*, revised translation, with introduction and notes by S. Fanous and H. Leyser (Oxford, 2008)

Thibaut of Provins (subject): 'De sancto Theobaldo, presb. Eremita diocesis Vicentinae in Italia', *Acta SS, Jun.* V, 592F–595F

—— 'Alia vita, bullae canonizationis adjuncta, De sancto Theobaldo, etc', *Acta SS, Jun.* V, 596A–598A

Thietmar of Merseburg: *Die Chronik des Bischofs Thietmar von Merseburg, und ihre korveier Überarbeitung*, ed. R. Holtzmann, MGH SRG, n.s. 9 (Berlin, 1935)

Thomas of Marlborough: *History of the Abbey of Evesham*, ed. and tr. J. Sayers and L. Watkiss (Oxford, 2003)

Vitas patrum: [*Auctores varii*], *Vitas patrum*, in PL, 73

Vogüé, A. de (introd. and tr.); Neufville, J. (ed.), *La règle de Saint Benoît*, SC, 181–6, 6 vols (1971–2)

Walbran, J. R. and Fowler, J. T. (eds.), *Memorials of the Abbey of St. Mary of Fountains*, SS, 42, 67, 130, 3 vols (1863–1918)

Walter Daniel: *The Life of Ailred of Rievaulx, by Walter Daniel*, ed. and tr. M. Powicke (Oxford, 1978)

Whitelock, D. (ed. and tr.), *Anglo-Saxon Wills* (Cambridge, 1930)

Wiborada (subject): *Vita s. Wiboradae*, in *MGH SS*, 4, ed. G. H. Pertz, 452–7

William of Malmesbury: *Gesta regum Anglorum = The History of the English Kings*, ed. and tr. R. A. B. Mynors; completed by R. M. Thomson and M. Winterbottom, 2 vols (Oxford, 1998–9)

—— *Gesta pontificum anglorum: The History of the English Bishops*, ed. M. Winterbottom, with the assistance of R. M. Thomson (Oxford, 2007)

—— *Saints' Lives: Lives of Ss. Wulfstan, Dunstan, Patrick, Benignus and Indract*, ed. and tr. M. Winterbottom and R. M. Thomson (Oxford, 2002)

—— *The Early History of Glastonbury: An Edition, Translation and Study of William of Malmesbury's De antiquitate Glastonie ecclesie*, ed. and tr. J. Scott (Woodbridge, 1981)

William of Newburgh: see *Chronicles*, ed. Howlett

William of Wycombe: 'Libri II De vita Roberti Betun, episcopi Herefordensis', in *Anglia sacra*, ed. Wharton, II, 295–322

Wilson, H. A., *Officium ecclesiasticum abbatum secundum usum Eveshamensis monasterii*, HBS, 6 (1893)

—— *The Pontifical of Magdalen College*, HBS, 39 (1910)

Wilson, J., *The Register of the Priory of St. Bees*, SS, 126 (1915)

Wulfstan of Winchester: *Wulfstan of Winchester: The Life of St Æthelwold*, ed. M. Lapidge and M. Winterbottom (Oxford, 1991)

Ziolkowski, J. (ed.), *The Cambridge Songs (Carmina Cantabrigiensia)* (London, 1994)

SECONDARY SOURCES

Aird, W. M., *St Cuthbert and the Normans: The Church of Durham, 1071–1153* (Woodbridge, 1998)

Alexander, D., 'Hermits and Hairshirts: The Social Meanings of Saintly Clothing in the *Vitae* of Godric of Finchale and Wulfric of Haselbury', *JMH*, 28 (2002), 205–26

—— *Saints and Animals in the Middle Ages* (Woodbridge, 2008)

Angenendt, A., 'How Was a Confraternity Made? The Evidence of Charters', in *The Durham Liber vitae*, ed. Rollason et al., 207–19

Arnoux, M., 'Un Vénitien au Mont Saint-Michel: Anastase, moine, ermite et confesseur († vers 1085)', *Médiévales*, 28 (1995), 55–78

—— 'Ermites et ermitages en Normandie (XIe–XIIIe siècles)', in *Ermites*, ed. Vauchez, 115–35

Baker, D., 'The Surest Road to Heaven: Ascetic Spiritualities in English Post-Conquest Religious Life', in *Sanctity and Secularity: The Church and the World*, ed. idem, *SCH*, 10 (1973), 45–57

—— (ed.), *Mediaeval Women: Dedicated and Presented to Rosalind M. T. Hill on the Occasion of Her Seventieth Birthday*, SCH Subsidia, 1 (1978)

Baldwin, J. W., Masters, *Princes and Merchants: The Social Views of Peter the Chanter and His Circle*, 2 vols (Princeton, 1970)

—— 'From the Ordeal to Confession: In Search of Lay Religion in Early Thirteenth-Century France', in *Handling Sin*, ed. Biller and Minnis, 191–209

Barker, K. (ed.), *The Cerne Abbey Memorial Lectures* (Dorchester, 1988)

Barlow, F., *The English Church 1000–1066: A History of the Later Anglo-Saxon Church*, 2nd edn. (London, 1979)

—— *The English Church 1066–1154* (London, 1979)

—— 'Folcard (d. after 1085)', in *ODNB*

Barrow, J. S., 'How the Twelfth-Century Monks of Worcester Perceived Their Past', in *The Perception of the Past in Twelfth-Century Europe*, ed. P. Magdalino (London, 1992), 53–74

—— 'The Clergy in English Dioceses c.900–c.1066', in *Pastoral Care*, ed. Tinti, 17–26

—— and Brooks, N. P. (eds.), *St. Wulfstan and His World* (Aldershot, 2005)

Batlle, C. M., *Die Adhortationes sanctorum patrum im lateinischen Mittelalter. Überliefer-ung, Fortleben und Wirkung*, Beiträge zur Geschichte des alten Mönchtums und des Benediktinerordens, 31 (Münster, 1972)

Benton, G. M., 'Discovery of an Anker-hold at Lindsell Church', *Transactions of the Essex Archaeological Society*, n.s. xix (1930), 316–20

Berschin, W., *Eremus und Insula. St Gallen und die Reichenau im Mittelalter – Modell ein lateinischen Literaturlandschaft*, 2nd edn. (Wiesbaden, 2005)

Biller, P. and Minnis, A. J. (eds.), *Handling Sin: Confession in the Middle Ages* (Wood-bridge, 1998)

Blair, J., *Minsters and Parish Churches: The Local Church in Transition, 950–1200* (Oxford, 1988)

——'Saint Cuthman, Steyning and Bosham', *Sussex Archaeological Collections*, 135 (1997), 173–92

——'A Saint for Every Minster? Local Cults in Anglo-Saxon England', in *Local Saints and Local Churches in the Early Medieval West*, ed. A. T. Thacker and R. Sharpe (Oxford, 2002), 455–94

——*The Church in Anglo-Saxon Society* (Oxford, 2005)

——and Sharpe, R. (eds.), *Pastoral Care before the Parish* (Leicester, 1992)

Blum, O. J., *St. Peter Damian: His Teaching on the Spiritual Life* (Washington, 1947)

Bonner, G., Rollason, D. W., and Stancliffe, C. (eds.), *St Cuthbert, His Cult and His Community to AD 1200* (Woodbridge, 1989)

Bott, A., *A Guide to the Parish Church of Saint Nicholas, Compton, Surrey* (Compton, 2000)

Bottomley, F., *St. Robert of Knaresborough* (Ruddington, Notts., 1993)

Boüard, M. de, 'Notes et hypothèses sur Maurille moine de Fécamp, et son élection au siège métropolitain de Rouen', in *L'abbaye bénédictine de Fécamp: Ouvrage scientifique du XIIIᵉ centenaire, 658–1958*, 3 vols (Fécamp, 1959), i, 81–92

Brakke, D., *Demons and the Making of the Monk: Spiritual Combat in Early Christianity* (Cambridge, MA, 2006)

Bretel, P., *Les ermites et les moines dans la littérature française du Moyen Age (1150–1250)* (Paris, 1995)

Brett, C., 'A Breton Pilgrim in England in the Reign of King Æthelstan', in *France and the British Isles in the Middle Ages and Renaissance: Essays by Members of Girton College, Cambridge, in Memory of Ruth Morgan*, ed. G. Jondorf and D. Dumville (Woodbridge, 1991), 43–70

Brett, M., *The English Church under Henry I* (Oxford, 1975)

Briggs, B., 'Expulsio, proscriptio, exilium: Exile and Friendship in the Writings of Osbert of Clare', in *Exile in the Middle Ages: Selected Proceedings from the International Medieval Congress, University of Leeds, 8–11 July 2002*, ed. L. Napran and E. van Houts (Turnhout, 2004), 131–44

Brito-Martins, M., 'The Concept of *Peregrinatio* in Saint Augustine and Its Influences', in *Exile*, ed. Napran and van Houts, 83–94

Brooks, N. P., 'The Career of St Dunstan', in *St Dunstan: His Life, Times and Cult*, ed. N. Ramsay, M. Sparks, and T. Tatton-Brown (Woodbridge, 1992), 1–23

——and Cubitt, C. (eds.), *St Oswald of Worcester: Life and Influence* (London, 1996)

Brown, P., 'The Rise and Function of the Holy Man in Late Antiquity', *Journal of Roman Studies*, 61 (1971), 80–101

—— *The Making of Late Antiquity* (Cambridge, MA, 1978)

——*Authority and the Sacred* (Cambridge, 1995)

Bull, M., *Knightly Piety and the Lay Response to the First Crusade: The Limousin and Gascony, c.970–c.1130* (Oxford, 1993)

Bulst, N., *Untersuchungen zu den Klosterreformen Wilhelms von Dijon (962–1031)* (Bonn, 1973)

Burton, J. E., 'The Eremitical Tradition and the Development of Post-Conquest Religious Life in Northern England', in *Eternal Values in Medieval Life*, ed. N. Crossley-Holland, *Trivium*, 26 (1991), 18–39

—— 'The Monastic Revival in Yorkshire: Whitby and St Mary's, York', in *Anglo-Norman Durham*, ed. Rollason et al., 41–51

—— *The Monastic Order in Yorkshire, 1069–1215* (Cambridge, 1999)

——'Selby Abbey and Its Twelfth-Century Historian', in *Learning and Literacy in Medieval England and Abroad*, ed. S. Rees-Jones (Turnhout, 2003), 49–68

Bynum, C. W., *Jesus as Mother: Studies in the Spirituality of the High Middle Ages* (Berkeley, 1982)

Chadwick, H., 'The Ascetic Ideal in the History of the Church', in *Monks, Hermits and the Ascetic Tradition*, ed. W. J. Sheils, 1–23

Charles-Edwards, T. M., 'The Social Background to Irish *Peregrinatio*', *Celtica*, 11 (1976), 43–59

Chenu, M. D., *Nature, Man, and Society in the Twelfth Century: Essays on New Theological Perspectives in the Latin West*, sel., ed., and tr. J. Taylor and L. K. Little (Chicago, 1968)

Chibnall, M., 'History of the Priory of St Neots', in C. F. Tebbutt, 'St Neots Priory', *Proceedings of the Cambridge Antiquarian Society*, 59 (1966), 33–74, at 67–74

Christy, A., 'The Hermitage in the High Woods, Writtle: Some Facts and Fancies', *Essex Review*, 18 (1909), 129–36

Clanchy, M. T., *From Memory to Written Record: England 1066–1307*, 2nd edn. (Oxford, 1993)

Clark, C., 'Notes on a Life of Three Thorney Saints, Thancred, Torhtred and Tova', *Proceedings of the Cambridge Antiquarian Society*, 69 (1979 for 1980), 45–52

—— *Words, Names and History: Selected Writings of Cecily Clark*, ed. P. Jackson (Cambridge, 1995)

Clay, R. M., *The Hermits and Anchorites of England* (London, 1914)

Clayton, M., 'Hermits and the Contemplative Life in Anglo-Saxon England', in *Holy Men and Holy Women: Old English Prose Saints' Lives and Their Contexts*, ed. P. E. Szarmach (New York, 1996), 147–75

Clemoes, P., 'Ælfric', in *Continuations and Beginnings: Studies in Old English Literature*, ed. E. G. Stanley (London, 1966), 176–209

Coens, M., 'Un document inédit sur le culte de S. Syméon, moine d'orient et reclus a Trèves', *AB*, 68 (1950), 181–96

Colish, M. L., *Peter Lombard*, 2 vols (Leiden, 1994)

Conner, P. W., 'Source Studies, the Old English Guthlac A and the English Benedictine Reformation', *RB*, 103 (1993), 380–413

Constable, G., *Religious Life and Thought, 11th–12th Centuries* (London, 1979)

—— *Three Studies in Medieval Religious and Social Thought* (Cambridge, 1995)

—— *The Reformation of the Twelfth Century* (Cambridge, 1996)

—— *Culture and Spirituality in Medieval Europe*, Collected Studies Series (Aldershot, 1996)

Cooper, T.-A., 'Lay Piety, Confessional Directives and the Compiler's Method in Late Anglo-Saxon England', *The Haskins Society Journal*, 16 (2005), 47–61

Cowdrey, H. E. J., *The Cluniacs and the Gregorian Reform* (Oxford, 1970)

—— *The Age of Abbot Desiderius: Montecassino, the Papacy and the Normans in the Eleventh and Early Twelfth Centuries* (Oxford, 1983)

—— *Lanfranc: Scholar, Monk, and Archbishop* (Oxford, 2003)

Cowley, F. G., *The Monastic Order in South Wales, 1066–1349* (Cardiff, 1977)

Cox, D. C., 'Evesham, Dominic of (d. in or before 1150)', in *ODNB*

Crouch, D., *The Reign of King Stephen, 1135–54* (Harlow, 2000)

—— 'The Troubled Deathbeds of Henry I's Servants: Death, Confession, and Secular Conduct in the Twelfth Century', *Albion*, 34 (2002), 24–36

Cubitt, C., 'Bishops, Priests and Penance in Late Saxon England', *Early Medieval Europe*, 14 (2006), 41–63

Darwin, F. D. S., *The English Mediaeval Recluse* (London, 1944)

Dauphin, H., 'L'érémitisme en Angleterre aux XIe et XIIe siècles', in *L'eremitismo*, pub. Università cattolica del Sacro Cuore, 271–303

Davies, J. R., *The Book of Llandaf and the Norman Church in Wales* (Woodbridge, 2003)

Davies, R. R., *The Age of Conquest: Wales, 1063–1415* (Oxford, 2000)

Dawtry, A., 'The Benedictine Revival in the North: The Last Bulwark of Anglo-Saxon Monasticism?', in *Religion and National Identity. Papers read at the nineteenth summer meeting and twentieth winter meeting of the Ecclesiastical History Society*, ed. S. Mews, *SCH*, 18 (1982), 87–98

Déchanet, J.-M., 'La contemplation au XIIIᵉ siècle', in *Dictionnaire de spiritualité ascétique et mystique*, ed. M. Viller, F. Cavallera, J. de Guibert et al., 17 vols (Paris, 1932–95), II.2: 1948–66

Deeming, H., 'The Songs of St Godric: A Neglected Context', *Music and Letters*, 86 (2005), 169–85

Dereine, C., 'Odon de Tournai et la crise du cénobitisme au XIᵉ siècle, *Revue de moyen âge Latin*, 4 (1948), 137–54

—— 'Ermites, reclus et recluses dans l'ancien diocèse de Cambrai entre Scarpe et Haine (1075–1125)', *RB*, 97 (1987), 289–313

Deswick, E. S., 'On the Discovery of an Ankerhold at the Church of St Martin, Chipping Ongar, Essex', *The Archaeological Journal*, 45 (1888), 284–8

Diekstra, F. N. M., 'The Flight of the Exile's Soul to Its Fatherland', *Neophilologus*, 55 (1971), 433–46

Doble, G. H., *Cornish Saints Series*, 46 vols (pub. various, 1924–41)

Doerr, O., *Das Institut der Inclusen in Süddeutschland*, Beiträge zur Geschichte des alten Mönchtums und des Benediktinerordens, 18 (Munster, 1934)

Dunn, M., 'Eastern Influence on Western Monasticism in the Eleventh and Twelfth Centuries', in *Byzantium and the West c.850–c.1250: Proceedings of the XVIII Spring*

Symposium of Byzantine Studies, Byzantinische Forschungen. Internationale Zeitschrift für Byzantinistik, 13 (Amsterdam, 1988), 245–59

Edwards, G. R., 'Purgatory: "Birth" or Evolution?', *JEH*, 36 (1985), 634–46

Eickhoff, E., 'Otto III. in Pereum. Konzept und Verwirklichung seiner Missionspolitik', *Archiv für Kulturgeschichte*, 83 (2001), 25–35

Elkins, S. K., *Holy Women of Twelfth-Century England* (Chapel Hill, NC, 1988)

Evans, J. W., 'St David and St Davids and the Coming of the Normans', *Transactions of the Honourable Society of Cymmrodorion*, n.s. 11 (2004), 5–18

Fanous, S. and Leyser, H. (eds.), *Christina of Markyate: A Twelfth-Century Holy Woman* (London, 2005)

Fell, C. E., 'Saint Æðelþryð: A Historical-Hagiographical Dichotomy Revisited', *Nottingham Medieval Studies*, 38, ed. M. Jones (1994), 18–34

Finucane, R. C., *Miracles and Pilgrims: Popular Beliefs in Medieval England* (Basingstoke, 1995)

Fleming, R., 'Rural Elites and Urban Communities in Late Anglo-Saxon England', *Past and Present*, 141 (1993), 3–37

——'The New Wealth, the New Rich and the New Political Style in Late Anglo-Saxon England', *ANS*, 23 (2001), 1–22

Follett, W., *Céli dé in Ireland: Monastic Writing and Identity in the Early Middle Ages* (Rochester, NY, 2006)

Foot, S., *Veiled Women I: The Disappearance of Nuns from Anglo-Saxon England; Veiled Women II: Female Religious Communities in England, 871–1066*, 2 vols (Aldershot, 2000)

Frank, K. S., 'Grimlaïcus, "Regula solitariorum"', in *Vita religiosa im Mittelalter: Festschrift für Kaspar Elm*, ed. F. J. Felten and N. Jaspert (Berlin, 1997), 21–35

Frantzen, A. J., *The Literature of Penance in Anglo-Saxon England* (New Brunswick, NJ, 1983)

Fulton, R., *From Judgment to Passion: Devotion to Christ and the Virgin Mary, 800–1200* (New York, 2002)

Gameson, R. and Leyser, H. (eds.), *Belief and Culture in the Middle Ages: Studies Presented to Henry-Mayr Harting* (Oxford, 2001)

Gazeau, V., 'Recherches sur l'histoire de la principauté normande (911–1204). I. Les abbés bénédictins de la principauté normande. II. Prosopographie des abbés bénédictins (911–1204)', Dossier d'habilitation, Université de Paris, I– (Paris, 2002)

Geary, P. J., *Furta Sacra: Thefts of Relics in the Central Middle Ages*, new edn. (Princeton, 1990)

Geddes, J., 'The St Albans Psalter: The Abbot and the Anchoress', in *Christina*, ed. Fanous and Leyser, 197–216

Genicot, L., 'l'Eremitisme du XIe siècle dans son contexte economique et social', in *L'eremitismo*, pub. Università cattolica del Sacro Cuore, 45–69

Gilchrist, R., *Contemplation and Action: The Other Monasticism* (London, 1995)

Godfrey, W. H., 'Church of St. Anne, Lewes: An Anchorite's Cell and Other Discoveries', *Sussex Archaeological Collections*, 69 (1928), 159–69

Golding, B., 'Hermits, Monks and Women in Twelfth-Century France and England: The Experience of Obazine and Sempringham', in *Monastic Studies: The Continuity of Tradition*, ed. J. Loades (Bangor, 1990), 127–45

Golding, B., *Gilbert of Sempringham and the Gilbertine Order, c.1130–c.1300* (Oxford, 1995)

—— 'The Hermit and the Hunter', in *The Cloister and the World: Essays on Medieval History in Honour of Barbara Harvey*, ed. J. Blair and B. Golding (Oxford, 1996), 95–117

Gougaud, L., *Devotional and Ascetic Practices of the Middle Ages*, English edition prepared by G. C. Bateman (London, 1927)

—— *Ermites et reclus: Études sur d'anciennes formes de vie religieuse, Moines et monastères*, 5 (Vienne, 1928)

Gransden, A., 'Traditionalism and Continuity during the Last Century of Anglo-Saxon Monasticism', *JEH*, 40 (1989), 159–207, reprinted in *idem, Legends, Traditions and History in Medieval England* (London, 1992), 31–80

—— 'The Growth of the Glastonbury Traditions and Legends in the Twelfth Century', in *idem, Legends*, 153–74

Greenfield, S. B., *Hero and Exile: The Art of Old English Poetry*, ed. G. H. Brown (London, 1989)

Gretsch, M., *The Intellectual Foundations of the English Benedictine Reform* (Cambridge, 1999)

Grundmann, H., 'Deutsche Eremiten, Einsiedler und Klausner im Hochmittelalter (10–12. Jahrhundert)', *Archiv für Kulturgeschichte*, 45 (1963), 60–90, translated into Italian as 'Eremiti in Germania dal x au xii secolo: "Einsiedler" e "Klausner"', in *L'eremitismo*, pub. Università cattolica del Sacro Cuore, 311–29

Hamand, L. A., *The Ancient Windows of Gt Malvern Priory Church*, 2nd edn. (St Albans, 1978)

Hamilton, B., 'S. Pierre Damien et les mouvements monastiques de son temps', *Studi Gregoriani*, 10 (1975), 175–202

Hamilton, S., *The Practice of Penance, 900–1050* (London, 2001)

—— 'The Unique Favour of Penance: The Church and the People, *c.*800–1100', in *The Medieval World*, ed. P. Linehan and J. L. Nelson (London, 2001), 229–45

—— 'Rites for Public Penance in Late Anglo-Saxon England', in *The Liturgy of the Anglo-Saxon Church*, ed. H. Gittos and M. B. Bedingfield, HBS Subsidia, 5 (2005), 65–103

Hart, C., 'Eadnoth, First Abbot of Ramsey, and the Foundation of Chatteris and St. Ive', *Proceedings of the Cambridge Antiquarian Society*, 56–7 (1964 for 1962–3), 61–7

Hayward, P. A., 'Translation-Narratives in Post-Conquest Hagiography and English Resistance to the Norman Conquest', *ANS*, 21 (1999), 67–93

—— 'Saint Albans, Durham and the Cult of Saint Oswine King and Martyr', *Viator*, 30 (1999), 105–44

Hayward, R. and Hollis, S., 'The Anchorite's Progress: Structure and Motif in the *Liber confortatorius*', in *Writing the Wilton Women: Goscelin's Legend of Edith and Liber confortatorius*, ed. S. Hollis (Turnhout, 2004), 369–83

Heale, M., *The Dependent Priories of Medieval English Monasteries* (Woodbridge, 2004)

Helvétius, A.-M., 'Ermites ou moines: solitude et cénobitisme du Vᵉ au Xᵉ siècle (principalement en Gaule du Nord)', in *Ermites*, ed. Vauchez, 1–27

Henderson, G., 'The Imagery of St Guthlac of Crowland', in *England in the Thirteenth Century: Proceedings of the 1984 Harlaxton Symposium*, ed. W. M. Ormrod (Woodbridge, 1986), 76–94

Herbert, J., 'The Transformation of Hermitages into Augustinian Priories in Twelfth-Century England', in *Monks, Hermits and the Ascetic Tradition*, ed. W. J. Sheils, 131–45

Heuclin, J., *Aux origines monastiques de la Gaule du Nord: ermites et reclus du Ve au XIe siècle* (Lille, 1988)

Hillaby, J., 'St Oswald, the Revival of Monasticism, and the Veneration of the Saints in the Late Anglo-Saxon and Norman Diocese of Worcester', *Transactions of the Worcestershire Archaeological Society*, 3rd ser. 16 (1998), 79–132

Hodson, M. O., 'East Ham Church: Remains of an Anker-hold', *Transactions of the Essex Archaeological Society*, n.s. 22 (1940 for 1936–9), 345–6

Holdsworth, C., 'Christina of Markyate', in *Mediaeval Women*, ed. D. Baker, 185–204

—— 'Hermits and the Power of the Frontier', *Reading Medieval Studies*, 16 (1990), 55–76

Howard-Johnston, J. and Hayward, P. A. (eds.), *The Cult of Saints in Late Antiquity and the Middle Ages: Essays on the Contribution of Peter Brown* (Oxford, 1999)

Howe, J., 'The Awesome Hermit: The Symbolic Significance of the Hermit as a Possible Research Perspective', *Numen*, 30:I, n.3. (1983)

—— *Church Reform and Social Change in Eleventh-Century Italy: Dominic of Sora and His Patrons* (Philadelphia, 1997)

Huchet, J.-C., 'Les déserts du roman médiéval: le personnage de l'ermite dans le romans de XIIe et XIIIe siècles', in *Littérature*, 60 (1985), 89–108

Hunt, N., *Cluny under Saint Hugh, 1049–1109* (Notre Dame, IN, 1967)

—— (ed.), *Cluniac Monasticism in the Central Middle Ages* (Hamden, CT, 1971)

Iogna-Prat, D., 'La femme dans la perspective pénitentielle des ermites du Bas-Maine (fin XIème début XIIème siècle), *Revue d'histoire de la spiritualité*, 53 (1977), 47–64

Ireland, C. A., 'Some Analogues of the OE "Seafarer" from Hiberno-Latin Sources', *Neuphilologische Mitteilungen*, 92 (1991), 1–14

—— 'Penance and Prayer in Water: An Irish Practice in Northumbrian Hagiography', *Cambrian Medieval Celtic Studies*, 34 (1998 for 1997), 51–66

Jackson, P., 'The *Vitas patrum* in Eleventh-Century Worcester', in *England in the Eleventh Century: Proceedings of the 1990 Harlaxton Symposium*, ed. C. Hicks (Stamford, 1992), 119–34

—— 'Ælfric and the "*Uita patrum*" in Catholic Homily I.36', in *Essays on Anglo-Saxon and Related Themes in Memory of Lynne Grundy*, ed. J. Roberts and J. Nelson (London, 2000), 259–72

—— 'Osbert of Clare and the *Vision of Leofric*: The Transformation of an Old English Narrative', in *Latin Learning*, ed. O'Keeffe and Orchard, II, 275–92

Jayatilaka, R., 'The Old English Benedictine Rule: Writing for Women and Men', *ASE*, 32 (2003)

Jestice, P. G., *Wayward Monks and the Religious Revolution of the Eleventh Century* (Leiden, 1997)

Johnston, P. M., 'Low Side Windows in Churches', in *Transactions of the St Paul's Ecclesiological Society*, 4 (London, 1900), 263–76

—— 'Hardham Church, and Its Early Paintings', *Sussex Archaeological Collections*, 44 (1901), 73–115

Jones, C. A., 'Envisioning the *Cenobium* in the Old English *Guthlac A*', *Mediaeval Studies*, 57 (1995), 259–91

Jones, E., 'Rotha Clay's Hermits and Anchorites of England', *Monastic Research Bulletin*, 3 (1997), 46–8

——'The Hermits and Anchorites of Oxfordshire', *Oxoniensia*, 63 (1998), 51–77

——'Anchorites and Hermits in Historical Context', in *Approaching Medieval English Anchoritic and Mystical Texts*, ed. D. Dyas, V. Edden, and R. Ellis (Cambridge, 2005)

Jotischky, A., *The Perfection of Solitude: Hermits and Monks in the Crusader States* (University Park, PA, 1995)

Kennedy, A., 'The Portrayal of the Hermit-Saint in French Arthurian Romance: The Remoulding of a Stock-Character', in *An Arthurian Tapestry: Essays in Memory of Lewis Thorpe*, ed. K. Varty (Glasgow, 1981), 69–82

Keynes, S. D., 'The Cartulary of Athelney Abbey Rediscovered', *Monastic Research Bulletin*, 7 (2001), 2–5

——'Ely Abbey 672–1109', in *A History of Ely Cathedral*, ed. P. Meadows and N. Ramsay (Woodbridge, 2003), 3–58

Kirby, D. P., 'Notes on the Saxon Bishops of Sherborne', *Proceedings of the Dorset Natural History and Archaeological Society*, 87 (1965), 213–22

Knowles, M. D., *The Monastic Order in England: A History of Its Development from the Times of St Dunstan to the Fourth Lateran Council, 940–1216*, 2nd edn. (Cambridge, 1963)

Koopmans, R. M., 'The Conclusion of Christina of Markyate's *Vita*', *JEH*, 51 (2000), 663–98

Lambert, M. D., *Medieval Heresy: Popular Movements from the Gregorian Reform to the Reformation*, 3rd edn. (Oxford, 2002)

Lang, G., 'Gunther, der Eremit, in Geschichte, Sage und Kult', *Studien und Mitteilungen zur Geschichte des Benediktiner-Ordens*, 59 (1941), 3–83

Lapidge, M. and Love, R. C., 'England and Wales (600–1500)', in *Hagiographies: histoire internationale de la littérature hagiographique latine et vernaculaire, en Occident, des origines à 1500*, ed. G. Philippart (Turnhout, 1994–), III, 203–325

——'Acca of Hexham and the Origin of the *Old English Martyrology*', *AB*, 123 (2005), 29–78

Lawrence, C. H., *Medieval Monasticism: Forms of Religious Life in Western Europe in the Middle Ages*, 3rd edn. (Harlow, 2001)

Leclercq, J., 'La contemplation dans la littérature chrétienne latine', in *Dictionnaire de spiritualité*, ed. Viller et al., II.2: 1911–48

——'L'exhortation de Guillame Firmat', *Analecta monastica, textes et études sur la vie des moines au moyen age, troisième série*, Studia Anselmiana, 31 (Rome, 1953), 28–44

——'Saint Antoine dans la tradition monastique medievale', in *Antonius magnus eremita, 356–1956*, ed. B. Steidle, *Analecta monastica, textes et études sur la vie des moines au moyen age, troisième série*, Studia Anselmiana, 38 (Rome, 1956), 229–47

——'Pierre le Vénérable et l'érémitisme clunisien', in *Petrus Venerabilis 1156–1956: Studies and Texts Commemorating the Eighth Centenary of His Death*, ed. G. Constable and J. Kritzeck, *Analecta monastica, textes et études sur la vie des moines au moyen age, troisième série*, Studia Anselmiana, 40 (Rome, 1956), 99–120

——'Saint Pierre Damien, ermite et homme d'église', *Uomini e Dottrine*, 8 (Rome, 1960)

——'Saint Romuald et la monachisme missionaire', *RB*, 77 (1962), 307–22

——'"Eremus" et "eremita": pour l'histoire du vocabulaire de la vie solitaire', *Collectanea Ordinis Cisterciensium reformatorum*, 25 (1963), 8–30

——*Aux sources de la spiritualité Occidentale: Étapes et constantes*, Les Éditions du Cerf, 21 (Paris, 1964)

——'Le cloître est-il une prison?', *Revue d'ascétique et de mystique*, 47 (1971), 407–20

Le Goff, J., *The Birth of Purgatory*, tr. A. Goldhammer (London, 1984)

Lefèvre, J.–A., 'Saint Robert de Molesme dans l'opinion monastique du XIIe et du XIIIe siècle', *AB*, 74 (1956), 50–83

Leyser, H., *Hermits and the New Monasticism: A Study of Religious Communities in Western Europe 1000–1150* (New York, 1984)

——'Hugh the Carthusian', in *St Hugh of Lincoln: Lectures Delivered at Oxford and Lincoln to Celebrate the Eighth Centenary of St Hugh's Consecration as Bishop of Lincoln*, ed. H. Mayr-Harting (Oxford, 1987), 1–18

——'Two Concepts of Temptation', in *Belief and Culture*, ed. Gameson and Leyser, 318–26

L'Hermite-Leclercq, P., 'Les reclus du Moyen Age et l'information', *Zeitgeschehen und seine Darstellung im Mittelalter: L'actualité et sa représentation au Moyen Age*, ed. C. Cormeau (Bonn, 1995), 200–20

——'Aelred of Rievaulx: The Recluse and Death According to the *Vita inclusarum*', *Cistercian Studies Quarterly*, 34 (1999), 183–202

——'La réclusion dans le milieu urbain Français au moyen âge', in *Ermites*, ed. Vauchez, 155–73

Licence, T., 'The Benedictines, the Cistercians and the Acquisition of a Hermitage in Twelfth-Century Durham', *JMH*, 29 (2003), 315–29

——'The Gift of Seeing Demons in Early Cistercian Spirituality', *Cistercian Studies Quarterly*, 39 (2004), 49–65

——'Suneman and Wulfric: Two Forgotten Saints of St Benedict's Abbey at Holme in Norfolk', *AB*, 122 (2004), 361–72

——'Evidence of Recluses in Eleventh-Century England', *ASE*, 36 (2007), 221–34

Limone, O., *Santi monaci e santi eremiti: alla ricerca di un modello di perfezione nella letteratura agiografica dell'Apulia normanna* (Galatina, 1988)

Little, L. K., *Religious Poverty and the Profit Economy in Medieval Europe* (London, 1978)

Lohmer, C., *Heremi conuersatio. Studien zu den monastichen Vorschriften des Petrus Damiani*, Beiträge zur Geschichte des alten Mönchtums und des Benediktinertums [BGAM], 39 (Münster, 1991)

Macquarrie, A., 'Early Christian Religious Houses in Scotland: Foundation and Function', in *Pastoral Care*, ed. Blair and Sharpe, 110–33

Martin, J.-M., 'L'érémitisme Grec et Latin en Italie mériodionale (X^e–XIIIe siècle)', in *Ermites*, ed. Vauchez, 175–98

Mayr-Harting, H., 'Functions of a Twelfth-Century Recluse', *History*, 60 (1975), 337–52

——'Functions of a Twelfth-Century Shrine: The Miracles of St. Frideswide', in *Studies in Medieval History Presented to R. H. C. Davies*, ed. H. Mayr-Harting and R. I. Moore (London, 1985)

Mayr-Harting, H., *The Coming of Christianity to Anglo-Saxon England*, 3rd edn. (Pennsylvania, 1991)

McAvoy, L. H. and Hughes-Edwards, M. (eds.), *Anchorites, Wombs and Tombs: Intersections of Gender and Enclosure in the Middle Ages* (Cardiff, 2005)

McLaughlin, M., *Consorting with Saints: Prayer for the Dead in Early Medieval France* (Ithaca, 1994)

McRoberts, D., 'Hermits in Medieval Scotland', *Innes Review*, 16 (1965), 199–216

Meens, R., 'Introduction, Penitential Questions: Sin, Satisfaction and Reconciliation in the Tenth and Eleventh Centuries', in *Early Medieval Europe*, 14 (2006), 1–6

—— 'Penitentials and the Practice of Penance in the Tenth and Eleventh Centuries', in *Early Medieval Europe*, 14 (2006), 7–21

Micklethwaite, J. T., 'On the Remains of an Ankerhold at Bengeo Church, Hertford', *The Archaeological Journal*, 44 (1888), 26–9

Milis, L., 'Ermites et chanoines réguliers au XIIe siècle', *Cahiers de civilisation médiévale X^e–XIIe siècles*, 22 (1979), 39–80

—— 'L'evolution de l'érémitisme au canonicat régulier dans la première moitié du douzième siécle: transition ou trahison', in *Istituzioni monastiche et istituzioni canonicali in occidente (1123–1215)*, Miscellanea del centro di studi medioevali, IX (Milan, 1980), 223–38

Millet, B., 'Women in No Man's Land: English Recluses and the Development of Vernacular Literature in the Twelfth and Thirteenth Centuries', in *Women and Literature in Britain, 1150–1500*, ed. C. M. Meale (Cambridge, 1993), 86–103

Morin, G., 'Rainaud l'ermite et Ives de Chartres: un épisode de la crise du cénobitisme au XIe–XIIe siècle', *RB*, 40 (1928), 99–115

Moore, J. S., 'Family-Entries in English *Libri vitae*, *c*.1050 to *c*.1350, Part 1', *Nomina*, 16 (1992–3), 99–128; Part 2, *Nomina*, 18 (1995), 77–117

Moore, R. I., 'Literacy and the Making of Heresy *c*.1000–*c*.1150', in *Heresy and Literacy, 1000–1530*, ed. P. Biller and A. Hudson (Cambridge, 1994), 19–37

—— *The First European Revolution, c.970–1215* (Oxford, 2000)

Morris, C., *The Discovery of the Individual, 1050–1200* (Toronto, 1987)

—— *The Papal Monarchy: The Western Church from 1050 to 1250* (Oxford, 1989)

Morris, R., *Monks and Laymen in Byzantium, 843–1118* (Cambridge, 1995)

Mulder-Bakker, A. B., *Lives of the Anchoresses: The Rise of the Urban Recluse in Medieval Europe*, tr. M. H. Scholz (Philadelphia, 2005)

Murray, A., *Reason and Society in the Middle Ages* (Oxford, 1985)

—— 'Confession before 1215', *Transactions of the Royal Historical Society*, 6th ser., 3 (1993), 51–81

—— 'Counselling in Medieval Confession', in *Handling Sin*, ed. Biller and Minnis, 63–77

Nightingale, J., 'Oswald, Fleury and Continental Reform', in *St Oswald*, ed. Brooks and Cubitt, 23–45

—— *Monasteries and Patrons in the Gorze Reform: Lotharingia c.850–1000* (Oxford, 2001)

Nott, J., *Malvern Priory Church: Descriptive Accounts of Its Ancient Stained Glass, Old Tombs, Tessellated Pavements, and Other Antiquities* (Malvern, 1896)

O' Dwyer, P., 'The Céli Dé Reform', in *Irland und Europa: Die Kirche im Frühmittelalter = Ireland and Europe: The Early Church*, ed. P. Ní Chatháin and M. Richter (Stuttgart, 1984), 83–8

O'Keeffe, K. O'B. and Orchard, A. (eds.), *Latin Learning and English Lore: Studies in Anglo-Saxon Literature for Michael Lapidge*, 2 vols (Toronto, 2005)

Olsen, G., 'The Idea of the *Ecclesia Primitiva* in the Writings of the Twelfth-Century Canonists', *Traditio*, 25 (1969), 61–86

Orchard, A., 'Parallel Lives: Wulfstan, William, Coleman and Christ', in *St Wulfstan*, ed. Barrow and Brooks, 59–91

Orme, N., *The Saints of Cornwall* (Oxford, 2000)

Ortenberg, V., *The English Church and the Continent in the Tenth and Eleventh Centuries: Cultural, Spiritual, and Artistic Exchanges* (Oxford, 1992)

Payer, P. J., 'The Humanism of the Penitentials and the Continuity of the Penitential Tradition', *Medieval Studies*, 46 (1984), 340–54

Peers, C. R., 'Finchale Priory', *Archaeologia Æliana*, 4th ser., IV (1927), 193–220

Penco, G., 'L'eremitismo irregolare in Italia nei secoli xi–xii', *Benedictina*, 32 (1985), 201–21

Pertusi, A., 'Aspetti organizzativi e culturali dell'ambiente monacale Greco dell'Italia meridionale', in *L'eremitismo*, pub. Università cattolica del Sacro Cuore, 382–417

Pestell, T., *Landscapes of Monastic Foundation: The Establishment of Religious Houses in East Anglia c.650–1200* (Woodbridge, 2004)

Pfaff, R. W., 'Lanfranc's Supposed Purge of the Anglo-Saxon Calendar', in *Warriors and Churchmen in the High Middle Ages: Essays Presented to Karl Leyser*, ed. T. Reuter (London, 1992), 95–108

—— 'The Anglo-Saxon Bishop and His Book', *Bulletin of the John Rylands University Library of Manchester*, 81 (1999), 3–24

Philippart, G. (ed.), *Hagiographies: histoire internationale de la littérature hagiographique latine et vernaculaire, en Occident, des origines à 1500* (Turnhout, 1994–)

Phillipe, P., 'La contemplation au XIIIᵉ siècle', in *Dictionnaire de spiritualité*, ed. Viller et al., II.2: 1966–88

Piper, A. J., 'The Early Lists and Obits of the Durham Monks', in *Symeon of Durham: Historian of Durham and the North*, ed. D. W. Rollason (Stamford, 1998), 161–201

Pope, J. C., 'Second Thoughts on the Interpretation of *The Seafarer*', *ASE*, 3 (1974), 75–86

Poppe, E. and Ross, B. (eds.), *The Legend of Mary of Egypt in Medieval Insular Hagiography* (Blackrock, Co. Dublin, 1996)

Powell, M., 'Making the Psalter of Christina of Markyate (the St Albans Psalter)', *Viator*, 36 (2005), 293–335

Powicke, F. M., 'Loretta, Countess of Leicester', in *Historical Essays in Honour of James Tait*, ed. J. G. Edwards, V. H. Galbraith, and E. F. Jacob (Manchester, 1933), 247–72

Quivy, P. and Thiron, J., 'Robert de Tombelaine et son commentaire sur le Cantique des cantiques', in *Millénaire monastique de Mont Saint-Michel*, ed. J. Laporte, R. Foreville, et al., 4 vols (Paris, 1966–71), II, 347–56

Raison, L. and Niderst, R., 'Le mouvement érémitique dans l'ouest de la France à la fin du XIᵉ siècle et au début du XIIᵉ', *Annales de Bretagne*, 55 (1948), 1–45

Raw, B. C., *Anglo-Saxon Crucifixion Iconography and the Art of the Monastic Revival* (Cambridge, 1990)

Ridyard, S. J., *The Royal Saints of Anglo-Saxon England: A Study of West Saxon and East Anglian Cults* (Cambridge, 1988)

Ridyard, S. J., 'Functions of a Twelfth-Century Recluse Revisited: The Case of Godric of Finchale', in *Belief and Culture*, ed. Gameson and Leyser, 236–50

Roberts, J., 'An Inventory of Early Guthlac Materials', *Medieval Studies*, 32 (1970), 193–233

——'Hagiography and Literature: The Case of Guthlac of Crowland', in *Mercia: An Anglo-Saxon Kingdom in Europe*, ed. M. P. Brown and C. A. Farr (London, 2001), 69–86

Robinson, J. A., *Somerset Historical Essays* (London, 1921)

Roffe, D., 'The *Historia Croylandensis*: A Plea for Reassessment', *EHR*, 110 (1995), 93–108

Rollason, D. W., *The Mildrith Legend: A Study in Early Medieval Hagiography in England* (Leicester, 1982)

——*Saints and Relics in Anglo-Saxon England* (Oxford, 1989)

——Harvey, M. and Prestwich, M. (eds.), *Anglo-Norman Durham, 1093–1193* (Woodbridge, 1994)

——(ed.) *Symeon of Durham: Historian of Durham and the North* (Stamford, 1998)

——Piper, A. J., Harvey, M., and Rollason, L., *The Durham Liber vitae and Its Context* (Woodbridge, 2004)

Rosenwein, B. H., *Rhinoceros Bound: Cluny in the Tenth Century* (Philadelphia, 1982)

Rubenstein, J., 'The Life and Writings of Osbern of Canterbury', in *Canterbury and the Norman Conquest: Churches, Saints and Scholars 1066–1199*, ed. R. Eales and R. Sharpe (London, 1995)

Sackur, E., *Die Cluniacenser in ihrer kirchlichen und allgemeingeschichtlichen Wirksamkeit: bis zur Mitte des elften Jahrhunderts*, 2 vols (Halle, 1892–4)

Sansterre, J.-M., 'Le monachisme bénédictin d'Italie et les bénédictins Italiens en France face au renouveau de l'érémitisme à la fin du Xe et au XIe siècle', in *Ermites*, ed. Vauchez, 29–46

Scarfe Beckett, K., 'Worcester Sauce: Malchus in Anglo-Saxon England', in *Latin Learning*, ed. O'Keeffe and Orchard, ii, 212–31

Schmidtmann, C., 'Romuald von Camaldoli: Modell einer eremitischen Existenz in 10./11. Jahrhundert', *Studia Monastica*, 39 (1997), 329–38

Searle, W. G., *Ingulf and the Historia Croylandensis*, Cambridge Antiquarian Society, 27 (Cambridge, 1894)

Sharpe, R., 'Goscelin's St Augustine and St Mildreth: Hagiography and Liturgy in Context', *Journal of Theological Studies*, n.s. 41 (1990)

Sheils, W. J. (ed.), *Monks, Hermits and the Ascetic Tradition: Papers read at the 1984 summer meeting and 1985 winter meeting of the Ecclesiastical History Society*, SCH, 22 (1985)

Sims-Williams, P., *Religion and Literature in Western England, 600–800* (Cambridge, 1990)

Smith, W., 'Iwi of Wilton: A Forgotten Saint', *AB*, 117 (1999), 297–318

Stroud, D., 'Eve of Wilton and Goscelin of St Bertin at Old Sarum', *Wiltshire Archaeological and Natural History Magazine*, 99 (2006), 204–12

Tabacco, G., 'Romualdo di Ravenna e gli inizi dell'eremitismo camaldolese', in *L'eremitismo*, pub. Università cattolica del Sacro Cuore, 73–119

Tentler, T. N., *Sin and Confession on the Eve of the Reformation* (Princeton, 1977)

Thacker, A. T., 'Bede's ideal of reform', in *Ideal and Reality in Frankish and Anglo-Saxon Society: Studies Presented to John Michael Wallace-Hadrill*, ed. P. Wormald, D. Bullough, and R. Collins (Oxford, 1983), 130–53

——'Æthelwold and Abingdon', in *Bishop Æthelwold: His Career and Influence*, ed. B. Yorke (Woodbridge, 1988), 43–64

——'The Cult of King Harold at Chester', in *The Middle Ages in the North-West: Papers Presented at an International Conference Sponsored Jointly by the Centres of Medieval Studies of the Universities of Liverpool and Toronto*, ed. T. Scott and P. Starkey (Oxford, 1995), 155–76

——'Saint-Making and Relic Collecting by Oswald and His Communities', in *St Oswald*, ed. Brooks and Cubitt, 244–68

——and Sharpe, R. (eds.), *Local Saints and Local Churches in the Early Medieval West* (Oxford, 2002)

Thompson, S., *Women Religious: The Founding of English Nunneries after the Norman Conquest* (Oxford, 1991)

Thompson, V., *Dying and Death in Later Anglo-Saxon England* (Woodbridge, 2004)

——'The Pastoral Contract in Late Anglo-Saxon England: Priest and Parishioner in Oxford, Bodleian Library, MS Laud Miscellaneous 482', in *Pastoral Care*, ed. Tinti, 106–20

Thomson, R. M., *Manuscripts from St Albans Abbey 1066–1235*, 2 vols (Woodbridge, 1982)

Tinti, F. (ed.), *Pastoral Care in Late Anglo-Saxon England* (Woodbridge, 2005)

Townsend, D., 'Anglo-Latin Hagiography and the Norman Transition', *Exemplaria*, 3 (1991), 385–433

Tsurushima, H., 'The Fraternity of Rochester Cathedral Priory about 1100', *ANS*, 14 (1991), 313–37

Tudor, V. M., 'Durham Priory and Its Hermits in the Twelfth Century', in *Anglo-Norman Durham*, ed. Rollason et al., 67–78

Università cattolica del Sacro Cuore (pub.), *L'eremitismo in Occidente nei secoli XI e XII: Atti della seconda settimana internazionale di studio, Mendola, 30 agosto–6 settembre 1962, Publicazioni dell'Università cattolica del Sacro Cuore*, Contributi Serie 3: Varia 4, Miscellanea del Centro di studi medioevali, 4 (Milan, 1965)

Van Engen, J., 'The "Crisis of Cenobitism" Reconsidered: Benedictine Monasticism in the Years 1050–1150', *Speculum*, 61 (1986), 269–304

Van Houts, E., 'Genre Aspects of the Use of Oral Information in Medieval Historiography', in *Gattungen mittelalterlicher Schriftlichkeit*, ed. B. Frank, T. Haye, and D. Tophinke (Tübingen, 1997), 297–312

Vauchez, A., *La sainteté en Occident aux derniers siècles du moyen age d'après les procès de canonisation et les documents hagiographiques* (Rome, 1981)

——(ed.), *Ermites de France et d'Italie (XIe–XVe siècle)* (Rome, 2003)

Vincent, N., 'Some Pardoners' Tales: The Earliest English Indulgences', *TRHS*, 6th ser., 12 (2002), 23–58

Voigt, H. G., *Brun von Querfurt: Mönch, Eremit, Erzbischof der Heiden und Märtyrer* (Stuttgart, 1907)

Wada, Y. (ed.), *A Companion to Ancrene Wisse* (Cambridge, 2003)

Walter, J. von, *Die ersten Wanderprediger Frankreichs: Studien zur Geschichte des Mönchtums*, 2 vols (Leipzig, 1903, 1906)

Warren, A. K., *Anchorites and Their Patrons in Medieval England* (Berkeley, 1985)

Watkins, C. S., 'Sin, Penance and Purgatory in the Anglo-Norman Realm: The Evidence of Visions and Ghost Stories', *Past and Present*, 175 (2002), 3–33

—— *History and the Supernatural in Medieval England* (Cambridge, 2007)

Webber, T., *Scribes and Scholars at Salisbury Cathedral, c.1075–c.1125* (Oxford, 1992)

—— 'The Patristic Context of English Book Collections in the Eleventh Century: Towards a Continental Perspective', in *Of the Making of Books: Medieval Manuscripts, Their Scribes and Readers. Essays Presented to M. B. Parkes*, ed. P. R. Robinson and R. Zim (Aldershot, 1997), 191–205

Wenskus, R., *Studien zur historisch-politischen Gedankenwelt Bruns von Querfurt* (Münster, 1956)

Whitelock, D., 'The Conversion of the Eastern Danelaw', *Saga Book of the Viking Society for Northern Research*, 12 (1941), 159–76

—— 'The Interpretation of *The Seafarer*', in *The Early Cultures of North-West Europe: H. M. Chadwick Memorial Studies*, ed. C. Fox and B. Dickins (Cambridge, 1950), 261–72

Williams, A., *The English and the Norman Conquest* (Woodbridge, 1995)

—— *Land, Power and Politics: The Family and Career of Odda of Deerhurst*, Deerhurst Lecture 1996 (Deerhurst, 1997)

—— 'Thegnly Piety and Ecclesiastical Patronage in the Late Old English Kingdom', *ANS*, 24 (2002), 1–24

Wilmart, A., *Auteurs spirituels et textes dévots du moyen âge latin: études d'histoire littéraire* (Paris, 1931)

Wilson, S. E., *The Life and After-life of St John of Beverley: The Evolution of the Cult of an Anglo-Saxon Saint* (Aldershot, 2006)

Woolf, R., 'The Ideal of Men Dying with Their Lord in the *Germania* and in *The Battle of Maldon*', *ASE*, 5 (1976), 63–81

Wormald, P., 'Æthelwold and His Continental Counterparts: Contact, Comparison, Contrast', in *Bishop Æthelwold*, ed. Yorke, 13–42

Wright, C. D., *The Irish Tradition in Old English Literature* (New York, 1992)

Yorke, B. (ed.), Bishop Æthelwold: His Career and Influence (Woodbridge, 1988)

Index

LIBRARY, UNIVERSITY OF CHESTER

Lightning Source UK Ltd.
Milton Keynes UK
UKOW030604090512

192215UK00004B/20/P

LIBRARY, UNIVERSITY OF CHESTER